George Bruce Malleson

The Battle-Fields of Germany

From the Outbreak of the Thirty Years' War to the Battle of Blenheim

George Bruce Malleson

The Battle-Fields of Germany
From the Outbreak of the Thirty Years' War to the Battle of Blenheim

ISBN/EAN: 9783337014230

Printed in Europe, USA, Canada, Australia, Japan

Cover: Foto ©ninafisch / pixelio.de

More available books at **www.hansebooks.com**

THE BATTLE-FIELDS OF GERMANY.

FROM THE OUTBREAK OF THE THIRTY-YEARS' WAR
TO THE BATTLE OF BLENHEIM:

WITH MAPS AND ONE PLAN.

BY

COLONEL G. B. MALLESON, C.S.I.,

AUTHOR OF "THE DECISIVE BATTLES OF INDIA," ETC.

"Ich sage Ihnen, dass grosse Fragen, nicht durch Reden und Majoritätsbeschlüsse, sondern durch Blut und Eisen, gelöst würden."—*Speech of* PRINCE BISMARCK *in 1862.*

LONDON:
W. H. ALLEN & CO., 13 WATERLOO PLACE. S.W.
PUBLISHERS TO THE INDIA OFFICE.

1884.

(All rights reserved.)

PREFACE.

A FEW words of explanation seem necessary to introduce to the public a work which, taking to itself the ambitious title of the Battle-fields of Germany, stops short after the battle of Blenheim.

A little reflection will, I think, prove that, beginning with the battle-fields of the Thirty Years' War, the subject naturally divides itself into three great series or epochs. The first of these, treated of in this volume, deals with the principal military events of the Thirty Years' War, with the battle which was the final turning point in the history of the House of Hohenzollern, with the decisive overthrow of the Turks before Vienna, and with the famous battle-field which gave the first check to the ambitious designs of Louis XIV. on Germany. From that moment we enter upon a new epoch. The Porte and France had alike ceased to be mortally dangerous to the Empire, and we arrive at a period when the North and the South of Germany, the former represented by Frederick II. of Prussia, the latter by the House of

Habsburg, began their long struggle for predominance. That struggle was still undecided when the old order of things in Europe was swept away by the wave of the French Revolution. Whilst, then, the history of the battles of that epoch would form the second, that of the battles of the epoch subsequent to the year 1739 would form the third, series, of the subject which constitutes the major title of this work.

To the political history of the Thirty Years' War I have referred as little as was possible. My object has been rather to describe the battles and the events which led to those battles. Englishmen have, no doubt, read in their own language accounts of Leipzig (Breitenfeld) and of Lützen; but of Duke Bernhard's campaign in the valley of the Danube; of Banner's daring and all but successful raid upon Ratisbon; of that battle of Jankowitz which made possible the capture of Vienna; of the surprises of Tuttlingen and Mergentheim; of the battle of Zusmarshausen; of the closing scene of the Thirty Years' War, the splendid defence of Prague; of that Fehrbellin which was the turning point in the history of the Hohenzollerns; they can have read, in the same tongue, but little save the barest outline, and sometimes not even that. To resuscitate these battle-fields from the oblivion into which they had fallen, and to describe them in the English language, has been to me a labour of love. I have had, indeed, to delve into many musty documents, and to pore over many forgotten folios in German and French; but never, I can truly assert, have I found the early hours of the morning pass more pleasantly than when I was engaged in a work which carried me, mentally, into the inspiring company of some of the greatest men who have trodden this earth. A list of some of the authorities which I have consulted follows this short introduction.

The eighth chapter, under the title of Fehrbellin, gives a complete sketch of the history of the House which now occupies the most prominent position in Germany. The reader will not fail to note how the qualities which are conspicuous in the ruling Emperor of Germany characterised the most able of his many eminent ancestors.

The ninth chapter sketches the history of Hungary under the Habsburgs and the several invasions of the Turks, until their last attempt in 1683 shattered before the walls of Vienna. The volume concludes with a sketch of the political occurrences which, from the time of the accession of Louis XIV., preceded and led up to the battle of Blenheim.

This battle-field closes the series. Whether, with Carlyle's "History of Frederick II." before the world; with Colonel Brackenbury's work upon the same subject, very recently issued; and with the early promise of a work guaranteeing, under the title of "Marshal Loudon," a sketch of the Austrian side of the Seven Years' War; it would be wise at the present moment to enter upon the second series, seems more than doubtful. It is one of those points upon which the opinion of the public must be decisive.

I may add that, with the exception of Fehrbellin, I have visited all the battle-fields treated of in this volume.

G. B. M.

8th May 1884.

LIST OF SOME OF THE WORKS CONSULTED.

Pelens: Histoire de la dernière guerre de Suède. Paris, 1622.
De Prade's L'Histoire de Gustave Adolphe, dit le Grand. Paris, 1686.
Raumer's Geschichte Europas seit dem Ende des fünfzehnten Jahrhunderts.
Gförer's Gustav-Adolf, König von Schweden und seine Zeit.
Schiller's Dreissigjähriger Kreig.
Harte's History of the Life of Gustavus Adolphus.
Pufendorf's Commentaria de rebus Suecicis, &c.
Le Soldat Svédois, ou Histoire de ce qui s'est passé en Allemagne depuis l'entrée du Roy de Suède en l'année 1630, jusques après sa mort, 1633.
Dictionnaire Historique des sièges et batailles mémorables, 1808.
Lebenslauf Herzog Bernhards, 1639.
Le Mercure françois.
Bazin's Histoire de France sous Louis XIII. et Mazarin.
Geijer's Svenska Folkets Historia (German translation).
Ramsay's Histoire de Turenne.
France Protestante. Haag Frères.
Leben des Marschalls von Turenne.
Histoire de Madame de Longueville.
Mémoires du Maréchal de Gramont.
Œsterreichische National-Encyklopädie.
Die Kaiser aus dem Hause Habsburg-Lothringen von Dr. Rupert Precechtel.
Brockhaus' Conversations Lexikon.
Alterthümer und Kunstdenkmale des Erlauchten Hauses Hohenzollern.
Genealogische Geschichte der Burggrafen von Nürnberg.
Histoire d'Éméric, comte de Tököly.
Histoire de l'Empire Ottoman, de Hammer.
Histoire de Mahomed IV., deposé en 1687 : Devize.
Prinz Eugen von Savoyen. Arneth.
Siècle de Louis XIV. Voltaire.
Mémoires du duc de Saint-Simon;
and several other memoirs of the period.

CONTENTS.

	PAGE
CHAPTER I.—BREITENFELD	1
CHAPTER II.—THE LECH AND NUREMBERG	40
CHAPTER III.—LÜTZEN	79
CHAPTER IV.—NÖRDLINGEN	102
CHAPTER V.—JANKOWITZ	125
CHAPTER VI.—TUTTLINGEN AND FREIBURG	158
CHAPTER VII.—MERGENTHEIM, ALLERSHEIM, ZUSMARSHAUSEN, PRAGUE	187
CHAPTER VIII.—FEHRBELLIN	226
CHAPTER IX.—VIENNA	257
CHAPTER X.—BLENHEIM	292

THE BATTLE-FIELDS OF GERMANY.

CHAPTER I.

BREITENFELD.

The city of **Leipzig** lies on a broad and fertile plain watered by three rivers, the Pleisse, the Elster, and the Parthe, which unite in its vicinity. The waters of these rivers and of their many arms have made the broad plain so rich and fertile, that, within a radius of six or seven miles, many flourishing villages have risen to house the cultivators of the fields, the meadows, and the orchards which cover its surface. To the north-west, for instance, along or near the line of the Magdeburg road, are the villages of Möckern, Wahren, Lindenthal, **Podelwitz**, Soehausen, and Breitenfeld—the last some five miles from the city. To the direct north lie Eutritsch, and, some two miles further, **Wiederitsch**. To the north-east are Schönfeld, **Mockau**, Neutzsch, Plösen, Cleuden, **Portitz**, Plaussig, and Seegeritz. A little more to the east, but in an almost parallel line, a direct road traverses the plain by Volkmansdorf and **Heiterer Blick** to the considerable village of **Taucha**, six miles from Leipzig. To the east, south-east, and south, are many more villages, the best known of which to students of history are Thonberg, Probstheida, Meusdorf, **Dölitz, and** Wachau; to the direct west, Plagwitz, Lindenau, **and** Leutzsch. The extent of the plain, the fact that on it has risen one of the richest cities of Germany, that it is the centre point of many converging routes, that its surface is generally level, that the banks of the streams which intersect and the villages which cover it might be utilised for warlike operations, have attracted to it, during the many wars which have desolated Germany, the commanders of armies. On two memorable occasions it served as the battle-field on which were decided the most important questions agitating the minds of mankind. In 1631 Gustavus Adolphus fought there to secure to his fellow-men freedom of conscience in matters of religion. In 1813 Austria, Prussia, Russia, and Sweden, combined to rescue the sovereigns and peoples of Europe from the thraldom of Napoleon. The first battle, fought near the village and manor of Breitenfeld, was followed, eleven years later, by a second, fought on the same spot, by the representatives of the same cause, to assert the same principles. Both these battles, though sometimes called after the city on the plain, bear in Germany the name of Breitenfeld. I propose, in this chapter, to examine the causes which led to them, and to narrate, as concisely as may be consistent with clearness, the events which preceded and illustrated the first.

The Reformation, in Germany, received the first authoritative acknowledgment of its political existence only when the electors, princes, and **nobles** of the Empire, assembled by Ferdinand I. at Passau, signed, the **31st July 1552,** the Peace of Religion. Three years later, **the 26th September 1555, the main conditions** of this agreement were detailed and confirmed by the Imperial diet assembled at Augsburg. But this peace, valuable to the Protestants as a recognition of their rights, by no means concluded the strife between the professors of the two religions. On the one side the **Catholics** complained of the secularisation and suppression of foundations belonging to their church. On the other, Protestants raised their voices against **the arbitrary** enforcement of claims which, **in spite of** the **Peace of Religion,** Catholic princes allowed **to be enforced** against them. Everywhere the Jesuits bestirred themselves to induce those princes to carry out with zeal and vigour the policy of forcible conversion. It thus came about that at the close of the sixteenth century the entire public life of Germany was completely dominated by religious machinations, and these machinations led to serious tumults and even, in certain instances, to war. To the feelings thus aroused an occurrence in the town of Donauwörth, 1606–7, gave considerable impulse. In consequence of the forcible prevention by its Protestant population of a procession headed by the Abbot from the monastery of the Holy Cross, the Emperor Rudolph placed the town under a ban (3rd August 1607), and committed to Maximilian of Bavaria the execution of the sentence. Maximilian in consequence occupied Donauwörth with his troops the 17th December following, and, condemning the inhabitants to pay the entire expenses of the occupation, used all the means in his power to force them to return to the old religion. This act of tyranny roused the Protestant princes. Many of them—the Elector Palatine, Frederic V., at their head—met together, 4th May 1608, at the monastery of Ahausen (in the Bavarian district of Schwaben-Neuburg), and there formed the Protestant Union. To this, besides the Elector Palatine, eight princes and fifteen imperial cities of Germany gave their adherence. The Catholics replied by constituting at Munich, 10th July 1609, a holy league, of whose decrees Maximilian of Bavaria was to be the executor. Meanwhile the Bohemians, two-thirds at least of whom had embraced the reformed religion, had taken advantage of the division * in the Imperial family between Rudolph II. and Matthias, to wring from the former, by letters patent dated 11th July 1609, conditions of almost unlimited religious freedom. These conditions, Matthias, on his accession to the Government in 1611, had confirmed. One of these granted to the cities and

* Caused mainly by the preference shown by Rudolph for his cousin Ferdinand, afterwards known as Ferdinand II., whom he not only summoned to his side to aid him in the government of the country, but designated, to the prejudice of his brother Matthias, as his successor in the Austrian dominions.

to the order of nobility the privilege of erecting Protestant churches and schools. But when, in opposition to the wish and orders of their landlords the Archbishop of Prague and the Abbot of Braunau, the inhabitants of Klostergrab and Braunau ventured to build churches, the archbishop did not hesitate, with the support of the Imperial authority, to have the church at Klostergrab pulled to the ground, whilst the abbot, with the same support, closed that at Braunau. In vain did the aggrieved inhabitants petition the Emperor. But the reply they received was couched in terms so harsh that, acquitting their imperial master, they drew the conclusion that it had been dictated, without his knowledge, by his councillors. When, then, the Estates of the kingdom met in the Hradschin on the 23rd May 1618, the Protestant nobles, headed by Count Thurn, came thither armed, and demanded from the Imperial councillors an account of their high-handed proceedings. Violent words ensued, complaint was answered with defiance, till at last, unable further to restrain themselves, the Protestant deputies seized the obstructive councillors, Martinitz and Slavata, and their secretary, Fabricius Platter, and hurled them from the window into the dry ditch, some fifty feet immediately below it! This act precipitated a war which had been long pending, and could not, under any circumstances, have been much further delayed. When the minds of all parties are embittered a slight incident will always suffice to bring about resolute action. In 1618 the minds of kings and nobles, of traders and peasants, were in a state of irritation scarcely to be controlled. The incident at Prague removed the barrier which had till then restrained the forcible expression of their indignation.

For the moment Bohemia was virtually independent of the House of Austria. The Estates administered the internal affairs of the kingdom and invested Count Thurn with the command of the army. The Protestant princes of the Union and the nobles of Moravia and Silesia supported them. The Emperor Matthias, a tolerant and well-meaning man, endeavoured, by

smooth words and promises of pardon on repentance, to conjure
the storm. His action only encouraged the revolters to make
further encroachments on the imperial authority. When at
last he resorted to force and ordered an army into Bohemia, the
Protestants replied by secretly offering the crown of that country
to the Elector Palatine, Frederic V.; by inviting the republic of
Venice and Savoy to declare war against Austria; and by entering into a stricter alliance with their brethren in the neighbouring provinces.

The death of Matthias (20th March 1619) brought matters between the two parties to a still more direct issue. His successor,
Ferdinand II., then in his forty-first year, was one of the most
bigoted of Catholics and the most resolute of men. When still
in his early manhood he had made a pilgrimage to Loretto, and,
prostrate before the altar of the Virgin, had solemnly vowed to
re-establish Catholicism throughout his dominions. The period
between the death of Matthias and his election as Emperor
(28th August 1619) was spent by both parties in the preliminary
strife. The Protestants of Bohemia despatched an army into
Moravia, formally set aside Ferdinand, and nominated the
Elector Palatine as their King. Their efforts, however, were
shattered by the dogged resolution of Ferdinand. On the 10th
June a mercenary army favouring the Union, led by Mansfeldt,
was completely defeated by the Imperial General Bucquoi, at
Zablati, near Budweis. Nine days later, however, Thurn,
marching through Moravia and Upper Austria, laid siege to
Vienna. Had Thurn been a great general the subsequent fate
of Austria had been changed. Whilst his army, marching to the
cry of "Equal rights for all Christian churches," had been greatly
strengthened in its progress through the hereditary dominions,
not a finger had been raised for Ferdinand. The latter had at
his beck but a handful of soldiers, far too few, even could they
have been trusted, to resist an attack. The population were
shouting all around him for Protestantism. That Ferdinand
was aware of the danger was proved by the despatch of his

children to a place of security in Tirol. But, recognising that for himself flight would be the renunciation of his claims to the empire—abdication of his rights over Bohemia—he refused to stir. Never did the dogged resolution of a man assert itself to greater purpose. Almost alone in his capital, exposed to the bullets of the besieging soldiers, virtually a prisoner in the Hofburg, he yet bade to his enemies a haughty defiance. Had Thurn only pushed into the city and seized his person, it had been all over with him and his pretensions. But Thurn, delaying to take the decisive step, preferred to incite sixteen Austrian barons, with Andreas Thonradl at their head, to compel Ferdinand to sign the conditions on which the Union had agreed. Forcing themselves into his private chamber, the parchment in the hands of their leader, the barons surrounded Ferdinand, and pressed him to affix to it his signature. As he still refused, one of them, bolder than the rest, seized him by the button of his doublet, exclaiming, "Sign, Nandy, sign." Ferdinand was still persisting in his refusal when suddenly a cavalry trumpet sounded on the Place below. In another moment the news spread that five hundred cuirassiers, led by Henry Du Val, Count of Dampierre, had arrived, the vanguard of a relieving army. One by one the rebellious barons sneaked away. Ferdinand's obstinacy had preserved his position for himself, had regained Catholicism for the hereditary states—and for Bohemia!

Thurn hastily retreated from Vienna. Thenceforth the game was in Ferdinand's hands. Though Bohemia, still in revolt, absolved itself from allegiance to Ferdinand on the 17th August, and chose the Elector-Palatine as its King on the 27th, Ferdinand was, the day following, elected Emperor of Germany at Frankfurt. No soon had he assumed this high position than he united himself by the strictest alliance with Maximilian of Bavaria to crush Protestantism throughout Germany. In their efforts to this end the two sovereigns were greatly assisted by the imprudence of their enemies. A Calvinist and a foreigner, deficient in judgment and possessing no counterbalancing ability, Frederic V. conciliated but little support in Bohemia. It is true that the Bohemians, in concert with Bethlen Gabor, who had proclaimed himself King of Hungary, again (October–November 1619) besieged Vienna. They were compelled, however, by want of supplies and stress of weather, to retreat—and at that season retreat meant demoralisation. The Protestant Union, moreover, was rent by internal dissensions.

In June of the following year the superior organisation of the Catholics had, without striking a blow, materially altered the condition of affairs. The Elector Palatine, foiled in his hopes of foreign aid, but very faintly supported by the other princes of the Protestant Union,—who, either from fear of the Emperor, or from a selfish regard to their own personal interests, affected to dissever the cause of Bohemia from that of their confederacy generally—was doubting whether he had acted wisely in accepting responsibilities which might involve the loss even of his hereditary domains. Saxony and Hesse-Darmstadt had been won over by Ferdinand. Lower Austria, once the focus of Protestant feeling, had submitted. A truce had been concluded with Bethlen Gabor. Denmark had been cajoled, and Sweden had been entangled into a war with the Poles. Venice, Savoy, and England remained inactive. One after another the hopes of the Protestant Party had disappeared! But the Protestant Party had still an army—a powerful army—assembled at Ulm, under the command of the Margrave of Ansbach. Opposed to it was the army of the League, collected at Donauwörth, under the orders of Maximilian. A battle between the two seemed impending. Every consideration impelled the Protestant princes to seek one. Every consideration prompted Maximilian to induce his enemies to disband without daring a fortune which might prove adverse to himself. Could he but bring about such a result he would turn upon Bohemia, drive thence the usurper, and re-establish the Catholic faith. Again did the Protestant princes play into his hands. Influenced partly by the interested advice of Catholic

France, partly by the fear of seeing another imperial army called up from the Low Countries, on their hands, they signed (3rd July) with the Emperor a peace, in the most important article of which they agreed to renounce all interference in the affairs of Bohemia, and not to afford any aid to Frederic V. beyond the borders of the Palatinate.

This fatal treaty was at once utilised by Maximilian. He immediately summoned Frederic V. to renounce his pretensions to the crown of Bohemia, and, when Frederic refused, he, after making doubly sure of Lower Austria, and arranging for the simultaneous action of a Saxon army in the Lausitz and a Spanish army in the Palatinate, entered that kingdom at the head of 30,000 men. As far as Prague his march was a succession of triumphs; but on the White Hill, three quarters of a mile west of that city, he found Frederic's army intrenched and ready to give him battle. Guided by one of the most skilled and successful generals of the age, the famous Count Tilly, he at once attacked it (8th November 1620), and, in less than an hour, not only drove it from its position, but so completely defeated it that it was never able to rally.

This battle put an end to the short reign of Frederic.* Another immediate consequence was the complete submission of Bohemia, Moravia, and Silesia to the Emperor. The religious freedom granted by Matthias was abolished; many of the promoters of the rebellion were punished in life and property. The year following (1621) all members of the sect of Protestants known as the Reformers—a sect analogous to the Calvinists— were forced to quit the country. A similar edict drove out the Lutherans in 1622. In that year likewise the Jesuits were recalled; and in 1627 the exercise of all religious forms, except those of the Catholic Church, were forbidden. It was calculated that these severe measures drove into exile thirty thousand of the wealthiest of the industrial, and two hundred of the noblest,

* Frederic fled with his children to Silesia, thence to Holland.

families of the kingdom. The confiscations alone amounted to between five and six millions sterling. A similar policy was pursued in the Austrian hereditary lands, especially in Upper Austria, where the shedding of much blood was required before the old religion could be firmly re-established.

After the conquest of Bohemia the interest of the war was transferred to the Palatinate. On the side of the Protestants appeared the partisan leader, Ernest of Mansfeldt, Duke Christian of Brunswick, and Margrave George Frederic of Baden-Durlach. Frederic V. returned to his hereditary lands and defeated a detachment of the League army at Wiesloch (27th April 1622). The defeat, however, was more than avenged nine days later when Tilly smote the Margrave George Frederic at Wimpfen; and again, when, on the 20th June following, after having forced the Duke Christian to abandon the Palatinate, he overthrew him at Höchst. The Protestant cause, however, would not have been lost in the Palatinate had Frederic V. displayed ordinary vigour and energy. But this prince, weak by nature, was induced by his father-in-law, James I. of England, to abandon the contest and trust to the tender mercies of Ferdinand. On the 13th July following he dismissed his army, and quitted the country. Thenceforward Tilly could plunder and pillage unmolested. The Palatinate was speedily reduced to the same condition as Bohemia; and at the Diet held at Ratisbon, the 6th May 1623, the electorate was conferred, despite the protests of Brunswick and Saxony, upon Maximilian of Bavaria! Had the Emperor been as wise as he was resolute, it is probable that, victorious in every direction, he might have been able to conclude a permanent peace with the Protestant Party. But the bigotry which was a very part of his nature was spurred on by his easy triumphs to refuse to sheathe the sword until heresy had been rooted out from the land. In vain did the Protestant princes, who had maintained a selfish and foolish neutrality, remonstrate against the continuance of hostilities after the avowed object for **which** those hostilities were undertaken had **been** gained. In the opinion of **Ferdinand II. the** real object still remained to be accomplished.

Under these critical circumstances **the** emigrants, now **grown** numerous, **and the** awakened Protestant princes, earnestly besought **the aid of a foreign power.** It was their representations **which at length induced three** nations of the reformed faith—England, Holland, **and Denmark—to** ally themselves to assist their oppressed brethren. England agreed to send subsidies, Holland to supply troops. **The** command **of the** delivering army was confided to Christian **IV.,** King **of** Denmark (1625). He was to be supported **in** Germany by the partisan Mansfeldt, **by** Prince Christian **of** Brunswick, **and by** the Protestants of Lower **Saxony, who had armed** themselves **to resist** the exactions of **the Emperor.**

Ferdinand II., after vainly endeavouring **to ward** off hostilities **by** negotiations, despatched Tilly **to the Weser to meet** the **enemy.** Tilly followed **the course of that river** as far as Minden, **causing to be occupied, as he marched, the** places which commanded **its passage.** Pursuing his course northwards, he crossed **the river at Neuburg (midway** between Minden and Bremen), and occupied **the** principality of Kalenberg.* The King of Denmark **was near at hand, in** the duchy of Brunswick, anxious, for **the moment, to avoid** a battle. Tilly, superior to him in numbers, was as anxious to fight one.

As though the position of the King of Denmark were not already sufficiently embarrassing, the Emperor proceeded **at** this period to make it almost unendurable by launching upon **him** likewise **an** imperial army. **Whatever** minor reasons might have combined **to** induce Ferdinand **II. to such a** course, **there** was one over-riding **them all. Up to the period** of the complete overthrow and expulsion **from the Palatinate** of Frederic V., ex-King of Bohemia, **Ferdinand had been indebted for all** his **successes**

---

* Kalenberg has long ceased to exist as a principality. **Since 1705 it has formed a** district of Hanover.

to Maximilian of Bavaria. It was Maximilian who, as head of the Holy League, had reconquered Bohemia for the Emperor: it was Maximilian's general, Tilly, who had driven the Protestant armies from the Palatinate; and it was the same general who was now opposing the Protestants of the north in the lands watered by the Weser. Maximilian had been rewarded by the cession to him of the Palatinate, but it was not advisable that so near a neighbour of Austria should be made too strong. It was this feeling, this jealousy of Maximilian, which now prompted Ferdinand to raise, for the first time in this war, an imperial army, and to send it to the north.

This army was raised by and at the expense of Albert Wenzel Eusebius of Waldstein, known in history as Wallenstein. A Czech by nationality, born in 1583 of noble parents, who belonged to one of the most advanced sects of the reformers but who died whilst their son was yet young, Wallenstein had, when yet a child, been committed to the care of his uncle, Albert Slavata, an adherent of the Jesuits, and by him educated at Olmütz in the strictest Catholic faith. When he had finished his course of studies at Olmütz, Wallenstein spent some time at the University of Altdorf, and then frequented in turn the schools of Bologna and of Padua. His next step was to travel through Italy, Germany, France, Spain, England, and the Netherlands, carefully observing the military condition and tactics of each country. Almost immediately after his return to Bohemia he took service under the Emperor Rudolph, and joined the army commanded by General Basta in Hungary. Soon advanced to the rank of captain, he distinguished himself greatly at the siege of Gran.

On the conclusion of peace in 1606, Wallenstein returned to Bohemia and married there a widow, well stricken in years, Lucretia Nikessin of Landeck, the owner of large properties in Moravia, all of which, upon her death in 1614, devolved upon him. Two years later he raised, at his own cost, two hundred dragoons, to support the heir presumptive to the empire, Ferdinand of Gratz, in his war against the Venetians. It was owing mainly to his skill and exertions that the beleaguered fortress of Görz (Gorizia) was saved from their hands. For this and for other services, scarcely less signal, he was promoted to be a colonel. His generosity, his daring, his quick insight, had made him the idol alike of officers and men. On the conclusion of the war he contracted a second marriage, this time also with an heiress, the bride being Isabella Katherina, daughter of Count Harrach, a favourite of the Emperor Matthias. This union not only greatly augmented his influence, but it procured for him the title of Count. On the breaking out of the religious disturbances in 1618, Wallenstein adhered to the cause of the Emperor, saved for his master, and carried to Vienna, despite the efforts of the Protestant nobles, the contents of the State Treasury, raised a regiment of cuirassiers, and fought at its head with success against Thurn and Bethlen Gabor. In 1620 he was appointed Quartermaster-General of the army led by Maximilian and Tilly against Frederic V.; and although, for personal reasons, he took no share in the battle of the White Hill, yet, on its favourable result, he marched at the head of an independent force into Moravia, and completely re-established there the imperial authority. In the following year he purchased from the Emperor Ferdinand, for the sum of 7,290,228 florins, sixty properties, great and small, which that prince had confiscated from patriots whom he had either executed or banished.

For his faithful services, Ferdinand in 1623 nominated Wallenstein to be Prince, a title changed, the year following, into that of Duke, of Friedland. At this time the yearly income he derived from his various estates, all economically managed, was calculated to be thirty millions of florins—little short of two and a half millions sterling. When, in 1625, the invasion of Christian IV. of Denmark threatened to derange the plans of the Emperor, that prince, anxious to find a counterpoise to the influence of Maximilian, turned his thoughts to Wallenstein. But the Duke of Friedland had anticipated his sovereign. It was he, who, divining his master's wishes, and animated by the ambition born of natural ability, offered to raise and maintain, at his own cost, an army of 50,000 men, and to lead it against the enemy. Ferdinand, eagerly accepted the offer. Named Generalissimo and Field Marshal in July of the same year, Wallenstein marched at the head of 30,000 men, a number which increased almost daily, first to the Weser, thence, after noticing the positions of Tilly and of King Christian, to the banks of the Elbe, where he wintered.

Of the campaign which followed in the spring, it is necessary to give but the briefest outline. It will suffice to say that Mansfeldt, with the view to prevent a junction between Tilly and Wallenstein, marched against the latter, and, though his troops were fewer in number, took up a position at Dessau in full view of the imperial camp, and there intrenched himself. Here Wallenstein attacked (25 April 1626) and completely defeated him. Not discouraged by this overthrow, and still bearing in mind the main object of the campaign, Mansfeldt fell back into Brandenburg, recruited there his army, called to himself the Duke of Saxe-Weimar, and then suddenly dashed, by forced marches, towards Silesia and Moravia, with the intention of reaching Hungary, where Bethlen Gabor had promised to meet him. In spite of his desire to finish the war in the north, Wallenstein recognised the necessity of following the daring adventurer, as the only means of preventing him from carrying the war into the very heart of the Imperial dominions. He marched, then, with all possible speed, and pressed him so hard, that, though Mansfeldt did effect a junction with Bethlen Gabor, it was with but the skeleton of his army. Despairing of success against numbers vastly superior, Bethlen Gabor withdrew from his new colleague, and Mansfeldt, reduced to despair, disbanded his remaining soldiers, and sold his camp-equipage to supply himself with the means of flight (September). He died soon after (30th November). His companion, the Duke of Saxe Weimar, followed him to the grave on the 4th of the month following. Wallenstein then retraced his steps to the North.

Meanwhile Tilly, left to deal with Christian IV., had followed that prince into Lower Saxony, had caught, attacked, and completely defeated him at Lutter (am Barenberge), the 27th July 1626. This victory gave him complete possession of that disaffected province, and, despite a vigorous attempt made by the Margrave George Frederic of Baden to wrest it from him, he held it till the return of Wallenstein from the pursuit of Mansfeldt. As two stars of so great a magnitude could not shine in the same hemisphere, it was then decided that Tilly should carry the war into Holland, whilst to Wallenstein should be left the honour of dealing with the King of Denmark and the Protestant princes of the north. Wallenstein carried out his task with great thoroughness. During the two years that followed, he drove the remnants of the enemy from Silesia, took military occupation of Brandenburg and Mecklenburg, then advanced into Pomerania and laid siege to Stralsund. Here, however, he met with his first check. In the splendid resistance which they made the Stralsunders were aided by the genius and the energy of Gustavus Adolphus, the young King of Sweden. Mainly in consequence of this aid, Wallenstein, after a siege of upwards of three months—May to July 1629—was forced to renounce his efforts. A year later he concluded with King Christian at Lübeck a peace, by which the latter bound himself to interfere no more in the affairs of Germany. For his services in the war Wallenstein received in fee the Duchy of Mecklenburg.

Germany lay apparently at the feet of the Emperor. Freed alike from Protestant opposition and from the yoke of Maximilian, Ferdinand began now, in consultation with the Jesuits, to put in action the policy dictated by the fanaticism which swayed his narrow mind. Before even the peace of Lübeck had been signed he had issued (6th March 1629), an edict, known as the Restitution Edict, in virtue of which the Protestants were required to restore to the Catholics all the monasteries and church lands of which, since the peace of Passau, they had become possessed; it further directed that, in the States immediately subject to the Emperor, the Catholic services alone should be performed in all churches, that the Reformers should be excluded from the operation of the Peace of Religion, and that the Catholic princes of the empire should be permitted to constrain their subjects to conform to their faith. This decree was put in force, under the pressure of the sword, in all the Imperial cities: in Augsburg, in Ulm, in Ratisbon; in Kaufbeuren and in other towns; and it was plainly intimated to the Protestant princes that they would be required equally to carry it out.

It was not to be supposed that an edict of this tremendous character would be submitted to without opposition. Already the preponderance obtained by the Emperor in Germany by the victories of Wallenstein had given umbrage to the more independent of the Catholic princes. Maximilian of Bavaria especially, who had really given Ferdinand his throne, was resolved in no sense to become that prince's vassal. His views, strongly supported by those of the French court, represented by the illustrious Richelieu, found expression at the Diet held at Ratisbon in 1630. The opposition which developed itself on this occasion forced the Emperor to consent to diminish his army, and to withdraw from Wallenstein the patent of Generalissimo. On the 30th September following, then, Wallenstein's army was disbanded, and Wallenstein himself withdrew to private life in his princely residence at Gitschin.

Before even this step had been taken a new difficulty had confronted the Emperor. Neither the Electors of Brandenburg and Saxony nor the representatives of the Hanse towns had attended the diet at Ratisbon. Almost the sole representatives of the Protestant feeling in Germany able to raise their voice against the new persecution, these champions of the Reformation had secretly urged upon the prince who had saved Stralsund to aid them in devising means to conjure the danger which threatened them all alike. These solicitations, supported by

Denmark and by France, fell on no unwilling ear. The very month which saw the re-formation of a Catholic League at Ratisbon, witnessed likewise the declaration of Gustavus Adolphus at Stockholm espousing the cause of the oppressed Protestants of Germany.

The son of Charles IX. of Sweden and of Christine of Schleswig Holstein, born the 9th December 1594, Gustavus Adolphus had succeeded to the throne of Sweden at the early age of seventeen. Nature had endowed him with beauty of form, with the strength that defies fatigue. She had bestowed upon him likewise the still more precious gift of a mind full of intelligence, of noble sentiments, and of courage. These qualities had been developed by a most judicious course of education. At the age of sixteen Gustavus Adolphus was well versed in the science of arms, he knew almost all the languages of Europe, he assisted his father alike at the head of his armies, and in the Council chamber. Called to the throne (8th November 1611) before he had attained the age of seventeen, at a time when his country was engaged in war against Russia, Denmark, and Poland, he displayed a rare prudence. With the advice of his friend, Axel Oxenstierna, whom, his senior by eleven years, he had made minister, Gustavus proceeded in the first instance to strengthen the bases of his own authority. He effected this important object by making concessions to his nobility, by restoring to them the privileges of which he believed they had been unjustly deprived. The good policy of this reform soon made itself practically felt. Before the close of the year following his accession his popularity had obtained for him all the assistance in men and money necessary to carry on the war. Deeming himself, however, not yet strong enough to combat three enemies at the same time, he took an early opportunity to conclude peace with Denmark (28th January 1613). He found it comparatively an easy task, then, to drive the Russian fleets from the Baltic, and to conquer from the Czar, Michael Romanoff, the provinces of Ingria and Carelia, and a part of Livonia. A less well-balanced mind than his own might possibly, at his age, have yielded to earnest advice pressed upon him by one of his oldest generals, Jacques de la Gardie,* to expel the Romanoffs, and to gain the imperial throne of Russia for himself. Gustavus contented himself with the more safe and solid project of expelling Russia from the shores of the Baltic, and of annexing Finland. He secured both these objects by a treaty which he concluded with the Czar in 1617.

The war against Sigismund III., King of Poland, known in Polish history as the sixty years' war, still, however, continued. So fiercely did Gustavus press it, that by the end of 1626 he had conquered the whole of Polish Livonia, and of west Russia as far as Thorn. Before Dantzig, which he proceeded then to besiege, he was wounded, and his troops were repulsed. Gustavus, however, took his revenge by inflicting several defeats on the enemy, and, although again wounded, and then again, he had driven them almost to extremity when Wallenstein, after having expelled the Danes from North Germany, entered Pomerania and laid siege to Stralsund. How the action of Gustavus, aiding the valour of the defenders, forced him to raise the siege and to retreat, has been already related. Gustavus pursued his advantage, captured Neuburg, Marienwerder, Graudenz, and other places, when, on the intervention of the Elector of Brandenburg, he agreed to a twelve weeks' suspension of hostilities (8th March to 1st June 1629). On the expiration of this term hostilities were renewed, but the diplomatic action of France induced the contending parties to come to terms, and on the 1st September following a truce for six years, very advantageous for Sweden, was signed at Altenmarkt.

The proceedings at the Diet of Ratisbon the following year, the renewal of the league against the Reformers, the solicitations of many leading Protestant nobles, and the promised sup-

---

* Second son of the renowned Pontus de la Gardie, Baron of Eckholm. Jacques is described as having been a type of those illustrious men who distinguish themselves no less by their great military services than by the protection they afford to letters and art.

port of France, determined the young Swedish monarch to take the bold step of declaring war against the Emperor. He felt, as he explained to his Estates, that the step was in reality purely defensive; that he would have to look on calmly whilst north Germany was being swallowed up, certain that his turn would come next, or to interfere; that of the two courses interference was the nobler and the more humane. On the 19th May 1630, then, he presented his only child, Christina, then six years old, to the Estates assembled at Stockholm; confided her to their care and to their fidelity as the heiress to the throne, and addressed them in the most touching language. Calling God to witness that he was undertaking this war solely in order to make common cause with the oppressed reformers of Germany in resisting the tyranny of their Catholic persecutors, he added: "I hope to ensure the triumph of the cause of the oppressed; but as it sometimes happens that the pitcher is broken whilst being carried to the water, it is possible that I may not succeed. I, who have exposed my life to so many dangers, who have shed my blood so often for my country, without receiving, thanks be to God, a mortal wound—I feel that, at last, I shall have to pay the sacrifice. That is why I make now my adieux to you all, and express my hope that we shall meet in a better world." Eleven days later he embarked at Elfsnabben.

The fleet collected at that port to convey the army to the shores of Germany consisted of twenty-eight ships of war of various sizes and a large number of transports. Considering the end in view, the might of the enemy, the extent of the country to be traversed, the army itself was ridiculously small in numbers. The three arms which composed it fell somewhat short of twenty thousand. Of these, in round numbers, fifteen thousand were infantry, two thousand cavalry, and the remainder artillery. But the army led by Gustavus was not to be judged by numbers alone. The men, trained to the perfection of discipline by the long wars with Russia and Poland, occupied the first rank in the esteem of military

Europe. They were led by officers tried and proved in several campaigns, and the reputation of many of whom was to become an immortal heritage to the generations that were to follow. Amongst them may be named Gustavus Horn, a Swede, who had "made his proofs" under Prince Maurice of Nassau; Banner or Banér, also a Swede, who avenged himself for the execution of his father by Charles IX. by rendering the most splendid service to the son of that monarch; Baudissin, a representative of the Lusatian family of Luppau; Falkenberg, Mutsenfahl, Ortenburg, Kniphausen, Teufel, and Tott, all men of great ability; Henry Matthias, Count of Thurn, the same who had flung the councillors and their secretary from the window at Prague; the Rhinegrave Otto Ludwig. The list could be lengthened, for there was scarcely a man in that army who was not a hero.

Detained by contrary winds, the fleet cast anchor off the little island of Rügen, separated only from the Pomeranian mainland by the Strela Sound, on the 24th June. Gustavus was the first to leap upon the land. Kneeling, in the presence of his following, he thanked the Almighty for having brought his army and his fleet in safety to German ground. With the utmost expedition, and in spite of a violent storm, he landed his troops, marched upon and occupied Stettin, Damm, Stargard, Cammin, and Walgart, almost without the semblance of opposition. Before the end of July he had become virtually master of Pomerania.

For the moment the Emperor had no army to oppose him. Wallenstein had been dismissed, and the army which Wallenstein commanded had vanished with their leader. A few troops had indeed garrisoned the towns of Pomerania, but these, drawn together by the Imperial commander in those parts, Torquato Conti, were in no condition to make head against the invader. Conti, whose cruelty was surpassed only by his avarice, used then unhesitatingly the only means at his disposal to check the progress of the Swedes. He ordered the laying waste of the country on both sides of his line of retreat, the burning of the more opulent villages; then, to render the possession of Stettin useless to Gustavus, he intrenched himself at Garz, south of that place, on the left bank of the Oder, hoping by that means to sever the communications between the Swedes and the rest of Germany. Further, when he saw that Gustavus had no intention of attacking him, but, leaving him intrenched at Garz, had proceeded to complete the conquest of the province, Conti suddenly quitted his position and made a dash at Stettin. Repulsed with loss, and seeing the impossibility of carrying on the campaign successfully, he sent a messenger to Gustavus to propose a truce during the autumn and winter months, on the ground that it would be too cold to fight. "The Swedes can fight in winter as well as in summer," was the reply of the Swedish king. It was sufficient for Conti, who resigned his command and left his troops, under the Count of Schaumburg, to make the best of their way into Brandenburg. This march thither they only accomplished with great loss of men, of guns, and of baggage.

The circumstances of the empire, the absence of an imperial army, the knowledge that more than one-half of the people of Germany gave him their sympathies and their prayers, and were prepared, as soon as he should have developed his capacity by beating the armies of the League, to render him their active aid, would have justified Gustavus, being the man he was, to march through Germany and finish the war in Vienna. The idea was considered by his generals and himself. Gustavus rejected it, not because he considered the plan impracticable, but because, were he to act upon it, he would appear to some, and he would be represented to all, as a foreign sovereign whose selfish aim was to expel Ferdinand only to assume his place; whereas, by confining himself to driving the Imperialists from the north and the west of Germany, where they were harassing and oppressing the people, he would occupy the position which he coveted above all others, that of a deliverer. He resolved rather, then, to make himself master, **in the** first instance, of the strong **places in** the northern and western portions **of the** country, to **rouse to** co-operation with him the **princes and** people **of** those portions, to close the Baltic **to the Imperialists, to** deprive the Emperor of all his allies **in the** country, and, **when this** had been accomplished, to **deal** the House of Austria **a** blow which should force it, under the penalty **of** destruction, **to** abandon the policy of persecution—to respect **the** rights and **the** consciences of others.

The resignation of **his** command by Torquato Conti, and the disorderly **retreat of the** troops **he had** commanded, were events which played **the** game of Gustavus. He took Greifenhagen—a considerable **town on the Oder,** between Stettin **and** Garz—by storm, occupied **the** latter place, abandoned by **the** Imperialists; then, marching nearly directly eastward, seized Pyritz. **Before the end of** the year the only places **in Pomerania** which **still held out for** the Emperor **were Greifswald, Demmin,** and Kolberg, **and Gustavus** was making **energetic** preparations for besieging these.

If **the** Imperial generals were, on the **plains in the north of** Germany, playing the **game** of Gustavus, not the **less so was** Ferdinand II. in his Cabinet of Vienna. It has been **already** stated how Wallenstein had over-run Mecklenburg, and **how the** Emperor, to reward his services, had pronounced that duchy to be forfeited, and had bestowed it upon **his** victorious general. But **the** expelled dukes of Mecklenburg still possessed power and influence **in** their hereditary domains. Gustavus, conqueror **of** nearly **all** Pomerania, **stood on the** borders **of** Mecklenburg prepared, there could be no doubt, **to restore** the **duchy to its** rightful lords. **The** expelled dukes, however, **endeavoured** rather to win from their **master the** boon which **the foreigner would** have placed in their hands. Through **the princes of the** Diet, **still** assembled **at** Ratisbon, they **expressed** their determination not only to give no aid, but **to offer the** strongest opposition to the foreign invader, provided **the Emperor** would restore to them their rights. But obstinacy was a great characteristic of Ferdinand. Though he knew what a refusal would cost him, he refused. One consequence was that Mecklenburg, the province adjoining Pomerania, was gained for Gustavus, and Prince Charles of Sachsen-Lauenburg proceeded thither to raise troops for him.

In other respects the affairs of Gustavus prospered. On the 13th January 1631, he concluded, at Bärwald, a treaty for six years with France, in virtue of which he was to receive a hundred and sixty thousand thalers on the spot, and an annual subsidy of four hundred thousand on condition of maintaining in the field an army of thirty thousand infantry and six thousand cavalry, and of assuring to the princes and people whose territory he might occupy the free exercise of their religion. He opened the campaign in the March following, took Neubrandenburg, Loitz, Malchin, and laid siege to Greifswald, Demmin, and Kolberg. To cover these last operations he formed an intrenched camp of Schwedt, on the Oder. He was still in that camp when he received information that an Imperialist army under Count Tilly was rapidly approaching to relieve the beleaguered towns.

A short, lean man, with hollow cheeks, a long nose, a broad wrinkled forehead, heavy moustachios, and a pointed chin, Tilly had the reputation of being the most successful soldier of the age. A Netherlander by birth, he had learned the art of war under Alba and, especially, under Alexander Farnese. In the school of that great captain he had learned alike how to obey and how to enforce obedience, to shrink from no measures, however opposed they might be to the dictates of humanity, which were necessary to obtain his end. He was a bigoted Catholic, and thought all means lawful for the extirpation of heresy. He had made his first military studies in the Netherlands against the Protestants: he had then served in Hungary against the rebels of that country and the Turks; then again in Bavaria, in Bohemia, and in the Palatinate against the Protestants. He had never been beaten. Though not, in the strict sense of the word, a great general, he was yet a man to be feared; for he combined quickness of movement with daring, possessed a very clear military vision, never shrank from striking when he thought a blow might be effective, and his execution was always "thorough."

Such was the man who, at the head of twenty thousand men, hastily collected from the different parts of Catholic Germany, was hastening, in the middle of the winter of 1630-31, by forced marches, to relieve the beleaguered towns of Demmin and Kolberg. At Frankfurt-on-the-Oder he met the shattered remnants of the small army which, under Conti, had endeavoured to stay the progress of the invader, and subsequently, under Schaumburg, had roused against itself, by its terrible excesses and unsparing exactions, the indignation of the people of the provinces through which it had retreated. Leaving Schaumburg with a sufficient garrison in Frankfurt, Tilly pressed forward to Pomerania. But before he could quit Brandenburg he heard of the surrender of the places he had been so anxious to save. The first object of his march, then, had vanished. There could be no question of attacking, with his comparatively small force, the intrenched camp of Gustavus at Schwedt. But he could still strike a blow under which Protestantism would reel. The considerable city of Magdeburg, known for its zeal for the reformed religion, had re-elected, as its administrator, Christian William of Brandenburg, a prince who had been placed under the ban of the Empire, had received a Swedish general, Dietrich of Falkenburg, and with him a small Swedish garrison. He resolved, then, that Magdeburg should feel the first vengeance of the Catholic League. Renouncing, accordingly, his march to Pomerania, Tilly struck westwards towards that city.

No sooner had Gustavus become aware that the direction of Tilly's march had been changed, than, as anxious as his opponent to deliver a blow which should be felt, he quitted his intrenched camp and marched on Frankfurt-on-the-Oder. His troops were on their march inflamed to fury by the tidings which reached them, that Tilly, on his march westward, had stormed the town of Neubrandenburg, recently taken by them, and had put to the sword every man of the Swedish garrison which had defended it. They arrived before Frankfurt determined to enforce a heavy retribution; attacked the city with vigour and resolution; and stormed it the third day (3rd April 1631). They captured all the enemy's guns and meted out to the soldiers who demanded mercy the same quarter which their own countrymen had received at Neubrandenburg.

Meanwhile, in view of the invasion of Germany, of the declared intention of the Emperor Ferdinand to enforce with the utmost strictness,the resolutions of the Diet against heresy, many of the Protestant princes had, on the invitation of John George, Elector of Saxony, met in consultation at Leipzig (6th February 1631). Neither John George nor George William, Elector of Brandenburg—though the latter had been one of those who had invited the intervention of the Swedes—had, up to this time, displayed the smallest desire to aid Gustavus in his enterprise. Both weak men, they were alike governed by their ministers—the Elector of Saxony by Field Marshal von Arnheim, a devoted friend of Wallenstein; George William by Count Adam of Schwarzenberg, a Catholic and an Imperialist. But the determination of Ferdinand to push to the utmost the Catholic crusade had alarmed them; and whilst the one summoned, the other was foremost in attending the congress at Leipzig. Besides the Elector of Brandenburg there were present also on the same occasion the Elector of Hesse-Cassel, and all the more important adherents of princely and noble rank of the Reformed connection. In spite of the intrigues of Ferdinand, the assembled notables declared their fixed resolution to maintain their rights; to summon the Emperor to abrogate the edict known as the Restitution Edict, to withdraw his troops from their towns and fortresses, to suspend his arbitrary executions, and to redress the grievances of which they complained:—and, should he refuse, to raise an army of forty thousand men to assert their claims.

The alliance which Gustavus had made with France, and more particularly the conditions of that alliance, had contributed more than anything else to the solidarity of the confederation of the princes and nobles of northern Germany. The important condition that the Catholic religion should be respected in all the places which might submit to or be conquered by Gustavus, that religion should be everywhere free, did as much to bind northern Germany to his cause as the reputation of his soldiers and his own fame as a warrior. Even the less bigoted Catholics who regarded with apprehension the increasing power of the Emperor, were ready to fight for a programme which, whilst it promised them protection against arbitrary power, ensured to them the exercise of their conscientious beliefs.

Meanwhile Tilly was marching against Magdeburg. Commanding a separate army, acting in conjunction with rather than in subordination to the Imperial commander, was Godfrey Henry, Count of Pappenheim. Tilly was the general of the Catholic League. Pappenheim, subsequently to 1630, represented the Empire. One of the best cavalry officers of the age, Pappenheim had distinguished himself on many a well-fought field. It was when returning from the pursuit of the Duke of Saxe-Lauenburg that Pappenheim received from Tilly notice of his movement against Magdeburg. Instantly he changed his course in that direction, drove in the troops with whom Falkenstein had occupied the outlying points, and had already invested the place when Tilly arrived. The regular siege began on the 30th March.

Gustavus, we have seen, had stormed Frankfurt-on-the-Oder on the 3rd April. Little apprehensive, probably even ignorant, of Tilly's designs against Magdeburg, he had marched from Frankfurt against Landsberg, an important town on the Warthe. He captured this place on the 16th April. The same day he learned that Tilly and Pappenheim were pressing Magdeburg hard. A glance at the map will show that to reach Magdeburg from Landsberg, Gustavus would have to march by Küstrin, Berlin, and Spandau, all belonging to the Elector of Brandenburg. Now, not only were Küstrin and Spandau strongly fortified, but the Elector of Brandenburg, influenced by his minister, had, some time before, opened the gates of the former to the fleeing Imperialists, and had shut them to the pursuing Swedes. It was impossible, then, that Gustavus should pass these two places to attack Tilly at Magdeburg, unless he were assured of the dispositions of their garrisons. Marching beyond them without such assurance, he would place himself between two fires. He had claims on the Elector of Brandenburg—not claims based merely on common religious convictions, but claims resting on the fact that he had freed his ancestral province from the presence of the enemy, and on the knowledge that he alone stood between the Elector and the Emperor. He sent to him, then, as soon as he had learned the peril of Magdeburg, a proposition whereby he engaged to march at once to relieve that city, provided only that the strong places of Küstrin and Spandau were placed in his hands. The Elector, George William, who was then at Berlin, hesitated long before he gave a favourable reply. He was dominated by his fears and by his minister. If he should comply, and if then Gustavus were to be beaten, what would become of himself? How could he hope to escape the wrath of the narrow-minded but bigoted and determined Emperor? He was still hesitating, still parrying the requests of Gustavus with evasive answers, when the Swedish hero reached Berlin. At the interview which followed, Gustavus scarcely attempted to control himself. He plainly told the Elector that the relief of Magdeburg was a matter which concerned not himself personally, but the cause of the reformed religion; that if the reformed princes of Germany declined to help him, he would return to Stockholm, make peace with the Emperor, and then, he added, "in what a position would you find yourself?" These arguments, to which the presence of the highly-disciplined and well-ordered Swedish army gave weight, decided at last George William, and he gave orders for the surrender to his ally of Küstrin and Spandau.

But all the difficulties were not yet surmounted. From Berlin to Magdeburg were two roads; the shorter to the west, through a country eaten up and occupied by the enemy, who would be able to dispute the passage of the Elbe; the longer, southward, by Dessau or Wittingen, through a land, easy and unexhausted, and belonging to a professing ally, John George of Saxony. But like George William of Brandenburg, John George, timid by nature and influenced by his minister, refused a free passage to the Swedish troops; and whilst Gustavus was negotiating to induce him to withdraw his objections, Magdeburg fell.

Magdeburg was stormed by the troops of Pappenheim and Tilly on the 10th May. For three days the city was a scene of blood for which, to use the words of Schiller, "history has no description." It was the most barbarous act of, in a military sense, a barbaric age. It is computed that thirty thousand persons, in total disregard of sex, or age, or condition, were ruthlessly massacred. It was not until the 14th, the fifth day after the storm, that Tilly himself ventured into the city. The evil had then been consummated. A deed had been done which rendered reconciliation impossible, which marked in broad and bloody lines the demarcation between Catholic and Reformed!

This sanguinary stroke produced, for the moment, results highly favourable to the Imperial cause. With the panic which spread throughout Protestant Germany flew also the feeling that the disaster might have been prevented, that the lingering of Gustavus at Berlin had assured the triumph of Tilly. For the moment men did not stop to enquire whether the Electors of Saxony and Brandenburg were free from blame. The latter prince, far from regarding the matter from the standpoint of religion, seemed in the first instance most anxious only to clear himself from all connection with the Swede. He had made over Spandau to Gustavus that Gustavus might march to relieve Magdeburg. Now that Magdeburg had fallen, he demanded in imperative terms the restitution of Spandau. But Gustavus, who had quitted Berlin, was equal to the occasion. He announced his intention to comply with the demand of the Elector, but to treat that prince as an enemy. Sending, then, instructions to the commandant of Spandau to evacuate that place, he marched against Berlin. Before the gates of that city he declared his ultimatum. He desired, he said, to be treated not worse than the Imperial generals; to be allowed to ensure the safety of his army by the occupation of the places necessary for that purpose, to be furnished with a moderate sum of money and bread for his troops. Were these conditions complied with, he would be the true friend of the Elector, and would engage to protect him against all his foes; were they refused, he would become his enemy. This message, which conveyed likewise to its recipient the conviction that it would be followed by action, decided the Elector, and he subscribed to the terms dictated by Gustavus.

Circumstances soon brought about a similar result in the councils of the Elector of Saxony.

The capture of Magdeburg had left Tilly free to direct his arms against the two most formidable of the reformed princes in that part of Germany, the Elector of Saxony and the Landgrave of Hesse. So long as these should maintain the power of independent action, the triumph of the Catholic cause was still uncertain. Tilly selected the Landgrave as the first object of imperial vengeance. From the ruins of Magdeburg he marched into Thüringen and desolated that beautiful country with fire and the sword. Frankenhausen, the capital of the principality of Schwarzburg-Rudolfstadt, was plundered and reduced to ashes under the very eyes of the imperial general. Erfurt purchased its exemption from a similar fate by a plentiful supply of money and provisions. Having exhausted the Saxe-Ernestine and Schwarzburg principalities, Tilly turned to the

Landgrave of Hesse-Cassel, and threatened his lands with the
same fate unless he would immediately disband his troops,
renounce the Leipzig contract, receive imperial troops in his
country and fortresses, pay up the contributions demanded, and
declare himself a friend. But the Landgrave of Hesse-Cassel
was made of firmer stuff than many of his colleagues in the
princely families of Germany. "I will not," he answered,
"admit foreign soldiers into my cities and fortresses; my
troops I require for myself; if I am attacked, I shall know
how to defend myself; if Count Tilly requires money and
provisions, he had better get them from Munich." More than
that, he repulsed two detachments which Tilly, on receiving
this answer, sent into his lands, and prepared to defend himself
to the last, when the movements of Gustavus forced Tilly to
renounce his intentions.

Gustavus, in fact, having concluded his arrangements with
the Elector of Brandenburg, prepared to move forward. Greifswald, the last place in Pomerania which had held out for
the Emperor, had fallen; a reinforcement of 8,000 men
from Sweden, and a corps of 6,000 Scotchmen, led by the
Marquis of Hamilton,* had arrived. Thus strengthened,
Gustavus marched against Pappenheim, who still held the
country about Magdeburg. It was Pappenheim's call for aid
which saved the daring Landgrave of Hesse-Cassel from a
conflict with Tilly. The latter, hastening back to Magdeburg
by forced marches, effected a junction with Pappenheim, and
took up a position at Wolmirstädt on the Elbe, between nine
and ten miles north of Magdeburg, and not much further
from that occupied by Gustavus on the same side of the
river at Werben, near the junction with it of the Havel.
In the skirmishes which followed, the Swedes invariably had
the advantage. At last Tilly issued from his position, and
marching to within cannon-shot of that occupied by Gustavus,
offered him battle. But, with an army inferior in numbers by

* Afterwards, 1643, the first Duke of Hamilton.

one-half to that of the enemy, the Swedish king was too prudent to accept the invitation. Knowing his position to be strong enough to resist attack, he remained behind his intrenchments. After a fruitless cannonade and some skirmishes, which were again favourable to the Swedes, Tilly then returned to his camp, losing in his retrograde movement many men by desertion.

Whilst Gustavus was thus watching the main imperial army, his lieutenants, General Tott and Duke Adolphus Frederic I. of Mecklenburg-Schwerin, had re-conquered almost the whole of Mecklenburg, and Adolphus Frederic had resumed the government of the Schwerin division of the dukedom. Just then Tilly fell back in the moment already related, and Gustavus thought the moment opportune personally to re-instate the other duke, John Albert, in the Güstrow portion. He rode for that purpose to Güstrow, and, surrounded by a retinue of princes and nobles, amid the heart-felt rejoicings of the people, replaced the dispossessed prince upon his ducal throne. On his return to his camp of Werben, he welcomed with great joy Landgrave William of Hesse-Cassel, the first of the princes of Germany who had offered, of his own free will, to make an offensive and defensive alliance with the invader. The alliance was concluded then and there.

This action on the part of Landgrave William produced in the mind of Tilly the fear lest it should become contagious. If Saxony, for instance, were to declare for Gustavus, his own position at Wolmirstädt would become dangerous in the extreme. He resolved to conjure this peril by making demands upon the Elector John George, the answer to which would be decisive. He required him, therefore, to admit the imperial army into Saxony, and either to disband the Saxon army or to unite it to his own. John George, knowing from experience that the tender mercies of the Emperor were cruel, embittered by the treatment dealt out to Magdeburg, and encouraged by the proximity of Gustavus, refused point blank. Upon this, Tilly broke up his camp at Wolmirstädt, and pressed on to

Halle, devastating the country as he marched. Thence he despatched another and more threatening message to the Elector. Its effect was directly the contrary of that which he had intended. It forced John George—who till then had regarded Gustavus with jealousy, distrust, even aversion, and who had preferred the sacrifice of Magdeburg to union with him— to throw himself into the arms of the King of Sweden. He had, on the receipt of the first message, despatched Arnheim to treat with that prince. The second message made him still more eager for an alliance, and he concluded one on terms dictated by Gustavus (3rd September 1631). The King then crossed the Elbe, and effected the day following, at Torgau, a junction with the Saxon army.

Tilly, far from endeavouring to prevent this junction, had pressed on to the important city of Leipzig, and had summoned it to surrender. As the commandant hesitated, Tilly reduced the suburb, called the suburb of Halle, to ashes. This severe measure, the recollection of the fate of Magdeburg, and the bad condition of the fortifications, combined to influence the commandant to yield. On the second day, Leipzig opened her gates. The city and inhabitants were mercifully treated by the conqueror.

The news of the occupation of Leipzig reached Gustavus and his allies at Torgau. They held at once a council of war, and resolved, at the pressing instance of John George of Saxony, to set the fate of Protestant Germany on the issue of a single battle. The order to march was then given, and early on the morning of the 7th September the Swedish-Saxon army came in sight of Leipzig.

Tilly, who was daily expecting the arrival from Italy of Aldringer and Tiefenbach, at the head of 12,000 veterans, was very anxious to avoid a battle until those reinforcements should reach him. He had therefore originally taken up a position close to and resting upon the city of Leipzig. The earnest representations of Pappenheim, backed by Fürstenberg and the younger generals, induced him, against his better judgment, to quit this unassailable post, and to move forward to the fair champaign plains of Breitenfeld. The ground which he selected for his new encampment is diversified here and there with small elevations and declivities. In front of two of these elevations, south-west of the village of **Podelwitz**, Tilly now ranged his army. He placed his **guns, consisting of forty pieces**, on the heights, in such a manner that their fire would pass over the heads of his right, commanded by Fürstenberg, and of his centre, commanded by himself. Behind the heights, in rear of his right centre, was likewise a very thick wood. His left, commanded by Pappenheim, and consisting of cavalry, was free in front and in rear. Notwithstanding that he had relinquished his advantageous position near Leipzig to post himself in the open plain, Tilly was secretly resolved to avoid a general action till his reinforcements should arrive. But the rashness of Pappenheim disconcerted his plans. To take up the position marked out by Gustavus, the Swedish-Saxon army had to cross a little rivulet called the Loder, near Podelwitz, to the north-east of the imperial army. The opportunity to harass the enemy whilst they should be engaged in this operation was so tempting that Pappenheim proposed to Tilly to attack them. Tilly gave a most unwilling consent, and only on the condition that Pappenheim should employ no more than 2,000 cuirassiers, and should not bring on an action. Pappenheim so far conformed that he charged the Swedes, advancing obliquely across his front, with only the number of men specified. But he made no impression on their serried ranks. Gustavus had noted the possibilities, had hastened to the point of danger, and, present there when Pappenheim swooped down, had first broken his attack, and finally forced him to retire badly smitten. Pappenheim, in his retreat, had set fire to the village of Podelwitz to check the Swedes' advance. It did not check it, however. The gallant soldiers of Gustavus traversed the burning village, and reached a position which enabled them to form up fronting the enemy's line.

Returning to the main body after his repulse, Pappenheim ordered his entire cavalry to form, with the intention of falling with force upon the enemy whilst they should be still in motion. But the allies had too well employed the interval to grant him a second chance. Their whole army had, under the fire of the imperial guns, cleared the dangerous point, and had taken their position opposite to the imperialists: the Saxons, numbering 15,000, of whom one-fourth were cavalry, were in two lines opposite Fürstenburg; the Swedes, counting nearly 20,000, in three lines, including the reserves, opposed to Tilly and Pappenheim. Of the front line, Gustavus Horn commanded the left, Colonel Teufel the centre, and Gustavus the right. The cavalry were not massed in one compact body, as with the imperialists. Sometimes between each regiment, sometimes between every two or three regiments, was posted a regiment of musketeers, trained to act with the horsemen. The centre was composed of four brigades of pikemen. The guns were ranged immediately in front of the first line. The second line consisted of five regiments of cavalry, immediately behind and supporting Teufel's brigades of pikemen. On their right, behind the wing commanded by Gustavus, were three regiments of horse led by Banner. The centre of the third line, or reserve, was composed of three brigades; two of which were British, under Hepburn. It was flanked on the right by four regiments of horse, under Baudissin; on the left by three regiments under Halle, and supported in the rear by two more at Hepburn's disposal. It may here be stated that there was no great disparity between the numbers on both sides. The imperialists counted but few more than 35,000.

The more compact formation of the allied army gave the imperialists an apparent advantage, for it enabled their longer line to outflank that of their enemy. Tilly was so impressed with this, that he was anxious to await their more forward movement. But Pappenheim and Fürstenburg forced his hand. Smarting under his repulse from Podelwitz, Pappenheim had, as I have said, returned to his camp, and ordered out all his horsemen, with the view to renew his attack in full force. Fürstenburg likewise no sooner viewed the Saxons formed up in front of him than he charged upon them with seven regiments of cavalry. These two attacks were made almost simultaneously, Pappenheim on the King's troops, Fürstenburg on the Saxons, the latter having perhaps a slight, but very slight advance.

By a special arrangement made by Gustavus, who had had no experience of his allies, and who therefore was inclined to doubt their discipline and steadfastness and the capacity of their general, a considerable space separated the Saxons from the Swedish army. This isolation was not, perhaps, calculated to increase the confidence of young troops having in front of them a serried line of infantry, on their left flank strong brigades of cavalry, and whose eyes were blinded by dust and smoke—for the wind blew strongly from the south. The result was just that which might have been anticipated. Attacked with great fury on their left flank, the Saxons made but a feeble resistance. Their Elector, John George, was the first to give evidence that the practice of war often differs vastly from its theory. He fled with all speed in the direction of Torgau, and first drew rein at Eilenburg, about midway between that place and Leipzig. In the space of twenty minutes the Saxon half of the Protestant army had disappeared; the Croats were engaging in pillaging their camp, and couriers were on their way to Munich and Vienna to announce a great victory.

For, at that supreme moment, Tilly never doubted but that victory was within his grasp. The only enemy still remaining on the field was inferior to him in numbers by nearly one-half. Pappenheim was engaging them on their right. He had only to push forward his numerous infantry, and assail them on their front and their now exposed left, to crush in Germany, for a long time to come, the cause of freedom of conscience.

But the Tilly of that day was not the Tilly who had triumphed on many a well-fought field, who had never known defeat

"The determination," writes Schiller, "which had never left Tilly before, failed him on this day." Certain it is that he allowed a grand opportunity to slip from his hands.

Another moment, and it was too late. Pappenheim, always in the front of danger, had launched, as already stated, his whole cavalry against the Swedish centre. Here, we have seen, the King commanded in person. Under him was an officer worthy to serve under such a chief, the cool-headed and daring Banner. The Swedes met the charge with so much steadiness that Pappenheim, unable to make any impression upon them, fell back baffled. Seven times, however, did he renew the charge, but seven times was he driven back. It was on the occasion of the last of these charges that Gustavus, noting the rout of the Saxons, and feeling certain that in a few minutes he would have Tilly on his hands, turned the repulse into a complete defeat by launching his own cavalry from his right wing and forcing Pappenheim to quit the field.

This, then, was the situation after a hand-to-hand engagement which had lasted about half an hour: Tilly had disposed of the Saxons, and Gustavus had driven Pappenheim from the field. If the left flank of the King was uncovered, his front was clear, and the traversing by the enemy of the space which he had designedly left between him and the Saxons would give him time, with his troops well-trained for movements of celerity, to offer a new front to the enemy.

Before even the Saxons had been completely driven from their ground, and before Pappenheim's repulse had been changed into a decisive rout, Gustavus, noticing the disorder of his allies, had strengthened his left flank, where Horn commanded, by detaching to it, from the centre, three of his best infantry regiments. On receiving this welcome reinforcement, Horn had distributed the pikemen, of which it was composed, in companies or sections between each squadron of cavalry, the pikemen slightly in advance. He had but just made this disposition when the imperial cuirassiers, their swords dripping with Saxon

3 *

blood, dashed upon him. The Swedish pikemen received the shock, however, with the same firmness and resolution with which, but a few minutes before, they and their comrades had met the charge of Pappenheim. The cuirassiers were drawing back, baffled, with the intention of renewing the attack, when Gustavus appeared on the scene, and, launching his own horsemen against the retreating imperialists, completed their discomfiture. They fled from the field, not again, that day, to reappear.

Having thus disposed of the enemy's horsemen, Gustavus, wheeling his troops and making a long sweep to the left, charged the extreme and now uncovered right front of the enemy, immediately below the high ground in front of which Tilly's army had been posted. To hew down and disperse the infantry there, to charge the high ground and to drive thence the gunners, to capture the guns, to turn them against the central mass of imperial infantry, now hesitating between two fires, was the work of a few minutes. A moment later and Horn's pikemen advanced from the front to deal the finishing blow. The imperialist infantry, assailed now on three sides, had no heart left to continue the battle. Four famous regiments excepted, they broke and fled. The four regiments alluded to, who belonged to the force which Fürstenberg had brought from Flanders, where they had "grown grey with victory," cut their way fighting to the wood of which I have spoken, in rear of their right centre, and eventually, after losing more than half their numbers, succeeded in effecting their retreat. The rest of the imperialist army fled, I have said, in disorder. They were, on the order of Gustavus, hotly pursued by the Swedish cavalry till night-fall. Their losses, when the pursuit ceased, had been enormous. Of the thirty-five thousand who had marched out of their camp that morning, one-fifth lay dead on the field; one-seventh were either wounded or prisoners. So complete was the defeat, that Tilly, who was badly wounded, and who had narrowly escaped capture, could not muster more than six hundred men to accompany him in his retreat to Halle and Halberstadt; whilst even Pappenheim only rallied fourteen hundred horsemen. The Swedes lost but seven hundred men, the Saxons about two thousand.

On his knees, amidst the dying and the dead, Gustavus returned thanks to God for his great victory. He then marched from the field, took possession of and occupied the still standing camp of the imperialists, near to and resting on Leipzig. That same evening, the Elector of Saxony reappeared to congratulate the conqueror. Gustavus received him with the greatest courtesy, thanked him for having so earnestly urged him to fight, and entrusted to him the task of re-capturing Leipzig. The next day he himself marched to Merseburg and Halle, defeating on his way thither a body of five thousand imperialists. At Halle he was rejoined by the Elector, who had recovered Leipzig without striking a blow.

Such was the first great encounter on the field of Breitenfeld. If the greater battle which was to follow it, at an interval of a hundred and eighty-two years, may be truly called the "Volkerschlacht"—the battle which delivered peoples from tyranny—this, its forerunner, may as truly and as fairly be designated a battle which freed Germany from the thraldom of religious intolerance. It was necessary, certainly, in both cases to follow up the victory, to supplement the first great initiative battle by others. Breitenfeld was, in fact, the first of a series of battles which brought about the great result of allowing Catholics and Protestants to live together in harmony, of ensuring to every man freedom of conscience, of rooting out and destroying the principle which gave one man the right to say that because he himself believed certain dogmas therefore all the German people should be compelled to believe them. This was the principle which Ferdinand II. had introduced into Germany. This was the principle which Gustavus Adolphus invaded Germany to destroy. These two men were the embodiments of those opposite ideas. The one, trained up from his

earliest childhood to hate the Reformers with the most bitter
hatred, viewed all the affairs of State through spectacles of
extreme Catholic prejudice. To force other men to believe as
he believed was the aim of his life. To effect this aim no
instrument was too vile. Persecution, confiscation of property,
banishment, sentence of death, torture, were all legitimate
weapons. From Ferdinand there issued no rebuke for the
slaughter of thirty thousand unarmed people at Magdeburg.
He read, on the contrary, with sympathy, the report of Tilly
that "since the taking of Troy and of Jerusalem no such
triumph had been achieved." The embodiment of the very
worst features of the worst form of Roman Catholicism, he
was unfortunately in a position, and he possessed, unfortunately,
the iron resolution, to give effect to his convictions—and he gave
effect to them with a vengeance.

Never, in the history of the world, has the influence of one
man been greater upon a people than was the influence of
Ferdinand II. on the hereditary states and kingdoms of the
House of Hapsburg. At the time of the death of his predecessor,
the Emperor Matthias, the reformed religion preponderated,
not only in by far the greater part of Bohemia, but in the
two Austrias and in Moravia. It was a living force in
Hungary, in Carniola, in Carinthia, even to a certain extent
in Styria. In Hungary the life remained: but by persecution,
by banishment, by the harrowing of armies, this one man did
succeed in rooting out, almost completely, the new faith from
the hereditary provinces and from Bohemia. He tried to
produce the same result all over Germany.

The living embodiment of the other principle, the principle of
toleration, was a far nobler character. If Ferdinand would have
enslaved men's consciences, Gustavus would have freed them.
Firm in his own convictions, he did not, like Ferdinand, force
those convictions down the throats of other men. He was willing
to grant to the various peoples of Germany the same freedom of
thought on questions of religion which he claimed for himself.

He loudly declared himself, when he entered Pomerania, the protector of all established religions, even of the Catholic. From that declaration he never swerved.

An age which has recognised toleration as a cardinal principle cannot be indifferent to an event which first breathed life into the scattered materials on which that principle has been built up, which gave to it a power of cohesion, and welded it into a material shape. The battle of Breitenfeld, or, as it is sometimes styled in this country, of Leipzig, was the first effective blow struck in the Germany of the seventeenth century for freedom of conscience. As such it deserves a permanent resting-place in the thoughts and memories of the descendants of those who so nobly fought to free themselves and their children from a yoke which they had found intolerable.

CHAPTER II.

THE LECH AND NUREMBERG.

THE victory of Breitenfeld had given Catholic Germany into the hands of Gustavus. With the remnants of his beaten army Tilly had retreated into Westphalia, and between Leipzig and Vienna there was no other army to oppose the progress of the conqueror. Had Gustavus marched directly from the battle-field to the capital of the hereditary states of the house of Austria, he might there have dictated terms of peace alike to Ferdinand and Maximilian.

From such a march Gustavus was deterred by the consideration that he would leave behind him, ready and able to reconquer and to harass the states of North Germany, so experienced a general as Tilly. There could be no question but that, left to himself, Tilly, rallying his beaten soldiers and joining to them the garrisons of some of the places still held for the League, would soon again be formidable. Had Gustavus been able to dispose of the Saxon army, to place it under the command of a general such as Banner, or Horn, or Bernard of Saxe-Weimar, he might have ventured on the daring step, a step the sound principle of which was, in a later age, vindicated by the genius of a warrior greater even than the hero King. But he was not able to dispose of that army. The jealousy of John George had but little abated, and although in his first moments of enthusiasm he had offered to use all his influence to have

Gustavus elected King of the Romans, he soon relapsed into the suspicious mood natural to him. Another consideration had great weight in deciding Gustavus against the bolder course. An imperial diet was at the moment sitting at Frankfurt to consider the Edict of Restitution, and Ferdinand was using all his influence to compel the members of that diet to a speedy and disadvantageous agreement with him. The certainty of the approach of Gustavus alone would prevent such a result. The march, too, of a Swedish army through Franconia and the Rhine provinces—a part of Germany which had been till then traversed only by the armies of the League—could not fail to produce a happy effect upon the minds of friends, of waverers, and of foes. Gustavus then charged the Elector of Saxony to carry the war into Silesia, Bohemia, and the hereditary states of Austria, his other German allies to maintain and extend their influence in Lower Saxony and Westphalia, resolving himself to win the lands ruled by the princes of the Catholic League. In accordance with this plan Gustavus set out to lead his army through Thüringen and lower Franconia, and thence to the Rhine.

The battle of Breitenfeld had been fought on the 7th September. On the 20th Gustavus presented himself before Erfurt, an important and fortified town on the Gera. Though this place was dependent upon the Catholic bishop of Worms, and possessed a large Catholic population, the magistrates surrendered it at discretion. Gustavus granted the inhabitants the free exercise of their religion; then, nominating William Duke of Saxe-Weimar to be governor of the district and of the province of Thüringen, and the Count of Löwenstein to be commander of the garrison, which consisted of Colonel Fowle's Scottish regiment, fifteen hundred strong, he, for convenience sake, divided his army into two bodies, and pushed forward across the Thüringen forest, which boasted of no great town and of but a few villages, into lower Franconia. The left column of his divided force he committed to General Baudissin, under whom served Colonel Hepburn; the King himself led the right. The difficulties of the march were considerable, for there were no roads, and the transport of artillery over the rocks and through the defiles caused the exercise of much labour and ingenuity. Nevertheless on the evening of the third day Gustavus reached the south-west boundaries of the forest. The next morning he attacked and carried the town of Königshofen, on the Saal, belonging to the Bishop of Würzburg. This town contained the magazine and arsenal of the diocese of that prelate, was victualled for twelve months, and was held by a strong garrison. Its easy capture, then, was a matter of great importance to the Swedes. Marching twenty-six miles the day following, Gustavus invested and forced to capitulate the free imperial town of Schweinfurt. Here he came again into communication with Baudissin who, in his march, had mastered the towns of Smalkalden, Meiningen, Neustadt, Hammelburg, Gemünden, and Karlstadt, the latter being the fortified frontier town of the see of Würzburg.

Gustavus now had his army once more united on the right bank of the Main, the famous river which constitutes the natural line of demarcation between northern and southern Germany, within striking distance—for it is only twenty-three miles—of the important city of Würzburg. The bishop of that diocese was absent, acting as ambassador in France on behalf of the Catholic League, but his brother of Bamberg was on the spot to represent him. This prelate was quite equal to the occasion. Whilst on the one hand he offered to treat with Gustavus, on the other he despatched messengers to Tilly, who was hurrying to the relief of Würzburg, urging him to hasten his march. His overtures to Gustavus—overtures in which he offered, in consideration of being left in peaceful enjoyment of his lands and dignities, to pay down a sum equal to £27,000, to furnish monthly to Gustavus the same sum which up to that time he had paid to the League, to recall his forces from the League army, and to surrender in pledge the strong fortresses of Forcheim and Kronach—did indeed impose upon and cause delay to the Swedish king; for when, after having agreed to the conditions, he pressed for their execution, the bishop, who had received certain intelligence of the near approach of Tilly, threw off the mask and declined to complete the bargain.

Tilly, who by means of reinforcements headed by Aldringer, Fugger, and other generals had increased his army, to the number of thirty thousand, was indeed approaching Würzburg, but he was still three days' march from it, not so near but that a determined general commanding determined soldiers might not venture an attack upon that town before he could arrive. Comprehending this on the moment, Gustavus, as soon as the negotiations with the Bishop of Bamberg had been broken off, marched directly on to Würzburg and invested it. The next day he obtained a firm footing on the south bank of the Main, poured in an incessant fire on the fortifications during that night and the two following days, carried the gate of the castle of Marienberg and the stone bridge over its ditch on the second day, and the castle itself the same night. The capture of Marienberg caused the instantaneous surrender of Würzburg, for the castle dominated the town. In Würzburg Gustavus obtained large supplies of corn, of wine, and of money.

Tilly, after his defeat at Breitenfeld, had fallen back, with an army reduced to eight thousand men, into Westphalia. Receiving there a strong reinforcement of cavalry and infantry from the Elector of Cologne, he had marched in a southerly direction to Warburg (on the Diemel), and, pushing into Hesse, had joined there the reinforcements brought from Italy by Aldringer and Fugger. He had reached Fulda when he heard of the investment of Würzburg by Gustavus. His army now amounted to somewhat over thirty thousand men, exceeding that of Gustavus by five or six thousand. A brave man, anxious to wipe out the defeat of Breitenfeld, Tilly was about to push on by forced marches to succour Würzburg, when he received an imperative order from Maximilian of Bavaria to avoid a combat if possible, and by no means to attack. The army commanded by Tilly was, in fact, with the exception immediately to be referred to, the only army left to the League, and Maximilian felt, and felt justly, that its destruction would expose the whole of southern Germany to be over-run by the victorious Swede.

The one exception spoken of was the army of Duke Charles IV. of Lorraine, a prince who, with the view to win for himself the electoral rank, had warmly espoused the Catholic cause, and who was, at the moment, marching at the head of seventeen thousand men to join Tilly. The boastful character of the Duke, and the indiscipline of his army, brought, however, no real assistance to the Catholic commander. Both the Duke and the army disappeared, too, almost as suddenly as they had appeared; for a little later the Swedish cavalry fell, during the night, upon the Duke's camp, and so terrified his soldiers that they hastened back, with all possible speed, to their own country. As, still panic-stricken, they approached the Rhine at Strasburg, a waggoner, passed on the road, struck the Duke's horse with his whip, calling out: "You must go faster than that if you would escape the great King of Sweden."

Tilly had been forced to allow Würzburg to succumb without making an effort to save it; but the arrival of Duke Charles had increased his army to nearly fifty thousand men, and he hastened then to the north bank of the Main, nearly opposite Ochsenfurt, at the angle of the very sharp bend made by the river, a bend so strongly marked that both flanks of an army marching on Ochsenfurt from the north would be covered. Gustavus, who was very anxious to save that town, placed in it a Scotch brigade under Hepburn and Monro. Meanwhile, he sent a detachment of cavalry to beat up the Lorrainers in the manner already referred to. Tilly, finding Gustavus prepared at all points and vigilant, made only a demonstration against Ochsenfurt, and then withdrew his army. It was only when the Swedes had, in the manner now to be described, placed a considerable distance between themselves and the Main, that Tilly ventured, in virtue of a secret agreement with the Bishop of Bamberg, to cross the river and occupy the strong places which that prelate had previously offered to Gustavus. There, and in the neighbouring marquisate of Ansbach, he remained for some time, living on the country and watching events.

No sooner had Tilly fallen back from Ochsenfurt than Gustavus, always bearing in mind the real object of the campaign, began his march towards the Rhine. Following the course of the Main, he occupied, without serious opposition, Seligenstadt, Aschaffenburg, and Steinheim. The capture of these places brought with them the possession or the submission of the districts which they represented on both sides of the river. Whilst he was thus advancing, one of his lieutenants had captured, by collusion with its ruling count, Philip Ludovic, the town and citadel of Hanau. Gustavus himself was marching with eight thousand men in a north-westerly direction towards the valley of the Neckar, whilst Tott and Banner were engaged in securing the more northerly districts. The Saxons likewise were still marching towards Prague.

One effect of the influence gained by Gustavus at this period was the adhesion, just as he was quitting Würzburg, of the important city of Nuremberg. Nuremberg, the English rendering of the true name Nürnberg, was a free city of the empire, famous even in those days for the wealth, the order, the industry of its people. Rising from a sandy plain, rendered fertile by the application to it of the waters of the Pegnitz, it was surrounded by a wall having more than a hundred towers, culminating in a castle which, built on rising ground, dominated the city and commanded an excellent view of the country around it. The beauty of its churches, the splendour of its private houses, its reputation as the home of art, added lustre to a city which then, in the commercial world, occupied a place inferior only to that of Venice and Genoa. It had been famous almost from its birth. In the year 1050-1 it was heard of as obtaining from the Emperor

Henry III. the **rights of coining money, of** holding markets or fairs, of imposing **duties. The establishment** of these fairs, **the** worship **of wonder-working Sebaldus,** the repeated visits, **always for a lengthened period, of the emperors, drew** the **industrial classes to the rising town. With the other possessions of the** Franconian **imperial house of Germany Nuremberg came, by the death of Henry V. (1125) into the possession of the House of Hohenstaufen;** and the **representatives of this** family, **Conrad and** Frederic, had, two years later, **to defend the** castle against **the Emperor Lothair. Lothair was repulsed, but the** odds against the Hohenstaufens **were too great, and, in 1133, Nuremberg was taken by Henry, "the proud," of Bavaria. But the election** of Conrad **of Hohenstaufen to the imperial throne (1138), restored** Nuremberg **to its position** as **an independent fief of the empire.** Greatly favoured **by** the Hohenstaufens, **the city soon** extended **beyond** the Pegnitz, **and its new** boundaries speedily came to be surrounded by a wall **with towers and** ditches. **In 1219 Frederic II.,** grandson **of the famous** Barbarossa, granted **the city** a patent **of** freedom. **In 1324, 1356,** and 1390, imperial **diets were** held within **its walls. At the last of** these the principle **of having one coinage for all Germany was** established. **Diets** assembled **there likewise in** 1522 and in 1523. **On the** 23rd **of July 1532, the first** religious peace was concluded, **and six** years **later the Emperor Charles V. and** the Catholic **princes** formed **there a league to suppress Protestantism throughout** Germany. **The political history of the city had** meanwhile undergone a **material change. The Hohenstaufens** had passed away, to be **succeeded by the Hohenzollerns. The** latter, after an administrative **rule of** nearly **two** centuries, **had removed to** Brandenburg. Their departure **left** the **city a prey, for** a long time, **to constant wars, but** the independent **spirit of** the citizens **at** length asserted **itself.** They had, at an early period **of** the Reformation, adopted, in their truest form, the principles of Luther, **and, whilst denying a** residence in the city **to all** who were not **of** the reformed persuasion, had carefully preserved from iconoclastic fury the beautiful churches and symbols which were amongst the precious ornaments of the city. When the thirty years' war broke out, the disturbance of its commercial prosperity by the discovery of the Cape route to the East had been but slightly felt, and the city still maintained nearly all its old influence and pre-eminence.

This city, on the retreat of Tilly, had declared openly for Gustavus. Its example had been followed by Ulm, Strasburg, and Frankfurt (on the Main). The Swedish monarch considered it, then, advisable to push on to the last-named city, important even then, as the recognised seat of the diet for the imperial election. He had taken Steinheim on the 13th, and joined his lieutenant at Hanau on the 14th November. He pushed on, thence, to Offenbach, some four miles from Frankfurt. Here he concluded an agreement in virtue of which his army was allowed free entrance into the city, the magistrates took an oath of fidelity, and the suburb of Sachsenhausen was placed absolutely in his hands. The following day, the 17th, he made a triumphal entry into Frankfurt with great pomp and ceremony, amid the plaudits of the people.

Three days were occupied by the passage of the Swedish army, its material, its baggage, its sick and wounded, through Frankfurt. Fully aware, as he was, of the impression which would be produced by the surrender of so important a city, Gustavus was determined to utilise that feeling by following up his success. The very evening of the day, then, on which he made his triumphal entry, he sent troops against Höchst, six miles beyond Frankfurt, and belonging to the Elector of Mainz, a strong adherent of the League. Höchst surrendered that night. The day following, Landgrave William of Hesse-Cassel, who had done good service in Westphalia and Lower Saxony, joined the Swedish king with six thousand foot and three thousand horse. Amongst other men of note who found refuge in his camp at this period, was the unfortunate Elector Palatine Frederic V., titular King of Bohemia.

The King stayed at Frankfurt only a sufficient time to prepare, at Höchst, materials for crossing the Rhine at Mainz, and for mastering the strong places on both banks of the Main. On the 1st December he quitted Frankfurt, and in three days over-ran the district known as the Bergstrasse *—a district which, in the more comprehensive application of the term, includes the country between Darmstadt and Heidelberg. He then made as though he would besiege the last-named city, with the view of restoring it to the Elector Palatine; but, knowing all the inconvenience of attacking a place whilst an enemy lay on his communications, he turned short off to his right, and attacked Oppenheim, an important town on the left bank of the Rhine, and the strong connecting fortress of Landskron. Whilst his troops were engaged against that place, he secured boats for the crossing of the river at Gernsheim, some few miles higher up the stream. The passage of the Rhine was successfully effected, in spite of the opposition of a strong detachment of Spanish infantry, forming portion of a corps which, under Don Philip de Sylvan, was serving in the Lower Palatinate. He then, after a very short siege, stormed Oppenheim and its fortress (8th December). The opportune fall of this place allowed Gustavus to march with his main body on Mainz, whilst a detachment secured Worms. Mainz, though defended by two thousand men under Don Philip de Sylva in person, surrendered on the second day. Gustavus made his triumphal entry into the city the day following, the 13th December.

The surrender of Mainz marks the close of the first portion of the campaign which followed the battle of Breitenfeld. Politically it was an event of the highest importance. It secured for Gustavus not only the command of the Rhine, but enormous supplies of every description, the possession of the electorate of

---

* In its narrow and strictly literal application, the Bergstrasse signifies only the old Roman road, about thirty-seven miles in length, at the foot of the Odenwald, between Bessungen, near Darmstadt, and Heidelberg; but, as stated in the text, it has come to comprehend the fruitful lands on both sides of it.

which Mainz was the capital, and the submission of two-thirds of the Lower Palatinate. It enabled him to gather up all the threads of the forces of which he disposed, and to strike out such a line as would tend to finish the war.

A glance at the positions of the various forces at his disposal will give the reader a clear view of the position of the Swedish monarch at this moment. Banner and Tott and the Marquis of Hamilton had been acting with the Duke of Mecklenburg and the Landgrave of Hesse-Cassel in endeavouring to clear northern and north-eastern Germany of the Imperialists. Opposed by Pappenheim, Gronsfeldt, Boninghausen, and others of less note, they had nevertheless been fairly successful. Pappenheim, indeed, had maintained his hold on Westphalia, but in the other provinces the Swedish arms had made progress. South of the Main, Tilly, watched by Gustavus Horn with nine thousand men, was asserting the cause of the League in Upper and Central Franconia, and now that the Swedish king had made a decided movement in the direction of Mainz, was even threatening Nuremberg. The Chancellor, Oxenstierna, accompanied by the Queen Eleonora, had marched through North Germany with considerable reinforcements to Mainz, and had there joined the King. On the other side, the Saxons, after much delay, had over-run the Lausitz, and, beating down the resistance of the imperial generals, Tiefenbach and Götz, had entered Bohemia and occupied Prague without resistance. Here the Elector, John George, quitted his army, and left the further conduct of the war to his minister, Field Marshal von Arnheim.

Between Prague and Vienna the road, if not quite open, was at the moment barely defensible; for Wallenstein had not yet reappeared on the scene, and Tilly's army was in Franconia. Had the Elector of Saxony been a strong man, he might, at this period, have finished the war. But John George, fickle, irresolute, timid, and fond of pleasure, far from looking at the opportunities before him, was at the moment debating within

4

himself whether it would not be more for his ease and advantage to come to terms with the Emperor. The success of Gustavus alone prevented him from taking this course. It may be reasonably asked now, as it was asked at the time by generals of great ability, how it was that, in planning the campaign after Breitenfeld, Gustavus should have allotted to his Saxon allies, whose feebleness and capacity he had thoroughly gauged, the direct and comparatively undefended route to Vienna, whilst he accepted for himself the less decisive road through Franconia to the Rhine. The question was put in so many words to Gustavus by Oxenstierna when he joined him at Mainz. "Sire," he said, at their first private interview, "I should have been better pleased to pay my duty to you at Vienna than at Mainz." The answer of Gustavus, whilst it reveals as much as any act of his life the profound statesman-like capacity of the man, is a thorough justification of his conduct. "I gave," he replied, "the fullest consideration to the question. I recognised that in the Elector of Saxony and in his minister, Arnheim, I had to deal with two men, one of whom was irresolute and bore me no love, the other was insincere and hated me. Such men would serve to keep the Protestant feeling alive in Bohemia and the Lausitz, and hold their own there against the few imperial troops opposed to them, until Providence should afford me the opportunity of striking a second and decisive blow at the enemy. But, suppose for a moment that I had taken the route through Bohemia, and assigned to them that which led to the Rhine. The whole bearings of the question would then have been changed. In Bohemia there is not a single Protestant prince on whom the Elector of Saxony can exercise influence. Here he would be in the very centre of all the princes and states who entered into the confederacy of Leipzig. He, and Arnheim, who leads him blind-folded, and is a better Jesuit than a soldier, are both timid enough to submit meanly, if defeated, and self-interested enough to sell me and my cause in exchange for some acquisition of territory. In either of these events, what would be my position if I were at Prague? The Elector of Saxony is the first Protestant power in Germany. The princes of the Union, if he were here amongst them, would naturally shape their conduct after his. Upon the Elector's defection, then, how could I conduct a retreat from Bohemia, Moravia, and Austria to the Baltic—the only course which would then be left to me, with the Imperialists on my rear and Arnheim in front? No; in the game which Gustavus has to play, it is Gustavus who must be amongst the Protestant princes of Germany—and the first man amongst them too."

This, then, was the position. The Saxons, at Prague, with the road to Vienna but feebly occupied at the moment, but which the Emperor was making strenuous efforts, in the manner about to be related, to occupy strongly, before they could force it: Gustavus, largely strengthened at Mainz, and from Mainz reconquering the Palatinate: Gustavus Horn watching Tilly in Franconia: the other subordinate generals and allies maintaining and improving the position in northern and north-eastern Germany. On the side of the enemy, Tilly, after a futile attempt to surprise Nuremberg, had left one half of his army under Aldringer to watch Gustavus Horn, whilst, with the other half, he had taken post at Nördlingen, an imperial town in Bavaria, close to the frontiers of Würtemberg, and which covered the principal road by which the Swedes must advance into the former country. Pappenheim, the number of whose troops was being gradually raised to eighteen thousand, was holding his own in Westphalia and on the lower Rhine, whilst the Emperor Ferdinand was, as already stated, employing his most strenuous efforts to levy an army which should enable him to re-assert all his former power.

It was in the month of November, 1631, when the Saxons were already at Prague, when Gustavus, after having baffled Tilly at Würzburg, was making his triumphal progress to the Rhine, that Ferdinand II., driven to desperation, stooped to make overtures to the powerful subject whom, but eighteen months before, he had subjected to the indignity of a curt dismissal. The story of the previous overtures made by Wallenstein to the Swedish king, their failure, of the solicitations addressed to him by the Emperor, of the first refusal of Wallenstein (November 1631), of the conference held between them at Znaim in the following January, and of **Wallenstein's guarded consent to raise an army in three** months but not to **command it, of the new** negotiations conducted on **the part of the Emperor by Father Quiroga, by the** Bishop of Vienna, **and by Count** Eggenberg, which resulted in an agreement whereby, **on the acceptance without** reserve of **his** conditions, one of which assured him **a royal** title and **a sovereign state*** on the conclusion **of peace,** Wallenstein finally agreed **to command the army he had meanwhile been engaged in** raising,—belongs rather **to the life** of that great commander **than to** these pages. **It must** suffice here **to state that on the** 15th April **the final compact was signed, and on the last week of** that month **the new** imperial **army, led by the greatest captain of the age, entered into the campaign.**

Before these negotiations could be brought **to their perfect conclusion, Gustavus had quitted Mainz** for **Frankfurt, the fortifications of which he** greatly strengthened. Having arranged **for the levying of** fresh troops in **Sweden and in** the German **provinces on the left** bank of the **Rhine, he** opened thence **the campaign** of 1632 by marching **to** undertake the **seige** of Kreuznach. Kreuznach, defended by a garrison **of** six hundred **veterans, was one of** the strongest **places** in the Palatinate, one of **the few which had not been** attempted by the Swedes during **the** earlier winter months. **It** was regularly **fortified, in the most approved** manner **of the** time. On one **side, defence rose** above **defence in such a way** that it was **difficult for a besieger to gain** a position commanding it. The

---

* The conditions actually **ran** as **follows:** The Emperor pledged **himself to** bestow upon Wallenstein "as ordinary reward an imperial fief, as **an extra**ordinary reward sovereign jurisdiction in all the lands to be **conquered."**

other side was, though very strong, still open to attack. To this side Gustavus directed his efforts. For a whole fortnight the place resisted him, and it was only when the springing of a mine offered to his troops a small but very steep breach, full of loose rocks, and difficult of ascent, that he ordered a storm. Volunteers from the ranks of the Anglo-Scottish brigade sprang forward to claim the honour of leading the attack. Led by Lord Craven, then very young, Colonel Talbot, and Mr. Masham, they performed this service, supported by the Swedes, with signal gallantry. After a very sharp and obstinate contest, which lasted two hours, the garrison surrendered. The loss, however, of the stormers was considerable. Not only was the number of killed excessive, but Gustavus had to lament the death of one of his best officers, Colonel Halle. Not one of the British officers escaped uninjured. Lord Craven, whose conduct particularly attracted the favourable notice of Gustavus, was wounded by a pike in his thigh; Sir Francis Vane, brother of Lord Westmoreland, was shot in the hip-bone; Masham received a severe hurt from a large stone and a fire-brand; Talbot was killed close beside Lord Craven. Partly to testify his opinion of the gallantry of his English allies, partly in appreciation of the merits of the officers concerned, Gustavus appointed Mr. Alexander Ramsay to be governor of the conquered town; about this time, too, he nominated Sir Patrick Ruthven to be governor of the free imperial city of Ulm, which had just then pronounced in his favour, and had consented to receive a garrison of twelve hundred men.

With almost the sole exception of Heidelberg, the strong places of the Lower Palatinate were now in the hands of the Swedes and their allies. Gustavus was anxious, before marching into Bavaria, to complete the expulsion of the Spaniards from that Electorate; then to deal finally with Cologne, as well to punish the Bishop-Elector of that city as to confiscate the enormous amount of property deposited therein by the princes and nobility of north-western Germany. To attack Cologne, however, would have necessitated a deviation from his true course; and he was, perhaps fortunately, deterred from attempting it by the receipt of information that Tilly had struck his lieutenant in Franconia, Gustavus Horn, a very severe blow.

We left Tilly at Nördlingen, on the borders of Bavaria and Würtemberg, prepared to protect the former country against Gustavus and his army. But, whilst lying at Nördlingen, Tilly received secret intelligence that Horn, who had recently taken Bamberg, was occupying that city and its neighbourhood in such manner as would, with the connivance of the inhabitants, facilitate an attempt to surprise him. The Bambergers, or people of Bamberg, were as intensely and devoutly Catholic as the neighbouring people of Nuremberg were intensely and devoutly Protestant. Their ruler and bishop, clothed in armour like a common cavalier, was at the time serving in the ranks of the League army. By communications initiated by him it was arranged that the people of the city, aided by armed bands from Forcheim and Kronach, should plan an insurrection, in which they should be supported by the sudden appearance of Tilly and his army. There was some miscarriage in the plan, for the insurrection had already broken out and been repressed when Tilly, at the head of sixteen thousand men, arrived before the place. Horn had nine thousand, a sufficient number, had his orders to concentrate been obeyed, to repel the invader. But his orders were not obeyed. Baudissin, instead of falling back on the city, moved against Tilly. Attacked and overwhelmed, his men drew with them in their flight the newly-raised corps of Count Solmes; and Tilly's veterans, led by Cratz and Farenbach, followed them so closely as to gallop on to the bridge leading into the city pell-mell with them. But here Horn showed himself worthy of his great sovereign. By strenuous exertions he maintained during the rest of the day the barricade at the other end of the bridge, in spite of all the efforts, repeatedly renewed, of his adversary's horsemen. When, however, towards nightfall, Tilly brought up his artillery, and began to place it in position, Horn thought it expedient to retire. He embarked his guns, his ammunition and baggage, on boats, despatched them down the Main, and then, himself commanding the rear-guard, conducted an orderly retreat in a westerly direction, crossed the Main at Eltmann, and, breaking down the bridge there, halted only when he reached Schweinfurt. Thence he despatched a courier to the King, bearing a report of the mishap.

This report effectually dispelled from the mind of Gustavus any lingering desire he might have had to move against Cologne. Leaving Oxenstierna with a division to finish with the Palatinate and to protect the middle Rhine, he marched without delay (4th March) on Aschaffenburg, and, pushing on thence, effected a junction with Horn between that place and Schweinfurt, and then advanced, his army increased now to forty thousand men, to Kitzingen. Tilly, who had been harassing and pressing Horn, on the first information of the King's approach fell back hurriedly on Neuburg (on the Danube), and crossing that river, marched to the town of Rain (on the Lech), breaking down the bridges behind him, two alone, to be hereafter referred to, excepted. At Rain he was within striking distance of Donauwörth.

Gustavus had marched very closely on the track of Tilly, sleeping often in the bed which his opponent had occupied the previous night. At Weissenburg he had halted to storm the strong castle of Wülzburg, on the west slope of the Jura, about a mile from the town, which was held for the League. But as the siege of this stronghold seemed likely to involve a longer delay than he had anticipated, and as he judged it especially advisable to secure Donauwörth, not only because that town was the key into that part of Swabia which leads into Bavaria, but because it would afford him a secure place upon which to fall back in case of a reverse, Gustavus decided to leave Wülzburg to itself, and to hasten on to the Danube. He arrived, then, before Donauwörth on the 26th March.

Donauwörth, a small town on the left bank of the Danube, at the junction of that river with the winding Wörnitz, was held by a garrison of about two thousand men, commanded by Rudolph, Duke of Saxe-Lauenburg. This prince declared that he would hold the place to the last; but after sustaining an attack of twenty-four hours duration, seeing no signs of Tilly's approach, and receiving no communication from that general, he cut his way through the Swedish army and escaped.

During this time Tilly was on the Lech, having his head-quarters at Rain. He might undoubtedly have reached Donauwörth, only seven miles distant, in time to enter the place before it could be stormed. But many considerations induced him to prefer to meet Gustavus on the Lech. At Donauwörth he would have fought with the river in his rear. Defeat would have meant absolute destruction, whilst the position on the Lech was very defensible, had been carefully studied, and he had occupied its strong points. He was aware that by not marching to the relief of Donauwörth he left to Gustavus a position assuring him an entry into Bavaria. But it was the lesser of the two evils, and he still fondly hoped that he might prevent him from taking the second step, without which the first would be comparatively fruitless, by erecting a barrier to his further progress on the Lech.

The Lech, a tributary of the Danube, rises in the Rothwand, where that precipitous mountain towers over the Formarin-See in the Voralberg. Swiftly flowing thence in a north-easterly direction, its turbid waters reach, by a multitude of curves and windings—at a distance of fifty miles—the little town of Reute. Leaving Reute, the valley takes a northerly direction, and, widening, affords scope for a broader development of the river, as it flows, still rushing and winding, past the magnificent scenery which intervenes between that place and Füssen.* A very short distance beyond Füssen the Lech enters Bavaria, flowing still, and until it joins the Danube beyond Rain, almost due north. At Schongau, some twenty miles beyond Füssen, it

---

* Near Füssen are the finest rapids in Germany, and a good waterfall. Füssen is likewise the head-quarters of a lake country of its own.

attains a breadth of over thirty yards, and becomes navigable for boats. Between that place and Landsberg the valley gradually expands, and thence to Augsburg and from Augsburg to Rain the river courses over an open plain with flat but often high banks, its surface covered with many islands. In this plain, however, the Lech still maintains the character of an Alpine stream. So irresistible is the rush of its waters that no dams can stop them; they continually overflow the banks, and form, in their midst, large and constantly changing islands of rubble. The same cause produces astounding differences in the breadth of the bed of the river, which, whilst it averages about forty-four yards, amounts at the confluence with it of the Wertach near Augsburg, to more than nine hundred. The height of the water changes too, continually and quickly, whilst the stream itself offers sometimes the appearance of a considerable mountain torrent, sometimes that of a rapid river. A careful study of all these particulars would give to the man who had studied them a considerable advantage over an enemy new to the ground. Tilly was influenced by this consideration when he decided to leave Donauwörth to its fate, and to meet Gustavus on the Lech.

No sooner, then, had the general of the League heard of the fall of Donauwörth than, anticipating the action which he felt would at once commend itself to the great commander to whom he was opposed, he broke down the bridge across the Danube by which his position could have been turned between Rain and Neuburg, and destroyed that over the Lech, close to the former town. Occupying then Rain with a portion of his right wing and Augsburg with a strong detachment, he distributed the remainder of his army at the assailable points between the two places. Small bodies of cavalry were placed at intervals to give warning as to the movements of the enemy. The distance thus covered was sixteen miles. His army, strengthened by all the troops which Maximilian of Bavaria, who joined him at Rain, had been able to raise, was forty thousand strong.

Gustavus, immediately after taking Donauwörth, had despatched the flower of his dragoons and musketeers to seize the bridge over the Danube between Rain and Neuburg. But, as we have seen, they were too late. He then resolved, if possible, to repair the bridge near Rain, over the Lech. But this operation was likewise found to be impracticable. Baffled here, he made, then, a long and careful reconnaissance, examining every bend and every peculiarity of the river. But here, too, he was forced to acknowledge the genius of his adversary, for he found the enemy's troops posted so as to command every likely point. A demonstration, which he made as a test, proved that Tilly was on the alert. He had recourse, then, to another method. Throwing up intrenchments along a portion of the left bank, where the river made a sharp bend almost in the form of a half-moon, the outer rim of which he occupied, he posted behind those intrenchments a strong detachment, whilst with the bulk of his army he encamped in the rear close to the little village of Nordheim. He then erected in the intrenchment three batteries—one on the centre of the half-moon, the others on the two faces, and armed them with seventy-two pieces of cannon. The fact that the left bank of the Lech was here higher than the right bank, gave Gustavus a marked advantage, and when, on the morning of the 1st April, he opened fire, he inflicted great damage on the enemy, who were posted in a wood behind a little rivulet called the Ach, and effectually prevented them from occupying the ground between that stream and the Lech. This cannonade, in which, though it was replied to, the Swedes had all the advantage, continued four days. Whilst it was progressing, Gustavus was engaged in preparing, at the little village of Oberndorf, near the place he had selected to cross the river, and which was concealed from the enemy's view by a declivity, on a plan of his own invention, the means wherewith to effect that purpose. These took the shape of strong wooden trestles, of various heights and with unequal feet, which could rest on the bottom of the river supported by piles, and form the basis on which to rest a bridge. To facilitate the driving in of these piles, he caused several fires to be lighted between the village and the river, and had these continuously fed with smoky combustibles. A favourable wind blew the smoke thus caused towards the enemy, and completely hid his workmen from their view.

Having made everything ready, Gustavus, very early on the morning of the fifth day (the 5th April), whilst it was still dark, despatched across the river in two boats which he had managed to secure, covered by a heavy fire, a thousand picked men, amongst whom were the most skilled workmen of his army. These speedily made a lodgment, and proceeded forthwith to throw up a bridge-head. This work had been completed when the rising light of the sun disclosed it to Tilly. That general, without an instant's delay, brought two batteries to bear upon it, but the low and swampy ground on which they rested diminished the efficacy of their fire. But this low and swampy land told in other respects in his favour, for it lay directly between his own intrenchments and the Swedes, and to attack him they must traverse it. To render such an attack more hazardous Tilly proceeded to strengthen his position by hewing down large trees to form breast-works, causing their branches to be sharpened and pointed near the trunk into a form of *chevaux de frise.*

Meanwhile, under a heavy fire from both sides, the bridge was completed, and about noon was crossed by the advanced guard of the Swedes, led by Colonels Wrangel and Gassion. As other brigades continued to follow the advanced parties, Tilly directed Aldringer to move round the swampy ground, charge with the flower of his cavalry those who had already crossed, and seize the bridge-head. Aldringer obeyed the order with great alacrity. He turned the marsh, and led his men with splendid daring against the enemy. But the Swedes, divining his intention, had time to form up, and Aldringer, notwithstanding the prowess of his men, failed to make any impression upon them. Falling back, then, for a moment, he rallied his troops, and then charged again at their head with splendid courage. In vain, however; a cannon-ball grazed the temple of Aldringer, and he was carried senseless from the field. His men, shaken, and exposed to a tremendous fire, broke in confusion. Tilly, noticing the catastrophe, and having no one at hand efficiently to replace Aldringer, descended from the wood with a fresh body of veterans, renewed the attack with indescribable fury, he himself fighting with all the ardour of a boy. The combat had lasted about twenty minutes, and its result was still uncertain, when a shot from a falconet struck him on the knee and shattered the bone. The old general, who had fallen swooning to the ground, was at once carried off the field, and his troops, now without a leader, gave way. Their retrograde action was hastened by the conduct of two considerable parties of Finland horse, who, eager for action, swam their horses across the river, and threatened to take them in flank.

By this time the shades of evening were falling. The Swedes had, indeed, secured the passage of the river; but the army of the League still held its intrenched position in the wood behind the Ach. Gustavus, then, decided to content himself with bringing across the remainder of his army, and with maintaining his position on the Bavarian side of the river.

Tilly, meanwhile, had been carried, with the agony of a painful death upon him, to the wood behind the Ach. There, during the fight, had remained his old master, the nominal commander-in-chief, **Maximilian, Duke of** Bavaria. To a great general there was still a chance, for the position was strong, was unassailable on the right, and covered in its front by the marshy ground.* Under other circumstances Tilly would undoubtedly have made an effort to defend it. But under the influence of excruciating pain his spirit had given way, and he advised

---

* "If I had been the Bavarian," exclaimed Gustavus when he **visited next day** the strongly fortified abandoned **intrenchment,** "never—even if a **cannon-ball had** carried away my beard and **my** chin—never would I have abandoned a post such as this; **never would I have** thus opened **a way into my own country to an** enemy."

Maximilian to save himself as best he could. That same night, then, the army of the League evacuated its position, and fell back in good order on Neuburg and Ingolstadt.

Firm now on Bavarian soil, Gustavus took Rain and Neuburg; then, sending Horn to follow the remains of the League army to Ingolstadt, marched himself with the remainder of his army up the Lech to Augsburg. He arrived at Lechhausen, a village two miles from the imperial free city, and separated from it by the Lech, on the 8th April. Its Governor, Colonel Breda, who held it with four thousand five hundred men, had broken down the bridge; but Gustavus immediately built two others, the one above, the other below, the city, and summoned it to surrender. Breda, hearing that Tilly was dying, that Aldringer was severely wounded, and that no help was to be expected from the League army, complied after a decent interval, and Gustavus on the following day, April 14th, made a triumphal entry into the city, considered then the birthplace of the Reformation,* attended by the titular King of Bohemia, and many other princes of note.

Leaving a garrison in Augsburg, and enlisting in his own ranks five hundred men belonging to the force which he had thence expelled, Gustavus hastened to retrace his steps along the banks of the Lech to Neuburg, and marched thence to Ingolstadt. This town, one of the strongest places in Germany, possessed a virgin reputation. Never had an enemy been able to force his way behind its walls. Not only did it possess a formidable garrison, but Tilly himself was there, and the League army, led now by Maximilian of Bavaria, covered it on the north. More than this, Tilly had implored Maximilian to maintain that town and Ratisbon at all hazards. The presence of the League army forced Gustavus, who appeared before it on the 19th April, to confine his efforts to an attack upon its southern face. The following morning, whilst inspecting the outworks,

---

* The Confession, called the Augsburg Confession, had been presented to Charles V. in that city just above a century before—in the year 1530.

the King of Sweden met with an adventure which is thus recorded by one of the chroniclers of the seventeenth century.* "But all these advantages did not compensate for the fright in which the Swedes were thrown the 20th April, when they just missed receiving a fatal and irreparable blow; for the King, having advanced that day to reconnoitre more closely the approaches to the place, mounted, as was his wont, on a grey hackney, the gunners of Ingolstadt, conceiving that something extraordinary was taking place, took so good an aim that a ball carried away the hackney's quarters, and covered the King with blood and dust. All his suite were in indescribable terror at the occurrence, but their fears were immediately changed into joy when they saw that the King was unhurt."

The day following this incident was memorable for two incidents. A cannon-ball carried off the head of Christopher, Margrave of Baden Durlach; and the veteran Tilly expired. With his last breath the old soldier urged upon the Elector two things: the first, never to break his alliance with the Emperor; the second, to bestow the command of the army upon Cratz. "That officer," he said, "has courage to serve you, fidelity to content you, and parts to assist you. He will conduct your troops with reputation, and, as he knows Wallenstein, will traverse his designs."

Gustavus remained eight days before Ingolstadt; then, finding the reduction of the place would require time which might be more usefully employed, he raised the siege, and hastened with the bulk of his army, by way of Geisenfeld, to Moosburg. Thence he detached Horn to take possession of Landshut on the Isar, forced that place to pay a hundred thousand thalers and to receive a garrison; then, drawing from it eighteen guns, hastened by way of Freising to Munich. The Bavarian capital surrendered without a blow on the 17th May. Into it Gustavus made a triumphal entry, and availed himself

* *Le Soldat Svedois,* or *Histoire de ce qui s'est passé en Allemagne depuis l'entrée du Roy de Suede en l'année* 1630, *jusques après sa mort.* Published in 1633.

of the large amount of treasure and stores found there. From this central point he employed himself, either in person or by his generals, in reducing the remaining strong places in Bavaria, and in sending succours to his generals in the north. He was at length called thence by the movements of Wallenstein.

Wallenstein, I have said, had concluded his final treaty with the Emperor the 15th April of that year. I have also stated that whilst the treaty was negotiating, indeed during December and the three following months, the agents of the Duke of Friedland, who had thoroughly forecast the future, had been engaged in levying troops in his name. It soon appeared that that name possessed a power greater than that of the Emperor. From all parts of the Austrian dominions there flocked thousands to his standard, some possibly enticed by the advantages held out to them, but the greater number drawn thither by a desire to renew the ties which had bound them by reverence and affection to so great a commander. When, then, on the 15th April, the compact was signed, Wallenstein found an army ready to his hand. At the head of this army he entered Bohemia, expelled thence with scarcely an effort Arnheim and the Saxons, and formed a junction near Eger with the remnants of the army which had been beaten on the Lech, and which, after leaving a strong garrison in Ratisbon, had marched northwards, through the Upper Palatinate, towards that frontier town. This junction increased the strength of his army to nearly sixty thousand men. Viewing the situation with the eye of a great general, he noted that although Gustavus had conquered the whole of Bavaria, and had occupied its principal towns and fortresses, yet that his position north of the river Main was by no means secure; that whilst the Saxons had been removed by his own action from the scene of combat, Pappenheim more than held his own in lower Saxony and in Westphalia. He perceived, then, that the surest way to force Gustavus to abandon his hold upon Bavaria was to march on some important point between him and northern Germany—a point which his enemy would not relinquish, but would strain every effort to maintain. Could he draw Gustavus to such a point, he would endeavour to hold him there whilst Bavaria should recover from its alarm, and Pappenheim, reinforced, should re-establish the Imperial hold on northern Germany. For this purpose he selected as a point of attack the important city of Nuremburg.

Wallenstein had recovered Prague the 4th May, had forced the Saxons to make a hazardous retreat to Pirna on the 30th, had effected a junction with the Bavarian army on the 11th June, and he appeared before Nuremberg the 30th of that month. There he found Gustavus, with what force he could command, intrenched, and ready to receive him.

Gustavus fully recognised the skill of his great opponent. He had, we have seen, occupied Munich on the 17th May, just when Wallenstein was engaged in driving his allies from place to place in Bohemia. His own forces had, from the despatch of Horn to the Lower Palatinate and other causes, been greatly diminished, and when the junction of Wallenstein with the Bavarian troops near Eger proved to him that that general had given up the idea which, it was supposed, he had first entertained, of following up the Saxons, he had felt certain that he would have to bear the brunt of the next movement. Indications not to be doubted soon convinced him that Nuremberg would be the point of attack. He could not but see how very advantageous to the Imperialists would be the possession of that city. For not only would the moral effect be enormous, but it would ensure the destruction of the allied troops in Swabia, which, under Banner, William of Weimar, and Ruthven, were then on the march to join him. Although, then, he could at the moment dispose only of about seventeen thousand men, he hesitated not for an instant, but hurried with all speed to the threatened city.

Gustavus arrived at Nuremberg the 19th June. His apprehensions that Wallenstein had immediate designs on the place were confirmed by the infomation which there reached him,

Three considerations then forced themselves upon him. The first, how, being as it were in a hostile country, to support his army; the second, how, his troops numbering fewer by more than two-thirds than those of Wallenstein, successfully to resist an attack; the third, by what line to direct the generals, who were marching to join him, to advance so as not to be intercepted. He met all these difficulties in the manner which might have been expected from one of a generous and manly nature, who had confidence in the justice of his cause, confidence in the effect which the same belief would induce in others, confidence in his soldiers and in himself. To meet the first difficulty he appealed with open heart to the citizens of Nuremberg; showed to them the necessities of the case, and asked them to supply his army with food and money until he should have strength to meet the enemy in the open plain. In this dread crisis the citizens of Nuremberg were true to the cause they had espoused. They entered heart and soul into the plans of Gustavus, and agreed to all his proposals. The third difficulty was to the Swedish King the most formidable, because the solution of it depended very much upon the action of others. All he could himself do under the circumstances was to send messengers to Horn, to Banner, and the other detachments, indicating his own position and the route which he heard from time to time Wallenstein was taking, to warn them to avoid, as much as lay in their power, a decisive conflict with the enemy: he refrained, in a word, from trammelling their action by too precise orders. The second he met in a manner which has stamped his reputation as a great military commander.

Gustavus was at Nuremberg with, at the most, seventeen thousand men. Wallenstein was marching on that place from Eger with nearly sixty thousand. Were Gustavus to quit Nuremberg and fall back on his several detachments beyond the Main, he would save his army, be in a position very shortly to affront Wallenstein, but he would sacrifice the free city which had been the first, south of the Main, to declare in his favour, he would give up Bavaria, and he would deal heavy discouragement, possibly a fatal blow, to the cause of freedom of conscience. On the other hand, by remaining to protect Nuremberg, he would occupy a position materially and politically strong, would give time to his detachments and partisans to rally, and would keep Wallenstein at bay until, either he were strong enough to assume the offensive; or, should he in the end be forced to quit his position, he would have given confidence to Protestant Germany by his long retention of it in the face of vastly superior numbers, and have afforded his lieutenants a rendezvous at a point where a junction was always feasible.

He set to work, then, without delay, to select and fortify a camp which, occupied by his soldiers, should defy Wallenstein. Round the city, at a distance of about thirteen hundred yards from it, he dug a ditch, for the most part twelve feet wide and eight deep, in some particular parts eighteen feet wide and twelve deep. Behind this ditch, at intervals, not fixed, but varying according to the conformation of the ground and the points to be guarded, he erected eight distinct forts, and armed them with his heaviest guns. He connected these with each other by long and thick earthen parapets, strengthened at intervals and wherever required with bastions and half moons, and mounted these also with cannon, of which there were, when the camp was completed, three hundred pieces in position, mostly supplied by the city of Nuremberg. The Pegnitz traversing the camp, divided it into two not unequal parts, and to reunite these, numerous bridges were thrown across the river. The whole camp, not including the spaces allowed for irregular angles, outlines of defence, intrenchments, and redoubts, was computed to cover two hundred and nineteen square acres. In such a space, it was comparatively easy to concentrate, without delay, in case of attack, a very large number on the decisive point. The whole of these works were designed and completed in exactly fourteen days.

Gustavus had, I have stated, reached Nuremberg on 19th June.

The works of his intrenched camp were very far advanced towards completion when Wallenstein and Maximilian of Bavaria appeared before it, the 30th June, with the full intention of attacking it. But the works, though not quite complete, were still so formidable, that Wallenstein recognised at once that the issue of such an assault would be, at the best, doubtful, and made up his mind on the spot, in spite of the earnest entreaties of Maximilian, to endeavour, in preference, to starve out his enemy. When Maximilian pushed his arguments beyond a certain limit, Wallenstein offered, in a cold and haughty manner, that if the Elector would begin the attack with his Bavarians, he would support him with his army. This remark ended the discussion, and the plan of starving out was agreed to.

With this view, Wallenstein took up a position near Zirndorf, about two miles south of Fürth,* upon a low, wooded hill, surmounted by a fortress, now in ruins, and which gives to the hill the name of Alte Veste. Round this, and enclosing a tract of country sufficient to make a circumference of seven miles, he threw up only light defences, surrounding the camp with a ditch of comparatively small dimensions, and covering it with an interlacement of forest trees, baggage waggons, and gabions. Behind these he ranged his army, formed into eight divisions, each about seven thousand strong. Besides these, the camp contained fifteen thousand women, nearly as many carters, sutlers, and servants, and thirty thousand horses.

To support this army and this following Wallenstein had little difficulty. He had with him large supplies of grain; the country behind and on both sides, belonging to the Bishop of Bamberg, was devoted to him; he possessed all the towns and passes in the circle of territories which surrounded him, except that little segment occupied by Gustavus. He received, likewise, provisions and ammunition from Vienna. To make assurance doubly sure, he stationed two considerable bodies of troops in the diocese of Bamberg and the upper Palatinate, and caused his Croats to

* Fürth is five miles from Nuremberg; Wallenstein's camp was only three.

scour the country day and night in a cross line from Bamberg to Munich. In this manner, and by sending daily parties from his own camp to prevent foraging on the part of the enemy, Wallenstein at once increased his own store, and compelled the Swedes to confine themselves to the resources of Nuremberg.

Between the two camps, three miles apart, flowed the Pegnitz, which, after traversing the Swedish camp, formed a sort of bow in front of it. The waters of this river supplied both armies, though the Imperialists were not absolutely dependent upon it, for, flowing to the north-west of, and partly through their position, and parallel with the Pegnitz, was the Rednitz, a small, narrow, unnavigable stream, but still constituting a provision for their camp.

From these positions, for nearly three months, the two armies looked one another in the face: Wallenstein resisting every incitement to attack; calmly asserting his own supreme position; not hesitating to lay waste for the support of his army the dominions of Maximilian of Bavaria, always vainly clamorous for action; occasionally parading his troops in battle array, provoking his enemy, but not going one step beyond. Gustavus, on the other hand, eating up the resources of Nuremberg, carefully watching his enemy, in the hope of a false movement which was never made, or of the consequences of a disagreement between Wallenstein and Maximilian which were never manifested; now despatching couriers to his detached generals, with routes for their guidance carefully marked out by himself, yet always leaving them freedom of action*; reviewing his troops daily; endeavouring too, by means of carefully planned raids, to intercept, and sometimes succeeding in intercepting, the enemy's supplies; devising, for the first time, I believe, in military

---

* "Your king," it was his habit to add at the close of these despatches, "can only direct his absent disciples in general terms. Incidents will arise which no human foresight can predetermine. Seize the moments, snatch the proffered opportunities which take birth and flight in one instant. I resign into your hands full discretionary power; use it in a manner worthy of me and of yourselves." Life was indeed worth living under such a commander!

history, a scheme for mounted infantry, by mounting on horseback the men who carried a shorter musket, and who were called "dragoons," and intermingling them with his light cavalry, so that on an expedition the former could, if necessary, dismount and serve as footmen*; and doing everything in his power, by a display of his natural gaiety and example, to encourage his men.

It must be admitted that on the Imperial side the courtesies of war were more conspicuously displayed than on the other. On one occasion a foraging party led by Colonel Dubatel had attacked and dispersed a party of Croats, when it was suddenly assailed by a largely superior number of Imperialists, many of its number were slain, and Dubatel was taken prisoner. Wallenstein, who knew the great affection which Gustavus felt for Dubatel, released him forthwith without a ransom. On another occasion he similarly released a Captain Reischel, and sent him back with a complimentary message to the King. A few days after the first occurrence, Colonel Darmitz, an officer high in the confidence of Wallenstein, was captured by the Swedes. Far from releasing him, Gustavus used his opportunity to press him to disclose his general's secrets, and wrung from him the admission that Wallenstein intended to remove into his camp a large convoy which had been collected for him at Freystadt, a small town near Neumarkt (on the Sulz) sixteen miles from Nuremberg on the Ratisbon road. Promptly he detached two parties to secure that convoy. They did secure it, and Gustavus then personally, after a very sharp encounter with the enemy, escorted it safely into his camp.

The strictest discipline was at the outset maintained on both sides, and on that of the Imperialists continued, according to the testimony of their opponents, to the end. But in the Swedish camp, whether from the habit of making constant raids, or from the occasional opportunities of plundering which were offered, a

---

* This system was found very efficacious in dealing with the Croats, who formed the loose light infantry of the Imperial armies.

feeling of rapacity began to manifest itself, from general down to the commonest soldier. Gustavus, who knew well that want of morale would soon lead to want of discipline, and that his hitherto invincible army would then soon cease to deserve that epithet, issued a strong order upon the subject, in which, appealing to the nobler instincts of those serving under him, he forbade all personal plundering. When this order did not suffice, he hanged the officer, a lieutenant, who was the first offender after it had appeared. When, a day or two later, a peasant complained that a common soldier had stolen a cow, which was the sole support of his family, Gustavus seized the fellow with his own hands, and, calling for the executioner, commanded him to perform his office. The man was hanged on the spot.

By degrees, the continued stay in one spot began to produce the inevitable result in both camps, especially in that of the Swedes, who were more shut in than their enemy. The waters of the Pegnitz, too, whilst their volume was greatly affected by the continued drought, became putrified by the carcasses of dead horses and other causes. The consequence was the prevalence of fever to an extraordinary extent. In the Swedish camp, moreover, there was an absence, first of green forage, and then of all forage. The state of affairs became every day more and more strained. Wallenstein was master of the situation. Apparently he had only to sit still on the Alte Veste and see the army of the Swedes perish from sickness before his eyes.

But the 21st of August brought a change in the situation. On that day four of his detached corps succeeded in joining Gustavus. It will be necessary to devote a brief space to the previous movements of these.

To the commander of the principal detached corps, the Chancellor Oxenstierna, had been committed the care of the Middle Rhine and the Lower Palatinate. Here he had been confronted by the Spanish troops under Don Philip de Sylva. The summons sent by Gustavus from Nuremberg reached him the last day of June. He was not, however, in a position to move before the

11th July. On that day, leaving Horn with a small force to oppose the Spaniards, Oxenstierna set out to join his master.

Not, however, by the most direct route. Taking into consideration all the possibilities of an attack by a superior force he had resolved to unite himself with the second detachment commanded in Westphalia by the Landgrave of Hesse Cassel. This junction would, under ordinary circumstances, have been difficult, for the Landgrave was opposed in that part of Germany by the vigilant and daring Pappenheim. Fortunately, however, Pappenheim had rushed, for the moment, to attempt to relieve Maëstricht, then besieged by Frederic of Nassau, and the Landgrave was thus at liberty to march unmolested to the Main and join Oxenstierna.

Two Scotchmen, **Ballandine** and Alexander Hamilton, who commanded two regiments of their countrymen, were in the duchy of Magdeburg when the news of the King's danger reached them. Without waiting for instructions they marched at once direct to Halle, met there a portion of the division commanded by the general to whom they were attached, **Duke** William of Saxe-Weimar. The division then pushed on through Lützen to Zeitz—on the Elster, nearly thirty miles south-west from Leipzig—was joined there by the Duke, who had hurried for the purpose from Lake Constance attended only by his guards, then traversing the forest of Thüringen, and strengthened in Franconia by the junction of five Saxon regiments, had pressed on to Würzburg, and had met there, on the **10th** August, **Oxenstierna**, who, having picked up the Landgrave of Hesse-Cassel on the Main, near Aschaffenberg, had directed his march to that important town.

Banner, who commanded the fourth corps, was at Augsburg opposed to Cratz, who commanded in that part of Bavaria a remnant of Tilly's old army. On receiving the King's summons he crossed the Danube, and gliding by the western side of the King's camp at Nuremberg, advanced to the free imperial town of Windsheim, on the Aisch, with a view of giving a hand to

Oxenstierna, who would naturally take that place in his route from Würzburg. To his surprise he found that the King had anticipated his intention by detaching thither a body of troops under Bernhard of Weimar. There, then, the junction of all the detached corps was effected, and these, amounting to forty-nine thousand men, marched, under instructions from Gustavus, by way of Herzogenaurach to Bruck and Eltersdorf, ten miles to the north of Nuremberg, at the junction of the Aurach with the Pegnitz. There they encamped and fortified themselves. On the third day (16th August) Gustavus rode into their camp, and five days later led them triumphantly, under the very nose of Wallenstein, into Nuremberg.

Why Wallenstein allowed those reinforcements to pass unscathed, even unthreatened, can only be surmised. He reckoned, probably, that they were marching to destruction in another form; for he was aware that the King's supplies were all but exhausted, that he could not feed, even for a week, in the position he occupied, the additional number of mouths thus brought upon him; further, that having detached ten thousand of his own men, under Holk, into the Meissen country for supplies, he could not bring into the field a number equal to that of the reinforcements, and that it would be more advisable to await an attack from them in his intrenchments. He resolved, then, simply to maintain the blockade.*

But Gustavus had brought his several detached corps to Nuremberg with the sole purpose of forcing that blockade. The day following, the 21st August, was, then, employed by the King in endeavouring, by means of a brisk cannonade, to force Wallenstein to quit his position and give him battle. But Wallenstein was far too great a commander to allow himself to be forced to do that which his enemy evidently desired. The

---

* Harte, the English biographer, *par excellence*, of Gustavus Adolphus, rates the reinforcements at only twenty-six thousand men, and calculates that Wallenstein had still a superiority over the increased army of Gustavus of fourteen thousand but Schiller gives the number of the reinforcements as about fifty thousand, and this view is fortified by the testimony of contemporary writers.

more persistently the Swedes cannonaded, the more eagerly did
he set his men to work on the one side with the spade; on the
other to threaten the King's flanks, and to engage his detached
parties at advantage, without, however, permitting themselves
to be drawn into an engagement which might become general.
The orders given to them were to be always prepared to fall back
behind their intrenchments. These directions were executed
with such exactness of discipline that Gustavus, baffled, was
forced to adopt other measures. The next day he brought his
guns nearer to the enemy's camp, and for twenty-four hours
poured upon it an unintermitting fire. The only result, however,
was that Wallenstein fell back a few hundred yards on to the
two ridges on one of which was the castle—now a ruin—
higher than the eminence he had before occupied—the other
known as the Altenberg. The ascent to these was steep and
craggy, and they were covered by a thick forest. Here
he covered himself with a three-fold barrier of trees, each
rising in a semicircle one above the other. Before Gustavus
had ceased the cannonade, the new position had become in-
accessible.

Again was the King baffled. But it had now become for
him a necessity to deliver, without delay, a blow which should
be decisive. His supplies, scanty before, could no longer suffice
for his augmented force. The city, though previously well-
stored, possessed now a bare sufficiency for its own wants, and
low diet, fever, and other forms of disease had already laid
low many there and in the camp. All the mills in and about
Nuremberg could not grind a supply of corn sufficient for such
a multitude, and the bread furnished daily by the town excited
rather than allayed the cravings of hunger. Horses in great
numbers were dying daily from starvation, and the casualty list
of the men was rapidly increasing. Forced, then, to compel
Wallenstein to fight, Gustavus quitted his intrenched camp
at Nuremberg, and, making over the defence of that city, and the
care of his sick and wounded, to its armed citizens, numbering

thirty thousand, crossed the Rednitz and took up a new position above Fürth, lodging himself in that town.* Thence he reconnoitred Wallenstein's position. What he saw has been described in language so vividly descriptive by the great German historian that I feel impelled to translate his words:—

"On the two steep heights between the Biber and the Rednitz, called the Alte Vesto and the Altenberg," writes **Schiller,** " rested the chief force of the enemy, their camp, **commanded by** these heights, spreading, impenetrable to view, over the fields between **them.** Their entire artillery was massed on the heights. Deep ditches surrounded **unscalable earthen parapets;** strong and closely laid abatis and sharply pointed **palisades** added enormously to the **difficulties** of climbing slopes, already steep and rugged, from whose summits **Wallenstein, calm** and secure as a god, launched his thunderbolts through thick clouds of smoke. Behind the ramparts lurked the insidious fire of the muskets, and certain death from a hundred open cannons' mouths envisaged the forlorn stormers."

Whether, beholding such a position, Gustavus, pressed as he was by famine, would, in his cooler moments, have made a direct attack upon it, may, perhaps, be doubtful. But after he had returned from reconnoitring, information was brought to him that the enemy had begun a retrograde movement; that only a few regiments had been left in camp to hold the Swedes in check until the guns and baggage should be well to the front. Hastening again to reconnoitre, Gustavus beheld the Imperialist army in motion, and, concluding too hastily that his information was correct, ordered a general advance.

The information was not correct. The whole was a device on the part of Wallenstein to entice the King to attack, and the brisk movement seen by the King was only a part of the same plan.†

Under a very heavy fire from two hundred pieces of artillery the Swedish and German soldiers advanced (24th August), to the attack of the Attenberg hill. Sword in hand, Gustavus, who had ordered his dragoons and part of his cavalry to dismount,

---

* In the inn called Grüner Baum in the street still named after the King.

† Harte states that in the general opinion it was Aldringer who purposely threw the false information in the way of **the King.** Other writers state that Gustavus received it from "his prisoners and **his spies."** Schiller does not mention the story.

directed the assault. This was made by the whole body of the musketeers of the army, drafted from the several brigades, subdivided into battalions five hundred strong, each commanded by a colonel.* Steadily and in good order did these gallant men advance, undeterred neither by the steepness of the hill, nor by the artificial obstacles which impeded their ascent. In a few minutes, the smoke of the cannon hid them from view. Then they were discovered endeavouring to force their way across the ditch which covered the hostile position. Vainly did they try to storm those well-defended intrenchments. Man and nature were too strong for them. After a fruitless struggle they fell back exhausted, broken, and in disorder.

Enraged at this repulse, Gustavus then led in person his own Finlanders to the storm; but neither could his Finlanders, nor the Livonians who followed them in the attempt, produce any impression upon that fatal hill. A fourth, a fifth, and a sixth attack met with a similar result. But still the fight went on; still Gustavus hoped that pertinacity would at length triumph. Every regiment in his army tried that day to conquer the impossible.

Wallenstein, when he heard that Gustavus had committed himself to an assault, had expressed, it is said, in words peculiar to the age, his conviction of the certainty of his failure. Calm and collected, mounted on horseback, he directed the defence, encouraging his men, even forcing, with the point of his sword, the weak-hearted to return. Whilst thus employed, a cannon ball struck his horse in the flank and brought him to the ground. To mount another, to show himself to his men uninjured, his resolute face as resolute as before, was the work of an instant. Well, too, was he supported. His men, for the most part, displayed in him that blind confidence which leaders of their fellows always attract from the multitude.

For ten hours the battle raged. The King himself never left

---

* It deserves to be noted that before ascending to attack, these battalions left their colours with the reserve

the front of his line, but stood there calmly directing every assault. Before nightfall there was not a man of his infantry or dismounted cavalry who had not been engaged in attempting to storm the position. The nature of the ground forbade action to the cavalry as cavalry. Gustavus, as we have seen, had utilised his in the manner which made them most available for his purpose. On the other side, one imperial regiment, reputed as the best in Wallenstein's army, had been completely shattered in an attempt to break through the sturdy Finlanders. A bullet had struck the sole of the King's boot; Duke Bernhard of Weimar had had his horse shot under him, Banner, von Erbach, de Castell, von Eberstein, de la Tour, and many other superior officers had been wounded; several, scarcely less deserving, had been killed; the hill-side was covered with the bodies of the dead and dying; when, happily, night threw her dark curtain over the scene. The battle was over. For the first time Gustavus had been repulsed. The repulse had but just been recognised when heavy rain fell. It continued all night. The next morning, leaving two thousand dead on the field, Gustavus recrossed the Rednitz.

From the first, success against such a position had been all but impossible. Bernhard of Weimar, who on that day commanded the cavalry, had indeed during the heat of the battle seized a height which, he reported, commanded the Alte Veste, and had sent word of his success to the King. But by that time Gustavus was too much in the toils of his original attack. Whilst recognising the importance of the post seized by Duke Bernhard, he could not, he said, leave his actual position without exposing his army to a double attack from the enemy.

Wallenstein, it is said, lost about a thousand killed and fifteen hundred wounded. The total loss of the Swedes, including the two thousand dead already referred to, could scarcely have been less than eight thousand. But these numbers can only be approximate, as no actual return was ever made.

Gustavus crossed the Rednitz on the morning of the 25th, but he did not return to his old camp at Nuremberg. He took up, rather, a new position within long cannon-shot of the Altenberg, and from that new position looked his enemy in the face. But Wallenstein, true to his policy of starvation, would not stir. Constant skirmishes ensued between the foraging parties of the two armies, but they led to no action of real consequence. At last, in sheer desperation, Gustavus formed a plan by means of which he hoped to lure Wallenstein into the open. With this end in view, he proposed to detach two small corps under Bernhard of Weimar and Banner to take up a position at Lichtenau, a strong fort on the Rezat some seven miles eastward of Ansbach, and which was held for the Burgrave of Nuremberg by Scheverlin, a patrician of that town. Had the plan succeeded, the Swedes, by obtaining the command of the foraging country, would have forced Wallenstein to action or to retreat. But the conduct of one man spoiled it. Scheverlin had proved himself to be a good soldier by repulsing on a previous occasion an attack made by a division of the imperial army. But the defeat of Gustavus on the 24th August had unnerved him; and when, after that event, Wallenstein caused Lichtenau to be again invested, he surrendered it without striking a blow, just at the moment when the two Swedish corps referred to were on the point of setting out to relieve him. Fourteen days had elapsed since the battle of the 24th, and it became absolutely necessary that one or other of the great leaders should decide to move.

The summer had been more than ordinarily hot; the waters of the Pegnitz had become putrid; the stench caused by the carcases of dead horses poisoned the air; a pestilence prevailed in both camps, and in the Swedish camp supplies were exhausted. Under such influences discipline had become greatly relaxed. To move had become a necessity. Leaving, then, Kniphausen with eight thousand men to defend Nuremberg, Gustavus quitted his position on the 8th September, and fell back by way of Neustadt (on the Aisch) to Windsheim. There he halted to watch the further movements of his enemy.

Five days later Wallenstein quitted his camp and marched to Forcheim. So far, the advantage of the campaign lay with him. His stern patience and unbending resolution had given the first check to the victorious career of the King of Sweden.

CHAPTER III.

LUTZEN.

WHILST the two leading actors were occupied before Nuremberg in the manner described in the last chapter, the war had been continued without interruption in Germany north of the Main. The Saxons and Swedes in the Lausitz; Holk, detached with ten thousand men from Wallenstein's army, in the Meissen country, and threatening Dresden; Pappenheim, Baudissin, and the Landgrave of Hesse-Cassel, in Westphalia and Lower Saxony; Gustavus Horn in Alsace and on the Upper Rhine; Ruthven in the vicinity of Ulm, and Wrangel in Pomerania; had been asserting to the best of their abilities the cause they respectively represented. The situation, in fact, at the time when Gustavus fell back on Windsheim (8th September), may be summed up in a single sentence. The Swedes and their allies had prevailed everywhere except in those places where Pappenheim commanded. Pappenheim, though he had gained no pitched battle, had made his presence felt wherever he appeared. It might even have gone hard with his opponent, Baudissin, had not the necessities of Maestricht, besieged by Henry of Nassau, withdrawn him for a time from Westphalia. On his return thither, Maestricht meanwhile having fallen, Pappenheim had at once recovered all the advantages of which his short absence had deprived him.

On the 9th September Gustavus had entered Windsheim; on

the 13th Wallenstein had quitted his intrenched position near Fürth to march to Forcheim. Although he had checked the victorious career of the Swedish king, he had not won from him a single stronghold. Gustavus was still in Bavaria, nearer to Munich than he was, his garrisons still holding Ulm, Nördlingen, and Donauwörth. Apparently he had gained nothing. But the keen instinct of a consummate warrior taught Wallenstein that, with so many places to maintain and his line of retreat to preserve, it would be impossible for Gustavus to keep together in one body the army which he had at Windsheim; that policy and the necessities of his position would force him to divide it. He resolved, then, still to keep in play the patient pertinacity of his nature, to wait till the event which he foresaw must happen should happen, then to sweep down upon Northern Germany, and, either crushing or bringing to himself the Saxons, re-establish there the imperial predominance, and bar the way to the return of the Swedish invader. It was a scheme worthy of a warrior.

Not suspecting the thoughts which coursed through the brain of his rival, Gustavus remained some days at Windsheim planning the continuance of the campaign. Far from entertaining the idea of quitting Bavaria, he was anxious to complete the reduction of the strong places of the country, and possibly even to push on to Vienna. The superiority he possessed in numbers over Wallenstein gave him hope that the result might not be impossible. For whilst, according to the best authorities, he still had, deducting the garrison of Nuremberg, from forty to fifty thousand men under his orders, Wallenstein, who had detached Gallas with four thousand men to reinforce Holk, by the most favourable statement counted only, before leaving his intrenchments, thirty-one thousand, and, of these, thirteen thousand were Bavarians, who quitted him at Bruck on his way to Forcheim. On arriving at that place his army numbered but seventeen thousand men.

Every circumstance, then, combined to induce the King to

continue his progress eastwards. But, fearful lest Wallenstein, released from his presence, should attempt to recover the strong places he had conquered in Franconia, he resolved—as that commander had foreseen—to despatch half his force, under Duke Bernhard, to dispute with the imperial general the passage of the Main; to march himself against the Ingolstadt which had before repulsed him, and penetrate thence into Upper Austria.

Gustavus had despatched Duke Bernhard, and had set out himself, when news reached him of the movement of Gallas. Leaving his army to continue its route towards Donauwörth, he hurried back with three thousand five hundred mounted troops to Nuremberg. Learning there that Gallas had stormed Lauf, ten miles to the east of that city, and was hurrying on to the Meissen country, Gustavus at once turned, and, proceeding by Ansbach, rejoined his army on the next day at Dinkelsbühl. Thence he marched nineteen miles to Nördlingen—where he was joined by five thousand Swiss levies—and thence, the day following, seventeen miles, to Donauwörth. From Donauwörth he proposed to cross the Danube and the Lech, and to besiege Ingolstadt.

Retaking Rain, which the imperial general, Montecuculi, had suddenly snatched,* but dared not fight an action to defend, Gustavus marched to Neuburg on the Danube (12th October), and halted there, awaiting the arrival of his siege-train from Augsburg and Donauwörth. He was still at Neuburg, endeavouring by the most vigorous exertions to hasten the necessary arrangements, when he received the most pressing solicitations to return to Saxony. Not only, was he informed, had Wallenstein penetrated into that province, but he was employing all his influence, and the influence of the Imperial Court, to detach the Elector from the cause of the King of Sweden; and there was great fear that John George, a weak

* Colonel Mitzval, who had basely surrendered the place, on the first summons, to Montecuculi, was tried, condemned, and executed a few days later at Neuburg.

man, alternately solicited and threatened, and secretly incited by Arnheim, who was devoted to Wallenstein, would succumb.

Wallenstein had, in fact, struck his blow. No sooner had he beheld the King of Sweden separated from him by the Danube, and entangled in sieges, than, after threatening Schweinfurt in a manner which drew to that place the Swedish army which Gustavus had confided to the leadership of Duke Bernhard, he suddenly marched directly eastward, and, passing through Bamberg, took Baireuth, and thence dashed against Culmbach. He took that town, then the residence of the Margraves of Brandenburg-Culmbach, and pushed on to Coburg. Coburg succumbed; but the Swedish colonel, Dubatel,* had had time to throw himself, with his dragoons, into the castle which commanded the town, called the Ehrenburg, and the defence which he made was so resolute and so protracted, that Duke Bernhard had time to reach Hilburgshausen, some twenty miles to the north-west of the place. His close vicinity forced Wallenstein, who had already been repulsed in one assault (4th October), to raise the siege.

Disappointed in an attempt which, had it succeeded, would have secured his march across Thüringen and his early junction with Pappenheim, Wallenstein, informing Pappenheim of his change of plan, made again a sharp turn to the east, and proceeded to Kronach; thence, nearly north, through the lands now the dominions of Prince Reuss,† to Weida, on the Elster. From

---

* Dubatel was a Scotchman: his real name was M'Dougal. He was a very brilliant officer.

† Forming a portion of what was in those days known as the Vogtland, regarded from the eleventh to the sixteenth century as the direct possessions of the German Emperor, which he administered by means of Vögte (anglice, prefects). In that period the Vogtland comprehended the districts which now form the south-western portion of the Zwickau circle, the domains of Weida and Ziegenrück in the Grand Duchy of Saxe-Weimar, the possessions of Prince Reuss, the district formerly known as the district of Hof, but which now belongs to Bavaria, and the present Saxe-Altenburg district of Ronneburg. The office of Vogt soon became hereditary in the House of Reuss. In 1373 the Vögte of Weida sold Hof to the Burgrave of Nuremberg. In 1560 Elector Augustus obtained by purchase the districts Weida, Arnshaugt, and Ziegenrück, and nine years later the counties of Plauen, Vogtsberg, and Pausa. It will be seen, then, that Weida, to which place Wallenstein took his army, formed a part of the dominions of the Elector of Saxony.

Weida he marched to, and summoned, Leipzig, and whilst the bulk of his troops were engaged before that place, took possession of Weissenfels, Merseburg, and the town, but not the fortress, of Halle. Leipzig held out only for two days. On its surrender Wallenstein marched to Eilenburg, midway to Torgau. Receiving there a despatch from Pappenheim notifying that he was marching on Merseburg, he retraced his steps to that place and joined him.

It was the news of this inroad into Saxony which summoned Gustavus just as he was about to attack Ingoldstadt. The fact that Wallenstein had chosen for his winter quarters the dominions of the German ally who, of all, was the most powerful, the most impressionable, the most easily cajoled, left him no choice of action. Between himself and John George of Saxony cordial relations had never existed. Necessity alone had forced the latter, in the first instance, to an alliance which had placed him before the world of Germany in a subordinate position to a foreign sovereign, and the superiority of Gustavus had never ceased for an instant to jar upon his petty nature. John George, then, was not only of the mould, but he was at the moment in the mood, which rendered him peculiarly accessible to the blandishments of the Imperial Court. Added to this, his natural dislike of war, the fact that there stood at his side, as his chief minister, a man once the pupil, now the devoted friend, of Wallenstein, the Field-Marshal von Arnheim, and we have a correct view of the situation as it presented itself to the Swedish monarch on the banks of the Danube.

The position required immediate decision and immediate action. Yet for a great commander such as Gustavus to arrive at a decision required no small sacrifice. He was called upon to choose between the relief of Saxony and the conquest of Vienna. Between him and Vienna the only army, a small force, the highest estimate of which makes it thirteen thousand strong—and it was probably much less—was shut up in Ingolstadt. Gustavus believed he could take Ingolstadt. That fortress captured, the way to Vienna lay open to him. Neither Ratisbon, nor Passau, nor Lintz, nor the fortifications of Vienna would have stopped him. From the capital of the dominions of the House of Austria, from the imperial seat of the Emperor of Germany, he could have dictated terms to Ferdinand II. Undoubtedly he would have had to fight Wallenstein in the spring; but the position of Wallenstein fighting for his own hand, would have been different from that of Wallenstein the agent and representative of the Emperor.

That he could reach Vienna before Wallenstein, were he to turn, could reach him, Gustavus himself never doubted. The only difficulty which presented itself to his mind had reference to the Saxons. At the moment John George was pressing him to march to his aid. Had John George been by his side, Gustavus might have convinced him that sound policy dictated the seizure of the capital of Ferdinand II. by the Swedes, whilst the Saxons should keep Wallenstein occupied in their own country. But no messenger, however exalted his rank, could produce the same result as that which might be hoped for from a personal interview, and it was quite possible that John George, stung by the neglect accorded to his earnest solicitations, might throw himself, with all the fervour of a convert, into the arms of Wallenstein. This consideration carried the day. With a heavy heart Gustavus abandoned the prospect of occupying Vienna, when Vienna was in his grasp, resolved to quit temporarily the Bavaria he had conquered, and to hasten with all possible speed to the aid of his dubious allies.

Once that his mind was made up, there was no uncertainty in his action. Banner, a general whom he greatly trusted, was suffering from a wound. Until he should recover, then, Gustavus appointed the Prince Palatine of Birkenfeldt to command a corps twelve thousand strong, which he proposed to leave on the Danube; then, strengthening the garrisons of Augsburg, Rain, and Donauwörth, he set out, the 7th October, with the remainder of his army, on his march to Saxony. From Donauworth he marched direct to Nuremberg, stayed there forty-eight hours to recover Lauf, and, after having forced the garrison of that place to surrender at discretion, pushed on with all possible speed to Erfurt, which he had fixed upon as the point of junction for his several corps. Gustavus reached Erfurt on the fifteenth day after leaving Donauwörth, just in time to prevent its citizens from acceding to an accommodation pressed upon them by Pappenheim. Here he halted some days, as well to rest his troops as to take stock of the actual position of affairs. News of good omen reached him from all parts of Germany. Everywhere his detached generals had been successfully asserting themselves. The news of his approach had given the Elector of Saxony courage to occupy on the Elbe the places where that river could be crossed,—Dresden, Torgau, and Wittenberg,—and so to diminish the arena whence the Imperial army could procure its supplies. Of that army he learned that it occupied the triangle formed by Merseburg, Weissenfels on the Saale, and Leipzig; that it was composed of three separate corps, that of Wallenstein twelve thousand strong; that of Pappenheim ten thousand; and that, united, of Gallas and Holk, numbering sixteen thousand, being a total of thirty-eight thousand. The day before reaching Erfurt, Gustavus was joined by Bernhard of Saxe-Weimar. This raised the number of the men under his orders to twenty thousand. His ally, the Elector of Saxony, was at Torgau with fifteen thousand.

The extraordinary speed with which Gustavus had accomplished his march from Nuremberg to Erfurt had prevented Wallenstein from receiving timely intelligence of his approach, and that general, confident that he would for some time to come meet no serious opposition, had, the very day after the arrival of Gustavus at Erfurt, despatched Gallas with twelve thousand men into Bohemia. A division of his troops was at the same time threatening Naumburg, the possession of which would assure to him a position which Gustavus could not assail, for Naumburg covered the only easy approach to Weissenfels. The other approach by way of Camburg abounded in defiles and narrow passages, and was shut in on one side by the Saale, and on the other by a mountain chain. In the face of Wallenstein's army it would be impossible to attempt to traverse these defiles and passes with any chance of success.

But it was in difficulties that Gustavus always showed himself great. At Erfurt he acquainted himself thoroughly with the geographical position of the country; at Erfurt he learned that Naumburg had not yet fallen; that, therefore, he might yet, by a sudden spring forward, secure that place. Success there would place in his hands the power of occupying an advantageous position until he could be joined by his Saxon allies. For the moment, the idea of attacking with his twenty thousand men the army of his enemy, had not presented itself to his mind. With the sole hope of securing Naumburg, then, Gustavus set out from Erfurt, and, marching very rapidly, reached the neighbourhood of that town before the Imperialists had heard that he had quitted the former place, cut up there a small detachment of the enemy, and, entering Naumburg, at once began to intrench himself. Wallenstein first heard of his arrival there from the fugitives of the beaten detachment.

Let us glance at Wallenstein's position. He still had under his orders twenty-six thousand men; he occupied a strong position on the Saale; in front of him was the Swedish army, inferior to him in numbers; at Torgau, on the opposite side of Leipzig, was the Saxon army, seeking for a junction with Gustavus; Franz Albert of Saxe Lauenburg, with two thousand cavalry, was feeling his way between Eilenburg and Grimma, both on the Mulde, with the same intention. He thus occupied a central position, against enemies who, when united, would outnumber him by some ten thousand men. But those enemies were not united. The most active of them was intrenching himself at Naumburg. His ally was beyond Leipzig. The time was the beginning of November. The belief then forced itself into the mind of Wallenstein that the Swedish leader did not intend to attack him, but rather designed to provide his army with safe quarters until the winter season should have passed.

In that view his own position was not very safe. The Saxon army on the one side, the Swedish on the other, very much restricted the area from which he could obtain supplies. He did not even command the great highway to the north, running through Halle; for though he held the town of that name, the fortress was occupied by the enemy. Feeling, then, that it was necessary that that highway should be absolutely in his command, and influenced, also, by the anxiety he had always felt to draw Gustavus further to the north, and thus to weaken the desire for co-operation with him of the Saxons, whose country would thus be freed from both armies, he determined, whilst Gustavus was yet intrenching himself, to despatch Pappenheim to secure the fortress of Halle,* and thence to proceed to the relief of Cologne, menaced by the enemy, whilst he himself, abandoning the line of the Saale, should distribute a portion of his army in the towns in the neighbourhood, and with the remainder fall back on the little town of Lützen. The plan was not his own, but he was over-persuaded to adopt it.

But Gustavus, far from dreaming of winter quarters, was planning a scheme of union with his Saxon allies. He had, on being assured of the possession of Naumburg, proposed to the Elector of Saxony that, if he would march to Eilenburg, midway to Leipzig, he himself would direct his course to the south of Wallenstein's position, by way of Pegau, to Grimma on the Mulde. Grimma was only fourteen miles from Eilenburg; and there was no enemy near to hinder the junction.

Too eager to await in his position a reply from the Elector of Saxony, Gustavus, leaving a sufficiently strong garrison in Naumburg, set out at one o'clock on the morning of the 5th November for Pegau. But he had scarcely marched the nine miles which constitute half of the journey to that place, when some country gentlemen and peasants of the district hastened

* Called the Moritzburg, now in ruins.

towards him with full and positive assurances of the extraordinary action taken by Wallenstein. Their story was confirmed by some straggling prisoners. They informed the King that Pappenheim was well on his march to Halle, that strong detachments occupied Weissenfels and Merseburg, that the remainder of the imperial army lay loosely and thinly dispersed in the various villages of the triangle formed by the two places named and Leipzig, and that Wallenstein himself was at Lützen. Gustavus at once summoned his generals and imparted to them the news; then, being informed that Lützen was but five miles distant—it was in reality nearly nine—he gave his men some refreshments, and, wheeling his army to the left, pushed on towards that village. On his march thither he was joined by Franz Albert of Saxe-Lauenberg, who, on the first intimation of the King's intentions to effect the junction by way of Grimma, had hastened with all speed to meet him.

Not till much later in the afternoon did the imperial scouts bring to Wallenstein the information that Gustavus was upon him. Taken by surprise, his troops scattered, the Duke of Friedland displayed to the full his wonted coolness and self-possession. It was then nearly five o'clock in the evening. Considering the heavy state of the roads; the fact that Gustavus would have, in his last three miles, to traverse a morass, crossed by a bridge, over which only two persons could pass abreast; Wallenstein felt absolutely confident that, whatever else might happen, he could not be attacked that day. His first care was to send mounted messengers to summon his men from the villages in which they were scattered. He then, as carefully as the light permitted, surveyed the ground. The high road between Weissenfels and Leipzig, by way of Lützen, with continuous ditches on both sides, seemed to offer a good defensive position if properly utilised. He therefore at once set to work to widen and deepen the ditches and to line them with his musketeers as they came up. His men worked at this all that night. Early the following morning he posted his left so as to be covered by the canal which joins the Elster with the Saale, and which runs from Merseburg to Zeitz: his right he drew up to the immediate left of, and thus covered by, the village of Lützen. On some rising ground to the left of that village, where there were several windmills, he planted fourteen small pieces of cannon, whilst, to support his advance, which was composed of the musketeers in the ditches on either side of the road, he ranged on the nearer side a battery of seven heavy pieces. The main body of his infantry he formed into four massive brigades in the centre, in a sort of irregular parallelogram, the second and third being echeloned with that in front in such a way that whilst the left-hand man of the leading rank of the second had touch with the right-hand man of the rear rank of the first, the right-hand man of the front rank of the third touched the left-hand man of the rear rank of the first. Immediately behind the first, but at an interval nearly double its own length, was the fourth. These brigades were flanked on both sides by musketeers interlinked with cavalry, and then by cavalry alone. Count Colloredo commanded on the left, Holk on the right, Terzky in the centre. These arrangements were completed gradually, that night and during the morning, as his men came up. Long before the Swedes appeared, the Imperial army was in battle array. That evening Wallenstein wrote a despatch to Pappenheim, directing him to return with all speed. It is certain, however, that the messenger to whom he entrusted it did not set out before the following morning.*

Meanwhile Gustavus had found the distance longer and the difficulties greater than he had anticipated. The roads were heavy, the delays caused by the morass were great. They might have been made greater still if the men of an imperial regiment

* Otherwise Pappenheim would have received the letter during the night, and have been able to reach the field before the battle had begun! Wallenstein's letter is in the Vienna archives. It was found in the pocket of Pappenheim's jerkin stained with his blood.

of cuirassiers and of a battalion of Croats, who were posted in a village on the further side of it, had done their duty. But these men, far from harassing the Swedes in their difficult passage, fell back to an eminence in rear of the village, and remained there calm spectators of their enemy's movement. Sunset arrived before the whole Swedish army had crossed. To dislodge and put to flight the Croats and cuirassiers did not occupy a very long time, but before it had been accomplished night had set in. It was impossible to move further. The surprise, in the sense contemplated by Gustavus, was no longer possible. The Swedish army, then, after dislodging the cuirassiers and Croats, bivouacked where it stood.

It was an anxious night. Unlike Napoleon before Austerlitz, Gustavus could not sleep. He passed the long hours, says Harte, partly in discourse with his generals, partly in profound contemplation. Immediately at his side were Kniphausen and Duke Bernhard. The former, it is said, seeing that there could no longer be a surprise, and feeling intuitively certain that Wallenstein would make every effort to recall Pappenheim; seeing, further, that the army would have to fight unrested and hungry, for no supplies were obtainable where they were : urged the re-passing of the rivulet and the re-taking of the route to Grimma. But Gustavus was resolved to fight. The battle, he reckoned, would be gained before Pappenheim could return; he would march at two o'clock in the morning and engage the enemy before daybreak.

But the extreme darkness of the night, a darkness extraordinary even for the time of year, and the density of a mist which accompanied and obscured the dawn, rendered impossible the carrying out of this plan. Nine o'clock struck before the sun had cleared away the fog. Then the King, addressed a few spirit-stirring words to his men and ordered the advance towards a village in front of them called Chursitz. Gustavus led the right wing, consisting of six regiments of Swedes, supported by musketeers, intermingled with cavalry;

the left, composed of cavalry and intermixed infantry, was commanded by Duke Bernhard; the centre, consisting of four brigades of infantry, and supported by Henderson's reserve of Scottish infantry, was commanded by Nicholas Brahé, Count of Weissenburg. The reserves, between each of these divisions, were formed entirely of cavalry, and were commanded on the right by Bulach, in the centre by Kniphausen, and on the left by Ernest, Prince of Anhalt. The field pieces, twenty in number, were disposed to the best advantage between the wings. With the King, on the right, was Franz Albert of Lauenburg, who had joined him the day before.

As the Swedish army advanced beyond the village of Chursitz—which served as a store-place for the baggage—towards the high road lined by the Imperial infantry in the ditches on either side of it, the men were greatly harassed by the fire of the seven heavy pieces of artillery drawn up close to, but on the further side of that road. Their own lighter guns could make no effective reply. Gustavus, most anxious to come to closer quarters, only pressed on the more quickly. His left wing, led by Duke Bernhard, was the first to reach the scene of action. Responding to the call of their commander, the men composing it forced the ditches, cleared the road, charged the death-dealing battery, killed or drove away the gunners, and, without waiting to render the guns useless, rushed, with full fury, on the Imperialist right. Here Holk commanded—a most resolute soldier. But on this morning all the efforts even of Holk to stem the irresistible advance were fruitless. His first brigade was overthrown by the shock of the encounter, the resistance of the second and the third was equally unavailing. Still pressed on the Swedes. Unless some great miracle could be performed, the battle was irretrievably lost.

On such an occasion a great general is divine. At this terrible crisis the individual appeared on the spot to work the miracle which alone could save the Imperialists from disaster. Suddenly, dashing through the three broken brigades, there faced the Swedes, disordered by their too rapid victory, the firm countenances and serried ranks of the fourth, led and animated by the Duke of Friedland in person. Instantly the victorious advance was checked; the fugitives rallied under cover of the solid resistance; the battle was restored; in their turn the Swedes fell back, and an opportune charge of three cavalry regiments on their flanks hastened their retrograde steps. At length, after a most desperate hand-to-hand struggle, the conquered guns were recovered, many of the Swedes were forced across the road, and the victory which had seemed a few minutes before to be within their grasp now appeared to smile on their opponents. But on the side of the Swedes there was likewise a man whose individuality ever worked an influence more potential than that allowed to the common run of humanity. Whilst Duke Bernhard was combating, now almost victorious, now almost decisively defeated, on the left of the Swedish line; Gustavus, on the right, had forced the road, and, charging the Croats and Poles opposed to him, had driven them from the field. He was on the point of wheeling to his left to take the Imperialist centre in flank, when a messenger reached him with the information that his left wing had fallen back, broken and in disorder, and that his immediate presence was necessary to save his army from defeat. Leaving to Colonel Stalhaus* to press the enemy where he was then fighting, Gustavus hurried to his left at the head of Steinboch's regiment of dragoons. Arrived on the spot, he waved his sword, and calling upon all who loved him to follow him, dashed to the front at a point where his men had not yet been forced across the road, and, riding amongst them, urged them to fresh exertions. By his side were Franz Albert of Lauenburg and a few other followers, but the pace had been

---

* Schiller says, "to Gustavus Horn"; but Horn was at the time far away engaged in Alsace. He had only succeeded on the 28th October, after a siege of eight weeks, in capturing Benfeld, sixteen miles south-west of Strasburg. It is impossible, had he attempted it, that he should have reached Lützen in time for the battle; but he did not attempt it.

so furious that Steinboch's **dragoons** had **not** yet arrived. **Urging on his broken men, and** endeavouring at the same time **to discover amid** the **tumult** and the smoke the true bearings **of the enemy, Gustavus** unguardedly approached **too near to** the latter, **when he was struck** in the shoulder by a musket ball. **Almost at** the same moment **the dragoons arrived. Noting the alarm** for himself which **they** displayed **at the** sight **of** their sovereign covered with **blood,** Gustavus **called** out, "It is **nothing;** follow **me!" and he directed a** charge against **the** enemy. But weakened **by loss** of blood and almost fainting, he begged **Franz Albert**—speaking **to** him **in** French **so** as not to be understood by his soldiers—to **lead** him **as** quietly and **with as** little parade **as** possible **from** the field. **The** Duke **complied,** led the King, accompanied **only by his page, Leubelfing, by a** detour, towards the road. **But Gustavus had scarcely moved a few paces,** when **he received another shot in the back. Calling out to Franz Albert that it was all over with him, and that he** must now **save** himself, **the mortally wounded King fell to the** ground. Franz Albert, believing **the battle lost, galloped** off **to** report, **it has** been asserted, **the death of Gustavus to** Wallenstein, **and then rode** on **to** Weissenfels. **But** the **page,** Leubelfing, remained. A minute later, three Austrian cuirassiers galloped to the spot and demanded the name of **the** dying **man.** As Leubelfing refused to give it, they discharged **their** pistols **at** him with such effect that he fell to the ground wounded to the death.* Then Gustavus, in an almost inarticulate voice, **declared his** name **and rank. Immediately** afterwards **the** Swedish cavalry were seen approaching; **then the troopers, eager to** save themselves, and yet **to finish the career of their** conqueror, discharged their pistols at **the King's temple, stripped** him,† **and** fled. Over his dead **body, a** little later, **a desperate cavalry encounter ensued, and when,** on the conclusion **of the**

---
* He died five days **later**
† His buff jerkin, stained **with his blood, was taken** to Ottavio Piccolomini, the colonel of the regiment of cuirassiers to **which the despoilers** belonged. By him it was sent to Vienna, where it is still preserved.

fight, it was borne away by his own men it was not recognisable, so covered was it with wounds and bruises.

Meanwhile, the battle had been raging with increased fury. The news of the fall of their King, which was carried rapidly through the ranks, far from disheartening the Swedes, inspired them with a firm resolution to avenge his death. Following up the line of attack which their beloved sovereign had indicated just before he was struck, they advanced with the firm step, the dogged resolution, the determined energy which had gained for them so many battles. Their general, the gallant Bernhard of Weimar, seemed to be animated by the very spirit of his dead commander, and in him the men silently recognised a leader whom they would be proud, on such a field, to follow. In vain did Wallenstein, Colleredo, Piccolomini, Mérode, and the other officers who fought under and with them, display tactical skill, bright example, and unsurpassed courage. The progress of that Swedish left wing was not to be stopped. The guns near the windmills were captured and turned against the enemy. Step by step the Imperial left wing was forced back, the centre was assailed in flank and in front, and by the guns from the rising ground, and, after a hard struggle, the centre gave way too. The battle was apparently lost for the Imperialists.

For the centre had been assailed, not on one flank alone, but on two flanks. Stalhaus, who had been commissioned on the right to finish the work of Gustavus, when Gustavus had been summoned to rally his then beaten left, had driven the Imperial left from the field, and had followed up his work by dashing with all his fury against the centre. This attack was aided by the fire, directed by Bernhard of Weimar, of the captured guns. The Imperialists were giving ground, hopeless of victory, when the explosion of one of their powder-wagons added new terrors to the fight. Those more distant from the actual scene of the explosion pictured to themselves a thousand terrible possibilities —an attack in rear—their retreat cut off—a general slaughter. It was now four o'clock. Every moment their vigour decreased, the defence slackened. Complete victory was in the very grasp of the Swedes, when, suddenly, the galloping of horse was heard; the sound approached nearer and nearer; it reached the very spot. Then, emerging from the smoke, Pappenheim, leading eight regiments of Imperial cavalry, rode up at full gallop to restore the fight!

Pappenheim had already attacked the citadel of Halle when the messenger of Wallenstein reached him. To wait until his infantry, engaged in plundering, should be collected, and then to proceed at their pace, was quite opposed to the fiery nature of the Swabian general. He had, however, eight regiments of splendid cavalry well in hand, and at the head of these he galloped at full speed to the battle-field, a distance of at least eighteen miles. As he approached the field he came upon the fugitives of the left wing, the men whom Stalhaus had driven before him. Addressing a few inspiring words to these men, he succeeded in rallying them. Ignorant of the death of Gustavus, and anxious to cross swords with the King, who, he was aware, commanded the Swedish right, he aided the efforts of the re-forming infantry, by dashing with all his force against the pursuing troops of Stalhaus, checking their pursuit, and forcing them in their turn to fall back. The experienced touch of Wallenstein, who throughout that day had displayed all the qualities of a consummate commander, was at once sensible of the relief caused by this splendid action. Leaving Pappenheim to deal with the Swedish right, he rallied and drew to his centre his right, and opposed a fresh front to the advancing troops of Bernhard of Weimar and of Kniphausen. Again did Fortune seem to smile on the Imperialists. Once more were the guns re-conquered, the Swedes forced backward beyond the road; and it seemed to need only the return of Pappenheim from the pursuit of the Swedish right to change that which had been a defeat into a decisive victory!

Very hopeful now of the result, the Imperial general waited anxiously for Pappenheim. But instead of Pappenheim there

came to him a messenger with the fatal intelligence that Pappenheim lay dying on the field; that his men, their horses tired and themselves disheartened, were falling back, that Stalhaus was resuming the offensive, and that he would have to look to himself!

It was even so. Pappenheim, whilst urging on the pursuit of the Swedes, had received two musket wounds through his body. Still keen for victory, still anxious to measure himself with Gustavus, he tried to sit his horse. In vain, however. As had sunk the enemy he sought, five hours before, so did he sink bleeding and helpless to the earth. Whilst lying there, the rumour reached him that Gustavus had been killed. His eye lighted up when, upon inquiry, the truth of the rumour was confirmed. "Tell the Duke of Friedland," he said to the officer nearest him, "that I am lying here without hope of life, but that I die gladly, knowing, as I now know, that this irreconcileable enemy of my faith has fallen on the same day." He survived only a few hours.

The fall of Pappenheim was fatal to the Imperialists. Discouraged, they could not withstand the energy which still animated the Swedes. The message brought to Wallenstein conveyed, indeed, a warning of real meaning. He had to look to himself. The appearance of Pappenheim on the field had procured him a temporary relief. The death of that general, and the discouragement of his men, rendered it incumbent upon him to provide for the safety of his army. All hope of victory had vanished.

Under these trying circumstances, Wallenstein still showed himself a great commander. His right wing and centre had indeed driven Duke Bernhard, the Count of Brahé and Kniphausen across the road, but the men under those leaders were by no means beaten: they still offered a stubborn and solid resistance; and it was evident that they would take advantage of any movement which might be made upon his left flank. That flank, by the falling back of Pappenheim's cavalry, was now uncovered; Stalhaus, his men refreshed by renewed hopes of victory, would at any moment be upon it, and his own destruction would be inevitable. To avoid such a catastrophe, Wallenstein fell back across the road, always fighting, and always in good order, extending his line to the left to give a face to Stalhaus, and giving the enemy no opportunity to turn him. The sun had set; darkness was fast approaching; if he could but maintain this order for half-an-hour longer, he could render the day—a day which had begun for him so inauspiciously, for he had been assailed when he was not prepared for an assault—at the least indecisive. In this action he was splendidly supported alike by his generals and his men. Whilst the Swedes, eager for the victory once again apparently within their grasp, pressed on with fury, the Imperialists showed the most stubborn obstinacy. Seven times did Piccolomini charge the advancing enemy. Seven times was a horse shot under him. Always re-mounting, he showed himself the type of the cavalier, daring, firm in reverse, unyielding. Nor was his a solitary example. Götzen, Holk, Terzky, Colleredo, Mérode, gave on that day, especially in the last retreat—a time which more than any other brings out a man—evidences of skill, of courage, and of conduct. But above them all towered their great leader. If, under the circumstances, he could not win a victory, Wallenstein gave, at Lützen, a brilliant example of the manner in which to conduct a retreat in the face of a victorious enemy.

At length, both armies exhausted, darkness—such a darkness as that of which it has been recorded that "it might be felt"—set in, and the combatants separated. After fighting for nine hours, each army still occupied the ground it had held before the battle. The result had been absolutely indecisive.

Victory belongs technically to the side which gains the field of battle, and, in that sense, the morning after the fight, the Swedes might fairly claim the honour. For, during the night, Wallenstein fell back on Leipzig, leaving behind him his colours and

7

all his guns. In thus falling back he displayed a precipitation wholly unnecessary, for hardly had he well quitted the battle-field when Pappenheim's six infantry regiments arrived from Halle. Had the Imperial commander only waited **for these** he would **have been in a position the** following morning to **claim the honours of the day, for,** during the night, the Swedish leaders were quite ignorant of their fortune. As it was, the fresh troops, finding no commander on the ground, took like-wise the road to Leipzig.

During the hours of darkness, indeed, Duke Bernhard and Kniphausen held an **anxious** consultation **as to** whether their army **should or** should not retire **upon Weissenfels, and** they only relinquished the idea because, **after much** argument, **they** concluded that the attempt would be barely practicable. Nor was it until the early morning light showed them that Wallenstein had disappeared, that they comprehended for the first time the advantages they had gained. So true is it that **in war** stead-fastness counts more highly than sensational valour!

The morning of the 7th November showed, indeed, the Swedes **to be the sole occupiers of the field of** Lützen and of the **Imperial** guns. But **what were these** advantages to the loss of **their great leader?** The **victory at Lützen** was but a poor com-pensation **for the death of Gustavus—the** hero whose name alone **was worth thousands of men, who had** initiated the great war **for freedom of conscience, and who, from** a small beginning, had **driven the Court of Vienna to its** very last resources. **A defeat** at Lützen might have been compensated for by a victory **else-where,** but the loss of Gustavus was irreparable!

The battle cost both sides nine thousand men in killed alone; the number of wounded was far greater; indeed, it is **said** that **hardly** a man on the Imperialist side remained without a scar. **The whole** field from Lützen to the canal was covered with **corpses.** The position of many of these indicated the valour and the discipline with which they had fought. It is said, indeed, that all the men **of** the yellow regiment of Swedish Guards, known as the Pretorian Brigade, lay dead on the field in the same serried order in which they had fought. The same story is told of the blue regiment, composed entirely of British soldiers. Those severely wounded did not survive the night, for the appliances to relieve them were few, and a hard frost which set in before morning finished the work which the hostile weapons had begun.

On both sides many men of eminent rank were hit. Amongst those killed there were, on the Swedish side, besides Gustavus, Count Milo, the Count of Brahé, Colonel Gersdorf, General Uslar, Ernest Prince of Anhalt, and Colonel Wildessein; on the side of the Imperialists, in addition to Pappenheim, John Bernard Schenk, Prince and Abbot of Fulda, Count Berthold Wallenstein, General Brenner, Isolani general of the Croats, a prince of the house of Dietrichstein, and six colonels. Piccolomini received ten wounds, none of them mortal; Wallenstein was struck by a spent musket-ball; Holk received a severe hurt; indeed, so close, so desperate was the conflict, that, as already stated, there was scarcely a man in the Imperial army who escaped absolutely without injury.

The question as to who it was who fired the carbine the ball of which killed Gustavus has remained, and will ever remain, one of the vexed questions of history. The famous Pufendorf,* who was born the very year that Lützen was fought, and who, from his position, enjoyed the fullest opportunity of making inquiries on the subject, directly charges Franz Albert of Lauenburg with the murder. That he did commit it was the impression of many of his contemporaries. It may be worth while to state the question as it has appeared to modern writers.

Franz Albert was the youngest of four sons of Franz II., Duke of Lauenburg. Related on the side of his mother to the royal race of Vasa, he had in his early years been received in a friendly manner at the Court of Stockholm. An impertinent remark

---

* *Commentaria de rebus succisis, ab expeditione* **Gustavi-Adolphi** *in Germaniam ad abdicationem usque Christinæ*; Utrecht, 1686.

with reference to Gustavus, of which he delivered himself in the chamber of the Queen Mother was, it is said, rewarded by a box on the ear, and caused his departure from Sweden. On his attaining years of discretion he professed the Catholic faith, entered the Imperial army, obtained the command of a regiment, attached himself with the fullest devotion to Wallenstein, and obtained apparently the confidence of that general. Certain it is that whilst the negotiations between the Emperor and Wallenstein were pending, Franz Albert was employed by the latter in endeavouring to bring about a secret understanding with the Court of Dresden. After Wallenstein had levied his army, and, advancing to Fürth, had blockaded Gustavus in Nuremberg, Franz Albert, without any assigned cause, quitted his camp and presented himself to Gustavus as a convert to the reformed religion and anxious to serve as a volunteer under the King's orders. By his professions of religious zeal and other flattering ways he managed to win the King's heart; and although Oxenstierna, when he saw him, entertained a profound distrust of him and went so far as to warn the King, the hold he had gained was not to be shaken. After the assault made by the King on Wallenstein's position, Franz Albert quitted the King's camp to raise troops for his services in his paternal lands. He rejoined him, we have seen, though only with his personal attendants, the day before the battle of Lützen, and, though offered a command, preferred to act as orderly officer to Gustavus. He attended the King during that battle in that capacity. It was remarked that on that day Franz Albert, alone of all the officers on the Swedish side, wore a green scarf, the distinctive mark of the Imperialists. He was by the King's side when Gustavus received his first wound, and he it was whom the King requested to lead him out of the combat. He was close to him when the King received his second and fatal wound in the back, and he quitted him the moment after the discharge. Everyone but he in attendance that day on the King was killed or mortally wounded. He it was, it is asserted, who brought the news of the King's death to Wallenstein; very soon after the battle he exchanged the Swedish service for the Saxon; some eighteen months later he re-embraced the Roman Catholic faith, and re-entered the Imperial army. It is hardly possible that a case of circumstantial evidence could be stronger.

On the other hand, it has been proved by the evidence of the page Leubelfing that Gustavus, in his eagerness to ascertain the exact position and force of the enemy, had advanced much too far in front of his men, and that he fell, so to speak, in the midst of Piccolomini's cuirassiers. The chamberlain, Truchsess, has even gone so far as to affirm that he saw the fatal shot fired, at a distance of ten paces from the King, by an Imperial officer, Lieutenant-Colonel Falkenberg, who at once turned and fled, but was pursued and cut down by Luckau, squire of Franz Albert of Lauenburg. This story is confirmed by Harte, who, after stating the case very strongly against Franz Albert, adds: "To the best of my unbiassed judgment there appears one circumstance in Duke Franz's favour, namely, that his Master of the Horse, who was a gentleman, killed the cavalier who shot Gustavus." Again, in his report of the battle, Duke Bernhard makes no allusion to the supposed action of Franz Albert. The presumption against the latter seems to rest mainly upon his subsequent conduct.

The immediate result of the battle of Lützen was to deprive Wallenstein of the winter quarters for which he had striven in Saxony. Early on the morning of the 7th he despatched his Croats to take possession of the battle-field, if it should be unoccupied by the enemy. But when these light troops returned to report the presence there in full array of the Swedish army, Wallenstein hastened to evacuatei Lepzig and to fall back into Bohemia. His departure left the Swedes at liberty to enter into free communication with John George and the Saxons.

CHAPTER IV.

NÖRDLINGEN.

WHEN Gustavus affronted the Imperialists at Lützen, he had six detached corps combating for him in other parts of Germany. Gustavus Horn was in Alsace, making in that province considerable progress; Dubatel was in Silesia, Baudissin in the Electorate of Cologne; the Scotchman, Ruthven, in Swabia; the Palatine of Birkenfeld in Bavaria; and there was a sixth corps in Lower Saxony.

That Gustavus, had he survived the victory of Lützen, would have at once utilised the means which were thus at his disposal to finish the war, cannot, I think, be questioned. He had been accustomed to make winter campaigns in countries colder even than Germany; he would have been joined, a day or two after the battle, by the Saxon army; and knowing, as he did, that a victory not followed up is but a victory in name, he would have gathered all his strength to make the final spring which would have gained for him all the objects to attain which he had quitted Sweden.

But the death of Gustavus completely changed the position. It prevented that immediate concentration of forces, that single direction, which should have made Lützen, in its results, decisive. The first consequence of it was delay—a delay requisite to communicate with the great princes and nobles, to re-consider the situation, to appoint a chief to carry out the plan which might be agreed upon, to induce generals of different nationalities, some of whom had found it difficult to lower their pretensions sufficiently to serve under a king, to place themselves under the direction of one of the generals of that king. To arrange and order all these matters meant, I repeat, a delay which, at the least, lost for the cause of free conscience many of the advantages which immediate action would have wrung from the victorious battle-field of Lützen.

It is wonderful, notwithstanding, taking into consideration all the circumstances of the time, the slow method of communication, the individual ambitions, how short was that delay. Certainly the men who fought in that war were not all animated by the highest and purest motives. The princes, the nobles, and the generals who had served under Gustavus were human. They lived in an age when power was to him who wielded the sword. Like the generals of Alexander, each had his own peculiar ambition, and the death of the modern Alexander had apparently opened the way for its attainment. At such a crisis and in such an age, much would depend upon the man who should succeed the dead hero in the administration of his kingdom. Fortunately for the Protestant cause, that task devolved upon one the most eminently fitted, by character and by position, to take up and to direct to their proper issue the threads which had fallen to the earth at Lützen.

Gustavus Adolphus had bequeathed the largest share in the administration of his estates,* during the minority of his daughter, Christina, to his Chancellor, Axel Oxenstierna. Oxenstierna was the greatest master of policy, the greatest administrator, that Sweden ever produced. In a Europe which could boast of a Richelieu he stood in the foremost rank. His character—as drawn by two writers of widely different temperaments

---

* The will of Gustavus, which, although not signed, was allowed to take effect, confided the administration, during the minority of his daughter Christina, to five nobles, of whom Oxenstierna was one. To him was allotted a large share in the internal administration of Sweden and the full power for the carrying on of the war.

—the one his wayward, eccentric, yet highly-gifted daughter; the other the sober-minded, painstaking, and methodical historian, Anders Fryxell—stands out as almost unique in history. "An extraordinary perspicacity," wrote Fryxell, in his *History of Gustavus Adolphus*, "a calmness which nothing could disturb, presided at all his determinations. These he executed with energy and perseverance. Nothing was deferred to the morrow, and nothing was forgotten. This activity, which embraced everything, never relaxed. In this respect his faculties approached the marvellous. The influence of his activity, of his loyalty, of his will, is to be seen in all the important negotiations, in the diets, the affairs, the wars of the time. There was not a single branch of the Swedish administration which was not indebted to him for ameliorations. . . . Posterity rests stupefied at the sight of the enormous amount of state papers emanating from his hand. So vast an activity would have been impossible, but for the severe gravity of the writer—but for the exact discipline to which he subjected others as well as himself. . . . In the loftiest and noblest acceptation of the term, Oxenstierna was an aristocrat. Entirely penetrated by the ideas of his age, it never occurred to him to doubt the rights of the nobility to the exclusive possession of important posts, to manage the revenues and the administration of the kingdom. But by the side of these rights he placed duties not less elevated. He demanded, first and before everything, superiority in the sciences and in learning, and he complained loudly of the education which, to use his own words, 'confined itself to dancing and horsemanship, and to the manners of a court life.' He could not endure pride of birth without merit, and he used to say: '*Melius est clarum fieri quam nasci.*' It was for the nobility, he always affirmed, to give an example of patriotism, and to shrink from no difficulties and no sacrifices, when the country was in danger."*

* Compare with this the portrait of the same statesman drawn by Christina in her memoirs—unhappily never finished—vol. iii. p. 46.

Such was **the man** who was suddenly called upon to assume
the administration **of** affairs in Protestant **Germany.** His task
was a very difficult one. **The fact that Gustavus was dead had**
scarcely been realised when personal ambitions **rose on every**
side to confront him. Foremost amongst the **pretenders was**
John George **of Saxony; but there was in** reality scarcely a
man, Swede or German, **who had rendered** any service to the
common cause, who **did not, in some form or other,** put forth
a claim either for the vacant leadership, **or** for personal
aggrandisement. The alliance between Sweden and Protestant
Germany was in imminent danger of **being broken, and there**
can be little doubt but that **had** Wallenstein, **at this period,**
been able to take full **advantage of the situation, the war might**
then and there have **been terminated.**

Some weeks elapsed before Oxenstierna could **succeed in**
impressing upon the German allies **of** Sweden **that the sceptre**
of the dead king was, till the **majority of** that king's daughter,
then **six** years old, **to be** wielded by himself. To make them
feel this truth, he himself visited Dresden and Berlin, obtained
promises of adhesion from John George of Saxony, Ulric **of**
Brunswick, **and** George William of Brandenburg; **assembled**
then a congress of the reformed German princes at Heilbronn on
the Neckar, then a **free town of the Empire; received at that**
congress authority to carry on the war, gratified several personal
ambitions,* and **divided the command of** the army, entrusting
the forces south **of the Main to the care of Bernhard of**
Weimar, those north of that **river to Duke George of Brunswick-Lüneberg.**

The military operations which had taken place between the

* For instance, he promised to Duke Bernhard the possession of the Franconian
bishoprics; to the Landgrave of Hesse, the possessions attaching to the sees of
Paderborn, Münster, Fulda, and the abbey of Corvey; to the Duke of Würtemberg,
the Catholic foundations in his dominions. There were many others to be satisfied.
So great was the greed, that the Chancellor, disgusted, declared that he would have
the record entered in the Swedish archives that "a prince of the German Empire
made a request for such and such territory from a Swedish nobleman, and that the
Swedish nobleman complied with the request by granting him German lands."

battle of Lützen and the assembly of the congress at Heilbronn, require but a brief record.

Three days after that battle Duke Bernhard, who had assumed command of the Swedes, joined the Saxon army at Leipzig. At that city they had again separated: the Saxons to conquer, for the profit of their Elector, the Lausitz and Silesia, and thence, if possible, to act with Count Thurn in an invasion of Lower Austria; the Swedes and their North German allies, partly, under George of Brunswick-Lüneberg, to defend Westphalia and Lower Saxony; partly, under Duke Bernhard, to march into Franconia, to renew the plan of invasion through Bavaria which had already twice been interrupted by Wallenstein. That general had, as we have seen, effected a safe retreat into Bohemia, and he remained there up to the period at which we have arrived, and even later, perfectly quiescent, adding to the strength of his army, watching events, and endeavouring by secret means, to be presently described, to give to those events the turn he desired.

Before Duke Bernhard had been nominated, by the congress at Heilbronn, to the command-in-chief of the army which was to operate south of the Main, he had marched across Thüringen into Upper Franconia, to recover the conquests which Gustavus had made in that province the preceding year. The strong places of Kronach and Hochstädt submitted almost without a blow. Bamberg followed their example. Duke Bernhard was at that episcopal capital planning further conquests, when he received a pressing summons from Horn to join him on the Danube.

The reader will recollect that when, after the campaign of Nuremberg, Gustavus had proceeded southwards with the intention of, for the second time, besieging Ingolstadt, he, on the news of Wallenstein's march towards Saxony, renounced that idea and hastened after his enemy, leaving the Count Palatine of Birkenfeld and General Banner to maintain the Swedish conquests in and about Donauwörth. These generals had, in the first instance, pressed their conquests southwards as far even as Lake Constance. But in October and November the Bavarian general Aldringer, who had recovered from the wound received on the Lech, had been able to bring against them forces vastly superior in numbers to theirs. Towards the close of 1632 the pressure he exercised had become so strong, that Banner, very anxious at all risks to maintain the line of the Lech, sent most urgent requests to Horn to join him. That general was at the time in Alsace. We have seen that on the 28th October he had, after a siege of eight weeks, taken Benfeld. Not delayed by the winter, he had pursued his victorious career in that province, and had driven the enemy from Schlettstadt, Colmar, and Hagenau. It was just after the capture of the last-named place that he received from Banner the summons to which I have referred. It was a summons not to be neglected by a patriotic soldier. Confiding, then, to the Rhinegrave Otto Ludwig the care of defending his conquests in Alsace, Horn, at the head of seven thousand men, crossed the Rhine, and hastened by forced marches towards Swabia. Before he could join Banner, however, Aldringer had forced the line of the Lech, and, by the capture of the important town of Kempten, had secured a strong position on the Iller. There he, too, received a reinforcement, strong enough in numbers to neutralise the aid brought by Banner to Horn. Deeming it necessary, above all things, to bar the further progress of the enemy, Horn determined to leave his recent conquests in Alsace entirely undefended. He sent, then, orders to Otto Ludwig to join him with all the troops still remaining in that province. Finding himself still unable to check the progress of Aldringer, he despatched to Duke Bernhard the pressing request to which I have referred.

On receiving this request Duke Bernhard at once quitted Bamberg, and marched southwards without delay. At Eichstädt he came upon a strong detachment of the Bavarian army under John von Werth, or Weerdt, a man who—rare occurrence in those days—had raised himself from a low social position to a high command,* swept it from his path, took Eichstädt, and pressing onwards reached Donauwörth (March 1633).

At Donauwörth there was no enemy before him to prevent his march to Vienna. Aldringer was in Upper Swabia still threatening, by stealing along Lake Constance, to enter Würtemberg from the south. To prevent this movement Horn had taken a position at Stockach, a little town just beyond the north-western end of the lake. Here he was rejoined by Birkenfeld, from whom he had momentarily separated; and hence, on learning of the arrival of Duke Bernhard at Donauwörth, he had ordered back, to Alsace, the Rhinegrave Otto Ludwig to defend the Swedish conquests in that duchy against a Spanish corps of 14,000 men led, in support of the Catholic cause, by the Duke of Feria. I must leave these several corps in position and on the march, whilst I ask the reader to return to Duke Bernhard.

All the possibilities seemed to be before that commander on his arrival at Donauwörth. Aldringer was on the shores of Lake Constance; Wallenstein was in Bohemia; a promise made to him from behind the walls of Ingolstadt to deliver up to him that city was ringing in his ears; from Ingolstadt to Vienna three fortified places, the towns of Ratisbon, Passau, and Linz, formed the chief protection of the line of the Danube. To march, then, to Vienna, and extort from the fears of Ferdinand the concessions he denied to just demands, or to depose him in favour of another, appeared then not only feasible, but, under the actual circumstances, easy of accomplishment. For, never were circumstances so peculiar. To defend the allied interests of the Catholic League and of the Emperor there were but three armies, that commanded by Aldringer, that of the Duke of Feria, and that led by Wallenstein. It cannot be doubted but that

* He was the son of a Burgundian peasant, who took his name from the village (Weerdt—Germanised into Werth) in which he was born (about 1602). At the age of twenty he was serving in the ranks as a cavalry soldier, under the famous Spinola. From that position he had advanced, in ten years, to be general in the League army in Bavaria.

these three generals working together could prevent the march of the Swedes to Vienna. But, supposing that Wallenstein were to hold aloof, such a movement was feasible; supposing, further, that Wallenstein were prepared to assist it, it was easy. All this was to be possible; for although at the period at which I have arrived, March 1633, the overtures made by Wallenstein to Oxenstierna had been of the faintest character, they were soon to become more pronounced, pointing to a direct issue. Up to this time Duke Bernhard had before him the fact that Aldringer and Feria were not in a position to oppose his advance, and that Wallenstein, motionless in Bohemia, had refused further to strengthen Aldringer.

Why, then, did not Duke Bernhard advance? Duke Bernhard did not advance because he too, like Wallenstein, had his dreams of ambition. The successors of Alexander were not content merely to promote the ends to accomplish which their Alexander had invaded Germany. Duke Bernhard was young, the youngest of eight sons—he had seen but twenty-nine summers—capable, daring, and the darling of the army. The congress summoned by Oxenstierna was sitting at Heilbronn. For the moment Oxenstierna had in his hands the disposal of many conquered places, of all the high positions. The time, then, was opportune for Duke Bernhard to obtain all that his secret ambition prompted him to demand. He had only to make the situation so dangerous that it would be most difficult, if not impossible, to refuse him. The means to produce such a situation were at hand.

The army was in arrears of pay; the treasure-chest of Duke Bernhard was exhausted; the soldiers were discontented. It is probable that, under any circumstances, this state of things would have led to a demonstration. But, viewed in connection with the fact that the general was discontented too, that he forwarded to Oxenstierna, with the demands of the troops, his own demands, it is equally probable that the demonstration would not, had he taken pains to check it, have assumed a very violent character. As it was, it became, very soon after the arrival of the army at Donauwörth, very formidable indeed. The soldiers, forming themselves into groups, demanded that to each group a city which they could plunder should be assigned. They granted the Chancellor four weeks to consider their demand. Should it not at the end of that time be complied with, they would act for themselves. Meanwhile they declined to move.

Looking forward for a moment, we shall see that after Duke Bernhard's demands for himself had been granted, he experienced little difficulty in restoring discipline. It is fair, then, to conclude that, at the outset, not only did he not use all the means in his power to repress the mutiny, but he used it as a lever to forward his own views. For, by the courier who carried the next despatches, he forwarded to Oxenstierna a demand—(1st) that territories appertaining to the sees of Bamberg and Würzburg should be erected into a principality in his favour; (2ndly) that he should be nominated commander in chief of all the armies fighting in Germany for the Protestant cause, with the title of Generalissimo!

Oxenstierna had been alarmed by the receipt of the mutinous demands of the troops on the Danube. He was disgusted when he found those demands virtually supported by the one general who, by his influence, was the most competent to meet the difficulty. His first thought was to dismiss Duke Bernhard from the Swedish service. But the reflection that the disorder might spread, and spread the more quickly with Duke Bernhard as its secret instigator, modified this view, and he determined to treat. He offered, then, to Duke Bernhard the Franconian bishoprics, to be held by him as a fief of the Swedish crown, with the exception of the fortresses of Würzburg and Königshofen, which were to remain garrisoned by Swedish troops. He pledged himself further, on behalf of the Swedish crown, to defend Duke Bernhard in the possession of those territories. The demand to be made generalissimo the Chancellor refused; but he appointed

NÖRDLINGEN. 111

Duke Bernhard to command in chief south of the Main. Duke Bernhard accepted this modification of his demand, and, having accepted it, experienced, as I have already stated, little difficulty in restoring order in the ranks of his army. But in this intrigue many weeks had been wasted, and the month of October arrived before he was able to make a forward movement.

Whilst this intrigue was progressing the situation of Horn and Birkenfeld had materially altered. We left these two generals at Stockach, near the north-western end of Lake Constance, endeavouring to bar the entrance into Lower Würtemberg to Aldringer, whilst the Rhinegrave Otto Ludwig was speeding towards Alsace to defend the Swedish conquests in that duchy against the Duke of Feria. But the Duke of Feria, who was acting quite independently of Wallenstein, was anxious, before entering Alsace, to effect a junction, and to co-operate, with Aldringer. Aldringer, in spite of Wallenstein's orders on no account to quit the line of the Danube, lent himself to the Duke's view, and the two armies united in Upper Swabia. Horn and Birkenfeld, whose troops had been increased by various reinforcements to thirty thousand, marched at once to offer battle to the Imperialists. But the latter, declining the offer, outmanœuvred the Swedish leaders, and marched by way of Freiburg and Lörrach into Alsace with the hope of crushing Otto Ludwig. In this hope they were disappointed, for Horn followed on their footsteps and, harassing them at every step, completely re-established, before the end of the year, Swedish supremacy in the much-contested duchy.

Before returning to Duke Bernhard, it is necessary that I should relate very briefly the action during this period, from March to October, of the great Imperial commander in Bohemia. Whilst the congress was sitting at Heilbronn, Wallenstein, whose army, by losses at Lützen, had been very much reduced and who wished, before engaging in military operations, to raise it to a strength which could make it formidable, had entered into negotiations with **Oxenstierna and** the Saxons. On the 7th June he concluded with **the latter an armistice of a** fortnight's duration for Silesia alone, **and at the end of** July a second for a similar period. In his correspondence with Oxenstierna, whilst there were some expressions **which** might be interpreted as displaying his contempt for the Emperor personally, an anxiety for **a peaceful settlement** of the questions **at issue** predominated. **Oxenstierna** made no reply to these overtures, so completely did **he distrust** Wallenstein, and in writing to Duke Bernhard **he** warned him to be on his guard against **any** propositions which the Duke of Friedland might make to him. At the moment Duke Bernhard was not put to the test, **for at this** particular period Wallenstein was engaged **in** endeavouring, **by** all **the** means in his power, to seduce Saxony from her alliance with Sweden, and to persuade the Elector and Arnheim to join with him in driving **the Swedes from** Germany. **John George,** since the death of Gustavus, had, in spite of his promises to Oxenstierna, been working **in Lower** Saxony and the Lausitz solely for his own interests. **It was to be** presumed, therefore, that he would listen to an accommodation which would secure those interests. But whether it was that his mind was not then prepared **for** the step which he took some months later, or that, as is probable, **he** feared the Swedes more than **he** trusted Wallenstein, it is certain that he repulsed the **offers made** to him. Alike to intimidate him and to check the **progress of the Swedes** under the Count of Thurn, Wallenstein then marched suddenly into Lower Saxony, defeated Thurn at Steinau on the Oder (18th October), re-took Frankfurt **(on the** Oder) and Landsberg, sent **a detachment to** reconquer **Pomerania, and even threatened Berlin.** Before setting out on this expedition, he had sent orders to Aldringer not to join the **Duke of Feria,** but to cover Ratisbon. Aldringer, pressed in a **contrary** direction by the Emperor, disobeyed him, with the further result which has now to be recorded.

No sooner had Duke Bernhard, his ambitious hopes gratified, restored discipline in his army, than he resolved to take advan-

tage of the absence of any army in front of him to seize
Ratisbon. He marched then, at the end of October, with all
speed on that important city. The garrison, though small and
composed mostly of raw levies, would have sufficed to defend
the place for a considerable time had it been well supported by
the citizens. But a large majority of the people of Ratisbon
had embraced the creed of Luther, and they regarded the
freedom they claimed for their consciences with a love not less
burning than the hatred which they bore to the Bavarians who
had suppressed their civil rights. They welcomed, then, Duke
Bernhard as a deliverer. So great was their enthusiasm that
Maximilian of Bavaria, who was momentarily within the city,
dreading lest the appearance of the Swedish army before its
walls should prove the signal for a tumult which would open its
gates to the enemy, wrote alike to the Emperor and to Wallenstein, exposing his necessity, and pledging himself to maintain
Ratisbon if only he were to receive a reinforcement of five thousand men. The Emperor was powerless; he had not the men
to send: but he had, or hoped he had, some influence with
Wallenstein, and he despatched to that general seven messengers,
one following the other, to urge upon him the necessity of preventing at all hazards the fall of so important a place. But
Wallenstein, feeling, if we may believe the views set forth in his
correspondence, that he was not strong enough to divide his army,
and that he could best cover Vienna by maintaining a strong
position in Bohemia, possibly likewise secretly pleased at the
occurrence of a complication which would tend to make the
dependence of Ferdinand and Maximilian upon himself more
pronounced, did not afford the aid demanded. It is true that he
replied to the solicitations of the Emperor by an assurance that
he would do all in his power to forward his views, and that, in
the presence of the messengers, he ordered the Count of Gallas
to march with twelve thousand men on Ratisbon; but the secret
instructions which Gallas carried forbade him to attempt any
enterprise which should be likely to bring on a general action

8

with Duke Bernhard. Wallenstein, in **fact,** left Ratisbon to its fate.*

Meanwhile **Duke** Bernhard **appeared** before the place. The commandant, **buoyed up** by hopes **of relief,** did all that man could do. But he had difficulties **within as well** as without. These difficulties increased **when the Swedes opened fire upon** the city. At **length** they **became insupportable: the promised relief did not arrive; and he** capitulated **(5th November).** Prior to **the capitulation, Maximilian,** foreseeing the inevitable result, **had withdrawn.**

Fired by the easy conquest of a place which **secured** for **him the command of the Danube, and seeing in his mental vision Vienna already occupied by his troops, Duke** Bernhard, sending **a** corps **of his army across the river, with** directions **to** cover **his movements, pushed** on and **mastered Straubing, an** ancient **town,** twenty-five **miles** on the road **to Vienna, the** centre point **of the** most fertile **part of** Southern **Germany, and** called, on **that** account, **"the granary** of Bavaria." Still advancing, **he** reached Plattling, **sixteen miles further, on the** 9th. Beyond Plattling, commanding **the point where the Isar** flows **into the Danube, was** posted **the army of the League, commanded by**

---

* **In letters which he wrote to the Emperor** after the fall of Ratisbon, and after the **movements,** subsequent thereto, **of Duke** Bernhard—movements which were the **consequence of his own** action—Wallenstein explained at length to Ferdinand **the reasons which had guided** him. In reply, the Emperor accepted his justification **as most complete. The** correspondence is dated the 27th November and the **3rd and 24th December.**

This is not the place to enter into a history of the mysterious causes which led to **the premature close of the career of Wallenstein.** But it **may at least be** asserted **that every means were taken by the entourage of** the **Emperor to** prejudice that **sovereign** against **his powerful vassal. Richelieu, who possessed,** more than any **man then** living, the **knowledge of the secrets of the Courts of Europe,** has left upon record that " **the courtiers and adherents of Spain gave a bad** interpretation **to** all his actions; **they attributed every untoward occurrence to his** fault and to **his** malice. Were **the occurrences** favourable, they asserted that they would have been more favourable **still if only he had** willed it." **In** support of this assertion, Richelieu proceeds to cite the very facts which **have** formed the gravest charges **against** Wallenstein. The real truth is that the great **commander** was in advance **of his** age. What he **had most** at heart to secure, far more than personal aggrandisement, was toleration **for all** creeds, and the union of Germany. It was a noble dream, but, under Ferdinand **II., a dream** impossible of attainment.

John of Werth. Not strong enough to dispute the passage of the Isar, John of Werth hastened to save himself, and, crossing the Danube, fell back towards the Bohemian frontier, hoping to meet the troops which, he was aware, the Emperor had eagerly importuned Wallenstein to send to his aid, but which, for the reason already indicated, and presently to be referred to more particularly, never came. Duke Bernhard then crossed the Isar, and, always pushing forward, came, on the 12th, within sight of Passau.

Duke Bernhard had come within sight of Passau when a slight movement made by Wallenstein revealed to him the extreme danger of his position. That able commander, fresh from strengthening the imperial interests in the northern parts of Germany, had turned a deaf ear to the repeated solicitations of the Emperor—now to detach a corps to save Ratisbon, now to strengthen John of Werth, now to protect Upper Austria. In the first instance he had seemed to comply; in the other instances he had not gratified the Emperor by that semblance. In point of fact, Wallenstein did not feel himself sufficiently strong to divide his army. Had he, for instance, directed Gallas with twelve thousand men to join John of Werth, and had Duke Bernhard attacked and defeated those united forces, Wallenstein would have been too weak to save the empire. Keeping his army strong, he had, he felt, the key of the position. He encouraged Duke Bernhard, then, to approach Passau, feeling that if he attacked that place it would be his grave. What, in fact, would then be the position of the Swedish general? In front of him flowed the Inn, there a broad and deep river, protected by strongly-fortified places on its further bank; behind him the army of John of Werth, an unfriendly country, and the Isar; on his left rear, Wallenstein himself, marching across the Bohemian forest. That leader had indeed keenly watched the situation, had fixed the very point up to which Duke Bernhard should advance, but beyond which he should not move.* When, **then, he** learned **that** Duke Bernhard was hastening on **from the Isar towards Passau,** he marched southwards with **his whole army in the** direction of Cham (on the Regen), so as to **place himself on his left rear.**

Duke Bernhard **heard of this movement just as** he arrived within sight of Passau. What **was he to do? Even were** he able **to assure** the passage of the **Inn,** could **he,** dare he, push **on, at an inclement season of the** year, towards Vienna, his **retreat cut off by two armies, both** of which might **attack** him at any **time. There were** strong places yet between Passau and Vienna. **To be in front of one** of these, well defended, **whilst** Wallenstein **was behind him, would be** ruin. The **more he** looked at the **situation the less he** liked it. He recognised, **at** last, that **he** had **only just time to** save himself by a prompt retreat. Without **a moment's delay, then, he** acted on that conviction, hastened back with all **speed to** Ratisbon, and, not stopping even there, marched northwards **into** the Upper Palatinate to defend that conquered country against Wallenstein even at the cost of **a** battle!

But to engage in **a** decisive battle, the loss of which **by him would mean the loss** of the cause entrusted **to him, was** repugnant **to Wallenstein.** He had but one army, and, **were that army to be destroyed, it would not** be difficult **for** Duke **Bernhard to avail himself of** the *prestige* of victory **and** to **resume the march which** the action of that **one army had prevented. The winter season, a very severe one,** was upon **him, and it seemed advisable,** the **safety of the** hereditary **lands having** been secured, to delay further **military** operations till the spring. Such were the thoughts **of Wallenstein,** and in the sense of those thoughts **he acted; and, it must** be re-

* **It** appears to me **that** this action **of Wallenstein** completely disproves the **charge** of treason and connivance with the Swedes preferred against him. Certainly up to the end of November 1633 there had been **no such** connivance. When Duke Bernhard was before Passau the fate of **the** Emperor was in Wallenstein's hands. **Had** any understanding existed with Duke Bernhard, Wallenstein would have either joined him, or have facilitated his **advance.** But, by **a single** march southwards, he stopped his progress, **and saved the empire!**

membered, that in so acting he had the approval of the Emperor.*

The campaign of 1633 thus came to an end. If it had not borne to the Swedes the fruits which would certainly have resulted if Gustavus had survived Lützen, its general product was not unsatisfactory to the cause of the reformers. Alsace had been entirely subdued; Duke Feria's army had been almost destroyed. Duke Bernhard had secured Ratisbon, and maintained the Swedish conquests in the Upper Palatinate. And if, for a moment, Wallenstein had restored Imperial influence in Lower Saxony, Pomerania, and Brandenburg, and had recovered a portion of the Lausitz from the Saxons, these advantages had been balanced by others gained by the Swedes in Cassel and Westphalia. In the former Landgraviate, Duke George of Lüneberg had taken, after a desperate defence, the fortress of Hameln, and, a few days later, had gained a complete victory over the Imperialists at Oldendorf. In Westphalia, the Swedes and their allies had taken Osnabrück, Paderborn, and Bückeburg. On the other side of the account, the Imperialists could only point to Wallenstein's success in the north against the Saxons, and, what was of more consequence, to the opportune check he had given to Duke Bernhard.

The campaign of 1634 was to open, on the Imperial side, under a new leadership. On the 25th February of that year, Wallenstein was murdered, by order of the Emperor,† Ferdinand II., at Eger. In his place, the King of Hungary,

---

* In December, the Emperor, in reply to Wallenstein's statement of his reasons for the plans he had adopted, wrote thus: "Vu la saison avancée et le changement de circonstances, nous acquiesçons pour le moment à votre bon avis."

† The men, under whose direction the Emperor's orders were carried out, and their tools, benefited largely by the revulsion of feeling produced in their master's mind by the death of the man he had hated and feared. The estates of Wallenstein were divided amongst Gallas, Piccolomini, and Aldringer; the meaner conspirators received promotion and money. Later, the Irishman, Butler, who, though loaded with benefits by Wallenstein, had superintended all the details of the assassination, was presented to the Emperor, whose imperial and royal hand pressed that of the murderer. I have omitted, as not essential to my narrative, all reference to the later negotiations of Wallenstein with Oxenstierna and Duke Bernhard.

afterwards Emperor under the title of Ferdinand III., was nominated to the chief command, with the Count of Gallas as his chief adviser.

Gallas was the very reverse of a capable commander, but his services in the betrayal of Wallenstein had brought him to the front rank of Court favour, and he was at least devoted to the Imperial cause. Strengthened by troops from Lorraine, led in person by the Duke who had made so poor a show when serving with Tilly, and by ten thousand Spanish veterans, under the Cardinal Infanta, the new Imperial general entered the Upper Palatinate early in May by way of Cham, and pressed on, following the course of the Regen, to Ratisbon, the recovery of which place lay very near to the Emperor's heart. To oppose the Imperial army, which numbered nearly thirty-five thousand men, Duke Bernhard had not quite fifteen thousand. With so great a disparity he could not offer battle, but he employed all the means in his power, short of fighting a general action, to delay the advance of the enemy, whilst he sent pressing messages to Oxenstierna and Horn—to the former for men and money, to the latter to march with all haste to his assistance.

Then occurred one of those misfortunes of which abundant instances were seen in the French army in the time of Napoleon. The historians of that period have pointed to the instances without number in which, when Napoleon was absent, the most splendid opportunities were lost, on account of the rivalries and jealousies of his marshals. So it was in the Swedish army in 1644. Between Duke Bernhard and Gustavus Horn there was no love. Their temperaments did not correspond. The one, vivacious, enterprising, daring even to rashness, was ready to rush upon any service which might offer the smallest glimmer of success. The other, slow, over-cautious, hesitating, would not stir an inch until the horizon before him was clear. Added to this, Horn, a born Swede, was a little jealous of the preference given to Duke Bernhard, a German in the Swedish service, and this feeling tended to increase his caution and to delay his action.

Had Duke Bernhard occupied the position of Horn in Alsace, he would undoubtedly have reached the Swedish army in the Upper Palatinate in time to prevent the fall of Ratisbon. But the slow movements of Horn rendered the loss of that place inevitable.

Left, in fact, to his own resources, Duke Bernhard was unable seriously to check the progress of the Imperial army which, in spite of all his demonstrations on its flanks and even on its rear, marched directly to Ratisbon and laid siege to it. The garrison of Ratisbon fought bravely, but they could not withstand numbers, and the city surrendered on the 26th July. Gallas then marched directly upon Donauwörth, and this place, after a feeble defence, also capitulated. Duke Bernhard, meanwhile, heart-broken at seeing place after place fall without being able to strike a blow on their behalf, had marched into Swabia to hasten, if possible, the movements of Horn. As soon as he had effected the wished-for junction with that general, he turned quickly back and reached the vicinity of Nördlingen only to see the enemy posted behind the more advanced of the two heights which dominate the plain. By a skilful manœuvre he was able, however, to introduce within its walls a reinforcement to the garrison of eight hundred men.

Nördlingen was, at this period, an imperial free town, possessing a territory of about fifty square miles. Built on the south bank of the Ries, some eighteen miles to the north-east of Donauwörth, it was surrounded by a wall interspersed with numerous towers, sufficient to guard it against a surprise, if not to defend it against a regular attack. The vast plain on which it stands, one of the most extensive in Franconia, is cut, in its centre, by two heights, rising at a distance of three thousand yards the one from the other. Between these two heights is a valley, which terminates, from both directions, in a village about three hundred paces nearer to the town than either of them. This height is called Allersheim. The foremost of the two is known as the Weinberg; it is very steep and cragged.

Behind, but not upon, the Weinberg, Bernhard and Horn

beheld the Imperial army encamped, when, on the evening of the 26th August, they arrived within sight of Nördlingen. Many considerations prompted Bernhard to desire to attack it. The fall of Ratisbon and Donauwörth, after the display of confident audacity which had led the Swedes to the walls of Passau, had inflicted upon their Protestant adherents in Bavaria a discouragement scarcely less than that which had been occasioned in Northern Germany by the sacking of Magdeburg. To allow a third important place—a place, too, which had declared its zeal for the common cause in a manner that was unmistakable—to fall, without a blow, into the hands of the enemy, would not only be a disgrace—it would be an evidence of soft-heartedness, of fear, of selfishness, such as would damage the cause without remedy. Better, far better, on such an occasion to fight and be beaten, than tamely to yield Nördlingen to the Imperialists. In the one case honour, and, with honour, the opinion of the reformers of Germany, would be satisfied; in the other there could ensue only shame.

Such were the arguments of Duke Bernhard. The cautious Horn was of a different opinion. "We are outnumbered," he argued in so many words; "the enemy is superior to us by one-third; they have a strong position, which it will cost many men to gain. The odds are at least five to one against our success. To fight, then, will be a mistake. Granted that all you say is correct; that the fall of Nördlingen will damage us in the eyes of the reformed princes and people of Germany. With good management on our part, the feeling thus roused will be but temporary. Look at the composition of the Imperial army. Of the thirty-five thousand men of which it is composed, eight thousand at least are Spaniards, who are on their way to Flanders, and who will leave the Imperial army within a few days. On the other hand, the Rhinegrave, Otto Ludwig, is, with seven thousand men, within a few marches of us. What, then, will be our position, if we only exercise patience? We shall then outnumber the enemy as much as they now outnumber us. We shall recover our prestige here, as we recovered it after Magdeburg at Leipzig; we shall recover even our conquests, and, if the enemy should dare to accept battle, we shall beat him and be in a position to march on Vienna. But if we fight now and are beaten, all the conquests made by our late sovereign and by ourselves south of the Main will be most seriously jeopardised."

The words of Horn were the words of wisdom, but they fell upon an unwilling ear. The fiery nature of Duke Bernhard had suffered so acutely from the reproaches, not always tacit, of those whom he had been forced to abandon at Ratisbon and Donauwörth, that he could not endure further delay. His view, too, was supported by all the other generals present at the consultation. Horn, then, out-voted, was forced to give way.

A battle having been resolved upon, it became of enormous importance to occupy without delay the steep and cragged height to which I have alluded, and behind which the Imperialists lay encamped. This duty was intrusted to Horn. The choice was unfortunate; for Horn, though a brave and capable commander, was slow and cautious, and this particular service had to be performed in a dark night in a country with which he was not familiar, and yet it was a service upon the prompt carrying out of which victory depended.

Up to nightfall the Imperialists had shown no disposition to occupy the Weinberg. Believing, then, that he had an easy task before him, Horn, taking with him four thousand chosen musketeers and pikemen, and twelve guns, set out, about nine o'clock at night, on his errand. But the rough road, the dykes and ditches which intersected the country, impeded him; the fact that he was unacquainted with the lay of the land made him doubly cautious; his progress consequently in no way resembled that of a daring soldier bent upon an enterprise demanding rapid execution. At length, about midnight, all the obstacles were passed, and he was in a position to ascend the hill. But here another difficulty arose. Caution suggested to him that the time spent by him in crossing the dykes and ditches, might have been employed by the enemy in marching on and fortifying the coveted summit. What if he were to find it strongly occupied? A less slow thinker would have argued that, the summit being necessary, the best mode of obtaining it would be by ascending it without delay. But it was not in Horn's nature to think rapidly. On this occasion over-caution suspended the exercise of his reasoning powers; and he came to the resolution to halt where he was till break of day.

The resolution was fatal. Had Horn only continued his movement he would have carried the Weinberg, and the result of the battle would have been different. The Imperialist leaders, Gallas and the Cardinal Infanta Don Fernando, had not been unmindful of the commanding position of the hill upon which Horn was marching, and they had given orders that it should be occupied before daybreak by four hundred Spaniards. These four hundred Spaniards reached the summit about midnight. Had Horn, then, marched straight on he would have met these men with a vastly overwhelming force, and have driven them from the height. His fatal delay gave them time to intrench themselves, and of this the Spaniards, veterans from Italy, took the fullest advantage. When the day broke, they had thrown up intrenchments of a very formidable character.

Sensible, then, of his mistake, Horn hastened to repair it by ordering a general advance. With their accustomed valour, the Swedes mounted the hill, and, daring every danger, rushed at the intrenchment. Before their rush, it seemed as though the splendid courage of the Spaniards was not to prevail, for in one or two places the defences were forced. But as the assailants crowded to enter at this point, the accidental explosion of an ammunition-wagon almost in their midst caused great loss, and threw them into a disorder of which the Spaniards availed themselves to drive them from the vantage ground. They were still falling back when the Spanish cavalry, which, on the first sounds of the combat, the Cardinal Infanta had ordered to the spot, charged their flanks and forced them to a precipitate retreat.

Bitterly repenting his delay at midnight, Horn brought up fresh troops, and re-animating those who had been already repulsed, led the united body once more to the assault. But the Weinberg, which had been occupied in the early morning by only four hundred men, was now defended by the whole of the Spanish infantry. Vain, now, was the energy of Horn, ineffectual was the valour of his troops. Fruitless were the sacrifices made by Duke Bernhard to reinforce him. Seven times did the Swedish infantry climb that fatal hill, seven times were they repulsed. No impression could they make upon the stalwart troops of Spain!

Whilst Horn was thus vainly endeavouring to repair his faults, Duke Bernhard had attacked the enemy in the plain. Despite his inferiority in numbers, his daring and skilful leadership obtained some advantages, to improve which the possession by Horn of the much-debated hill was necessary. To aid his colleague in his attempt, Duke Bernhard had sent him all the infantry he could spare. He was still holding his own, waiting for the signal which should show him that Horn had been victorious, when he learned that that general, seven times repulsed, was in full retreat. Duke Bernhard recognised on the instant that the battle was lost; that Horn, if not speedily succoured, was doomed; for the Imperialists, flushed with victory, were using all their efforts to cut him off. To save his colleague, he made at once a strong demonstration against the enemy, hoping to draw upon himself their undivided attack. For the moment he succeeded; but he was too weak in numbers to bear the assault which he had thus provoked. John of Werth, who commanded the Imperial cavalry, met the Swedish horsemen in full shock, and overthrew them so completely, that these, forced back upon their infantry, threw them into complete disorder. With this repulse disappeared the last hope of saving the day. Horn, uncovered on all sides, and surrounded by an enemy ten times superior to him in numbers, was forced, with all his men, to surrender. Duke Bernhard narrowly escaped the same fate. In the end, he succeeded in shaking himself clear, and even managed to rally, as he retreated towards the Main, some nine thousand men. But the defeat was decisive. The loss of ten thousand men, killed, wounded, and missing, in addition to the four thousand under Horn taken prisoners, and all the guns, camp-equipage, and baggage, testified to its severity.

Nördlingen was to the Swedes what Breitenfeld had been to the Emperor. Nördlingen was even a more decisive battle than Leipzig. It virtually changed a war which had till then been really only a civil war, a war of religion, into a war with a foreign enemy. Nördlingen brought France into the field to check the aggrandisement, and to profit by the defeats, of the House of Hapsburg. Nördlingen dissolved the confederacy of the reformed German princes against Ferdinand II. As one of its consequences, John George, the irresolute, short-sighted Elector of Saxony, concluded with the Emperor at Prague a separate peace in the month of May following. The example of John George was followed by the Elector of Brandenburg, by Duke William of Weimar, the Princes of Anhalt, the Duke of Brunswick-Lüneberg, the Duke of Mecklenburg, by Pomerania, by the cities of Augsburg, Würzburg, and Coburg, and by others. Of all the leading members of the Protestant Union, Dukes Bernhard of Weimar, and William of Cassel, were almost alone in supporting the cause to maintain which Gustavus Adolphus had invaded Germany. To Duke Bernhard, personally, the overthrow at Nördlingen was fatal. The Franconian Duchy, acquired by the exercise of so much craft, disappeared for ever from his grasp. For the moment, the Swedish army, whose exploits had made the courtiers of Vienna tremble, and had forced the proud and obstinate Ferdinand to humiliate himself before Wallenstein, seemed annihilated. Well might the heart of the Emperor swell almost to bursting with gratitude when—not dreaming happily as yet of the action about to be taken by France—he joined in the *Te Deum* for Nördlingen!

CHAPTER V.

JANKOWITZ.

In the last chapter I indicated the main consequences of the battle of Nördlingen, the almost complete severance of the alliance between Sweden and the princes of Northern and Central Germany, and the introduction, on the field, of France—originally, as an ally, following the lead of Sweden; afterwards, as a principal, assuming the chief place in the contest. The first period, that of an ally fighting nominally for Sweden, terminated with the death of Duke Bernhard of Weimar (18th July 1639). The record of events which happened between the battle of Nördlingen and that period is full of interest. There is scarcely a more tempting subject for the pen of the historian. The noble despair of Oxenstierna; the splendid courage of Banner; the abilities, ripened by misfortune, of Duke Bernhard; the culpable weakness of John George, most prejudicial to the Saxony over which he ruled; the selfishness of the Protestant princes of Germany: combine to offer to the historian materials most effective. But I am not writing the history of the Thirty Years' War. It is my object rather to conduct the reader to battle-fields which, from the results obtained, from the character of the commanders who led the armies to fight, or from the extraordinary skill displayed by one or other of those commanders upon them, afford to the military student matter to interest and instruct him. I shall pass as lightly as I may, then, over the political events which separate the first period I have indicated from the second; and shall take the reader, as quickly as possible, into the camp.

Left, by the results of the fight at Nördlingen, without money, without allies, without resources, Oxenstierna had been forced, very much against his will, to appeal for material aid to France. France had responded by allowing, after an interval, Duke Bernhard to levy troops, which he should lead, professedly in the interests of Sweden, against the Emperor. Meanwhile, Saxony had concluded with the Emperor at Pirna, at the close of 1634, a convention which ripened into a treaty of alliance, to which almost all the princes of Northern Germany subscribed, at Prague, in the month of May following. The Electors of Saxony and Brandenburg were thus changed into enemies of Sweden. The Swedish General, Banner, who, at the period of the battle of Nördlingen, had been encamped side by side with the Saxon army on the White Hill near Prague, had, on the first indication of wavering on the part of its Elector, managed skilfully to withdraw his troops from the dangerous proximity. On the 22nd October 1635, he defeated the Saxon army, at Dömitz* on the Elbe, then invaded Brandenburg, took Havelberg, and even threatened Berlin. Compelled by the approach of a Saxon and Imperialist army to quit his prey, he turned and beat the combined army at Wittstock (24th September 1636). After that battle, he drew the reinforced Imperialists, commanded by Gallas, after him into Pomerania; there he caused them great losses by cutting off their supplies, then forced them back into Saxony, and, following them up closely, attacked and beat them badly at Chemnitz (4th April 1639).

Whilst Banner had thus been maintaining the glory of the Swedish arms, Duke Bernhard had been striving vigorously to repair his defeat at Nördlingen. Thrust back by that defeat, with the starving remnants of his army, beyond the Rhine, he had entered into negotiations with the French Court, and at the

---

* In the Grand Duchy of Mecklenburg-Schwerin.

end of twelve months had induced that Court to place six thousand French troops under his orders. Having, in the interval, restored discipline in the ranks of his own army, he crossed the Rhine, still nominal commander-in-chief, the 1st January 1635, with the view to force the Bavarians to raise the siege of Heidelberg.* Before, however, he could reach that place, the besieging army, strengthened by the Imperialists led by Gallas, had taken it, and the victor pressed forward so rapidly into the Lower Palatinate, that Duke Bernhard was compelled to beat a hasty retreat on Saarbrücken. French reinforcements having increased his force to twenty thousand men, he had again crossed the Rhine (July 1635), had forced the Imperialists to raise the siege of Mainz, and gained many advantages over them, when he was forced by want of provisions, the breaking out of an epidemic, and desertion, once more to fall back. In his despair he made an urgent appeal to Richelieu, and finally concluded with him, 17th October 1635, a secret treaty, whereby, in consideration of his placing himself wholly at the service of France, Duke Bernhard was to receive yearly four millions of francs (£160,000) to maintain an army of eighteen thousand men, with its proportion of artillery, a very considerable yearly income for his personal expenses, a guarantee that on the conclusion of peace his interests and the interests of his officers should be taken care of, and that he himself should receive the sovereignty over Alsace. To hasten the carrying out of those details of this agreement which immediately affected him, Duke Bernhard hastened to Paris (March 1636). Here he was received with great honours, but obtained scanty satisfaction. With such help as he could secure, however, he hastened back to the frontier, and, having concerted measures with La Valette, the French general who was to co-operate with him, he invaded Lorraine, drove the enemy thence, taking Saarburg and Pfalzburg, and then, entering Alsace, took Saverne. His career

---

* Heidelberg had been taken by the Swedes in 1633.

of conquest in Alsace was checked by the invasion of Burgundy by Gallas, with an army of forty thousand men. Duke Bernhard marched with all haste to Dijon, and forced Gallas to fall back, with great loss, beyond the Saone (November 1636). Pursuing his advantages, early the following year he forced the passage of the Saone at Gray, despite the vivid resistance of Prince Charles of Lorraine (June 1637), and pursued that commander as far as Besançon. Reinforced during the autumn, he marched towards the Upper Rhine, and, undertaking a winter campaign, captured Lauffenburg, after a skirmish with John of Werth; then Säckingen and Waldshut, and laid siege to Rheinfelden. The Imperialist army, led by John of Werth, succeeded, indeed, after a very hot encounter, in relieving that place; but three days later Duke Bernhard attacked and completely defeated it (21st February 1638), taking prisoners, not only John of Werth himself, but the generals, Savelli, Enkefort, and Sperreuter. The consequences of this victory were the fall of Rheinfelden, Rötteln, Neuenburg, and Freiburg. Duke Bernhard then laid siege to Breisach (July 1638). This place, owing to the avarice, and worse than avarice, of its commandant, who had traded with the public funds for his own purposes, was without provisions to stand a long siege. To supply the deficiency the Imperial general, Götz, advanced at the head of a force considerably outnumbering that of Duke Bernhard. Leaving a portion of his army before the place, Duke Bernhard then drew to himself Turenne, who was lying in the vicinity with three thousand men, fell upon the Imperialists at Wittenweiher (30th July), completely defeated them, and captured their whole convoy. Another Imperialist army, led by the Duke of Lorraine in person, shared a similar fate at Thann,* in the Sundgau, on the 4th October following. Götz, who was hastening with a strengthened army to support the Duke of

---

* About twelve miles to the west of Mülhausen. The Sundgau is the Southern portion of Alsace, known during the long period of its union with France, 1648 to 1871, as the Department of the Haut-Rhin. It now again forms part of Alsace.

Lorraine, attacked Duke Bernhard ten days later, but was repulsed with great loss. Breisach capitulated on the 7th December. Duke Bernhard took possession of it in his own name, and foiled all the efforts of Richelieu to secure it for France, by garrisoning it with German soldiers.

To compensate the French Cardinal Minister for Breisach, Duke Bernhard undertook a winter campaign to drive the Imperialists from Franche-Comté.* Entering that province at the end of December, he speedily made himself master of its richest part. He then returned to Alsace with the resolution to cross the Rhine and carry the war once again into Bavaria; and, holding out the hand to Banner, who had assumed a victorious position in Bohemia, to march, under better auspices than those which had before attended him, to Vienna. He had made all the necessary preparations for this enterprise, had actually sent his army across the Rhine, when he died very suddenly, not without suspicion of poison, at Neuburg am Rhein (8th July 1632). The lands he had conquered he bequeathed to his brother, to be maintained by him during the war, under Swedish protection; or, if that were not found possible, under the protection of France, on the condition that on the conclusion of a general peace, they should be constituted, under his brother's rule, a *fief of the German* empire. But Richelieu paid no attention to the wishes of the dead general. Before any of the family could interfere, he had secured all the fortresses in Alsace, even Breisach, which was its key, for France. The only consolation the family reaped from their protests against this high-handed policy, was permission to transport the body of Duke Bernhard to the family vault at Weimar.

With the death of Duke Bernhard began a new phase of the war. Every day subsequently to that event, France assumed on the Rhine more and more the position of the principal factor in the war. It was not so yet in middle and southern Germany.

---

* Comprehending the present departments of **Doubs** (excepting **Mömpelgard**, which then belonged to Würtemberg), the **Jura**, and the **Upper Saone**.

But before I proceed to record the events which occurred in those parts, and which will form the main subject of this chapter, it is necessary that I should allude very briefly to the political changes which threatened for a time to affect the contest.

The Emperor Ferdinand II. had died the 15th February **1637**. His son and successor, **Ferdinand** III., whom we have already met at Nördlingen, possessed a nature less warped by bigotry and more prone to conciliation than that of his father; at the period at which we have arrived, he was not indisposed to treat for a general peace. At the Diet assembled at Ratisbon in 1640, proposals were made with that object. But the passions on both sides were still too excited; and a pamphlet,* written at the instigation of the Elector of Brandenburg by a Swedish councillor, came to inflame still more the minds of the princes there assembled. The object of this pamphlet was to warn the several states against a peace which could not fail to be fatal to Germany, inasmuch as, to secure it, it would be necessary to make very great concessions to France. This appeal to patriotism effectually stifled the hopes of the peace party, and the war broke out with renewed energy.

We left Banner on the 4th April 1639 at Chemnitz, in Saxony, at the foot of the principal ridge of the Erzgebirge. From Chemnitz his victorious army poured into Bohemia and Silesia, carrying all before it. The Swedish soldiers showed themselves on this occasion unworthy of the cause which they had come to champion. Unrestrained by their leader, who never restrained himself, they plundered indiscriminately the monastery, the castle, and the cottage. At last the cry of desolated Bohemia reached **Vienna**, and Ottavio Piccolomini was ordered from the Netherlands, Count Hatzfeldt from Westphalia, to drive him from the kingdom. Of this force, when united, the Emperor's brother, the Archduke Leopold, took command.

---

* Entitled *Disertatio de ratione status in Imperio nostro Romano-Germanico.* Stettin, 1640.

Before it, step by step, Banner fell back, his soldiers more anxious to secure their plunder than to fight, until he had reached Saxony. But even here he was not safe. The Archduke followed him so expeditiously that he caught him at Plauen, and delivered him there so severe a blow that he was forced to take refuge in Thüringen, not halting till he had reached Erfurt. Safe here from farther pursuit, Banner made a vigorous attempt to restore discipline to, and to reinforce, his army. Once more Fortune smiled upon him. The Dukes of Lüneberg—who, after Nördlingen, had abandoned the Swedish alliance, and given their adherence to the Peace of Prague— now renounced that treaty, and brought to Erfurt the contingent which had just been fighting against him. From Hesse he received assistance; and, what was of more consequence, the Count of Guébriant joined him with the army of Duke Bernhard, to the command of which, by the death of that illustrious commander, he had succeeded. Thus strengthened, Banner resumed the offensive. The Imperialists, however, avoided a general action; and winter shortly afterwards setting in, both armies went into winter-quarters, the Imperialists, now led by Piccolimini, in Franconia, the Swedes and their allies in the principality of Lüneburg.

It was during this winter, 1640–41, that there sat at Ratisbon the Diet at which, I have related, so resolute an effort was made for the restoration of peace. At this Diet were present the Emperor, all the Catholic princes of Germany, some Protestant princes who had adhered to the Peace of Prague, and many bishops and ecclesiastics of the reformed faith. The news of their sitting, and of the turn the discussion was taking at those sittings, reached Banner in his winter quarters at Lüneburg. The idea suddenly occurred to him that if, marching warily, he could pounce upon Ratisbon before his march should be discovered, he would be able to finish the war at a blow. The design seemed easy of execution, for there was no army in his path: the Imperialists were scattered far and wide in their

9 *

winter-quarters. His own army was concentrated at Lüneburg. The plan was too tempting to be rejected.

Confiding in no one, save in his French colleague, **the Count of Guébriant**, Banner suddenly set out from Lüneburg in the depth of the winter of 1641. Marching with speed and secrecy through Thüringen, he appeared in front of Ratisbon before the Emperor or any of the members of the Diet had heard that he had quitted his winter quarters. Great was the consternation within the walls of the threatened city. With one exception, no one dreamed of defence; how to flee, to escape from the clutches of the Swede who had desolated Bohemia, was the uppermost thought. Fortunately the exception was the Emperor. Ferdinand III. was in a position not dissimilar to that in which his father had found himself when Vienna was besieged by Count Thurn in 1619. Then he, by his iron firmness, conjured the storm: Ferdinand III. offered it as bold a front now. Publicly declaring that, whatever might happen, he would not quit Ratisbon, he gave courage to the more courageous, new life and new hope to the weaker spirits. It is difficult, however, to conceive how the noble resolution of the Emperor could have availed to prevent his capture, and the capture of some of the most illustrious of his councillors, had the winter season pursued its ordinary course. Banner had made his splendid raid to the northern bank of the Danube with a success which left nothing but the passage of that river to be provided for. The success which he had so far achieved he owed entirely to his forethought, his daring, the celerity and secrecy of his movements. Of Fortune he asked but one thing, and that was that the intense cold which had added so much to the difficulties and privations of his march, which, up to twenty-four hours before his arrival on its banks, had covered the face of the Danube with an ice strong enough to bear his army, should continue but forty-eight hours longer. At that season of the year—it was the month of January—it was not a very extraordinary demand. But the words of Juvenal—"nullum numen abest si sit Fortuna"

—must have occurred to the mind of the Swedish general as he approached the banks of the Danube. Within the last twenty-four hours a thaw had set in sufficient to render the ice unsafe for the passage of troops, but insufficient to make it navigable for boats. All the other good influences, skill, daring, quickness of movement, reticence, discipline—all were with him; but Fortune had left him to preside over the destinies of the Kaiser, and her desertion left those other influences without power or avail. It must have been a bitter moment for Banner when he realised that all the advantages he had gained were thus neutralised; that the Danube, the thin streak of water which lay between himself and his prey, was not to be crossed!

In his first anger Banner opened upon the city a heavy fire with his artillery; but the distance being great, and the guns of small calibre, the fire produced but little effect, and the baffled general soon recognised that it would be useless to continue it. Still, though unable to take Ratisbon, Banner conceived that, in view of the season, of the surprise, of the fact that the enemy's troops were scattered, it was still possible to penetrate into Moravia, to give his troops winter quarters in a province as yet untouched by the war, and whence they would be in a position, on the breaking up of the winter, to march on Vienna. But to this view he met an unexpected opponent in his French colleague. The interests which Guébriant had to serve were not those which Banner had most at heart. Guébriant's mission was to secure for France the left bank of the Rhine. He had readily co-operated with Banner in the daring enterprise against Ratisbon, because the capture of the Emperor would, above all things, further the views of the great Cardinal. But that enterprise having failed, to move his army still further from the Rhine, to plunge it into Moravia, where he feared it would probably merge into the position of a corps of the Swedish army, was not to be thought of. Rather than accede to such a proposal, he separated from Banner, and fell back towards the Main. Skilful general though he was,

Guébriant had not mastered the principle to be impressed on the world more than a century and a half later, that the surest way for a general to secure the aims of his Cabinet is to demand their accomplishment in the conquered capital of the enemy!

Meanwhile the Imperialists had not been slow in summoning their troops from their winter quarters. Acting with the secrecy which had assured the success of their enemy's march, they very soon had assembled between Ingolstadt and Ratisbon an army far outnumbering that of Banner reduced by the departure of Guébriant. The difficulties which Banner had to face were becoming, in fact, every day greater. His march from Lüneberg to Ratisbon had been a great feat, but he was required now to achieve a greater—to retreat across a hostile country, at an unfavourable season, in the face of an enemy superior in numbers. With the boldness and the confidence which never deserted him, Banner set himself to this task. Following the course of the Regen till he reached the sharp angle made by the turn of that river beyond Nittenau, he there quitted it, and made for the Bohemian forest, hoping to gain Eger. Finding, however, that the enemy were pressing him hard, he left posted in the little town of Wald-Neuburg, a position covering the line of retreat, a brigade of three regiments. To the commander of this brigade, Colonel Schlangen, he gave orders that the place was to be defended to the very last man. Never were orders better obeyed. The town and the heights commanding it being very strong and very defensible, Schlangen and his three regiments kept the Imperial army at bay for four days. The time thus gained was used to the best advantage by Banner. By hasty marches he reached Eger, thence he followed the ordinary road across the Erzgebirge to Annaberg, a considerable town on the Saxon side, and at the very foot, of that range, some nineteen miles south by south-east of Chemnitz, and a rather less distance south-east of Zwickau. But before he could reach that place, a great danger awaited him. Ottavio Piccolomini, after forcing Wald-Neuburg, had followed with all haste in the track of the

Swedes as far as Schlackenwerth, ten miles beyond Carlsbad. Learning here that Banner had followed the ordinary road leading across the Erzgebirge to Annaberg, Piccolomini conceived the bold idea of pressing on by a more difficult but shorter route across the crest of the mountains to Pressnitz, then to occupy in force the passes which he would have turned, and which Banner must traverse. It was a brilliant idea, an idea to develop which required nerve, dash, and decision. Piccolomini possessed all three. He marched to his point with all possible haste. One short half-hour more—of such value is time in war—and he would have destroyed the Swedish army. Banner had no knowledge of his movements; but he, too, was marching quickly, and, having a very considerable start, he managed to clear the passes and occupy Pressnitz just before the Imperialists came in sight. At Pressnitz he was safe. Thence he made good his retreat to Annaberg, and from Annaberg to Zwickau. There he was rejoined by Guébriant, who, on learning of the hot pursuit of Piccolomini, had crossed the Main and hastened to his aid. From Zwickau the two generals fell back to Halberstadt in Lower Saxony.

At Halberstadt Banner sickened and died, 10th May 1641. His death, though attributed, as were, in that age, the deaths of all great men, to poison, was the combined consequence of great fatigue and an extremely dissolute life. His reputation as a general had reached its highest point. In that sense no one was more highly esteemed by his contemporaries. Daring even to rashness, he was ever ready to attempt that which seemed to offer a probability of success. His skill in withdrawing from a dangerous position, after having occupied it till the last chance of success had disappeared, forced admiration from his enemies. A strict disciplinarian on the battle-field and before the enemy, he allowed his troops when unopposed, as in the Bohemian campaign, relaxations which were extremely injurious alike to the morals of the army and to his own reputation. He always fought at the head of his men, and his influence over them was unbounded. So great was the power he was supposed to wield that the King of France, anxious to gain him for the furtherance of the interests for which he had entered into the war, addressed him as "cousin," and promised him, in case of success, the large estates which had at one time belonged to Wallenstein.

The loss of such a general following so closely the disappearance from the scene of giants such as Gustavus and Duke Bernhard would, in any other time, have been regarded as almost fatal to the cause for which he had fought. But the first half of the seventeenth century was singularly productive of great warriors. Cromwell and Blake in England; Guébriant, Condé, Turenne, in France; Tilly, Wallenstein, Piccolomini, Mercy, Duke Bernhard, John of Werth, Montecucculi, in Germany; Gustavus and his lieutenants in Sweden: form a long list which but one other period of the world's history has equalled. On the Swedish side especially, in that rôle of promotion by selection, an Amurath did always succeed to an Amurath. Gustavus was followed by Duke Bernhard, Duke Bernhard by Banner, and now, when, after one of the most brilliant feats of generalship of which history gives record—the attempt on Ratisbon and the subsequent retreat—Banner followed his predecessors, there arose a successor whose military achievements are not unworthy to vie even with theirs.

Lennart Torstenson, Count of Ortola, was born at Torstena, in the Swedish province of West Gothland, the 17th August 1603. From his early youth he was attached to the Court and camp of Gustavus Adolphus. He was by the side of that monarch at the sieges of Riga and of Dantzig, and he accompanied him to Germany, having then attained the rank of lieutenant-colonel of artillery. He took his part in the sieges of Demmin, of Frankfurt on the Oder, of Landsberg, and contributed to the victory of Breitenfeld, to the subsequent storming of Würzburg, and to the success of the battle fought with Tilly on the Lech. He had been promoted to the rank of general, and commanded in chief the artillery, when Gustavus attacked, without success, the position of Wallenstein on the Alte Veste, near Fürth. Taken prisoner on this occasion, he was consigned by Maximilian of Bavaria to a damp cell in the fortress of Ingolstadt. A detention in that cell of six months laid the foundations of the disease which tormented him during the remainder of his life. Released after Lützen, he joined Horn in Alsace, and was sent thence, in 1634, to Sweden to procure reinforcements. He returned with these the following year, joined the army of Banner, served for four years under that general as commandant-in-chief of artillery, was present at the battles of Wittstock (24th September 1636) and of Chemnitz (4th April 1639). His continued sufferings from rheumatic gout, contracted in the cell of Ingolstadt, and which interfered greatly with the proper use of his hands and feet, forced him to return, immediately after Chemnitz, for rest and advice to his own estates, and he would have remained there altogether—so great were his sufferings—but for the imperative call of duty. On the death of Banner the great chancellor made to him an appeal which he could not resist. Although unable, from his infirmities, to mount a horse, and forced to move about carried on a litter, he did not hesitate to quit his home and its comforts, and to set out for the army.

Banner had died the 10th May 1641: Torstenson joined the army the 15th November following. The interval of five months had been a long record of misfortune. Banner had scarcely been laid in his grave when the spirit of indiscipline, which he had known how to repress, broke out in its worst form. There were, in the first place, three generals, Wrangel, Pfuel, and Wittenberg, all eager for the command. Not one of these possessed, or cared, under the circumstances, to exercise, the influence which would have dominated the evil-doers. Officers and men were alike in arrears of pay, and the most prominent to demand payment were the officers. The camp became a bear-garden, in which every man seemed anxious to gain all that was possible for himself.

The actual command of the allied forces, on the death of Banner, had devolved for the moment on his French colleague, Guébriant. Guébriant was a capable general, but the circumstances were extremely difficult. He found himself, in a corner of Lower Saxony, menaced by an enemy superior in numbers. Gradually he had been forced to fall back on Wolfenbüttel, in the duchy of Brunswick. Here, on the 19th June, he delivered battle to the Imperialists, but, although he beat them, and caused them a loss of two thousand men and forty-five standards, the victory produced no decisive result. It served, however, to procure for the allies a much-desired respite.

Torstenson joined the army at Winsen on the Aller the 15th November. He found it in the worst possible order. Its growing indiscipline had rendered it impossible for Guébriant to attempt any military operation. Nor was this the worst. The same cause had loosened, and in some cases dissolved, the adhesion of its German allies. Once more had the Dukes of Lüneburg quitted the Swedish banners; the princes of the House of Brunswick had become reconciled to the Emperor; and the Landgravine of Hesse, though not proceeding to that extremity, had withdrawn her troops within her own dominions.

The first care of Torstenson was to restore discipline in his army. To bring about this result he had recourse to very severe measures. He brought Colonel Seckendorf before a council-of-war for holding intelligence with the enemy; he punished the officers who had failed to restrain their men; and to the men he declared his firm resolve not to lead them against the enemy until they should give substantial proofs that they were worthy of his leadership. When, by these and other means of the same character, the army had resumed its former character, Torstenson industriously spread abroad that he was about to march into Westphalia, made requisitions in that province, and indicated the line of country he was to traverse. When he had, in this manner, thrown dust into the eyes of the enemy and the public, he suddenly broke up his camp, and, traversing Brandenburg, **dashed through the Lausitz** into Silesia. He had resolved to **quit** the exhausted provinces of North Germany, and to carry the **war, if it** were possible, into those districts, the appanage **of the House of** Hapsburg, which had as yet but lightly felt **its horrors.**

Before he **had set out,** Guébriant, **always bent on** the interests of his **own** country, **had** quitted him (3rd December 1641) for the banks of the Lower Rhine. **But,** on the other hand, Colonel Stalhaus, whom we **have** seen leading the right wing of the Swedish army at Lützen when Gustavus quitted it **to dash to** the **aid of Duke Bernhard, was at** Sorau, **on the Silesian** frontier, **with a** corps of veteran troops. Torstenson, then, marching hastily, **as I** have said, through the **province of** Brandenburg, picked **up** Stalhaus at **Sorau, and** then **made a** dash at Glogau, in **Lower** Silesia. **He took** Glogau by assault (24th April 1642); **then,** turning southwards by way of Raudten, Lüben, Liegnitz, **Jauer, and** Striegau, he marched on Schweidnitz, **the most central and one** of the **most important** places in Silesia. Close to Schweidnitz was encamped the **Franz** Albert of Lauenburg, the same who had accompanied Gusvatus on the field of **Lützen, whom a long** chain of circumstantial evidence already accused **of being his** murderer, and who now commanded the imperial army. **Torstenson at** once engaged **him** (24th May). The attack—led, by an irony of fate, by Stalhaus—completely succeeded. The Imperial army was beaten, and Franz Albert, wounded to the death, was taken prisoner.* Schweidnitz surrendered the next day. Neisse, Glatz, and Troppau followed the example of Schweidnitz, and by the end **of** June Torstenson penetrated **into the** all-but-untrodden Moravia. **Still** pursuing his victorious **career, he took Olmütz on the** 7th July; **and his** flying parties **of cavalry, advancing** beyond that capital, **caused** consternation **even in** Vienna. **Expresses** were despatched in all haste **from that** city **to Archduke Leopold and** Ottavio Piccolomini to hasten **their** preparations, so **as to** prevent the

---

* He died of his wounds seven days later.

possibility of the fall of the Imperial capital. Before these
expresses reached them, the army commanded by those
generals, thirty-three thousand strong, was on its march to
compel the invader to retire.

Torstenson had, in fact, attempted a daring blow similar in
character to that which, the preceding year, Banner had but
just failed to deliver at Ratisbon. In both instances the blow
had met at the outset with brilliant success; in both, the want
of sufficient power had been acknowledged the moment the
Imperialists had had time to gather in strength. The distance
to be traversed before the heart of the enemy could be struck at
was, in both instances, too great for an army which had left its
base, and which had no supports. Already, after the capture
of Olmütz, had Torstenson recognised how thoroughly false, in
a military sense, was his position. He was in the air, enemies
in front of him, a superior hostile army marching on his flank,
and hostile countries intervening between himself and his real
base. Already had he given orders to fall back into Silesia, so
as not to be entirely cut off. He had fallen back, and he had
undertaken the siege of Brieg on the Oder (twenty-five miles to
the south-east of Breslau), when information reached him that
the Imperial army was upon him!

Torstenson was too able a commander to dream of accepting,
with twenty thousand men in an isolated position, a battle with
an enemy who counted thirty-three thousand. He raised, then,
the siege of Brieg, and, crossing the Oder, followed the right
bank of that river as far as Crossen, about eighteen miles nearly
north of Guben. At Crossen he was fortunate enough to receive
reinforcements from Sweden. Taking these with him, he
directed his march southwards, retook Glogau—which had been
captured in his absence—and penetrating into the Upper Lausitz, endeavoured to bring on a general action. This, however,
the enemy carefully avoided. His army was divided: Piccolomini
had marched westward; and the Archduke Leopold, now inferior
in numbers, was in no mood to accept a challenge. In vain did

Torstenson besiege and take Zittau under his very eyes. The Archduke was not to be enticed. Rather did he await on the slopes of the Giant Mountains the reinforcement of his army by that of Piccolomini, or the development of some new action on the part of the Swedes.

Too weak in the face of the now-awakened Imperialists to renew the march into Moravia, too prudent to attack the Archduke in an unassailable position, and yet most anxious to render efficient service to the cause the disposal of which was now to a great extent in his hands, Torstenson resolved to wrench Leipzig from the enemy. When we last heard of that city, it had been recovered by the Swedes for their Saxon ally immediately after the battle of Lützen. But the year following that battle, Saxony had made her peace with the Emperor, and Leipzig had since been occupied by a garrison which regarded the Swedes as enemies. The holding of the city by a hostile force—a strong post in the direct line between an army combating on the Bohemian frontier and its base—had been found over and over again by the Swedes to be full of inconvenience. To remove such inconvenience for the future, Torstenson suddenly broke up his camp about Zittau, and marched on Leipzig.

At a respectful distance the Archduke Leopold followed Torstenson on his march to Leipzig. At Dresden he had the satisfaction of reuniting himself with Piccolomini, and then the march of observation became a march of pursuit. So diligently was this pursuit followed, that, on the evening of the 22nd October, the Imperialists came in sight of the Swedish army encamped before, and besieging, Leipzig.

In numbers there was no great disparity between the two armies. Including the garrisons he had drawn to himself as he marched, and the reinforcements received at Crossen, Torstenson could dispose of nearly thirty thousand men, and the Imperialists had but few in excess of that number. But the difficulty of Torstenson's position lay in the fact that he was between two enemies—a hostile Leipzig in front of him, and an Imperial army behind him. He had to march out to fight or to be assailed at a great disadvantage. Torstenson did not hesitate for a moment. Leaving one corps to cover Leipzig, he marched, on the evening of the 23rd October, to the plain of Breitenfeld, to bid defiance to the enemy when they should advance in the morning.

Eleven years had passed since, on the same plain of Breitenfeld, the great Gustavus had gained his memorable victory over Tilly. On that plain now, one of the most trusted of his lieutenants—the lieutenant who had commanded his artillery in the first action—was about again to invoke the protection of the God of armies. But the position of the belligerents was almost exactly reversed. In 1631 the Swedes were advancing on Leipzig; Tilly was endeavouring on Breitenfeld to prevent that advance. In 1642 the Imperialists were advancing upon, the Swedes were defending, that famous field. The one difference in the two positions was very much to the advantage of the Imperialists. For, whereas in 1631 the city of Leipzig was held for the army which defended Breitenfeld, it was held, in 1642, for the army advancing to the attack.

The Swedish army, formed up close to the ground which Tilly had occupied in 1631, waited, on the morning of the 24th October, for the advance of the enemy. At length they appeared in brilliant array, led in person by the Archduke Leopold, himself, like all the princes of his House, a man of great courage, and, like many of them, possessing very considerable ability. Under him served Ottavio Piccolomini, whose name was already famous, and who was now about to fight the last battle in which, for five years to come, he was to be engaged on German soil.* Other officers whose names at a later period were to become prominent were there likewise. It should be noted, however, that the foreign element in the Imperial army was

---

* The year following the battle, he exchanged the Imperial for the Spanish service, but returned to the former in 1648.

extremely strong, constituting **a** considerable majority of the troops engaged.

To march to a position facing the Swedish army, **the** nature **of** the ground, covered with small canals and interspersed with villages, rendered it incumbent upon **the** Imperialists to break their formation. This necessity had occurred to the left wing **just as it came** within striking distance of the Swedish right. **The** generals who commanded these, Stalhaus and Wittenberg, **took** advantage of the slight confusion which was thus caused, **to** charge **with full fury on the** enemy. The charge was so unexpected, so sudden, and so fierce, that the enemy's left **wing was at once** thrown into disorder.

On the Swedish left, **a few** minutes later, the battle engaged, and here the German element of the Imperial army, led by **the** Archduke in person, **gained a** considerable advantage. In vain **did** the Swedish generals, Schlangen and Lilienhoek, do all that men could do. In **vain did** Torstenson, carried on his litter, re-animate the discouraged, and **urge his** men to the front. They **were** being gradually overpowered, when suddenly, as at Lützen, the victorious right, having driven the enemy in front of them from the field, came round to help their comrades.

They came but just in time. Their arrival, however, not only restored the battle, it enabled the Swedish left wing to assume **the offensive.** It was now the turn of the Imperialists to look to their own exertions. Their left uncovered, and their right falling back, it seemed impossible that they **could** escape total **defeat.** Yet on this day the conduct **of** the infantry of Southern Germany extorted the admiration even of their enemies. Assailed on all sides, they yet refused to give ground. In ranks always closing up, and **always** serried, **they still** offered **a** defiant opposition. When all their powder was spent, the musketeers, **reversing** their muskets, still used them as clubs.

Nor was the conduct of their commander, the Archduke Leopold, less worthy of admiration. To use the language of **a** contemporary writer, he " combined the duties of a commander-in-chief with the action of a resolute colonel. Wherever the fire was hottest, there he rode, encouraging and animating his men. Had he been supported by the foreign element as he was by the German, the result would have been different."

But neither the efforts of Archduke Leopold nor of his Austrian soldiers could change the result. Not less stubbornly than they fought, fought the Swedes. At last, uncovered still more by the falling back of their allies, the men of South Germany fell back sullenly. Their retreat was covered by the Archduke himself with a regiment of cavalry.

The battle had lasted three hours before the result was thus decisively declared. It was a great victory. The Imperialists lost five thousand men killed and wounded, and nearly as many taken prisoners; all their guns, forty-six in number, the silver service and the correspondence of the Archduke, and all their baggage. The victors lost more than three thousand killed and wounded: among the former, two generals—Schlangen who, it may be recollected, had at Wald-Neuburg, in 1641, barred the entrance into Bohemia to Piccolomini for four days; and Lilienhoek. The Archduke retreated at once into Bohemia.

Too weak to follow him, Torstenson turned all his energies to the reduction of Leipzig. The surrender of that place, nearly three weeks later, brought with it an enormous advantage. The city purchased its exemption from plunder by an abundant supply of good food, serviceable clothing, and money. Rest it would have given likewise, but the ardent nature of the crippled Swedish general would have no rest until the work he had designed had been accomplished. Allowing only time sufficient to re-clothe his army, Torstenson entered again into a winter campaign.

Before he set out Torstenson held, at Leipzig, a long consultation with his former colleague, Count Guébriant, who had travelled thither for that special purpose. The result of the consultation was an agreement that whilst Torstenson should pursue the course upon which he had decided, Guébriant should use all the means in his power to attract the attention of the enemy towards himself. Were I to follow strictly the order of dates, I should now describe the immediately antecedent action of Guébriant, and the action which followed this agreement. But it will be more convenient to the reader, and more germane to the general object of my narrative, if I continue to accompany Torstenson, leaving to the next chapter the record of the achievements of his French ally.

Guébriant having returned to the Rhine, Torstenson set out, in the depth of a hard winter (December 1642), on the road to Bohemia. The first place he attacked was the then important Saxon city of Freiberg, exactly midway between Dresden and Chemnitz. Freiberg resisted him bravely and successfully. Its long resistance had the effect of forcing the Imperialists to quit their winter-quarters and march to its relief; a movement which, however, undertaken by troops a large proportion of whom were Spaniards, in the depth of winter, caused them considerable losses. On their approach Torstenson raised the siege and fell back on Frankfurt on the Oder, there to recruit his army alike by the garrisons of the towns in the north, and by expected reinforcements from Sweden. These having been obtained, he again resumed the offensive, and, marching across Silesia with great rapidity, invaded Bohemia by way of Leitmeritz, and, without stopping to take Prague, penetrated into Moravia, relieved Olmütz, which was pressed by an Imperial army; then, forming an intrenched camp at Tobitschau, ten miles from that city, proceeded to subdue the strong places in that province. One after another, Tovacov, Kremsier, Wischen, succumbed. Brünn alone, though its suburbs and the Spielberg were burned, successfully resisted him. The pertinacity of the garrison of this place saved Vienna; for, whilst the Imperial army, now commanded by Gallas, covered the frontiers of Bohemia, not daring to attack, and ever avoiding an attack from Torstenson; that general, secure in his intrenched camp, had been meditating a blow which, if it could only be **carried out as he was** planning it, could not fail to be decisive.

Whilst Ferdinand III., alarmed at the close proximity of the Swedes to his capital, was vainly endeavouring **to** arouse the nobles of Hungary and to **induce them to** raise an army to fight for his cause, Torstenson was negotiating, in a far more **hopeful** spirit, with George I., better known as Rákóczy, Prince of Transylvania. A **very large** party in Hungary, discontented with **the rule** of the House of Hapsburg, had offered the throne of the kingdom to Rákóczy. Torstenson, informed of this intrigue, had sent at once the most pressing letters to that prince, urging him to accept the offer and promising him the support of the Swedish **arms. Mainly in** consequence of this advice and this promise Rákóczy complied. He had already entered Hungary to carry out his part of the agreement, when the sudden action of the King of Denmark rendered it impossible, for the moment, for Torstenson to co-operate with him.

On the 23rd September, **a** messenger from **Oxenstierna reached** Torstenson, informing him that war **with Denmark** was upon the point of breaking out, and that he must at once hasten northwards with all speed to strike a blow which should **be** decisive. The position was one which demanded the skill of the diplomatist more even than the resolution of the warrior. Torstenson was in Moravia, within a stone's-throw almost of Vienna. Between himself **and** Pomerania—whither he was bound now to proceed —lay Bohemia, covered by Gallas. Were he to succeed in outmanœuvring Gallas, no other enemy was to be apprehended. But **he had** at the same time so to direct **his march** that the Danes should **not** hear of it until he should make his presence sensibly felt. At the same time he had to reassure Rákóczy.

It is a striking proof of the great abilities, of the high mental power of Torstenson, that he carried out to the letter this apparently impossible programme. He began by concluding with Gallas **an** armistice for the entire winter. He then industriously spread **the report that he** was about to winter in

Bavaria. Having set his army in march, he marched into Silesia, making his way gradually to the Elbe. He followed the windings of that river as far as Havelberg, still giving out that Bavaria was his ultimate destination. But at Havelberg he threw off the mask, informed his soldiers of the task before them; then, entering Holstein by way of Trittau (11th December) speedily subdued the whole peninsula, the fortresses of Glückstadt and Crempe excepted. His arrival, in fact, was the first absolute declaration of war! When spring set in, he beat the Danish cavalry at Kolding, and occupied the whole of Jutland as far as Skagen. Gallas, meanwhile, had become aware of the deception, and had followed his enemy northwards. As soon as he discovered his destination, he too entered Holstein, captured Kiel, effected a junction with the Danish army, and then took a position which, he believed, would effectually enclose the Swedish army in Jutland. But Torstenson was again to show his great superiority as a general. As soon as he had finished his task with the Danes he returned into Holstein through an unguarded pass between Schleswig and Stapelholm (24th September 1644); then, marching against Gallas, forced that general, always anxious to avoid a general action, to fall back first along the Elbe, and then along its tributary the Saale as far as Bernburg on that river, the capital of the duchy Anhalt-Bernburg, where he had previously formed an intrenched camp. No sooner had Gallas firmly occupied that camp, than Torstenson passed the Saale, and took up a position to the south of Bernburg, which entirely cut off the Imperialists from Saxony and Bohemia.

In this position the Swedish general remained firm and fixed until Gallas had consumed all his supplies down to the very last crust. Driven then to despair, and shut out from the south, he quitted his camp and made a fierce effort to regain the Elbe and force his way into Brandenburg. Obtaining, by means of a dark night, followed by a day almost as dark, a considerable start, he did succeed (21st November) in crossing the Elbe.

But on the 22nd Torstenson was on his track. The half-starved Imperialists were no match in marching for their well-fed pursuers. At Jütenberg, nearly forty miles south of Berlin, Torstenson came up with, attacked, and defeated and dispersed (23rd November) the fugitive army. Of the whole force at the head of which Gallas had entered Holstein, some five thousand only cut their way back into Bohemia. With these was Gallas himself. He returned, carrying with him, records Schiller, the reputation of being the most perfect master in the art of ruining an army then living. The destruction of the Imperial army was followed by peace with Denmark.

Left free to act on the lines which the expedition to Denmark had forced him temporarily to abandon, Torstenson renewed his relations with Rákóczy, and, despite the inclement season, set out to act in concert with him. That prince had found himself unable, unassisted, to make good his pretensions. At the moment, after a campaign in which he had been foiled by the Imperial army under Götzen, he was in the valley of the Neutra, at the southern base of the Neutragebirge, awaiting the approach of Torstenson. That general did not give him cause for impatience. Rapidly traversing Saxony and Silesia, Torstenson entered Bohemia. His design was to traverse that kingdom likewise, and, entering the valley of the Danube, besiege Vienna, at the same time holding a hand to Rákóczy.

To baffle, if possible, this scheme, the Emperor Ferdinand had repaired in the early winter with Archduke Leopold to Prague. There he had received Gallas with the broken remnants of his army; thither he had summoned from Hungary Götzen, fresh from baffling Rákóczy; there, too, he had been joined by four thousand Bavarian cavalry under General Hatzfeldt. To Hatzfeldt he confided the command-in-chief of his army. For the moment it was the last army he could raise. Its mission was to prevent at all costs the march of Torstenson across Bohemia to the valley of the Danube.

Undeterred by these preparations, Torstenson invaded Bohemia by way of Eger, pushed on thence to Pilsen, and thence to the banks of the Moldau. He crossed the Moldau at Altsattel, and, entering the Tabor circle, marched to Jankau, or Jankowitz, a village nearly in the centre of the tract which is inclosed by the Moldau to the south-west, and by the Sazawa to the northeast.* Learning that the Imperialists, to the number of twenty-three thousand men, were close to him, barring his way southwards, Torstenson took up a position for the night on an isolated hill above the village, in and about which he stored his baggage.

The ground enclosed by the Moldau and its tributary the Sazawa may be roughly described as an undulating tract broken up by ranges of hills, in some parts by isolated hills, and abounding in tanks or ponds. Occasionally, indeed, the traveller comes upon a broad plain, free of incumbrances, and admirably adapted for cavalry purposes. In that part of Bohemia such plains, however, are rare. One of the isolated hills of which I have spoken rises about twenty miles to the north of Tabor. I have called it isolated because it is separated from the range immediately to its north by an open space, or pass, having on the east of it undulating ground broken up, in sympathy with the general features of the country, by hillocks, and interspersed by ponds. Separated by the pass from this undulating ground, on the north-western slope of the isolated hill of which I have spoken, is a village called by the Czechs, Jankov, by the Germans Jankau or Jankowitz. South again of this village is a broad, unsheltered plain, admirably adapted for the manœuvres of cavalry.

Bearing in his mind this description of the country, the reader will have no difficulty in understanding the plans of the Imperial commander-in-chief. General Hatzfeldt's mission was to stop the progress of Torstenson. He outnumbered the Swedish general principally in cavalry. He took up a position,

---

* The nearest railway-station to the field of battle is Wottic, on the Franz-Joseph's-Bahn.

therefore, commanding the road by which the Swedes must proceed, if, on quitting the village of Jankowitz, which they would naturally occupy, they should follow one or other of the roads; that by Tabor and Wittingau, or the alternative by Iglau and Znaim, leading to the Danube. But when, on the evening of the 23rd of February, it was reported to Hatzfeldt that Torstenson had occupied the isolated hill in front of Jankowitz, that general, fearful that he might escape him, agreed, after discussion, to the solicitations pressed upon him by the Count of Götzen, to spring upon him with all the infantry in the early morning; to surprise and drive him from the hill to the broad plain to the south of the hill, then to dash upon him with his cavalry and destroy him. The execution of the infantry portion of this daring scheme was committed to Götzen; the work of the cavalry was to be directed by Hatzfeldt himself.

Before daybreak the following morning, the 24th February, 1645, the Imperialist infantry, in pursuance of this plan, advanced to attack the hill. The Swedes were not expecting an assault, and they were taken at as great a disadvantage as, more than a century later, was Frederic II. of Prussia at Hochkirch. Götzen made the most complete use of the surprise. Allowing the Swedes no breathing time, he forced them from one position to another, giving them no chance to form, until he had driven them completely from the height. The victory had actually been gained, when a stray bullet struck dead the Imperialist commander.

The death of the Count of Götzen was fatal to the cause for which he had fought so well. His success had been too rapid to allow the cavalry, which had to make a long detour through difficult ground, to come up. There was no one on the spot to supply his place. General Hatzfeldt was with the cavalry, not yet in sight, and the infantry, flushed with their easy victory, was just in the condition in which men specially require direction. The victory was, I repeat, gained had it only been followed up. Certainly Götzen, who knew well the stubbornness of the

Swedish troops and the character of their leader, would have pressed on, giving the Swedes no time to re-form till the cavalry should arrive to complete the victory.

But to the minds of his men, left by his death without a leader, the case presented itself under a totally different aspect. They saw only the enemy, driven from his position, retreating in one direction, whilst beneath them, in and about the village of Jankowitz, was the baggage of the Swedish army, absolutely at their disposal. The temptation was irresistible. With a unanimity as remarkable as though it had been the result of a preceding discussion, they abandoned the pursuit of the Swedes and dashed at the baggage in the village!

This sudden move was Torstenson's opportunity. He used it to the utmost. Rallying, and forming up in their proper places, his men, more shaken by the surprise than beaten, he led them, the guns in the centre, to the assault. In their turn, the Imperialists were taken at a disadvantage. A tremendous fire of artillery opened upon the masses, now comprising the whole army of the enemy, engaged in plundering, in and about Jankowitz. A third and fourth discharge repulsed a charge made by the full strength of the Bavarian horsemen, as they arrived, too late, on the spot.

When the guns had done their work the Swedish infantry rushed forward, barring by their advance to the Imperialists the road by which they had descended from the hill, and drove them beyond the village into the tract covered with tanks and hillocks, where their superiority in cavalry could not make itself felt. In its turn, too, the Imperialist army was driven in disorder from position to position. For them there was no relaxation. Across the uneven plain were they forced, till, finally, the cavalry and the survivors of the infantry fled in wild disorder through the narrow pass which separated the isolated hill from the range adjoining the plain, near the position whence they had emerged that morning to assault the Swedes on the hill of Jankowitz!

The victory, a very bloody victory, was gained. The commander-in-chief of the Imperialists, Count Melchior of Hatzfeldt, five other generals, many officers, and three thousand men were taken prisoners. The killed alone, taking no record of the wounded, exceeded two thousand. The loss of the Swedes, though considerable in the earlier part of the day, did not equal one-fifth of that sustained by the Imperialists. Jankowitz was, in all respects, a decisive victory!

For the road to Vienna lay open. Torstenson did not delay an instant to take it. Sending expresses to Rákóczi, notifying his success and begging him to march on Vienna without delay, the Swedish leader took the direct road by way of Iglau and Znaim to the Danube. Whilst he is marching thither, I propose to glance at the situation of the Emperor Ferdinand and of Rákóczi.

Ferdinand, on hearing of the disaster of Jankowitz, proceeded with the utmost speed to Vienna. The outlook was as bad as it could be. He had lost his last army. With the greatest exertions he could not rally more than from five to six thousand men in and about his capital. Everywhere his allies were falling from him. John George of Saxony, who had abandoned the Protestant cause after Lützen to further, as he believed, his own selfish interests, had found an alliance with the Emperor more onerous than the dictation of Sweden. As one of the consequences of that alliance, Saxony had had to bear the main burdens of the war. Reduced to despair, John George had sued for and obtained from the Swedes a treaty of neutrality renewable from year to year. From no prince in North Germany was help to be expected. In the west, again, the French, after changes of fortune which I shall record in the next chapter, had reduced the Bavarian army to complete inaction, had captured Speyer, Worms, Mannheim, and Philippsburg. In that direction, then, Ferdinand could only cast despairing glances. Nor were the prospects from Hungary more comforting. Rákóczi, in compliance with the summons of Torstenson, was marching from Transylvania at the head of an army of twenty-five thousand **men**, laying waste the country through which he passed.

But, even **in** this extremity, Ferdinand displayed the dogged resolution, the pertinacity, the enduring power, which are innate in **the family of the House** of Hapsburg. Whilst Torstenson was subduing the strong places on the **Danube**, Ferdinand was **engaged, day and** night, in **repairing**, improving, and strengthening **the** fortifications of Vienna. In justice to the Empress, a daughter of King Philip of Spain,* **it should** be recorded that in this action Ferdinand had been anticipated by his wife, who, **on** hearing the result **of the** battle, had hastened from Linz to the capital (14th March) and given the orders which Ferdinand, on his arrival five days later, had confirmed and emphasised. The orders issued by the Emperor on this occasion were of the most stringent character. Vienna was to be defended to the last man. No one between the ages of sixteen and sixty was permitted, **on any pretence, to leave the city.** All craftsmen, apprentices, **and** students were **divided** into sections, each specially under the orders of a captain; the city militia was paraded and trained to defensive exercises. **All the** peasants within a circle of thirty miles **were** brought in to work at the fortifications. Every householder was required to lay in for himself and family a store of bread-stuffs which would be sufficient for one year's consumption. A general levy was issued to all the dwellers on the banks of the Danube to defend that river.

But these measures, vigorous as they were, would have availed but little if Rácóczy had responded vigorously to the call of Torstenson. Foreseeing this, Ferdinand had opened secret negotiations with the Transylvanian **chief, and** these, though they produced at the moment no apparent effect, paved the way to **a** disagreement, leading finally to a rupture, between the two allies.

Torstenson, taking the route I have indicated, had reached the Danube and taken in succession by storm the fortified places

* She died the 13th May of the year following.

of Dürrenstein, **Krems,** Stein, Kreuzenstein, **and Korneuburg.**
Seizing then the direct road from Moravia to the capital, he
approached Vienna by the tract known since 1775 as the Augarten,
but then **quite open.** **Crossing this,** he had entered the suburb
now known **as** Brigittenau, **and thence** had moved his army,
across a bridge,* into the Wolfau.†

Beyond that bridge, and holding it by a formidable work, the
Imperialists had thrown up intrenchments,‡ and placed behind
these one of their best regiments, the regiment Fehrenberg. On
the very night of his arrival in the Wolfau, Torstenson attacked
the bridge-head and **the intrenchment, and, after a very** severe
contest, captured **both.**

The panic which **this** success **produced in Vienna is scarcely
to be described.** The Empress, till then **so brave, started
immediately for Gratz,** taking with her her son **and her
daughter. Almost alone, the** Emperor and his brother, Leopold
William, displayed no fear. They showed themselves everywhere, **and declared their determination to** defend the city to
the very **last stone.**

After the capture **of the** bridge-head, Torstenson proceeded to
make steady but **slow** progress in **the** pasture-lands, along **the
inner** bank **of the arm of the** Danube—the lands known in the
present day as the Spittelauer lands. Every inch **of** this ground
at all defensible **was** disputed by the Archduke; **but as this
prince was never able to** bring into the field more than five or
six thousand men, he was unable **to check** materially the
advance of the Swedes. Torstenson, however, had not as yet
directed his efforts against the city itself. For this he was
waiting for the **advance, on the other side of** Vienna, of his
Transylvanian **ally.**

But that ally **did not** come. Two causes were at work, one

---

* Now the Brigittenbrücke.

† The syllable "au," **common** to the three suburbs mentioned, is the abbreviated **form** of "aue," meaning meadow-land **or** pasturage near running **water.** It is sometimes used for running water alone, as in the words Donau, Moldau, Sau, &c.

‡ Close to the existing site of the Franz-Joseph's Bahnhof.

of which would have been sufficient to prevent the advance of a man who was a poor general and a poorer politician. The first of these causes was the promises of the Emperor. As the price of peace, Rákóczy had made demands upon Ferdinand II. almost all purely personal. They were insignificant indeed compared to those which he could have dictated from the palaces of Vienna. The second was based on the reception of a mandate from the Sublime Porte, of which he was a tributary, to cease hostilities against Austria. Instead, then, of complying with the requisition of Torstenson, he wrote to him, under the influence of the two causes I have mentioned, to state that military considerations required rather that the Swedes should assist him in conquering Hungary, than that he should assist the Swedes in gaining Vienna and the towns to the west of that city on the Danube. It will easily be understood that this was a mere excuse to recede from his engagements. Shortly afterwards (July of the same year) he concluded peace with the Emperor.

Convinced by this reply that he must renounce the hope of receiving any aid from Rákóczy, and feeling too weak to assail, with his diminished army, the fortifications of Vienna, Torstenson fell back on the Brigittenbrücke, and, leaving only two hundred men to guard the bridge-head,* crossed the bridge, and, quitting the suburbs of the capital, marched (14th April) by way of Mistelbach on Brünn. That strongly-fortified city had already successfully defied him, and he was determined that this time there should be no failure.

Unfortunately for his scheme, Brünn was defended by a man who had deserted from the Swedish service, one Souches or de Souches; and this man, a very capable soldier, expecting no

---

* It was not till forty-five days had passed, or till the 29th May, that Archduke Leopold William succeeded in storming that bridge-head, and in taking as prisoners the surviving defenders. It may be added here, as a matter of historical interest, that, on the retreat of the Swedes, the Emperor conferred many liberties on the citizens of Vienna, bestowed upon the then members of the town council patents of nobility, and adorned the city arms with the double-headed eagle.

mercy, resolved to defend the place to the very last extremity. He so inspired citizens and soldiers with his own resolution that, although Torstenson lay before the place three months, and tried several assaults, he was forced, at the end of that time, to raise the siege. Sickness, caused by privations, by the **profuse eating of** unripe fruit, by the unwholesome atmosphere of a **camp** which witnessed daily many deaths, had combined with **the** fire of the enemy to diminish his army enormously. On the 15th August, then, he retreated into Bohemia, diminishing **his** army still further **as he fell back, by leaving** garrisons in all the conquered places. He marched only as **far as** Leutomischl, commanding the road into Upper Silesia, when he halted to give his army a long rest. His troops having been **refreshed, he** marched to and captured Brüx,* on the Biela. There his health broke down completely, the gout flew to his head, and quite incapacitated **him for work.** He was compelled to make over **command of the army to** Gustavus Wrangel, and to return to **his estates in Sweden.**

Torstenson had accomplished great things. Acceding to the **command** of the Swedish army when that army, by reason of its indiscipline and want of *morale*, was **on** the very verge of dissolution, he had restored order, re-introduced the lofty sentiments which had animated it in the time of his great sovereign, and recovered for it to a great extent its *prestige* by a daring march into Moravia. He completely restored that *prestige* by beating the Imperial army at Breitenfeld. A little later, by a brilliant **march, he** forced **Denmark** to **peace,** destroyed the Imperial army under Gallas, compelled the Elector of Saxony to neutrality, then, marching **into Bohemia,** fought and gained **that** battle of Jankowitz which, with a little befriending of **Fortune, might have been** made decisive **of** the war. It placed Vienna within the grasp of himself and his ally; and it was by **no** fault of his that, at the critical moment, that ally failed him. That alone and unsupported he could have succeeded is

* Nearly midway between Teplitz and Saaz.

highly improbable. **No more** daring general then lived; and if Torstenson **deemed** the task impossible, posterity may accept his opinion as final.*

Whilst the army, now led by Wrangel, after capturing Leitmeritz, Friedland, Teplitz, **Brandys, and Saaz, is** marching to take up its winter quarters in Thüringen, I must return to record the progress made by Guébriant and his successors on the Rhine and on the German lands watered by the Rhine.

* On his **return to** Sweden, Torstenson was raised to the rank of Count, and appointed Governor-General of Gothland and the neighbouring districts. He died at Stockholm on the 7th April 1651. "He was a great commander, and a friend of learning and of art," is the contemporary record of this illustrious man.

CHAPTER VI.

TUTTLINGEN AND FREIBURG.

I HAVE shown how, on the 3rd December 1641, General Count of Guébriant, commanding the army known as the Franco-Weimar army, had quitted the camp of Torstenson at Winsen (on the Aller) and had marched to the Lower Rhine. Guébriant crossed that river at the confluence with it of the Lippe, close to Wesel, defeated easily an attempt made by the garrisons of Venlo and Geldern to interfere with his progress, and was about to distribute his amy in winter-quarters, when he learned that the Elector of Cologne, in mortal terror of being attacked, had despatched an urgent message to General Hatzfeldt, who commanded the Bavarian army on the middle Rhine, to hasten to reinforce his own troops, who, led by Marshal de Lamboy, occupied an intrenched position at Kempen,* about forty miles from Cologne, and but six from Crefeld. On receiving this information, Guébriant resolved to anticipate Hatzfeldt and to attack Lamboy before that general could arrive.

Kempen—the birthplace of Thomas à Kempis, and now a chief town in the Düsseldorf district of the Rhine provinces—lies in a cultivated plain, offering but few obstacles to the advance of an army. The troops under Lamboy, drawn almost entirely from the Cologne electorate, had taken no leading part in the hostilities which had been raging in Germany for twenty-three years. Their leader, however, was a capable soldier. William of Lamboy belonged to one of the most ancient and noble families

---

* A great many writers, misled by the similarity of the name, have confounded this place with Kempten on the Iller, in Swabia.

of Liège. Entering the army as a volunteer, he had made his proofs under the Duke of Lorraine, and when in command of an army, had, after failing to relieve Breisach, made a retreat so masterly, that he had been rewarded by the bâton of Field Marshal. He had subsequently distinguished himself in several encounters on the soil of France. Serving under him on this occasion were several officers, soon to become famous. The chief of these was Francis, Baron of Mercy.

Lamboy's army numbered about twenty thousand men; that of Guébriant exceeded it by five thousand, but the men serving under him had been inured to war in many a campaign; some amongst them had fought at Nördlingen and in the campaign preceding Nördlingen. Since that fatal battle they had never known defeat. They had confidence in their leader, and they responded eagerly to the call made upon them by that leader to assail the intrenched camp of the enemy.

Guébriant led them to that assault early on the morning of the 18th January (1642). Lamboy was not prepared for it. His army, taken by surprise, made a brave and resolute resistance, but was completely defeated, losing two thousand men in killed and five thousand taken prisoners. Amongst the latter were Lamboy himself, Mercy, Landon, and all the colonels! This battle decided the fate of the Electorate. All its resources, in men, horses, provisions, guns, and clothing, were utilised by the victor to feed, strengthen, and re-equip his army.

But Guébriant—for whom the victory of Kempen procured the bâton of a marshal—was not the man to waste his time in unnecessary delays. No sooner had he drawn all that was possible from the Cologne Electorate, than, leaving in the towns he had taken strong garrisons to make head against Hatzfeldt, he recrossed the Rhine, and marched into Thuringen, to support the aggressive movement which Torstenson was then making towards Saxony, Silesia, and Moravia. Soon perceiving, however, that the progress of his Swedish colleague had taken the form of a triumphant march, he resolved to hasten to the middle Rhine, the real aim of French aspirations. Unfortunately for his projects, a Bavarian army under John of Werth—fresh from a splendid captivity, made enjoyable to him in a thousand ways in Paris*—had been beforehand with him, and occupied the Margraviate of Baden with a superior force. After exposing his army to many privations and suffering many losses, Guébriant managed to reach the Breisgau and to connect himself with Alsace. He had the solitary consolation of knowing that he had served in an indirect manner to favour the enterprise of Torstenson.

Having placed his troops in winter quarters, Guébriant hastened, in the beginning of December, to Leipzig to consult there with Torstenson regarding the campaign for the coming year. He found the Swedish general bent upon utilising to the utmost the victory he had just gained at Breitenfeld, by penetrating without delay into the dominions of the Emperor. The condition of the Franco-Weimar army did not permit Guébriant to co-operate in this enterprise. The most he could promise to do was to endeavour to attract as much as possible the attention of the enemy to Bavaria.

Guébriant returned to Alsace, and, having once again recruited his army, entered Swabia, and so occupied the Bavarian army, that for a long time it could render no help to the Imperialists on the one side, nor to the cities of the Netherlands, threatened by a French army, on the other. At length, however, Mercy—who had been released from the captivity to which the battle of Kempen had assigned him—made a great effort to force back Guébriant, so as to relieve Thionville, then very

---

* "Dès qu'il eut donné sa parole," wrote the *Mercure*, "on se fit un plaisir de lui laisser une entière liberté ; il alla faire la cour au roi, qui lui fit mille caresses ; il fut regalé par les seigneurs les plus considerables, et alla à tous les spectacles. Quand il restoit à Vincennes, on lui faisoit une chère magnifique, et les dames les plus qualifiées de Paris se faisoient un divertissement de l'aller voir manger. Il leur faisoit à toutes mille honnestetés qui cependant se ressentoient toujours de l'Allemand et du soldat. Il buvoit admirablement, et n'excelloit pas moins à prendre du tabac, en poudre, en cordon, et en fumée." John of Werth had been exchanged against Gustavus Horn in the month of March of this year, 1642.

hardly pressed by **the Duke** of Enghien. Guébriant, who **was**
now outnumbered, **made a retreat** so circumspect, so measured,
and so skilful, that **he** gave **time for** Thionville **to fall;** then,
reinforced by **some of** the troops **who had taken** part **in** the
siege, he resumed the offensive, **forced** the **Bavarian** army to
fall back, and, re-entering Swabia, **took** Rottweil, 8th November
1643, before its very **eyes. It was** Guébriant's last action.
In the capture of **Rottweil he received a wound in his arm,**
which, unskilfully treated, caused his death (13th November).
He died regretted by his troops and esteemed by his enemies.
The command of **the** Franco-Weimar army devolved upon Josias
of Rantzau, a member of the **noble** Schleswig-Holstein family
of that name.

Von Rantzau was no unworthy **successor** to Guébriant. **Only
thirty**-three years old, **he** had seen an amount of service such as
few veterans of the **more** modern days have enjoyed. After a
long training, first under **the generals of the** Dutch Republic,
then under Gustavus, then under the Emperor, and again under
Duke Bernhard, he, finally, in 1635, accepted the offers made **to
him by France, and** thenceforth remained **constant to her**
banner. His career, from **that time up to the moment of his**
introduction to **the reader, had been a blaze of** glory. **There**
were few important **actions in which he had** not taken a lead
ing part. His prominence in fight was remarkable, even in an
age **when personal adventure was a more** important factor on
the **battle-field than it has become in these** days **of** stricter discipline. He had received sixty wounds; **and had lost, in action,**
an eye, an ear, **an arm, and a leg.** Yet, notwithstanding that he
was the possessor, **at the age of thirty-three,** of little more than
one half of his original personality,* he was as active, as daring,

---

* On his death in 1650, the following epitaph was placed upon his tomb:—
  Du corps du grand Rantzau tu n'as qu'une des parts;
  L'autre moitié resta dans les plaines de Mars
  Il dispersa partout ses membres et sa gloire.
  Tout abattu qu'il fût, il demeura vainqueur;
  Son sang **fût** en cent lieux le prix de la victoire,
  Et Mars ne lui laissa rien d'entier que le cœur.

as efficient, as the strongest and soundest-limbed man in his army. So great, moreover, was his reputation, that not even the calamity which was about to happen to him, and which I proceed now to record, could detract from the estimation in which he was held by his contemporaries.

Fresh from the glorious field of Rocroi, on which he had borne a very prominent part, and from the capture of Thionville, Rantzau had commanded the French division by which Guébriant had been reinforced, had accompanied him into Swabia, and, on his death, five days after the capture of Rottweil, had, as I have said, succeeded to the command of the Franco-Weimar army. Winter had come, the ground was covered with snow, the Bavarian army had shown no disposition even to relieve Rottweil; there seemed no probability that it would now attempt to avenge the loss of it. Rantzau, then, did not hesitate to carry out the intentions of his predecessor; to march to Tuttlingen, seventeen miles from Rottweil, and distribute his army in winter quarters.

The town of Tuttlingen lies on a broad plain on the right bank of the Danube. Above it rose the castle, now in ruins, called the Hohenburg or Hohnburg, and a high range known as the Tuttlingen heights, both of which, especially the latter, commanded a complete view of the country and of the Alpine ranges beyond. To the north the plain was comparatively open; but on the south and south-west it was fringed by a series of heights, covered in some places with thick forest, and separated from each other by narrow gorges easily defensible. In such a position and in such a country, a general who should crown the heights bordering the plain, and should keep a good look-out, might confidently hope to maintain his army till the winter season should have passed away. It should be added that Tuttlingen was connected with the left bank of the Danube by the village of Möhringen on that bank, two and a half miles further up its stream. This village was also occupied by the French.

But the Germans had determined **not** only to **avenge** the loss of Rottweil, **they were** resolved that the French army should **not** winter on **the soil of the** Fatherland. **Very** solid reasons had they for their determination. **Mercy had not, indeed, been** able **to** prevent **the fall of** Rottweil; **but, two days** after the capture of that place, he had been joined first by the Duke of Lorraine (Charles IV.), then by a strong division of Imperialists, **commanded by Hatzfeldt—who** had been released from captivity at the same time as himself—and, **finally,** by John of Werth, with a body **of** splendid cavalry. This united force considerably outnumbered the **Franco-Weimar army.** It was led by three men who had **risen, by sheer merit, to the** height of their profession. **Of these,** Hatzfeldt **we know, and** John **of** Werth **we know.** Before describing **the action which they took upon this** memorable occasion, **I propose to say a few introductory words** regarding Mercy.

Francis, Baron of **Mercy, was born at the close of** the **sixteenth** century at Longwy—now **belonging to the** French department of the Meurthe-Moselle—about **forty** miles **to the** north-west of Metz. **At a very** early age he entered the military service of Bavaria and took a part in all the principal actions and **sieges** in which **the** army of that **country was engaged** during the earlier **phases of** the **Thirty Years' war. When** Ratisbon was besieged by Banner, Mercy, bearing **the rank of** general **of artillery**—feldzeugmeister—had commanded **the advance** of the army which **had** marched under Piccolomini **to** its relief. He it was who **had** assailed the four regiments which, under Colonel Schlangen, had delayed the pursuing army for four days **at** Wald-Neuburg; he had subsequently taken part **in** the defeats of Wolfenbuttel and Kempen. After his release from the captivity **to** which the latter defeat had subjected him, he had **been** placed at the head of the Bavarian army which had first driven Guébriant from Swabia, and later, after the fall of Thionville, had been forced to fall back before him into that province. He had already the reputation of

11 *

a skilful and daring commander, ready to risk much when much was to be gained, yet steadfast and full of **resources in** adversity.

Mercy had prudently declined to risk a battle with an **enemy** vastly superior in numbers to save Rottweil; yet when the conditions were reversed, when his army had been strengthened by the junction of Hatzfeldt, of the Duke of Lorraine and **of** John of Werth, he determined that the Franco-Weimar army should not rest in security in its winter quarters about Tuttlingen. At a consultation attended by the four generals referred to it was resolved to attempt to surprise the enemy. A reconnaissance, conducted with great **secrecy**, had satisfied Mercy that Rantzau was resting in the most perfect security; that, although **he** had placed his guns on the heights and in positions commanding the passes, yet that, trusting to the **prestige his army** had **gained** and to the discouragement of **the** Bavarians, he had not manned them; that he had not even taken the pains to inform himself of the position of the Bavarian **army,** nor of its recent accession of strength. This confident negligence of the French commander confirmed the allied generals in their determination to strike him **soon and to strike** him hard.

The allied army was during this time assembling about the **towns of** Aach and Engen, having detachments at Hattingen, to **the** south of the French position. **Late in** the evening of the **23rd of November the** whole force closed up about Hattingen. **Thence, early the** following morning, silently **and** in perfect **order, his own** distinctive task assigned to each general, **the allied** troops set out on the great expedition, Jean of Werth and **the** Croats leading **the van.**

They **were—for the** purpose they **had in** view—singularly **favoured by the** weather. The night **was dark, and** it snowed **heavily. The passes were** reached, were traversed without an **enemy being encountered.** Then the assailing columns came upon **the guns pointed** against the debouchment from those passes

TUTTLINGEN AND FREIBURG.   165

into the plain. They lay there undefended. **To secure these was the work only of a few minutes.** Then, **in the same silence, the** Germans, **secure** now **of victory,** divided **their** columns, spread-out so as to encircle the town of Tuttlingen and the **villages in which the** scattered **foe** still carelessly slept. **This, too, was** accomplished without sounding **the** alarm. Then, on the positions where **the enemy** lay **a rush was made. In** most of those on **the** rim of the **circle, the** startled **soldiers,** surprised in their sleep, **clutched vainly at** their arms. **The** generals and officers, **equally surprised,** did not fare better. Only the **cavalry,** whose horses stood saddled and **whose men were dressed, had a** chance **of** escape. The troopers had but time to jump into the saddle and, convinced that the situation was lost, to seek safety in a precipitate flight.

Of the others it remains only to be recounted, that, hopelessly in the **toils, they fell an easy prey to the enemy.** It is true that **in the best manner open to them** they offered **a** desultory resistance, **a resistance which** became more pronounced as those occupying the centre hamlets succeeded in forming. **But** those in the more advanced positions had been hewn down without mercy. The others, ranged, as they were able, in groups **without** order and without support, fought blindly and **madly, some** endeavouring to force their way through, some contenting themselves with a defence of **their position.** But, **as day dawned, they all** recognised the utter hopelessness of further resistance. Surrounded by superior numbers, without guns, without commanders—for their generals **had been** captured almost at the very **outset—they** despairingly **threw down their arms and demanded quarter.** The request was not refused.

The history of the world contains **no similar record of a** surprise so **complete, so well** managed, and so completely successful. **It is true that** the cavalry, **the** horsemen of Weimar, escaped **almost** to a man; but **all the guns were** captured. Of the infantry two **thousand had been** hewn or **shot down,** nearly eight thousand men, twenty-five staff officers, and ninety captains surrendered as prisoners. **Of the superior** officers, Rantzau himself and six generals **were** taken. Nor was this all. With the coming light of day **it** was noted that some hamlets **to the** north, in which **had lain the** rear-guard of the Franco-Weimar army, had not **been included in the** destroying circle, and that **the rear-guard itself, now on the** left bank of the Danube, was **hurrying with all speed towards** Lauffenburg. To pursue it, **to attack it, and to cut down the men** composing it—who, refusing **to surrender, fought bravely to the** last—was the completion of **the Tuttlingen tragedy of the 24th November** 1643. It need scarcely be added **that all** the impedimenta, public **and** private, of the conquered, **fell into the hands of the Bavarians.**

It was a **great achievement—a decisive victory gained almost** without **loss**—a fitting revenge **on the French for the devastation** which they had inflicted upon Germany. For the cause for **which** the French fought **was** widely different from that which had influenced Gustavus **and the** North Germans. These combated, at least **nominally, for** freedom of thought, for the right **of every man to pray in the manner declared** to him by his own **conscience, to upset the most grinding** of all tyrannies—the **tyranny which brings coercion into the** private chamber of **the subject. Far from the thoughts of** the French authors of **the war were such ideas as these. These men had** all but **established in France the uniformity** which the Habsburgs and **the Wittelsbachs were striving to** introduce **into** Germany. **They then assisted the Swedes, not to** aid **them in** gaining that **which in their hearts they hated, but the more** thoroughly to **render the** division **in Germany** permanent, **to gain** a portion of **her fair lands for** themselves. The strengthening of France, **the weakening of Germany,** were their sole objects. Little sympathy, **then, can we feel for** the conquered of Tuttlingen. Rather can **we** enter **into the** joy and self-congratulation **which** must have animated the hearts of Mercy, of Hatzfeldt, of John **of** Werth, **of** Duke Charles of Lorraine, when, **at ten** o'clock **on** that **snowy morning,** they recognised that the work for which they had nobly dared had been thoroughly accomplished!

One result of the battle of Tuttlingen was to free Swabia and Baden from the French; nor were these, in the following year, able to recover their preponderating position in the south-west of Germany. It is true that the Court of Versailles, on learning of the defeat, put on a very bold face, that it conferred upon Rantzau, whom it ransomed, the rank of lieutenant general* (22nd April 1644), and gave him the command of an army in the north; that it hastened to form a new army to replace that which it had lost. But with the sublime audacity which characterised its proceedings with respect to Rantzau were mingled prudence and forethought of the highest order; for, to command the new army, it selected Henry de la Tour d'Auvergne, Viscount of Turenne.

Turenne was one of the glories of France. Born at Sedan, the 11th September 1611, the second son of Henry, Duke of Bouillon, and of Elisabeth, daughter of William I., Prince of Orange, he was brought up in the Protestant religion. From an early age he panted for the profession of arms; and when his delicate health seemed to offer an obstacle to the carrying out of his wishes in this respect, he determined to prove to his father that he was well capable of enduring fatigue. With that view, one dark winter's night, he stole from the family house and lay down to sleep on the ramparts of the town. There he was found, sleeping, by his anxious tutor, the Chevalier de Vassignac. He was then only ten years old, and it is probable that this incident tended to cause his father to waive the objections which he had till then made. The Duke of Bouillon, nevertheless, relaxed no efforts to impart a sound education to the boy. It was not, however, until the examples of the heroes of ancient history fired his imagination that Turenne took kindly to his studies. The history of Rome, the exploits of her early heroes, the daring of Quintus Curtius,

* He was made a Marshal of France the year following.

the achievements of **the Scipios,** touched a chord which had remained **dormant. Thence-forward** he devoted himself eagerly **to his books. The** deeds of the great Macedonian completed the **spell. At the early age of** thirteen he was sent to serve as a **volunteer,** to **learn** his profession, in the camp of his uncles Maurice and Henry of Nassau. It was the first school of arms in Europe, and the young soldier knew how to profit from the opportunity. His conduct on every occasion **was of** a nature to obtain **for him** the approval of his uncles. It became at last so much talked of that his name **reached the ears** of Cardinal Richelieu, who, ever anxious to enlist **merit in** his own service, sent for the boy (November 1630), gave **him** the command **of a** regiment, **and ordered him** into **the field.** His splendid conduct there on **all occasions, but especially** when serving under the **orders of Marshal de la Force, the** coadjutor in Lorraine of Duke Bernhard, **procured for him** fresh promotion. On the **21st** June **1635,** before he had attained the age of twenty-four, he obtained the commission of brigadier-general ! *

Thenceforward Turenne was always employed **in the** most difficult undertakings. It would take too much space to recount all his **splendid exploits.** It must suffice to record that in the very year **of his** nomination to the **rank** of brigadier-general he covered **himself** with glory, **a glory** of the most imperishable **character, by the** manner in which **he covered** the retreat, of thirteen days' **duration, of the** French **army** from Mainz to Metz. Whilst constantly **repulsing the attacks** of the **enemy,** he showed an **equal assiduity** in the **care which he bestowed** upon his men, **then suffering greatly from** sickness and hunger. With them **he** shared **the small quantity of food he was** able to **obtain for himself.** To give **the** weaker amongst them rest from their sufferings he did not hesitate to sacrifice his own baggage and to mount the men upon his wagons, and on one occasion he

---

* **The commission** was that of "Maréchal de camp," **a** rank immediately above **that of colonel, and** below that of major-general. It **thus** corresponds to that of **brigadier-general in** the British army.

even gave his own horse to a wounded soldier. Conduct such as this gained for him the devotion of those whom he commanded.* We hear of him the following year fighting successfully in Franche-Comté; in 1637 in Flanders; in 1638 assisting Duke Bernhard to take Breisach; in 1639 and 1640-42 in Italy, always distinguishing himself, and almost always victorious. In the last-named year, then being thirty-one, he was nominated lieutenant-general.

Turenne was in Italy in 1643, when the Franco-Weimar army was surprised and almost destroyed at Tuttlingen (the 24th November). Without a moment's hesitation, Cardinal Mazarin, who had succeeded Richelieu in the direction of the destinies of France, directed Turenne, who had shortly before (16th May 1643) received the bâton of a marshal, to proceed at once to the seat of war in south-western Germany, and to use all the means in his power to form, from the wreck of Rantzau's army and from such other sources as might be available to him, a force sufficient to make head against the victorious enemy.

Rarely has a more difficult task been allotted to any general. Of Rantzau's army the cavalry alone, five thousand strong, had

---

* It is difficult to imagine a character more perfect than that of Turenne. "Turenne," writes a French critic, M. Grégoire, "was not merely an illustrious general; he was a good, a simple, and an honest man, true to his word, hating falsehood, full of kindness and attention towards his inferiors; always dignified without being proud, always holding his own without asperity in the presence of great personages. His equity, his spirit of moderation, his integrity have been proclaimed by all; he was generous and disinterested; he died without having added anything to his fortune after forty years of glorious services. He employed his own money in helping his officers and men, making it a condition that they should not divulge the name of the benefactor. His modesty always showed itself in his acts, in his words, in his writings. The basis of his character was calmness, coolness, kind-heartedness, respect for others and for himself."

"The greatest judges of the art of war," writes the same critic, "Condé and Napoléon, have left no bounds to their admiration of Turenne. Condé used to declare that Turenne was the only man with whom he would exchange his glory."

"Nothing in his exterior," wrote the authors of France Protestante, "revealed the great man. Of middle height, with very broad shoulders, eye-brows thick and almost joining, a big nose, eyes large but sunk in their sockets, thick lips, hair so long that it almost covered his face, he was ugly, and his ugliness, of a type common and even repulsive, was made more remarkable by the extreme simplicity of his dress."

escaped from the field; there remained, likewise, four thousand infantry who, left behind at Rottweil, had fallen back on the first news of the disaster; but they were all in a most terrible condition. The severity of the weather, the scarcity of forage, and the long marches had told upon horses and men alike, and when Turenne joined the fugitives the cavalry were all but unmounted, and the soldiers were in rags. His first care was to re-equip the whole force, and to remount the cavalry at his own cost. This task accomplished, he crossed the Rhine at Breisach (3rd June 1644), surprised and defeated a division of Mercy's army which had been sent to the front to observe him, and was on the point of taking means to relieve Freiburg, which town Mercy was besieging, when orders from Paris directed him to stay his action until he should be joined by the Duke of Enghien. Whilst he was awaiting the Duke's arrival Freiburg fell, and when, on the 3rd August, the allied armies appeared before the town, that town and the heights near it were occupied by the army of Mercy.

The prince who, at this critical moment, assumed the command of the French army, had but shortly before rendered himself famous by a feat of arms as brilliant as any of which the world has cognizance. Born in 1621, Louis II. of Bourbon, Duke of Enghien, was the son of Henry II., Prince of Condé, and of Charlotte de Montmorency. His natural great abilities had been developed by an education of the most extended character. To everything which he undertook in his early youth he devoted all his energies. The combined power and resolution to do this formed one of the chief causes of his success. When, at the age of seventeen, he entered the army, he applied the same rule to his conduct, and very soon gained a reputation for the possession of abilities far beyond the ordinary run of men. The fact was, that, joined to the power of application of which I have spoken, directing and controlling it, he possessed genius, genius of a very high order. He had, too, a very clear brain, and nerves of iron. He was endowed with that remarkable and rare power, a power without which no soldier, however gifted he may be in other respects, can be a general of the first order—the power to think as clearly and calmly in the midst of the flight of bullets, of the roar of cannon, of the trampling of cavalry, as a philosopher in the quiet of his study. This power has been possessed by all the first-class leaders of their fellows on the field of battle. It is a quality absolutely essential to success under difficult circumstances. To the perfect possession of it the Duke of Enghien owed the brilliant success which first marked his name in a manner never to be forgotten in history.

In the beginning of the seventeenth century the Spanish infantry enjoyed the reputation, gained under Charles V., and maintained under his successor, of being the best and steadiest in the world. In 1641 an army composed of the choicest of this splendid infantry, men who had fought side by side in many a hard campaign, and commanded by generals whose reputation as leaders was scarcely inferior to their reputation as soldiers, Don Francisco of Mellos and the Count of Fuentes, invaded France. The task of attacking and expelling these enemies was committed to the Duke of Enghien, who had but just attained the age of twenty-two.

Louis XIII. of France was then dying. On his death-bed he had used this expression to the father of the Duke, the Prince of Condé: "The enemy is at our gates; but your son will drive him away." Mazarin, on the other hand, had written to the young commander to risk nothing. A defeat, he saw, would be fatal to France. Nevertheless, Enghien, on the 19th May 1643, attacked the Spanish army. This is not the place to describe one of the most brilliant, and certainly one of the most instructive, battles ever fought. It must suffice to state that the Spanish infantry showed themselves worthy of their old renown. They were beaten, less by the prowess of the enemy, though that was not to be surpassed, than by the wonderful coolness and self-possession, the clearness of vision and ripeness of judgment, amid the hottest fire, of Enghien himself. Whilst the last two qualities enabled him **to detect**, as clearly as **on** a peaceful parade, the slightest mistake **on** either side, the **two** first enabled him quickly to repair or **to** use that mistake **so as** to bring superior numbers on the decisive point at the decisive moment. To him it was not fatal that, whilst he triumphed **on** the right, his left **was** beaten and his **centre was** uncovered. He waited patiently till **he** had completely destroyed the enemy's left, then, wheeling **to the** left, crushed in turn their centre and their right,* and gained one of the most brilliant victories on **record.**

Such was the man who, after taking the fullest advantage of his victory at Rocroi, had joined Turenne beyond **Breisach, and** in sole command of the French army, found himself, **on the 3rd August,** fronting the Bavarian army, commanded by **Mercy, on the** heights about Freiburg.

There are few travellers of the present day who, journeying **from** Baden to Basel, have not stopped to admire the wonderfully beautiful landscape presented by Freiburg. Immediately behind it rise, to a height of nine hundred feet, the dark green hills of the Schwarzwald, covering as it were **with** their picturesque forms the marble city, with its walks, **its** vineyards, its fruit-gardens, below them.

The valley of **the** Dreisam, **as it is called from** the little river which runs into the Elz near Riegel, **some** fourteen miles to the north of **Freiburg, is singularly** attractive. **There are,** indeed,

* " Any general before **the time of** Condé," writes **M.** Cousin, **in his** *Histoire de Madame de Longueville*—referring to the period of the battle when, triumphing on his right, Enghien was informed that on his left his cavalry had been driven from the field and his guns taken—" would not have hesitated to retreat—to re-traverse in an equivocal attitude the field he had gloriously won, in order to hasten to the rescue of his left and centre. Condé took a course entirely opposite: instead of falling back, he advanced further; then, when he had reached the furthest end of the enemy's line, where the Italian, Walloon, and German infantry were posted in reserve, he wheeled to the left, threw himself upon that reserve, crushed it, and then charged in rear the victorious right wing." The novelty of Enghien's movement, indicates another French writer, M. Amédée Renée, consisted in the fact that after having routed the enemy's left and centre he attacked their right, thus placed between two fires, in the rear.

few places, not in the circle of the loftier mountains, which so strike the traveller at the first view. And it is not too much to add, that longer acquaintance more than confirms the first impressions.

The heights immediately behind Freiburg are divided by the valley of the Dreisam, running eastward by way of the townlets Littenweiler, Ebnet, and Kirschzarten, until, still running eastward and assuming the name of Höllenthal, the valley passes Neustadt, Röthenbach, Löffingen, and Hüfingen, where it follows the Breg, and forms near Donaueschingen, the connecting link between the Rhine and the Danube.* In this valley, parallel to the road, flows the river Dreisam, now connected with the Rhine by a canal, which serves to drain the low tracts at the base of the mountain range and the tracts adjoining them to the westward. The demarcation between the range to the north and that to the south of Freiburg, is thus very pronounced. Freiburg itself clings to the extreme southern skirt of the northern range, and juts out from it into the plain at the angle where the Dreisam valley begins.

The road from Breisach to Freiburg, after taking a curve to the south, turns northwards through some marshy woods, the road traversing which was in those days very narrow and very defensible. These woods abut on a plain peculiarly well adapted for defensive military action. Whilst the marshy woods protect its south-west face, its right is covered by a rivulet, and it forms, so to speak, the glacis of a spur which rises abruptly behind it, and is on all four sides very defensible. This spur is called the Schönberg, and rises to a height of two thousand feet. It is about five miles south-west of Freiburg.

This plain and this height had been seized by Mercy. He had under him fifteen thousand good troops. A portion of these he had posted in the plain, and, to make their position there

---

* Parts of this valley were, in those days, too narrow to be traversed by an army. The main road to the Danube lay through the Glotterthal, and passed the monastery of St. Peter.

absolutely secure, he had thrown up defences along the rivulet which covered it to the north, and built a redoubt commanding the narrow road through the marshy woods. Nor had he been content with this. To render the mountain impregnable, he had erected on the top of its southern slope a palisaded fort. Into this he had thrown six hundred men, and had armed it with his heaviest guns. Further, he had connected this fort with the left of the hill by a line of redoubts, two hundred paces apart, and he had covered that line with abattis of a most formidable character. Between the position thus occupied and the range between it and Freiburg ran the valley called Günthersthal. This valley could, indeed, be reached from the south, but only by making a long detour, and Mercy conceived that he had sufficiently provided against an attempt in that direction by strongly fortifying its entrance, which covered the plain occupied by a portion of his army.

Turenne's force, composed mainly of the troops of Weimar, was ten thousand strong, in equal proportions of cavalry and infantry. Forbidden, by positive orders, to attack Mercy, he had taken up a position to the south of the height occupied by that general, and had waited there the arrival of the Duke of Enghien. On the 3rd August, Enghien joined him with the corps of the Duke of Gramont, ten thousand strong, of whom four thousand were cavalry. The very same day Enghien reconnoitred, and then summoned a council of war. Called upon for his opinion, Turenne pronounced against an attack. He would, he said, march northwards, enter the Schwarzwald by the Glotterthal, and take up a position at St. Peter. They would thus cut off the supplies of the Bavarian army, and force them to depend upon those which might be brought from Villingen, beyond the Black Forest, and only ten miles from the Danube. He added that it was as easy to starve them out as it was dangerous to attack them in a position so strong, and defended by such good troops. The Duke of Gramont and Count d'Erlac agreed with Turenne. But Enghien was bent on attacking. He went again to reconnoitre, and Turenne having pointed out to him a defile by following which, **and** thus making a long detour round the mountains the front spur of which Mercy occupied, it would be possible to issue from the Ganthersthal on to the plain **which formed the glacis** of the Bavarian position, he resolved to avail himself of the discovery **and to attack** on the morrow. He arranged, then, with Turenne, that whilst the latter should set **out early** the following morning to effect the turning movement, he should restrain his own ardour till three hours before sunset, **when,** Turenne being probably by that time within striking distance, he would attempt the southern face of the hill.

At daybreak **on the 3rd** August, Turenne set out. **Whilst he was** marching, Enghien proceeded to assign **to** the divisions **of** his army their positions. **In the** front line of attack he placed the Count **of Espenan,** with two battalions, each eight hundred strong; **in the** second line, to support **Espenan, the** Count of Tournon, commanding the regiments **of** Conti and of Mazarin. **Two regiments** Enghien kept himself **in** reserve, to employ them as he might consider best at the moment. Gramont and the Count of Marsin remained **by his side.** The cavalry were ranged in this manner. Whilst the Count of Pallnau was to support the infantry attack with one regiment—the regiment of Enghien —the gendarmes were pushed forward along the narrow road leading into the plain, to cover the left flank of **the** French. These dispositions having been made, Enghien ordered the men **to dine, and then** waited calmly for the hour agreed upon with **Turenne.**

At four o'clock in the afternoon, Enghien gave the order to attack. With great dash and vigour, Espenan dashed forward, drove back the advanced posts of the enemy, and, pushing his **way up the** terraces **of a** vineyard, reached, without a halt, the abattis which covered **the** enemy's line **of** redoubts. But here he was **met by a** fire so **hot** and so sustained, that his men could make no way. Whilst he was persevering in his endeavours to **force** the abattis, **the order** became broken, and the men were fast separating into groups, when Enghien, who had noticed the check and its cause, galloped to the front, dismounted, ran to the front of the regiment of Conti, rallied it, and led it to the charge. His example was followed by Gramont, by Tournon, and by all the principal officers and by the volunteers.

The men, animated by the conduct of their officers, rushed forward, forced the abattis, charged the enemy, and, advancing rapidly from their right, carried, one after another, the line of redoubts. Enghien was careful to have these occupied as they were won; then, calling to himself his cavalry, he pushed forward with great alacrity and made himself master of the left and centre of the plateau on the summit.

But the right of the plateau, including the palisaded fort, and the thick woods on either side of it, was still held by Mercy. Darkness was setting in. At any moment Mercy might mass his troops and attack in flank any force which might advance against the fort. Enghien felt very strongly the danger of the situation. Unwillingly, then, he halted his troops, contenting himself with announcing to Turenne, by bugle and trumpet, that he had gained the summit of the hill.

That general, meanwhile, had threaded his way along the gorge of a deep ravine which runs between the Schönberg and the heights rising behind it, had reached, about four o'clock in the afternoon, the point, near the village of Merghausen, where the ravine joins the Günthersthal. It will be recollected that, in view of the possibility of a turning movement, Mercy had posted here a strong body of infantry. This infantry now offered a very determined resistance to the further advance of the enemy. Turenne found that every vantage point had been occupied, that every possible precaution had been taken. Covered by a strong abattis in front, and occupying the slope of the mountain and the woods on both flanks, the Bavarians seemed so firmly lodged as to be immovable. But Turenne was just the man not to despair of conquering even the impossible. Distributing his light troops on either flank to clear the woods and the mountain slope, he pushed forward with his main body, forced the abattis, and, pushing on, gained, just as darkness was setting in, the entrance into the plain. He accomplished this just at the moment when Enghien, deterred from insisting further by the strong position held by Mercy in the palisaded fort and the adjoining woods, had ceased the combat. This cessation gave Mercy an opportunity such as, in the presence of a commander like the Duke of Enghien, only a general of the very first class, a general clear-headed, cool, possessing nerves of iron, would have dared to seize. The firing in the valley below had indicated with tolerable clearness to Mercy the progress of Turenne. He felt that the daring Frenchman, unless promptly checked, would advance still further, that such an advance would provoke a new movement on the part of Enghien, and that his fate and the fate of his army would then be sealed.

Leaving, then, the palisaded fort strongly guarded, he collected some seven thousand men, and, with rare judgment, stole down the northern slope of the hill, and faced the astonished troops of Turenne, just as the latter, forcing their way into the plain, had deemed their task accomplished. One of the most terrible combats in the whole war, fruitful as that war was in engagements of a desperate character, now took place. But forty paces separated the hostile armies from each other; the darkness was profound; and, to add to the horrors of the situation, it was raining as it can only rain in those dark mountain regions. Both sides were animated by feelings which incited them to do all they knew to conquer. A Protestant himself, Turenne was leading the troops raised in Protestant Weimar, the men who had fought at Leipzig, at Nuremberg, at Lützen, at Nördlingen, who had avenged the death of Gustavus, who had mourned the premature loss of Duke Bernhard, and who had transferred to their present leader the confidence, the affection, the devotion which they had borne to that illustrious soldier. On the other side, the troops of Mercy were inspired by a hatred of the French invader, by a profound indignation at the violation of their soil, by a fury at the action of the Weimar troops in aiding that invader. Both sides, then, were terribly in earnest. They gave their lives recklessly; each man bent on doing his utmost to achieve the end which he had at heart. For nearly seven hours the fight continued. Notwithstanding every effort, neither side could make progress. The French could not force their way across the plain, nor could the Bavarians drive back the French into the valley. At length, towards the small hours of the morning, the contest slackened, and Mercy, feeling that if he remained where he was, he would, with the morning light, have to deal with Enghien as well, sent orders to evacuate quietly the palisaded fort. Then, under cover of the still continued darkness, and a fire maintained by a line of musketeers whom he had drawn up for the purpose, he marched directly to take up a new position on a hill now called the Lorettoberg, nearer to Freiburg. He had lost in the two attacks, in killed and wounded, from five to six thousand men. The French loss had been at least as great.

The Schlier, or Lorettoberg, about a mile to the south of Freiburg, commands a very extensive view over the plains and valleys below it. The spur of which its summit is the apex, projects into the plain, between the Dreisam valley on the one side and the Günthersthal on the other. Whilst the former covers the sharp angle of its extreme projection, one of its branches separates it by a wide demarcation from Brombeerberg to the east, whilst the Günthersthal severs it completely from the hills to the south. But that it is securely linked on to the range from which it projects forward, it would be completely isolated. As it is, it somewhat resembles an inverted ∧, the two points forming the base of which are securely bound to the solid mass behind it, whilst the two sides and sharp point are in the air. A very thick pine forest covered the western slope of the Lorettoberg, from a point about one-third of its height below the summit down to the valley below. On the point above the forest is a ledge or plateau, capable of lodging some three to four thousand men in order of battle. It remains to add that a mountain path, running across the base of the Lorettoberg, connects the village of Merzhausen in the Günthersthal with the townlet of Littenweiler in the Dreisam valley.

It was to this hill that, in the early morn of the 4th August, just as day was breaking, Mercy led his wearied soldiers. Without giving them time to rest, never certain but that the pursuer might not be upon their heels, he ascended the hill. Upon the plateau of which I have spoken, he placed the great bulk of his much-reduced infantry; the remainder he disposed behind a wood, about midway down the western slope of the mountain; with his cavalry he maintained communications between the base of the hill and Freiburg, which thus formed, so to speak, an outwork covering his right. Fortunately he had, when besieging Freiburg, carefully noted the position, and had covered with abattis the front of the ground now occupied by his cavalry. Having made these arrangements, he prepared to await, with resolution, the next movement of the enemy.

Meanwhile, Turenne had been quite unable to profit by the departure of Mercy. His men had been on foot since daybreak, they had fought nearly seven hours, they had eaten nothing, they were wet, tired, and exhausted. Bravely had they struggled to maintain, as they had maintained, their position. Turenne contented himself, then, with remaining where he was till break of day, when, seeing no enemy, he pushed forward into the plain. There he was soon after joined by Enghien, who had likewise taken advantage of the morning light to move forward. For a moment Enghien was inclined to pursue the Bavarians, but the sight of his own men, wet, bleeding, tired out, restrained his ardour, and he resolved to give them a rest, and to pass the day in reconnoitring the new position taken by the enemy.

The more the Duke of Enghien examined the new position of the Bavarian general, the more was he penetrated by a conviction of its exceeding strength. Over and over again did he express his admiration for the genius which had enabled his

12 *

enemy, when almost in the jaws of destruction, not only to escape him, but to take a position so strong and so defiant. The cross road between Merzhausen and Littenweiler was so narrow and difficult that it was almost impossible to assail Mercy in the rear. The thick pine wood on the south-western face, intersected by paths of which he knew nothing, seemed to forbid an attack on that side, whilst the sharp front and the north-western face, the sound of the axes on which proved to him that they were being made more and more defensible, and the ground between the base of the hill and the town, appeared almost equally hopeless. Nevertheless Enghien was not a man to be baffled, and, long before the sun set, he had decided on his plan. He had determined to deliver three attacks; one, a false one, on the projecting slope; a second, which he would conduct personally, against the wooded face of the hill; a third, to be entrusted to Turenne, against the abattis guarding the entrance into the valley. He fixed the following morning for the attack.

The day which Enghien had thus spent in reconnoitring, Mercy had passed in strengthening his position. Seeing, from his lofty post, that the enemy did not intend to attack him that day, he directed his men to fell trees, to cut ditches, to throw up earthworks, to form abattis. Feeling confident that he would be attacked the following morning, he did all in his power to lessen the enemy's chances of success.

A little after daybreak on the morning of the 5th August, the two French corps of attack were ranged in the order decided upon; that of Turenne, on the left, about to take further ground in that direction to force the entrance into the valley, Enghien's waiting at the foot of the hill until Turenne should have gained a position of attack. The troops had not begun to march, and the two leaders were yet engaged in conversation, when a sound of uproar was wafted to them from the Bavarian camp. To ascertain the cause of this, Enghien and Turenne, giving orders respectively to their officers—Turenne to his, to move slowly to the left; Enghien, to those under him, on no account to make any movement till his return—galloped towards a height some little distance off, to reconnoitre. Had Enghien's orders been obeyed no calamity would have happened. But the Count of Espenan, who again commanded the advanced division of Enghien's corps, sent a detachment to take a redoubt which Mercy had erected on the slope of the hill, near its base. The Bavarians defended it bravely; Espenan reinforced his detachment, and, as he did so, Mercy reinforced the defenders. To such an extent did this proceed, that before long a very considerable body of French troops were engaged on the point which had not been intended by Enghien to be the real point of attack, and, to make it still worse, before he could return from reconnoitring, Enghien's entire corps had broken from the control of its leaders and had rushed, helter skelter, to the spot. Mercy, who had noticed their confusion, sallied down with his best troops from the plateau of which I have spoken, and, charging home, completed their disorder.

Such was the state of affairs when Enghien and Turenne returned. A glance convinced the former that whilst it was impossible to restore the old order, yet that success on the line which had been thus accidentally chosen was impossible; that his only chance was to associate his troops with the movement which had been originally consigned to Turenne. It was a difficult task; for not only were his own men thoroughly disordered, but the great bulk of the officers had lost their heads. But rarely has human influence—the influence, that is, of men who soar above their kind—been more wonderfully asserted than it was on this occasion. Turenne's corps was fortunately intact; it had continued steadily to take ground to the left. Throwing himself, then, amongst his troops, Enghien gave back to them their confidence; then, leaving a detachment to amuse the enemy, he hurried with the remainder to Turenne, then well on his way, and reached him in time sufficient to join him in his attack on the abattis. His coolness and conduct had given the French army a second chance.

Sustained by the gendarmes and the horsemen of Weimar, the two French leaders led their men, anxious to recover their laurels, against the abattis. But if their assault was full of vigour, the defence was not less stubborn. Three or four times were the abattis forced and the intrenchments beyond them stormed, as often were the assailants hurled back. To encourage his men, Gaspard Mercy, brother of the Bavarian commander-in-chief, dismounted all his cavalry, and led them to support his still nobly-fighting footmen. The slaughter on both sides was terrible, for neither would desist, the one from attacking furiously, the other from defending vigorously. Night at length came to put an end to the horrors of the day. With the darkness the combat, still undecided, for the French had not gained a lodgment in the intrenchments, ceased. The last glimpse we have of a battle in which both sides fought so well comes to us from the pen of the Duke of Gramont, himself an actor. "I saw him," he wrote, alluding to the Duke of Enghien, "falling back with a few men, the others having been killed by his side."*

The slaughter had been terrific. Gaspard Mercy, of whose action I have spoken, was killed, and with him about twelve hundred men. The loss of the French was much greater. It did not fall short of, and probably exceeded, two thousand.

During the night Enghien occupied the position on which he had fought, surrounded by the dead, the dying, and the wounded. Turenne, whose heart was as tender as a woman's, passed the night in visiting the wounded, without asking whether they were friends or enemies, and in having those who could be moved placed upon carts to be taken to Breisach. "In the midst of combats and of carnage," writes his biographer,† "humanity formed in him the base of heroism."

---

* Enghien, states Gramont, in his memoirs, never concealed the real reason of his repulse. He said to Gramont himself during the action, " Qu'un peu trop de chaleur avait emporté ses troupes, et que l'attaque ne s'était point faite de la manière qu'on l'avait resolue."

† *Histoire du vicomte de Turenne par Ramsay.*

Enghien was resolved, and the troops under his orders were resolved, that Mercy should not permanently profit from the mistakes which had robbed him and them of a great victory. But, unwilling to shed more blood than was necessary, Enghien recurred **now to** Turenne's plan of starving out his enemy. Mercy, it was certain, had with him, on the Lorettoberg, supplies for **a few** days only. **His only line** of retreat, and retreat would **speedily** be forced **upon him, lay** through the valley of St. **Peter** to Villingen. As it would **be** impossible **for** Enghien, without forcing the defences before which he had failed in the attack of the 5th, to prevent Mercy from retreating directly on St. Peter, he conceived the idea of marching northwards **by** the high road, passing Zähringen and Gundelingen to Denzlingen on the Glotter, commanding the **entrance** into the Glotterthal, then entering that valley to reach St. Peter before Mercy should **be driven** by famine **to march** thither across **the** Dreisam valley, **and wait there,** ready to pounce upon his prey.

Filled with this idea, Enghien gave his **army a** rest of four **days; then, early on the 9th, he** despatched Turenne with the Weimar troops along the road to the north, waiting himself to observe the dispositions **of Mercy.** Mercy made no sign. **A** message having reached him from Turenne **to** the effect that the few obstacles in the **march** northwards had been cleared away, Enghien followed **on the same** road, joined **his** colleague that night at Denzlingen and entered the Glotterthal, full of the hope that he had thoroughly deceived Mercy, the following morning.

But Mercy had not been deceived. That able commander had noted, from the summit of the Lorettoberg, the march, first **of Turenne, then of** Enghien, along the road leading northwards. **Not for** a moment did he imagine that **his** young **and** brilliant opponent had renounced his **designs. But** why should he march northwards? Suddenly **the** idea dawned upon **him.** It must be to gain St. Peter—his only line of retreat—by the Glotterthal. In a moment he recognised his danger. Unless **he** could reach St. Peter before the French he **was lost.** On the instant, then, he gave the order to march, and half an hour later, at the head of the six or seven thousand men—all who remained to him—began his descent into the Dreisam valley bound for St. Peter!

It was a terrible race. A messenger reached Enghien just as he arrived at Denzlingen, bearing the news of Mercy's movement. Instantly he detached from Turenne's army eight hundred horsemen of Weimar, under the command of a Livonian nobleman, Rosen of Grossopp, with orders to enter the valley of the Dreisam, to press upon Mercy's rear, to harass and retard him in every possible manner. Meanwhile he urged on his troops, marching at their head, encouraging and animating them. Rosen executed the orders confided to him with great intelligence. Hurrying on, he caught up the rear-guard of the Bavarian army just as it came in sight of the monastery of St. Peter, and charged it with terrible fury. So fierce was the assault that Mercy had to lead back troops from the front to repel it. Then, indeed, numbers told; but, as the Weimar horsemen still fought, there was the danger that the Bavarian army might be entangled in their pursuit. It was a very real danger, for at the moment Enghien and Turenne, though not in sight, were ascending the further slope of the heights which commanded the valley. Mercy, feeling sure that they could not be far off, checked the pursuit of Rosen; then, hurrying forward, careless of the still continued charges of his enemy, reached the point where the roads from the Dreisam valley and the Glotterthal unite, just in time to behold the heads of the men forming Turenne's advanced guard ascending the heights immediately above him. He had but just time. Another ten minutes and he had been lost. Turning sharply to the right, he marched with all speed for more than half a mile into a thick wood which bordered the road. Entering that wood he left there all his guns and all his baggage; then, issuing from the other side, made his way by the best paths he could find across the mountains. Enghien, who had promptly joined Turenne, saw his enemy disappear in the wood. He did not see him emerge from the other side. Knowing, however, the direction which he must take, he pursued him for several miles. But the unencumbered Bavarians either marched more quickly or found a shorter road, for they succeeded in eluding pursuit. By his retreat, indeed, Mercy allowed the French—to use the words of an English writer—"to reap all the advantages of a victory they had not gained."* Not the less, however, did he save the remnant of his army; and not a very long period was to elapse before it was to be shown that his skill and intelligence had, for the time, saved his country.

But for the moment events justified the remark of the English writer whom I have quoted. The Duke of Enghien did reap all the advantages of a victory which he had not gained. Thenceforth the right bank of the Rhine, the Palatinate, Würtemberg, lay at his feet. He speedily took advantage of the position. Anxious to gain, in return for the profuse bloodshed which had taken place, something substantial for his own country, he turned his steps northwards, and, marching down the Rhine, attacked, one after another, the fortresses which covered the German side of the Bavarian Palatinate. One after another Speyer, Mannheim, and Worms opened their gates to his arms. Philippsburg, invested by Turenne, alone offered a strenuous resistance, and did not surrender until the garrison had consumed their last bread-crumb. Turenne then marched to Mainz. The terror the recent battles had inspired was so great that Mainz at once opened her gates to the conqueror. Meanwhile Enghien had summoned Landau, and Landau, even then strong and destined to become, through the genius of Vauban, the strongest fortress in the Palatinate, surrendered after three days of open trenches. From Strasburg to Coblenz the Rhine was made French. Well might Enghien, in his account of this victorious campaign, triumphantly boast that that noble river had returned to her ancient masters!

Satisfied, and justly satisfied, with this result of the three

* Gardner's *Thirty Years' War.* London: Longmans.

hard days' fighting before **Freiburg, the** Duke of Enghien placed **the bulk** of his army in winter quarters and returned **to Paris.** To guard the **new** frontier against an enemy who **had ever** shown himself **daring and** enterprising, Turenne remained with six thousand men. It was calculated, not altogether without reason, **that the genius of the** commander would compensate for **the diminished strength of his army.**

CHAPTER VII.

MERGENTHEIM, ALLERSHEIM, ZUSMARSHAUSEN, PRAGUE.

WHILST Enghien and Turenne were pursuing their victorious career on the Rhine, Mercy, escaped from their clutches, had fallen back into Würtemburg. There he had gradually drawn to himself the corps commanded by the Duke of Lorraine, and detachments from the strong places in Bavaria. These additions made him sufficiently strong to affront even the united French army, much more the solitary corps of six thousand men which, under the command of Turenne, constituted, besides the garrisons of the fortresses, the sole defence of the Rhine between Strasbourg and Coblenz. Despite, then, the wintry season, Mercy marched, in the month of December, towards the Rhine, in the hope of profiting by the absence of Enghien and his army, and of repairing the losses of the autumn.

But though the French were few in numbers, the great ability of Turenne more than supplied the deficiency. Never did the qualities of a great leader make themselves more conspicuously felt than during this memorable winter. Did the Bavarian troops sit down before a fortress, Turenne was on their flanks, on their rear, disturbing their communications, cutting off their foraging parties. He had, by means peculiarly his own and without any aid from his Government, increased the strength of his army to eleven thousand; he still had, moreover, under his command the remnant, a remnant in very deed, of Duke Bernhard's troops, and these men, all cavalry, and in whose breasts the desire to secure freedom of conscience predominated over the love of German unity, fought for him with an energy, a resolution, and a courage not to be surpassed. They were proud of their leader, a Protestant like themselves, and in this short campaign that leader proved himself worthy of their fullest confidence. To seek a parallel to it in history, the reader must go forward to the campaigns of 1796 in Italy, and of 1814 in France. On this occasion, as in 1796, and as for a time in 1814, a small army in a central position baffled all the efforts of hostile forces greatly outnumbering it.

Mercy, animated doubtless by the desire to distract his enemy's attention, had made the great mistake of dividing his forces. Whilst with one corps he besieged Speyer, he sent a second against Bacharach and a third against Kreuznach (on the Nahe). Of this error Turenne promptly availed himself. The distance between Speyer and Kreuznach was considerable. Turenne threw himself between the two besieging corps, marched on the right flank of that before Speyer, forced it to raise the siege, and to fall back with some loss on the line leading to Würtemberg; then, hurrying by forced marches to Bacharach, the extreme end of the enemy's line, arrived there just in time to save it, and compelled the besieging corps to take a northerly line of retreat. Meanwhile Kreuznach had fallen. But Turenne, having driven in opposite directions the two wings, so to speak, of the enemy's line, experienced no difficulty in dealing with the centre. From Bacharach he pounced upon Kreuznach and retook it, the enemy's centre corps evacuating it, and retreating in a line apart from the other two, on the very rumour of his approach.

Having thus completely defeated the enemy's plan, and forced the three hostile corps to retrograde in different directions, Turenne proceeded to follow up his advantage. Completing, by two or three vigorous blows on the left flank of the one, and on the right of the other, the separation between the Bavarian right and centre, he marched with all speed on the left, which, commanded by Mercy in person, had begun to show symptoms of recovery. He gave that adversary no time to complete the process. Though the combined army of the enemy exceeded his own by nearly three to two, Turenne, throughout the operations I have recorded, had always been superior on the decisive point. He was so now. Mercy, hopelessly separated from his centre and right, was forced into Swabia, his men harassed and, owing to the superior numbers of the enemy's cavalry, hardly pressed for food. Followed up step by step, he was compelled at last to take shelter behind the Franconian ranges, and, not safe then, to fall back on Nuremberg, and from Nuremberg on Würzburg. In that city at last he found shelter. Behind its walls he could hope to give rest to his discouraged army.

It is not to be supposed that this brilliant campaign, in which, with numbers utterly out of proportion to those of the enemy, Turenne had not only saved the threatened frontier, but had forced the divided foe to a disastrous retreat to the fortresses and strong places in the interior of his fatherland, had been accomplished without great exertions and considerable privations. In fact Turenne had only been able to accomplish it by, so to speak, multiplying himself, by supplying, by the activity of the few, the want of numbers. His men, in fact, were worn out by fatigue. The cavalry needed fresh horses; the infantry, shoes and garments. It was the middle of April. The enemy had been even more exhausted than their pursuers. They were still, however, could they unite, superior in numbers. Turenne was very unwilling to give them any respite; but he was strongly urged, now that the Bavarians had received a lesson, to grant his troops the rest they so much needed. He was, I have said, very unwilling to comply. At last, however, moved by the state to which his German cavalry had been reduced, he silenced his better judgment, yielded to the strong representations made by those about him, and distributed his troops in quarters in the vicinity of Mergentheim.

Mergentheim, known originally as Marienthal, is a town in Würtemberg, situated at the junction of the Wachbach with the Tauber, some thirty-five miles nearly due south of Würzburg, and six from Königshofen. The fruitful valley in which it lies, called, from the river which is the main source of its fertility, the Taubergrund, was well adapted for the purpose of giving repose to an army. The northern approaches to it were covered by a wood some five or six hundred paces in length, and of a depth in proportion, and beyond this, again, was a vast plain incapable of giving cover to an advancing enemy. As no enemy could approach except from a northerly or north-easterly direction, the position of Turenne was secure, provided only he had the wood carefully occupied and its flanks guarded. Far from neglecting this precaution, the great Frenchman placed in the wood a strong body of infantry. The remainder of the army he distributed on the Taubergrund in and about Mergentheim.

One effect of the relaxation of the pursuit of the Bavarian army, foreseen by Turenne, was speedily produced. At Würzburg Mercy was, during the fortnight which followed his arrival there, joined by the centre and right of his army. His own men had recovered from their fatigues, and he was now in sufficient strength to deal a retaliatory blow on his pursuers. If he could but reproduce in the Taubergrund the day of Tuttlingen he would be fully recompensed for the toils, the privations, the fatigues he had undergone. Such a day, well followed up, might suffice to recover the losses which had resulted from the three days' murderous conflict at Freiburg. It was true, he felt, that the long bright days of May were less favourable for a surprise than the dark snowy night which had so contributed to his victory at Tuttlingen. But he had numbers on his side, and the information which reached him showed that the French were not at all expecting an attack.

Full of the hope based upon the grounds I have stated, Mercy set out from Würzburg with his army, now some sixteen thousand strong, on the afternoon of the 4th May. Marching all night, he arrived early on the morning of the following day at the further edge of the broad plain to the north of the wood of which I have spoken as covering the ground over which the French troops lay scattered. From their position in the wood the French scouts descried the Bavarian army advancing in order of battle across the plain. Information was at once despatched to Turenne, and Turenne at once ordered Colonel Rosen—the Rosen of Grossop who had attacked Mercy so vigorously during his retreat from Freiburg—to proceed at once to the wood, occupy it, receive there the reinforcements as they should arrive, and delay as much as he could the advance of the enemy, whilst he himself should mass the main body at Herbzthausen, three miles from Mergentheim. Had Rosen contented himself with obeying this order, it is probable that Mercy's enterprise would have recoiled on his own head, for the wood was very defensible, the French troops were fresh, and Turenne was eminently capable of taking the utmost advantage either from the lay of the ground or from the mistake of an enemy. Unfortunately, however, Rosen was one of those men who are never content with merely obeying orders, whose zeal and good intentions outrun their discretion, and who, bringing to bear upon the design of a master their own commonplace powers of reasoning, invariably spoil that design. So it was on this 5th day of May 1645. Had Rosen, I repeat, been content to hold the wood, he would have so delayed the enemy's advance as to give time to Turenne to come up; but, unaware of the close propinquity of the enemy, he advanced with his handful of men beyond the wood and began to form them on the plain.

Turenne, meanwhile, had succeeded in collecting the main body of his troops. Once assured of that, he galloped to the front to observe how Rosen had executed the orders he had given him. To his dismay, he beheld his advanced guard, so to speak, in the air, on the plain, and the enemy close upon it. It was too late now to withdraw Rosen; his only chance of success was to support him with the rest of his little army.

The extreme right of the plain was fringed by a small wood, standing quite isolated, and yet within reach of the French infantry. To regain the large wood covering the Taubergrund was, I have said, impossible, but this smaller wood was within easy distance. On to it, then, Turenne directed all his infantry, three thousand strong, under Rosen, caused them to occupy it, and covered their right with two squadrons of cavalry. At some little distance on the left of this little wood he drew up in a single line his whole remaining cavalry, consisting of eight weak regiments, with the exception of two squadrons which he placed in reserve. He had scarcely completed these dispositions when Mercy, who had changed his line of attack in accordance with the movements of his enemy, made a fierce front assault with his infantry, supported by his guns, on the wood. This the French resisted manfully. Turenne remained a passive spectator of the contest till he saw it well engaged; then, suddenly wheeling his horsemen to his right, he charged with full force the right flank of the Bavarians, composed of a great part of their cavalry. So successful was the attack, that the first line of the Bavarian cavalry was completely overthrown, their second was shaken, and they lost two standards. But before Turenne could loosen himself from this conflict the Bavarian infantry had carried the wood, and forced the French infantry to retreat in great disorder. Their retreat was precipitated by an opportune charge made by John of Werth at the head of the cavalry of the left wing, and in which he took Rosen prisoner. When Turenne, then, could shake himself free from the enemy's horsemen on the Bavarian right, he found himself with his cavalry face to face with the whole Bavarian army, and his retreat threatened. But never for an instant was his clear brain troubled. Despatching his cavalry to take a position which would cover his retreating infantry, he rode to the latter, rallied them, encouraged them, and, indicating to their commander the ultimate line of retreat to be taken, he returned with all speed to the front, placed himself at the head of his rearmost squadrons, and retarded the advance of the enemy by repeated charges.

Meanwhile, however, Mercy had detached several regiments of cavalry to turn the main wood, and to meet the French as they emerged on its further side. This order was punctually executed, but produced no result. With a brilliant charge Turenne overthrew the hostile squadrons. From that moment the pursuit relaxed, and Turenne, rejoining the infantry, led them, without further attack, towards the Main, with the intention of entering the duchy of Hesse. He had lost many of his infantry, twelve hundred horses, and all his guns and baggage.

By taking this line of retreat Turenne completely baffled Mercy. He rendered his victory strategically profitless. In Hesse the French expected allies and reinforcements. Mercy could not advance against the fortresses on the Rhine without exposing his flank. It was thus, in all essentials, a barren victory. "If," wrote Turenne to his sister, "anything could console a man for such a mishap, it would be the fact that the enemy derived no profit from it."*

In Hesse Turenne found the reinforcements he had expected. The Landgravine of that territory—who was his cousin-german—sent him her troops, and the Swedish general, John Christopher Königsmark—whose grand-daughter, Aurora, famed for her beauty, her wit, her artistic talent and her many bewitching qualities, was to make so great a sensation in the years that were to follow—brought him a fresh corps from Sweden. Thus strengthened, Turenne was on the point of re-taking the offensive, when he received orders from his Court to stay his

---

* During his long and brilliant military career, Turenne, when in chief command of an army, met with but this one reverse; for, at Rhétel, where he was beaten in 1650, he was only second in command. When he was asked how it was he had been beaten at Mergentheim, he answered: "By my own fault." He added: "If a man has made no mistakes in war, the reason is that he has not long made war." Turenne, in fact, recognised that he had had no right, notwithstanding the importunities which assailed him, to relax his pursuit of the enemy.

hand until he should be joined by the Duke of Enghien and his army. Turenne had sustained nobly all the difficulties and hardships of the campaign. Cardinal Mazarin was resolved that Enghien should enjoy its glorious fruits.

That prince was not less anxious to meet again the enemy who had so boldly withstood him at Freiburg. Since he had quitted the army in the preceding winter he had been content to enjoy, in the capital, the reputation he had acquired as the restorer to France of her true boundary. But, on the first news of the disaster at Mergentheim, he had drawn together an army of eight thousand men, and, invested with the title of Commander-in-Chief on the Rhenish frontier, and once more having the Duke of Gramont as his lieutenant, had entered Lorraine, and had thence pressed on to join Turenne, who, on his part, had re-passed the river Main, and, taking Weinheim on his route, had marched to Speyer. There the junction took place. Enghien, learning that Mercy was at Heilbronn, but two days' march from him, marched directly on Wimpfen am Berg, on the Neckar, stormed it, crossed the Neckar, pushed forward after Mercy. The skilful Bavarian general was in no humour, however, to accept a battle, unless on the ground he had himself chosen. He retreated then, as rapidly as possible, to Feuchtwangen, in Franconia, and fell back thence, as Enghien advanced, in the direction of Nördlingen. In the vicinity of that town he arrived at 9 o'clock on the morning of the 3rd August.

I have already given some slight description of the situation of Nördlingen. "The vast plain on which it stands, one of the most extensive in Franconia, is cut, in its centre, by two heights, rising at a distance of three thousand yards the one from the other. Between these two heights is a valley which terminates from both directions in a village about three hundred paces nearer to the town than either of them. This height is called Allersheim. The foremost of the two is known as the Weinberg."* I may add here that the ground between

---

* See *ante*, page 119.

the height of Allersheim and the village—which also bears that name—is, though smooth and level, traversed in its entire breadth by a very wide and deep ditch ; also, that between the Weinberg and the village the road is difficult and rugged ; further, that the summit of Allersheim is crowned by a castle, then very capable of defence.

Mercy utilised to the utmost these natural advantages. He was a great believer in the spade ; and it was his habit to include, as part of the equipment of his army, carts laden with that humble instrument, with pickaxes, and with shovels. No sooner, then, had he reached the plain about Nördlingen than, assigning to each division of his army its position, he set the men to work to render it impregnable. On the Weinberg, which formed his right, he placed the Imperial regiments, under the orders of General Gleen ; on the height of Allersheim, his left, under John of Werth. The space between the two heights, three thousand yards, and the village of Allersheim, were occupied by the troops under his own personal command. In the village immediately in front of him he placed his choicest infantry, occupying the church and the cemetery, both of which were enclosed by walls. His guns he disposed with great skill, so as to command the ground by which the enemy must advance. Some of them were placed behind the broad and deep ditch of which I have spoken as traversing the ground between the base of Allersheim and the village, and which Mercy had greatly strengthened ; thence to the Weinberg every advantage had been taken of the rugged nature of the ground to throw up intrenchments and to place batteries. Mercy having thus posted his troops, who numbered sixteen thousand,* all veterans, set them to work, as I have stated, with the spade and pickaxe, whilst the cooks prepared their simple meal. This had just been partaken of when the French army appeared in sight.

Enghien had followed up the retreating Bavarians with great expedition, but he, too, had met with obstacles which had

---

* He had thirty-six squadrons and eighteen battalions.

somewhat retarded his progress. Very young, the spoiled child of Fortune, he had not yet learned the necessity for the display of tact and moderation in dealing with men of a nationality different from his own. The open manner in which he spoke of the material advantages to France at the expense of Germany which would result from a victory over Mercy had so alienated Königsmark, a born German, that he had withdrawn his contingent. Nevertheless, Enghien pushed on, and about 3 o'clock of the afternoon of the 3rd August, twelve months within two days of the first desperate assault at Freiburg, arrived on the plains of Nördlingen to see the Bavarian army drawn up in the manner I have described.

At once Enghien, accompanied by Turenne and the Duke of Gramont, rode to the front to reconnoitre. Enghien and Gramont immediately declared themselves in favour of an attack. Turenne, more calm and sober in judgment—he had the blood of William of Orange in his veins—pronounced against it. The position of the enemy, he said, was so strong as to be almost impregnable; it would be the height of rashness to attack it in front, and impossible to turn it. In vain did Enghien and Gramont endeavour to change his opinion; to prove to him that the Bavarian centre could be pierced, and that then the wings separated from each other by a distance of nearly a mile and three quarters would fall an easy prey. Turenne was not convinced; it would be all but impossible, he thought, to break that strong centre. When at last he yielded to the importunities of his colleagues, he did so with a firm conviction that they were about to commit a grave blunder.

The military reader will not have failed to recognise that the key of the German position was the village of Allersheim. It was upon that village certainly that the French would direct their chief attack. Turenne had been the first to recognise this fact, and, after some discussion, Enghien came round to his opinion. He now disposed his troops accordingly. In the front line on the extreme right, facing the height of Allersheim, he

placed six squadrons **under the Duke of** Gramont. Gramont was supported by **six** battalions and six squadrons, led by the **Count of Chabot. On the left, facing the** Weinberg, was Turenne, **commanding** twelve squadrons of Saxe-Weimar cavalry —the **sole** remnant of **the army once** led **by the** gallant Duke Bernhard—supported **by six** squadrons **and six battalions of** the troops contributed **by the Landgravine of** Hesse. In the centre **was** ranged **the** greater part **of the** French infantry, consisting **of ten battalions, led** by Generals Marchin and Bellenave, **and Brigadier-General Castelnau-Mauvissière. Behind these, as** supports, **were five** squadrons of gendarmes and carbineers.*
The Duke of **Enghien** exercised **a general** superintendence **over** the whole. **Accompanied by the Marquis de la** Moussaie, **he** held himself **in readiness to dash to** that part of the **field where** the presence of **a commander-in-chief would be most required.**

Mercy, **as** he beheld **the approach of the French, could not** restrain **his joy. "You see," he said, turning to the** person **nearest him,† "those rash troops advancing: before** nightfall **they will be in my hands." But, confident** though he felt of **victory, he** neglected **no precaution to assure it. He** remained **motionless** till **he judged that the French were** within **fire.** **Then, about 5 o'clock in the afternoon, from the guns on both lines** leading **from the heights to the village of** Allersheim **he opened a deadly fire. In spite of that fire the French** infantry **of the centre, gallantly led by Marchin and Bellenave, continued to** advance; they reached **the village; there they were met by the best** infantry of Germany, **and a hand-to-hand** contest **ensued.** **Every** man of the two armies **felt that on his** individual efforts

---

* It will be seen that the French **were somewhat superior in numbers.** The squadron averaged one hundred and **eighty men; the battalion, five hundred and** twenty five. This **would** make **the Bavarian army six thousand** four hundred and **eighty** cavalry, **and nine** thousand **four hundred and fifty** infantry, or within **a** fraction of the number stated in the text, **sixteen thousand.** By the same calculation the French **would have had six thousand three hundred** cavalry and eleven thousand **five hundred and fifty infantry, or close upon twenty** thousand in all. All the French writers **admit a superiority of one to two thousand men.**

† French writers **state that the person was his wife, but there are reasons why** this is improbable.

depended victory or defeat. At length the French slowly gained ground; but when they approached the walled enclosures they were met by a fire so concentrated that they were forced to give way; as they fell back one of their leaders, Marchin, was dangerously wounded. It was just at this period that John of Werth, tired of waiting on the left an attack which was not made, descended with his cavalry from the hill of Allersheim, and charged the French right. So furious was the charge, and so well supported, that Gramont, despite all his efforts, was driven back on his reserves. Vainly did Chabot's battalions and squadrons, disordered by the rush amongst them of their own troops, try to repair the disaster. By degrees they were involved in it. John of Werth gave them no repose, but, driving them back, made charge after charge on their broken ranks. Had he at this moment wheeled his right and fallen on the enemy's centre, the day would have been lost for France. But for once in his life John of Werth was led from the true line of attack. Like a contemporary commander in England, the gallant Prince Rupert, he thought for the moment only of the enemy immediately in front of him. That enemy he pursued untiringly in a direction leading from the decisive point of the scene of action; nor did he desist until he had made Gramont and many other officers prisoners, and had absolutely rased from the battle-field the right wing—front line and reserves—of the French army!

Whilst John of Werth was thus occupied on the Bavarian left, the battle had recommenced with double fury in the centre. We left the French repulsed from the village of Allersheim, their leader, Marchin, dangerously wounded. Just then they were cheered by the arrival of reinforcements under La Moussaie. Again did they advance to the charge, again did they enter the village. Once more, however, were they met by the indomitable courage of the Bavarians, and by the splendid conduct of their leader. All the buildings in the village were occupied by sections. The fire from these in their flank combined with the fire from the church and cemetery in front to make advance impossible. Once again were the French hurled back from the village, broken and in disorder, La Moussaie and Castelnau-Mauvissière both badly wounded!

This, then, was the situation after nearly two hours' fighting: the French destroyed on the right, and that right still pursued by John of Werth; twice repulsed in the centre; on the left, under Turenne, to whom I shall presently refer, holding their own, and, perhaps, a little more.

To the Duke of Enghien, at the moment, the battle must have seemed lost, unless, by an heroic effort, he could force the defences of the village of Allersheim. That effort he resolved to make. Massing all the infantry which yet remained to him, he led them in person to their third assault.

But Mercy, certain now of victory, did not await that assault behind the walls of the village. He allowed the French to approach within musket-shot, then, calling upon his men to make the effort which should be decisive, he poured upon the enemy a volley, and charged. Before that charge the French reeled. In vain did Enghien display the courage and the presence of mind for which he was so famous, urging, inciting, commanding. His horse was killed under him; two others, which he mounted in succession, were wounded; his aides-de-camp were hewn down by his side; he received a severe blow in his thigh, and his dress was pierced through. Still he fought—still, too, the Bavarians gained ground. The last hour—as it must have seemed to him—had come, when suddenly the attack relaxed. A chance musket-ball had mortally wounded the gallant Mercy, and—John of Werth being still engaged in his mad pursuit, and Gleen being fully occupied by Turenne—the Bavarian army was deprived, at the most critical period of the battle, of its leader!

Then it was that there came into play that presence of mind under difficult circumstances which is the stamp of the real general. The sudden relaxation in the fury of the attack revealed on the instant to Enghien that something had occurred which might be utilised on the instant, but only on the instant. Calling to his men to make a last bid for victory, he made a fierce charge on the village. The Bavarians, stunned by their leader's fall, allowed themselves to be surprised; and though a few minutes later they recovered themselves and, burning for vengeance, pressed forward once more, it was too late. The French, in that short interval of inspired leadership, had gained the front of the village, and they would not let it go. The Bavarians, however, still held the church and the cemetery, and from these Enghien could not expel them. He could not boast, even then, of a decisive victory in the centre. The most that he could claim was that he had, for the moment, averted complete defeat! He was not, however, in a safe position, for at any moment the victorious cavalry of John of Werth might thunder on his rear and his right flank. The fate of the day, in fact, still lay in the balance, and the direction in which the scale would turn depended on the action of that leader and of Türenne.

Whilst these events had been passing on the French right and in the centre, Turenne, on the left, had marched to storm the defences between the village of Allersheim and the height of Weinburg. But the resistance on this side had been as obstinate and as determined as the resistance in the village. The first attack was repulsed. A second, in which Turenne was wounded, was equally unsuccessful. Despite of his wound, however, Turenne, learning what was passing in the centre, and assured that the fate of the day depended upon his carrying the Weinburg, once more massed his men, and led them, for a third time, to the base of the height. In this attack, the attention of the enemy in the village was so completely engrossed by the front attack made upon it by Enghien that they had no leisure to direct upon Turenne the flanking fire which he had found so galling in his first two attempts. Relieved from this obstacle, his men—Germans fighting against Germans—slowly made their way. They were still fighting fiercely when Enghien, all bloody from the fight in the village which he had only half won, brought them the last men of the Hessian reserve. He, too, had seen that unless the height of Allersheim could be secured before John of Werth should return the day would still be lost, and, in spite of the suffering caused by the severe contusion he had received, he had come to make the attack, if possible, decisive. Thus reinforced, the attacking troops made a supreme effort, gained the summit, took prisoner the Imperial general, Gleen, and forced the enemy down on the other side. Down that side Enghien pursued them; then, wheeling to the left, took the village in the rear. The attack, sudden and unexpected, succeeded. The Bavarians, attacked on two sides, evacuated the church and the cemetery, and the day, if not won, was saved!

For now the French had gained the centre and the Bavarian right. Scarcely had they succeeded, when the Bavarian left, under John of Werth, appeared marching towards them. That general had, by his inconsiderate pursuit of the French right wing, thrown away the day. But one half-hour earlier, and he would have been able literally to destroy the enemies of his country! He could have rolled up their centre when its front was engaged in the village, and have then galloped on to destroy Turenne whilst he was embroiled with Gleen. But now—such is time in war—the short delay had lost him that splendid opportunity, and he was now with the victorious left wing of the Bavarians face to face with the victorious left and centre of the French!

He might still have fought, possibly with advantage, for the French were terribly exhausted. But, ignorant of all the circumstances, knowing only that Mercy had been wounded to the death,* he deemed it more prudent to fall back on the height of Allersheim. There he encamped for the night. The French remained masters of the field of battle.

* He died the day following.

Enghien had gained the battle of Allersheim, so styled by the Germans to distinguish it from the first battle fought near Nördlingen, but called by the French after that town. But it was a victory absolutely without results. To gain it he had lost nearly four thousand men—one fifth of his army—killed or wounded, and several of his best generals. His own hurts were so great that he was forced to return to France for a rest which was indispensable to their cure, and he made over the command to Turenne, to whom, it is due to Enghien to add, the Duke attributed, in his letters, all the glory of the victory, and whose wound was not so severe as to incapacitate him for active command. But Turenne found that he had gained only the height and village where he had fought. During the night John of Werth had been joined by the right and centre of the Bavarian army, and before break of day he had begun a retreat upon Donauwörth. In that retreat he was feebly followed by three thousand French horsemen, who did not dare to attack him. At Donauwörth he was speedily joined by an Austrian corps led by the Archduke Leopold. Fearing to be cut off, Turenne then retraced his steps to the Neckar, across which he swam his cavalry, and felt secure only when he found himself under the walls of Philipsburg. There, for the present, we must leave him, to meet him once again in the following year, when, guiding the French army himself, he was able to act, and act decisively, on his own sure judgment. That judgment had been amply vindicated during the campaign I have recorded, for the sacrifices by which victory had been gained at Allersheim had made that victory worse than profitless to the conqueror!

It will, I trust, be recollected that the events recorded in this chapter were contemporaneous with the march of Torstenson through Moravia, after the battle of Jankowitz, with the attempt to occupy Vienna, with the abortive siege of Brunn, with his retreat on Leitmeritz, and with the transfer of the command of the Swedish army to Wrangel. As the campaign of the following year, 1646, will bring the latter prominently upon the stage in honourable conjunction with **Turenne, it** is fit that I should introduce him now more particularly to the reader.

Charles Gustavus Wrangel was the son of **Hermann** Wrangel, a Swedish general, **who** had served with distinction **in the** earlier periods of the **Thirty Years' War. By** the side of **his** father, Charles Gustavus had, from his **early youth,** fought in many battles. In 1629 he **was granted by the great Gustavus** a commission in the **Royal Guard of Sweden. After** the death of that sovereign **he served under Bernhard of** Saxe-Weimar, and afterwards under Banner. **He had, as Major-General, the** command **of a division when Banner fought** and gained the victory of Chemnitz (4th April 1639). In conjunction **with** Generals Pfuel and Wittenberg he commanded the Swedish army during the short interval between the death of Banner and the arrival **of** Torstenson. **He** accompanied the latter in his **first** invasion of Moravia, and **during his march into** Holstein. **He** then separated from him to take command of the Swedish fleet. With this he achieved a **great triumph over the Danes.** After peace **had been** signed **with Denmark** (13th August 1645) he reverted to a military **command, and proceeded** towards the end of the year, with the patent of reversion of **the** command, to join Torstenson at Leitmeritz, **which that general** had just taken. **On** his arrival Torstenson resigned **his charge** into his hands. Wrangel at once completed the task **begun by his** predecessor by occupying Friedland, Teplitz, Brandeis, and Saaz. **Having** placed garrisons in **these** places, he marched into **Thüringen,** there to take up his winter **quarters.**

During that winter great exertions were made **on both sides to raise** such a body **of troops** as would finish the **war. In** Vienna a resolution **was arrived at to** leave the **French for a** moment in order to concentrate **all** the energies **of** the Empire upon the crushing of **the** Swedes. That aim accomplished, the victorious army would march upon the Rhine. With this view the Archduke Leopold was placed **at** the head **of the** Imperial army, then twenty-four thousand strong ; **to** this was **joined** the Bavarian corps which, in the preceding year, had combated under John of Werth and Hatzfeldt, and which consisted in round numbers of four thousand cavalry and twelve thousand infantry. With a force so imposing it was calculated that the Archduke would obtain an easy triumph over a general whose capacity for command-in-chief had not then been tested.

But the winter-time had not been uselessly employed by the Swedes and their allies. The close of the last campaign without results—the Swedes having only just failed before Vienna, and the French having been only just prevented from taking advantage of the victory of Allersheim—had disposed the minds of the generals on both sides to a union of their forces, with the view to take advantage of the success in the field which they felt they were certain to attain. Turenne especially was very earnest on this point. This year he would be required, with the troops he had led under the walls of Philipsburg, to face the enemy alone, for Enghien had been placed at the head of the army to act against Spain. He was urgent, then, that he should be allowed to act in concert with the Swedish army; and, though the Cardinal-Minister for a long time refused his assent, on the plea that the entire strength of France was required in the Low Countries, it was ultimately, though somewhat tardily, given. To force his hand, whilst the question was still pending, Wrangel resolved to draw the bulk of his garrisons from Bohemia, and to march, by way of Westphalia, into Upper Hesse. Once there, he relied upon events to bring about the desired junction.

Excluding garrisons scattered in the principal towns the Swedes had taken, and the flying corps of Königsmark, about five thousand strong, Wrangel could dispose of fifteen thousand infantry and eight thousand cavalry. At the head of these troops, early in the spring, he broke up from Thüringen, and, marching upon the Weser, drew to himself the Hessians, four thousand six hundred strong, assured his line of communication by the occupation of Paderborn and other strong places, and

then marched into Upper Hesse. Shortly after his arrival in
that province, Mazarin yielded to the urgent representations of
Turenne and Wrangel, and gave to the former the required
authority to join, and to act in concert with the Swedish army.
The junction took place at Giessen on the 31st July. The
strength of the united army, which had been joined at Wetzlar
by the flying corps of Königsmark, amounted to close upon
forty-two thousand men.*

With such an army there seemed no limit to the possibilities,
more especially as at the express invitation of Wrangel and
Königsmark Turenne assumed the chief direction of the united
forces. Ascertaining that the Archduke Leopold, who had
failed, as he had hoped, to crush Wrangel before he should be
reinforced, had taken up a position at Friedberg, in the Wet-
terau, Turenne marched to the Main, distracted the enemy's
attention by feigned preparations for attack, then, by a dex-
terous flank march, turned his position, took Hanau and
Aschaffenburg by assault, crossed the Main, and marched with
all speed through Franconia into Swabia. Mastering in succession Schorndorf, Dinkelsbühl, and Nördlingen, and beating a
Bavarian corps near Donauwörth, Turenne took that place,
crossed the Danube, occupied Rain, seized the line of the Lech,
forced Maximilian to flee for refuge to Braunau, and sat down
before Augsburg to besiege it.

The Archduke, meanwhile, had, to the astonishment of the
world, remained, during this time, quietly encamped at Fulda.†
The danger which threatened Augsburg caused him at last, on
the earnest representations of Maximilian of Bavaria, to break
up his camp and proceed southwards. Marching by way of
Schweinfurt, Bamberg, and Nuremberg, he crossed the Danube
at Straubing, then, wheeling to his right, and drawing to himself large reinforcements from the hereditary states and from

---

* Thus: Wrangel, twenty-three thousand; Turenne, nine thousand; Königsmark
five thousand; Hessians, four thousand six hundred.
† On the river of the same name in the province of Hessen-Nassau.

Bavaria, crossed the Lech near Thierhaupten, just above Rain and some thirteen miles north of Augsburg, and took up there a position which forced Turenne and Wrangel, now considerably outnumbered, to raise the siege of that place and to retire to Lauingen. The Archduke then ascended the Lech, crossed that river below Landsberg, and encamped on the high road to Memmingen at a distance of fifteen miles from Landsberg, whence he drew his supplies. His idea was to wait until the allies should have exhausted the stores they had with them, and then to attack them.

But Turenne was too quick-witted for the Archduke. Penetrating his designs, he marched towards the Imperialists, and made as though he would attack them. Then, suddenly filing off to the left, he reached the Lech before the Archduke had time to follow him, crossed it by the bridge which Leopold had left standing, took Landsberg by escalade, seized the magazines of the enemy, and, dominating the whole country, sent out parties which carried their devastations to the very gates of Munich!

Maximilian of Bavaria had long been weary of the war. One after one the early friends, whose enthusiasm had acted upon his own, Ferdinand II. of Austria, his counsellors, his generals, had disappeared. He was left almost alone, and it was his country which had become the scene of desolation. South of the Danube he beheld the peasantry harassed and the lands devastated by two large armies. And for what was he now fighting? Ferdinand III. was in the hands of the Spanish faction, and it was that faction which had most strenuously opposed the cession to himself of the Palatinate. He had had enough of this miserable war. He besought, then, the Emperor to agree to a congress of deputies from the contesting powers to treat of the terms of peace.

With difficulty Ferdinand was persuaded. At length, however, a meeting of the representatives of all the powers took place at Ulm. But twenty-nine years of fighting had not sufficiently abated the several ambitions. For the moment, indeed, the French and Maximilian alone sincerely desired peace—the French, to enable them to employ in the Low Countries the troops employed in Bavaria; Maximilian for the reasons above stated. The Swedes, victorious everywhere, were anxious to dictate a peace, not to discuss its terms. A feeling not dissimilar animated Ferdinand III.

Under these circumstances, a general peace was not within the bounds of possibility. Yet the obstinacy of Ferdinand and the diplomacy of the French obtained for the latter and their allies a result more advantageous than would have been the terms of any peace then within prospect of attainment: it obtained the neutrality of Maximilian (14th March 1647).

Under the terms of this neutrality, to which Cologne and Hesse-Cassel likewise subscribed, it was agreed that the Swedes and the French should quit Bavaria, should withdraw their garrisons from the places they had conquered in that duchy; and, on the other hand, that Maximilian should renounce every part of Swabia, and confine himself to Bavaria and the Upper Palatinate. The allies were left free to continue the war against the Emperor in any other part of Germany.

Upon this, Wrangel and Turenne, who had, meanwhile, fallen back to the shores of Lake Constance, separated. The former retired through Franconia towards the Main, and, taking Schweinfurt, marched towards Bohemia, and, expelling the Imperial garrison, took up a position at Eger. Turenne, who had been urgently summoned by Mazarin to repair to the Low Countries, marched towards the Rhine, and overthrowing on his road the last ally of the Emperor, the Landgrave of Hesse-Darmstadt, forced him likewise to accept the treaty of neutrality. The difficulties which he encountered when he ordered the remnant of the bands led by the heroic Bernhard to cross the Vosges mountains, in order to serve in the Netherlands, will be related when I record his return as a combatant to the German soil.

The retreat of Turenne and the defection from the Emperor of Maximilian affected to a certain extent the relative strength of the hostile armies; and Ferdinand, full of hope that his presence with the army would be beneficial, assumed the command and led it towards Eger. Wrangel was not indisposed to a general action. Instead, then, of shutting himself up in the place, he took up a very strong position close to it, and awaited there the approach of the Emperor. Ferdinand marched forward, and encamped in front of the Swedes, a valley only separating the two armies. For some time daily and nightly skirmishes took place. Nothing more, however, came of it. The position of both armies was so strong that neither would give the other the advantage of attacking. A slight circumstance decided the movements of Ferdinand. One night a party of resolute Swedes penetrated into his camp, and arrived within a few yards of the Imperial tent before they were discovered. It is true they were cut down to a man; but the adventure decided the Emperor to retreat from so dangerous a propinquity. He fell back on Pilsen, and took up there a new position. But Wrangel followed him, and encamped opposite to him. Again a battle seemed imminent, when an event occurred which forced the Swedes to evacuate Bohemia.

Maximilian had signed the neutrality treaty on the 14th March. It had given great offence to his army. As time went on, John of Werth and General Spork formed a conspiracy—communicated to and encouraged by the Emperor—to march with the bulk of the Bavarian army to Ferdinand's camp, and place it under his orders. An accident revealed the conspiracy to Maximilian. John of Werth and Spork had time to take refuge with the Emperor, and the movement was checked. The discovery, though it proved to Maximilian that the Emperor had been plotting against him, gave vitality to some thoughts which had been passing through his mind. He was already tired of a situation which had left him an empty treasury, an impoverished country, and a numerous and dissatisfied army.

Probably, likewise, he reflected that by his action he had cast to the winds any chance of territorial aggrandisement which might be secured by the negotiations for a general peace, which were even then assuming some form at Münster and Osnabrück. As suddenly, then, as he had accepted the treaty of neutrality, he renounced it (September 1647), published a manifesto against Sweden, received back in his service John of Werth and Spork, sent the bulk of his army to join the Emperor, and re-occupied, with the remainder, the strong places in Swabia, which, six months' before, he had made over to the Swedes!

This was the event which induced Wrangel to evacuate Bohemia. He fell back, by way of Thüringen—in which province he was joined by the flying corps of Königsmark—into Weimar, pursued as far as that duchy by the allied Imperial-Bavarian army. That army was no longer led by the Emperor. Ferdinand had long since discovered that war was not his trade, and had, on the junction of the Bavarians, confided the command of the army to a Calvinist deserter, Peter Melander, Count of Holzapfel!

It was strange that such a man should have gained the confidence of the champion of the Roman Catholic faith! Stranger still, when it is remembered that Melander possessed within him no elements of greatness! A Hessian by birth, he had risen without service of special merit to the rank of lieutenant-general in the army of the Landgravine, and up to that period had fought always against the Emperor. On attaining that rank, his arrogant conceit aspired to a higher command than the Landgravine considered he was entitled to. On her refusal, he went over with his bigoted Calvinism, his exalted self-opinion, and his little talent, to the enemy against whom he had ever fought. The self-assertion, which Amalia of Hesse had seen through, so imposed on the Emperor, that he gave to the deserter his fullest confidence, and, as I have related, on his departure to Vienna entrusted to him the command of his army.

There could scarcely have been a more unfortunate selection. There were many signs pointing to a conclusion of the war, and it was evident that the conditions of peace would depend very much on the position occupied at the time by the several combatants. Never, since the defeat of Duke Bernhard at Nördlingen, had the hopes of the Imperialists stood so high as when Maximilian, renouncing his neutrality, had given the Catholic cause a superiority all along the line. The Swedes and their allies had been forced to evacuate Bohemia and Silesia; the Swedish garrison in Olmütz was hard pressed; in Alsace and in Swabia the French detachments were losing ground; the Imperialist army largely outnumbered that of Wrangel; Turenne was beyond the Rhine, under orders to march for the Netherlands. It needed only a resolute leader of the Imperial army to win back all that had been lost. John of Werth, Montecucculi, Hatzfeldt, the Archduke Leopold—any one of them would have accomplished the task. But, at such a conjunction, the Emperor set them all aside in favour of the Calvinist deserter!

In the first moments of his command, indeed, Melander seemed to show that he had fully recognised the points of the situation. He pressed Wrangel hard on his retreat through Thüringen; pressed him hard till he had reached Weimar. Had he continued to press him, Wrangel must have fought at a great disadvantage or have been driven into the sea. But the conduct of Melander, when he had forced back his enemy so far, proved that the Landgravine Amalia had read his character more truly than had Ferdinand III. Standing in front of Weimar he had on his left his native country, the Landgraviate of Hesse, uncovered and at his mercy. His desire to wreak his vengeance on the Landgravine for the slight he considered she had put upon him, triumphed over the instincts of the warrior and the sense of duty. He quitted, then, the pursuit of Wrangel, led the Imperial army into Hesse, and avenged himself on the ruler from whom he had deserted by devastating her lands—which

were the lands of his own country—and plundering her people
—who were his countrymen—in a manner which had not been
exceeded at any period even of that war!

This diversion saved Wrangel. He led his army northwards, and distributed his men in winter quarters about
Brunswick and Lüneberg, in undisturbed possession of his communications with Sweden. The winter was spent in endeavouring to impress upon Cardinal Mazarin the advisability, in view
of the approaching peace, of making a great combined effort
very early in the ensuing spring. Melander, on the other hand,
paid the penalty of indulgence—to the neglect of his clear duty
—in personal feelings. The Bavarian corps, under General
Gronsfeld, had quitted him as soon as he had turned from the
pursuit of Wrangel. His own army, distributed for the winter
in the districts which he had himself made desolate, literally
melted away. When the time for movement arrived, its numbers had so diminished that he was unable to make head
against the enemy whom, the previous autumn, he had had in
his grasp.

Wrangel was not slow to take advantage of the opportunity.
Well aware of the weakness of the Imperial army, and still
hopeful that Turenne would yet join him, he broke up from
Brunswick in February, and marched against Melander. The
Imperial general, his left flank always open to an attack from
the side of France, fell back on the Danube. Wrangel pressed
him hardly, was joined during the month by the last remnants
of the Weimar cavalry till then in the service of France,* and
on the 23rd March by Turenne himself. The allied army followed rapidly on the retreating foe, and finally, after a series of
manœuvres, overtook him at Zusmarshausen, a village on the
river Zusam, some sixteen miles to the west of Augsburg, on the

---

* The Weimar cavalry had refused to cross the Vosges to combat for France in
the Netherlands, and, on compliance being insisted, the greater number of them
had renounced the service of that country, and hastened to join the Swedish
army.

14 *

old road from that place to Ulm, and within the outer rim of the Streittheimer forest.

Melander had crossed the Danube at Donauwörth; Turenne and Wrangel had made their passage at Lauingen, nineteen miles higher up the river. It was an endeavour on the part of the former to be beforehand with the French and Swedes, to take them in the act of crossing, which brought on the battle which I am now about to describe.

The river Zusam, taking its rise in the Algauer Alps, flows northwards almost parallel with the Lech, until it empties itself into the Dannbe at Donauwörth. It increases considerably in volume as it approaches Dinkelscherben, and beyond that place to its mouth it is remarkable for the number of its sharp windings. Between those two points it forms constant repetitions of the letter S. At Dinkelscherben it is now traversed by a railway-bridge, but at the time of which I am writing the principal bridge was at Zusmarshausen, three or four miles nearer to Donauwörth, at a point where the river is deep and fairly broad. The village of Zusmarshausen is immediately on the river, on its right or Augsburg side. The shortest road to the river from Lauingen runs by Weissing, Holzheim, Ellerbach, and Fultenbach, to a point between the last-named place and Zusamzell. At that point it joins the main road to Donauwörth, and, branching southward, crosses the river at Altenmünster, and runs thence, skirting the Streittheimer forest, up its right bank, to Neumünster, and thence to Zusmarshausen. There is, however, another road from Lauingen, which, though longer, could not fail to recommend itself to generals in the situation of Turenne and Wrangel. This road runs parallel with the Danube till it cuts the old Ulm road at Gunzburg. The last-named road, running at a direct right angle to it eastward, takes the traveller by way of Burgau and Glöttwang, and through the Scheppbach forest, to Zusmarshausen.

It is important to bear in mind the existence of these two roads. The Imperialists, crossing at Donauwörth, had marched by that leading from that place southwards, with the general idea of taking up a position which would cover Augsburg against an enemy who should cross the Danube at a point higher than Donauwörth. **For** this purpose there was no better **point to** occupy than Zusmarshausen. An army occupying the village behind the Zusam, the passage of which would have been rendered most difficult if the bridge across **it had been** destroyed, with a corps at Neumünster, little more than a mile higher up to cover its right, and a detachment in observation, supported by a second corps at Altenmünster, would have secured the right. The left was covered **by** the nature of the country **and by a** remarkable bend made **at** this point by the river. Melander had only to sit still at Zusmarshausen, and employ **to the** utmost his scouts and reconnoitring parties.

Some dim idea of the advantages offered by the **position** of Zusmarshausen, and of retaining them, seems to have occupied at the outset the mind of Melander. **As long as he was** uncertain **of the movements of his enemy, he remained** quiet. Suddenly, however, certain **information reached** him that Turenne **and** Wrangel were seeking to cross the Danube at Lauingen. This information would, **had** he been a wise man, have confirmed him in his quiet attitude. **He should** not **have** stirred until he had ascertained, beyond question, the exact movements **of** the enemy. But Melander acted just as he should **not have acted.** Rendered nervous and fussy by **the** news about Lauingen, he resolved to seek out the enemy, not by means of his scouts, but with his main army. He quitted, then, Zusmarshausen, and marched by the second of **the two** roads which I have described to Glöttwang. Scarcely **had he** reached that place when **he received** certain information **that** the enemy, pressing **forward** in light order, was at Rosingen, within a few miles of him. Thoroughly alarmed **now,** Melander hastened **to** make a retrograde movement, with the view of reoccupying his old position at Zusmarshausen. **But** the French and Swedes marched more **rapidly** than he did; and **he had** only succeeded in transporting half his army—the Bavarian portion, led by General Gronsfeld—over the bridge across the Zusam, when Turenne and Wrangel attacked him. Those generals, in fact, had crossed at Lauingen the day before the information of their propinquity to that place had reached Melander, and, leaving there all their heavy baggage, had marched rapidly by the second of the two roads which I have described. The skirmishers in their front had given timely intelligence of the movements of Melander—of his rash advance, and of his still more rash retreat—and this intelligence had only served to quicken the already rapid movement of the allies. Turenne felt that the enemy was in his power, that the bridge over the Zusam would alone suffice to give them into his hands. Melander would have either to fight with his whole army, with an unfordable river in his rear; or, were he rash enough to transport a part of his army behind that river, he would expose it to be cut in two. Melander, we have seen, did display that rashness.

The Bavarians under Gronsfeld were just succeeding in making good the passage of the Zusam, when Melander was called upon to make head against the full force of the allied attack. He had been at the bridge and along the line leading to it hastening his men and endeavouring by all the means in his power to quicken their movements; but, at the first sound of attack, he galloped back to his rear-guard, and encouraged them to make such a resistance as would save his army. Before he could reach his rear-guard Montecucculi's cavalry had been put to flight. He found it impossible, then, to stem the torrent of that fierce assault, and his troops gave way under the very eye of their commander. Melander was still animating them when a bullet pierced his jerkin. For a few seconds he sat his horse; then, calling to his men to continue their resistance, he fell dead to the ground!

The fall of their leader, the absence from the front of the general, Raymond, Count of Montecucculi, who, as next in authority, succeeded him, **completed the discomfiture** which repeated **charges on the front and on** the flanks **of** the Imperial **army, whilst its more advanced columns were** engaged **in crossing a narrow bridge, had begun.** Some time elapsed before the news of the death **of Melander reached Montecucculi ; and when it** reached him, **the** pressure from the **front was too great to** permit him to make his **presence felt.** The battle **had, in** fact, been decided the moment when Turenne and Wrangel caught the Imperial **army,** *in flagrante delicto,* **on the ground** west of the Zusam!

Meanwhile **about one-half of the** Imperial army had **succeeded in passing to the right** bank. The fierce **and indiscriminate rush which** followed **the rout of** Montecucculi's **cavalry and the death of** Melander brought with **it a few** more. Then Gronsfeld, who had ranged his Bavarians in battle array on the **further side, saw very clearly that unless** he could stop that **rush, he, too, would be overwhelmed ; that, to save the cause, it was necessary to** sacrifice **the** Imperial troops—nearly **a moiety of** their army—**who were** still **on** the further side. **With a supreme** effort, **then, he** managed **to** utilise **the means which had been already provided** under more **favourable** circumstances, **to destroy a** portion of the bridge sufficient to render it impassable. **This** action—to be repeated at **Leipzig a** hundred and sixty-five **years later on one of the most momentous** occasions the world **has ever** witnessed—though it **saved, for a moment, the bulk of** the allied **army, left one-fourth of it a prey to** the enemy.

It **can** easily **be conceived how** Turenne and **Wrangel took the** fullest **advantage of their position ;** how not **an enemy on** the further side **of the** Zusam escaped death or surrender. But they did more. **They** brought **up** artificers to render the broken **parts of the bridge** traversable **by means of** fascines sunk in the stream. But Gronsfeld and Montecucculi, fully alive to the danger, had planted guns **and marksmen at points sheltered** from the enemy's fire, and which commanded the bridge throughout its length and breadth. Their fire effectually hindered the artificers. The two generals then despatched their cavalry to attempt, at some point or other, to cross the river. But the Bavarian horsemen, well led, followed their movements and baffled them. The victors were forced then to be content with the victory they had already gained. That such a necessity was imposed upon them proves the folly of Melander in quitting so strong a position to march against an enemy of whose movements he was ignorant! It was not sufficient that his folly caused his death. The death of a man is not always sufficient atonement for the disgrace, the loss, the dishonour, his actions may bring upon his country!

During the night that followed, Gronsfeld, who had now assumed command, fell back very rapidly, but in perfect order; nor did he halt until he had placed the river Lech between himself and his enemy. Turenne and Wrangel lost no time in following him; but the passage of the Zusam was long, and when they reached the left bank of the Lech, just above Augsburg, they found the enemy intrenched in a strong position on the opposite side. The Lech here being very broad * and difficult, the allies descended that river until they arrived at a point opposite Rain—the very point, in fact, whence Gustavus had made his successful passage of the river in the face of Tilly. In the hope to surprise the bridge across the river at this point, the allied generals had sent to the front a strong body of cavalry with orders to seize it. But before they could arrive, the commandant of the Bavarian garrison at Rain had caused it to be set fire to; and though it was still burning when the allied cavalry came in sight of it, it was already lost beyond redemption for practical purposes. But the loss of the bridge hindered Turenne and Wrangel as little as it had hindered Gustavus. Employing means similar to those used by the hero-king, they crossed the river in the face

* See *ante*, pages 56, 57.

of the enemy, and forced Gronsfeld, now commanding only the small Bavarian army, to a precipitate flight. Bavaria now lay defenceless at their feet. Universal terror reigned amongst the Catholic magnates of that country. There was no thought of further resistance. Maximilian himself gave an example to his subjects by fleeing, in despair, to Salzburg!

Two other misfortunes following upon the battle of Zusmarshausen and the passage of the Lech, came to complete the lowering of the pretensions of the Catholic party in Germany, and to force its leaders to accept terms of peace. The first of these was brought about by the action of Königsmark, the second the victory of Condé over the Austro-Spanish army at Lens. The action of Königsmark is so interesting and so little known that I propose to give it in some detail. After crossing the Lech, Wrangel had despatched Königsmark with his flying corps into Bohemia. Königsmark marched across the Upper Palatinate, entered that kingdom by way of Eger (9th July), and took Falkenau, Bischofteinitz, and Klattau. About that time, his head-quarters being still at Eger, an officer called Ernest of Ottwald, who had just quitted the Imperial service, came to him, demanded and obtained an audience, and represented that during his recent residence in Prague he had observed that whilst the repairs of the city-wall were progressing it was customary to leave the parts under repair unguarded at night, and that he was satisfied it would be easy for a party of Swedes to enter the city that way, and then by a rush to master one of the gates and admit the main army. Königsmark listened to the information with pleasure, resolved to act upon it immediately, and set off that very night by forced marches towards Prague. Pressing on with all speed, he surprised Rakovnik (Rakonitz) 26th July, closely guarded all the roads which communicated with the capital, then sent on Ottwald to conduct twelve hundred horsemen and musketeers, commanded by Colonel Koppi, to carry out the design, whilst he himself, with the rest of his flying corps, marched to, and occupied at midnight, Breonov (St. Margaretha), close to Prague. Meanwhile Ottwald, Koppi, and the horsemen advanced in order of attack to the fallen wall. A hundred musketeers were in front, closely followed by fifty sappers, and these as closely supported by two hundred chosen infantry, the rest of the cavalry and infantry bringing up the rear. As they approached they heard the call of the sentry followed by the sound of a bell. The Swedes for a moment thought they had been betrayed, but Ottwald assured them that the bell merely signified the summons to the monks to early matins, whilst the call of the soldier was the consequence of the relief of sentries. For a moment the party halted. No sooner, however, had the guards finished their rounds than the signal for attack was given. The advanced troops, led by Ottwald, cleared the rubbish, entered the city, cut down the sentries at the neighbouring gate (the Strahover Gate, now known as the Reichsthor) and lowered the drawbridge. In front of this were Königsmark and his troops. These now entered, mastered the remaining gates of the Kleinseite and the Hradschin, and in the midst of inconceivable alarm and disturbance occupied all the principal squares and streets.

On the first sound of tumult the Commandant of Prague, Count Colloredo of Walse, had fallen back with the garrison, eight hundred strong, into the Altstadt, and had blocked or occupied all the approaches to it. Aided by the major commanding the city militia, Turek of Rosenthal, he armed as quickly as possible the citizens, the students, and even the priests. He despatched messengers at the same time to the Count of Buckheim, who was proceeding to Glatz at the head of two thousand cavalry, to return; sent for a detachment then at Budweis, under Don Juarez Conti, and ordered the occupation of the island, Klein Venedig, by another detachment under Colonel Prichovsky. He had, however, only two guns, and to supply all the arms that were required he was compelled to ransack the gunshops in the Altstadt. He managed, however, to repulse the attacks which Königsmark had not ceased, from the moment he had established a semblance of order in the Kleinseite, to make upon him.

In the course of the forty-eight hours following, both sides received reinforcements. Buckheim returned with his two thousand horsemen from the road to Glatz, whilst General Wittenberg, who had commanded the Swedish cavalry at Zusmarshausen, and had been detached after the passage of the Lech into Silesia, arrived with a still larger body of men, and took post on the Ziskaberg. On that he planted five batteries, and opened fire from forty pieces of artillery on the Neustadt. Colleredo could not reply. His two solitary pieces had been early used up. But if he had no guns he had what on this occasion was not less valuable, the courage, the determination, the cool calm energy of the citizens. Not in after years, in Saragossa even, was a place defended by its citizens with greater resolution than were those quarters of Prague known as the Altstadt, Neustadt, and Josefstadt, separated from the Kleinseite by the Moldau, in July, August, September, and October, 1648.

During this time the inhabitants of Bohemia suffered terribly. Whilst from his vantage ground on the Kleinseite Königsmark was directing repeated attacks on the western portion of the city, his lieutenant, Koppi, was ravaging and plundering the country far and wide. The circles of Leitmeritz, Saaz, Schlau, and Bunzlau suffered terribly. Nor were these circles the only victims. The valuable library, known as the Rosenberg library, was transported from the Hradschin to Stockholm, where it still exists under the name of the Bohemian library.*

During the last days of July, the whole of August, and September, the occupants of the two sides of the city fought against each other with unremitting fury. On the 3rd October a new

---

* A few of the most cherished volumes, eight-and-forty in number, were recovered by the present Emperor, Franz Josef, and placed in the Brünn archives.

Swedish army, led **by Prince** Charles Gustavus, Duke of Zweibrücken, nephew **of the great** Gustavus and afterwards himself **King of Sweden, arrived to strengthen** Königsmark.

It was the news of the arrival of this reinforcement following the **defeat of the Austro-Spanish army at** Lens (20th August), which **decided Ferdinand III. to accept the best conditions of** peace then attainable. **He** forwarded instructions to this effect **to his** plenipotentiaries at Osnabrück and Münster, and the result **was** the signature, on the 24th October, of the treaty—at the **former** place with Sweden, at **the latter** with France—known **in history as the Peace of Westphalia, a peace** which remained **the basis of the general European concert until** the old order **of things was swept away by the mighty** wave of the French **Revolution.**

But meanwhile, whilst the articles of the Peace were still **being** debated, **the struggle between the** Swedes and the Imperialists **in** Prague **had continued with** unabated fury. It is **due, I think, to the memory of those who conducted a** defence unsurpassed in history **that the record of their daring** courage **should** be **continued up to the time when its** display was no longer needed.

The arrival **of Charles Gustavus** had given to the **Swedes an** overwhelming **superiority** in disciplined troops and in munitions **of war.** **That prince** hastened to use his advantage **to the** utmost. **On every spot of** ground which commanded the Altstadt **he erected** batteries. These poured forth their death-dealing **missiles** day and night into the city. **Yet, in spite of the** fire, **Don Juarez Conti, who** had charge **of the** defences, continued **to show a** bold front. He multiplied his earthworks, met mine **by countermine, distributed to** each officer **a district, or in** some instances even a **house,** for which he alone should be responsible. **To** the students, **placed** under the guidance of the Jesuit **Placky, and to** a **major of the** militia, John of Areizaga, he **committed the defence of** the banks of the Moldau. **Of the** priests and monks **of all** denominations, the Benedictines, the

Jesuits, the Carmelites, the Paulites, the **pupils, and the servants, he formed a** company, **two hundred** strong, which he **confided to the** charge **of Don** Florio **of Cremona, Provost of Zderaz, and of Rudolf Rhoder, Provost of Altbunzlau.** Of young men **of** noble **blood he formed a very strong troop of** cavalry. In this manner and **in** other similar **manners did the** Imperialist leaders **utilise the resources at their disposal.**

On the 5th October **Prince Charles Gustavus led the Swedes** across the Moldau, **and occupied the hill** then known as the Galgenberg. Königsmark took **up a** position on the Weinberg, whilst Wittenberg placed **his cavalry** behind the gate called **the Wyssehradthor,* his infantry on the** Weinberg, **opposite the gate known** as the Rossthor. **On** these positions **the Prince** planted his batteries, and **on the 6th opened fire.** After a cannonade which lasted all that day and the following night, he summoned **the city to surrender.** He received the following heroic **reply :** " Let the Prince come with his **people :** we are all ready to give him the **politest reception ! "**

The cannonade then continued. **On the third day the Prince** gave orders to storm **the gate known as the Galgenthor.** Obeying these orders, the **Swedes, in spite of** the most heroic resistance, mounted **the walls,** gained **a** position behind them, and mastered the Galgenthor **and a tower. Then was Conti's** opportunity. He fired a **mine which had been laid under the** tower, and having created **a panic by the explosion,** which **hurled into** the air about **a hundred Swedes, he came down** with fresh troops to complete **their** discomfiture. **This he did, and** recovered the lost gate. **Whilst he was** thus engaged, another party of the Imperialists had sallied from **the** Wyssehradthor and taken several prisoners.

Not disheartened **by** this **failure, the Swedes** renewed **the** fire the **next day, and** continued **it from five batteries** for two

---

* The Wyssehrad was a stronghold with **numerous towers,** then very much dilapidated, forming the southern extremity **of the city.** The Rossthor formed then the further extremity of the street **now known as the Wenzels-Platz.** The site of the gateway is now occupied by the **Bohemian National Museum.**

days and nights. The effect was very disastrous to the defenders. On the 13th October the Prince ordered **a general storm**. The gates known **as the Galgenthor, the** Rossthor, the Brückenthor, and the Wyssehradthor, **were, in** consequence, **simultaneously** attacked with great fury. But in spite of the courage of the assailants, of the fact that they were well supplied with **cannon,** whilst the defenders **had not one** single piece, the patriotism of the citizens prevailed, and **the** attack was beaten back at all points.

Once more did the Prince attempt negotiation. **On the 14th he summoned the** city to surrender, accompanying the summons **by a promise to treat with** consideration **all** the inhabitants. Again **was an** answer **similar to** that previously given returned. Enraged **at** this obstinacy, the **Prince** brought his batteries within pistol-shot of the **walls. In a few days** an enormous breach was effected.

On the 25th an attempt was made to storm **the** city by this breach. A select corps of **four** thousand men, supported by another of two thousand, formed **the** storming party. The advance of this party was covered by **a fire** from forty **guns. This time success** seemed assured. The stormers, after some hard fighting, **entered** the breach and, the defence suddenly collapsing, were **about to advance** in triumph, when suddenly Conti, **always on** the **alert,** fired **a mine.** The immediate effect of this desperate act was the destruction of five hundred Swedes, **blown into the** air; its almost immediate consequence the flight **of** the remainder. These did not recover from the panic until they had reached a spot well behind their reserves.

This was the last serious **attempt to** take the city. The heroic **defence of the** inhabitants had given them a **moral** superiority which completely dominated **the** assailants. The **prestige** was **now** on the **side** of the defenders, and, notwithstanding the **scorn with which sentimental** politicians have **tried to** overwhelm **that word,** it still counts for much in war. **If their** courage had required fortifying, and if the spirits of their assailants had needed still further to be depressed, both results would have been obtained from the knowledge of the fact that a relieving army, led by Feldzeugmeister Golz, was approaching.

It was well, perhaps, that that general did not arrive in time to take part in the contest. On the 3rd November messengers reached the head-quarters of both the hostile camps with the information that the war was at an end, that the Peace of Westphalia had been signed. After so many reverses sustained by the Imperialists, it was consolatory and fitting that the last warlike operation should have been a feat of arms never surpassed in the history of the world, which, for the firmness, the steadfastness, the heroism it displayed, for the triumph of resolution over numbers, deserves to rank with the achievements of Clive at Arkát, of Palafox and his heroic companions at Saragossa, of the immortal defenders of Lakhnau!*

At last the war was over! True it is that it had been a war of desolation; true it is that some of the parts of Germany which formed a constant marching and resting ground for the rival armies, notably Bohemia,† have not to this day entirely recovered from its effects; true it is that the sufferings of individuals were terrible; that culture and civilisation were thrown back; that crime received an impulse: and yet the result obtained was worth even those sacrifices. The battle of religion was so thoroughly fought out that thenceforward the Catholic

---

* I have been unable to find any English account of this siege of exactly a hundred days' duration. The account in the text is based mainly upon Austrian and Swedish records.

† A contemporary, Balbin, wrote of that kingdom "There was no town, no castle, no village even, in Bohemia, which, during this war, was not either completely wrecked (ausgeplündert) or burned, or laid in ashes." The Swedish general, Adam Pfuhl, boasted that he alone had burned eight hundred townships (Ortschaften). Balbin adds: "During the Thirty Years' War Bohemia was a prey alike to friends and foes. The only wonder is that any inhabitants remain in it." In his *History of Bohemia* Pelzel gives the following statistics. "Before the war the population of Bohemia consisted of three millions, inhabiting 738 towns and 34,700 villages. In 1648, the year of the conclusion of the war, the number of inhabited towns had sunk to 230; of villages to 6,000; of inhabitants to 780,000."

and Protestant could agree to live together in peace. The toleration obtained was not, indeed, absolute. It was of a kind which Gustavus and Ferdinand II. would have alike repudiated. It left remaining, indeed, as a guiding principle, the maxim, "*Cujus regio, ejus religio.*" But it took away from the Emperor of Germany the power of dictating to the consciences of the people of Saxony, of Hanover, of Brandenburg, and of parts of Germany other than those appertaining to the House of Habsburg. And with respect to all those other parts of Germany, it may be stated that the toleration secured was absolute. In them difference of religion ceased to be regarded in any other light than difference of opinion.

The bigotry which made of Ferdinand II. so strong a partisan in the war—though it did not cause it—incited his descendants to deny for many long years to their hereditary subjects the toleration which was enjoyed by the rest of Germany. Eighty years subsequently to the Thirty Years' War, 1729, the Emperor Charles VI. permitted the expatriation of a large number of industrious subjects merely because they professed the Protestant faith. Homes in North Germany were provided for these men by Frederick William of Prussia, father of Frederic II., and it is a fact that their descendants have, by their valour on many a battle-field, more than repaid to the House of Hohenzollern the hospitality denied to them by the House of Habsburg. But such strong measures were rare.

The Peace of Westphalia laid down definite rules which could not be evaded. It secured for Germany repose—a repose the more certain to endure because whilst it practically secured to every man the right to worship his Maker in the manner the most binding on his own conscience, it re-established the rule of law and order.

Politically the great gainer of the war was France. Lorraine and Alsace (Strasburg excepted) became permanently joined to her Monarchy. Sweden obtained a strong position on the Elbe and the Weser. Maximilian of Bavaria gained the Upper

Palatinate and with it the Electoral dignity. Brandenburg secured the first place, whilst Saxony descended to the second, in the Electorate. Of the three great Catholic Powers, Bavaria is the only one which permanently retained the fruits of her many exertions; and even Bavaria was forced, in 1779, to yield some portion of her territory to Austria!

CHAPTER VIII.

FEHRBELLIN.

TRADITION points to the **Swabian Count,** Thassilo of Zolre,* or Zollern, **as founder of the princely** house of Hohenzollern. Thassilo flourished about **the ninth century.** He built the castle **of** Zollern, and left, it **is** said, **four** sons, Denkmar, Eribald, Frederic, and Gottbold. **Of** these but little **is known.** We come first **upon their** descendants in the year 1064, **when** two Counts of Zollern, Burckhardt and Wezel of **Zolre, are returned** in **the record of those** killed in **one of the many battles which marked the minority of the Emperor Henry IV.** From the first **of** these **two descended Frederic I. of** Zolre (who died about 1120) ; from the second **Count** Adalbert **of Zolre. This** Adalbert was, about 1095, co-founder **of the** Monastery of Alpirsbach,† whilst **Frederic I. was its governor.** From **Adalbert descended the** collateral **line of** Hargieloch, which **was** extinguished **so early as** the twelfth century. **Of the six sons of** Frederic I. only two were founders of dynasties, **viz.** Frederic II., ancestor **of** the first Zollern Burgraves of Nuremberg ; and Burckhardt, **ancestor** of the **Zollern Counts** of Hohenberg, **whose** main line was, how-

---

* **The** castle of Zolre, or Zollern, is situated in the principality now known as the principality of Hoch-Hechingen. It rises about a mile **and** a quarter from Hechingen, on an elevation of two thousand eight hundred **and** forty feet, called the Zoderberg. The castle was destroyed in 1423, rebuilt in 1454, and again restored during the present century. It **became** Prussian in 1849.

† Alpirsbach is a town in the Black Forest **district, in the** valley of the Upper Kinzig, not far from the boundary of Baden. **The Benedictine** monastery, founded by Count Adalbert in **1095,** is still in good repair.

ever, extinguished in 1387, and its collateral line in 1486. Count Frederic III. of Zolre, son of Frederic II., was one of the trusted councillors of the Emperors Frederic I. and Henry VI. He is mentioned in the parchments of the time as being Burgrave of Nuremberg (11th July 1192). As such he assumed the title of Frederic I. Through his wife Sophia, heiress of Conrad, the last of the Burgraves of Nuremberg of the Austrian family of Rätz, he came into possession of the Franconian and Austrian freehold estates of that family. His two sons, Frederic II., who died in 1218, and Conrad I., who followed his brother twelve years later, were both alike designated Counts of Zolre and Burgraves of Nuremberg. According to the custom of those times, the two brothers administered their possessions in equal partnership; so much so that, when Frederic died, his son, of the same name, continued the administration on equal terms with his uncle. This lasted till 1226, when a division took place, Conrad taking the Nuremberg Burgraviate and the rich possessions more recently acquired; Frederic obtaining the old estates appertaining to the family of the Zollerns. This division of the family into Franconian and Swabian branches has descended unbroken to the present day. I propose in this paper to trace briefly the fortunes of the Franconian line up to the time of the decisive battles which established its claim to the regal rank.

Of the Franconian branch—in point of fact the younger—Conrad I. died in 1230, just after the division had been marked out. His son, Conrad II., is therefore historically regarded as its first representative. Conrad II. was one of the wisest and most influential men of his time. He administered his possessions with great care and prudence. From a fortune-marriage with Clementia, Countess of Habsburg, he had two sons, Frederic and Conrad. On his death in 1260 his possessions were divided between these two; Frederic, known as Frederic III., obtaining the Burgraviate, and Conrad, called Conrad III. "the pious," a portion of the Franconian estates, with the title of

Count of Abenberg. **Frederic married** Elisabeth, one of the heiresses of the freehold **possessions of the last** Count of Meran, **and on** the death **of the latter a** considerable portion of those possessions, including Baireuth, came **to his share.** From Rudolph of Habsburg, **to whose** election **to** the empire **he had powerfully** contributed, Frederic obtained an imperial investiture of a large number of lands and prerogatives, a portion of **which had** been purchased into the family **by** means of a wise **economy, the remainder by the product** of the very rich mines **in the territory of which Baireuth was** the capital. Frederic III. **was succeeded by his sons by his second marriage** with Helene, daughter **of Albert I. of Saxony—John I., who died** in 1299, **and** Frederic **IV., who survived his brother thirty-four** years. The last-named was **a very capable prince.** Following in the steps of his father, he acquired for his House several castles and **estates, and** purchased from the Count of Oettingen the city **of Ansbach.** He left (1332) four sons, of whom the **two elder, John, called the** second, and Conrad, called the fourth, succeeded **him** in joint possession. Conrad died **in 1334. The third son,** Frederic, having **entered** the Church,* the fourth, Albert, then **succeeded to the** joint inheritance with **John II.** The two brothers **could not, however, agree**; but, after **many** disputes, **they came, in 1341, to an** understanding noteworthy as constituting **the oldest family statute of the Zollerns.** John II. died in 1357, and **was succeeded in the joint** inheritance by his son **Frederic V., who, on the death of his** uncle, Albert IV., in 1361, became sole ruler. **Frederic** V. inherited all the acquisitive instincts **of his race.** His great **aim was to** round off the borders of his **territories by** filling up the gaps with fresh lands. His success in **this** policy procured **for him the title of "** The Conqueror." **The** height of his ambition **was attained when,** on the 15th April 1363, he was raised **by the** Emperor **Charles** IV. to **the rank** and dignity of a **Prince of** the Empire. Shortly before his death in 1397, **he abdicated, and made over** his possessions conjointly

* He was made Bishop of Ratisbon in 1341, and died in 1353.

to his two sons, John III. and Frederic VI. Five years later
(1403) these two princes agreed to a division of territory on the
principle that John should obtain the lands above the mountains and the principality of Baireuth; Frederic the lands below
the mountains and the principality of Ansbach. After the division had been made, both princes proceeded to enlarge their
borders in opposite directions. On the death of John, without
offspring, in 1410, the severed portions were re-united under the
rule of Frederic VI., and this prince shortly afterwards obtained
other steps on the ladder of greatness. In 1411 the Emperor
Sigismund bestowed upon him the possession in mortgage,* and
four years later the electoral hat of Brandenburg. Solemnly
invested, two years later, at the Council of Constance, with the
Electoral hat and the hereditary office of Lord High Chamberlain to the Emperor, the new Elector assumed the designation
of Frederic I. His eleventh successor in that dignity, the
Elector Frederic III., was the first King of Prussia, and as such
is known likewise to posterity as Frederic I.†

* The rescript is dated "Ofen, 8th July 1411." It appoints Frederick VI., of the
House of Hohenzollern, Burgrave of Nuremberg, to be "a fully-empowered general
administrator, and chiefest captain" (zu einem vollmächtigen gemeinen Verweser
und obristen Hauptmann), in the territories of Brandenburg, and endows him with
all the powers belonging to the Margraviate, the electoral dignity excepted. In the
same rescript Sigismund bound the Margrave of the day to spend one hundred
thousand golden gulden on the lands of the Margraviate, to enable him "to redeem
those lands from the warlike and destructive usage to which they had long been
subjected" (damit er diese aus solchem Kriegerischen und verderblichen Wesen,
darin sie lange Zeit beklagenswerthe Weise gelegen, desto besser bringen möge).
By this rescript, in fact, the lands of the Margraviate were really pledged to the
Burgrave—not in consideration of the loan which he made, under a different
arrangement, to Sigismund, but as a set-off for the money and trouble which he
engaged to devote for the restoration to a prosperous condition of those devastated
lands. By another rescript given at Constance (known then as Kostnitz) the 30th
April 1415, the Electoral hat of Brandenburg, and the hereditary office of Lord
High Chamberlain, with the reservation of redeeming them by purchase, were
bestowed upon the Burgrave; and on the 18th April, two years later, he was
solemnly invested, at the Council of Constance, with these dignities, without any
question being raised of the right of redemption by purchase. From that date
Frederic styled himself Frederic I., Elector of Brandenburg, and from it begins the
real rise and development of that Margraviate.

† It will be seen from the foregoing narrative that there were four Frederics I. in
the Franconian branch of the Zollerns: the first, Frederic I., Count of Zolre or

Nominated in 1411 to be "the fully-empowered administrator and chiefest captain" in Brandenburg, Frederic, then only Burgrave of Nuremberg, attempted to enter upon his duties the year following. But the rude nobles of the Margraviate received his pretensions with scorn, and, in reference to the even then world-wide trade of Nuremberg, mocked at him as the "Nuremberg toy." But Frederic soon proved to them that, granting the correctness of the nickname, the toy was worthy of the high reputation of the city whence it came. One by one he subdued the opposition of the nobles, and forced them at length (1414) to recognise the validity of the laws which he imposed to ensure the tranquillity of the country. It is to him, and his son and successor, Frederic II., that the Margraviate of Brandenburg is indebted for the first glimpses of returning prosperity. The rule of the second was but a continuation, in all respects, of the rule of the first. It extended, in the person of the first Elector, from 1411 to 1440, and in that of his son to 1471. The internal policy of that period of sixty years may be condensed in a few words. After the establishment of internal tranquillity, accomplished in 1414, every effort was made to repair the havoc which the extravagance of previous rulers had made, to re-people the districts which had been depopulated, to restore the industries which had been destroyed. Whilst, then, the two princes extended in succession the borders of the Margraviate by re-uniting to it the greater part of the northern portion of its ancient limits, known as the Ukermark,* which, in the time of trouble, had been secured first by the Dukes of Mecklenburg, and then by the Dukes of Pomerania;—whilst they took, likewise, from the former, seven districts of Priegnitz—the debatable land between

Zollern, who died about 1120; the second, **Frederic I.**, Burgrave of Nuremberg; the third, Frederic I., Elector of Brandenburg; and the fourth, Frederic I., King of Prussia.

* **The** Ukermark, the northernmost division of **the** Margraviate Brandenburg, is bordered on the south by Mid-Brandenburg; on the west partly by the same, partly by Mecklenburg-Strelitz; on the north and east by Pomerania and the Neumark. It is indicated now by the districts Prenzlau, Templin, and Augermünde, in the division of Potsdam.

Brandenburg on one side,* and Hanover, Mecklenburg, and Magdeburg on the other (1442); whilst, two years later, they secured, first as a pledge from the knights of the Teutonic Order, and a year later by purchase, Neumark, the long narrow strip of land watered by the Oder and the Warthe, and bounded on the north by Pomerania, on the east by Prussia and Poland, on the west by Ukermark, and on the south by Silesia and the Lower Lausitz, and which contains the important towns of Cüstrin, Soldin, and Königsberg; they planned likewise—with the view to bring new strength and blood and capital to the exhausted districts of Brandenburg proper—and partly carried out, a large scheme of emigration from Anhalt, the sober, steady, and persevering character of the people of which country—and who were known as the Askanier—promised much for the objects they had in view. Nor did their expectations remain unfulfilled. Brandenburg owes much of the prosperity it now enjoys to the infusion of the pure German blood of the Askanier.

It is not to be supposed that all these measures of aggrandisement were favourably regarded by the sometimes jealous, sometimes suspicious, eyes of the emperors of the period. Albert II., son and successor of Sigismund, compelled the second Frederic to restore all that he had taken from the Lausitz—the small districts of Lübben and Kottbus excepted. Similarly he forced him to renounce his designs upon Pomeranian Stettin. But, for all that, the two first Electors accomplished great things. They implanted law and order, introduced a system of equal justice between man and man; restored industry; re-populated, by the introduction of an outside German race, whole districts; made themselves respected within and without; and recovered for the Margraviate more than its ancient borders. These were the material results of the transfer to Brandenburg of the "Nuremberg toy"—the outcome of sixty years of well-directed energy on the part of two energetic members of the noble house

* These were Perleberg, Pritzwalk, Witlstock, Kyritz, Havelberg, Lenzen, and Plattenburg. Priegnitz is called also Vormark.

of Zollern. No one will deny that, regard being especially had to the century in which it was accomplished, it is a great record.

Albert Achilles, the successor of Frederic II. (1471), did not inherit the great qualities of his two illustrious predecessors. To the interests of the Margraviate he devoted little attention. Circumstances, however, forced him to action, and he then showed that the spirit of the race, if it lay dormant, was still strong within him. The Dukes of Pomerania had thought the occasion opportune to recover some of the territory which the two Frederics had forced them to relinquish. But Albert Achilles met them in the field, beat them, and forced them to acknowledge (1479) the feudal supremacy (Lehns-oberhoheit) of Brandenburg. The claim to that supremacy was, however, renounced (1493) by his son, John—who had succeeded his father in 1486—in favour of a compact whereby, under certain circumstances, the succession to Pomerania should devolve upon the Zollerns, or, as they came to be called, the Hohenzollerns. In other respects the reign of John was uneventful. His son and successor (1499), Joachim I., was a strong, in many respects a great, man. During his rule of nearly thirty-six years the great schism between the Church of Rome and her followers, of which Luther was the leader and the exponent, took place in Germany. A Catholic by conviction, Joachim detected in the movement the germs of that general revolt against supreme authority which broke out a century later and was the main cause of the Thirty Years' War. Loyal to the core to the Empire and the Emperor, he declared war against a creed which to him was not only a pestilential heresy but a canker-worm gnawing the base of the edifice of authority. He suppressed, then, as far as he could, all manifestations in favour of the new religion, and denounced conformity as a political crime. Not even to his own wife, Elisabeth of Denmark, who had embraced the faith of Luther, would he allow the practice which he sternly refused to others. And when she, strong in her faith, persisted, he proceeded to acts of violence which forced her to flee for refuge into Saxony.

In these proceedings he showed himself, rightly or wrongly, a strong man; in others he was really great. He put down, at once and for ever, the high-handed practices in which his nobility had been in the habit of indulging, and compelled them to respect the law; he founded (1506) an university at Frankfort on the Oder, and established at Berlin (1516) a supreme court of judicature. If he was stern and unbending, he was, according to his convictions, just to all, and during his reign Brandenburg made a remarkable advance in prosperity and power.

In one respect Joachim I. displayed a weakness in favour of his own family, when its interests came in contact with those of the country over which he ruled. The male line of Schleswig-Holstein died out, and his wife became heiress to that duchy. As well by the existing family law, laid down by his grandfather, Albert Achilles, known as *dispositio Achilles*, as by the Golden Bull of the Emperor Charles IV.,* the Elector of Brandenburg possessed the right, under such circumstances, to add that duchy to the actual territories of his House. But Joachim had two sons, and he could not resist the temptation to provide for the younger. In spite, then, of the law, he deliberately severed the Neumark† from the Electoral lands and transferred them to his second son, Hans of Cüstrin.

Joachim I. died in 1535. His sons, Joachim II. and Hans, embraced the Reformed religion; but whilst the former adhered very zealously to the League of Smalcald, and introduced the new faith into the Neumark, Joachim, in his reverence for and desire to live in good understanding with the Emperor, held aloof from the League. Not the less, however, did he promote the spread of the doctrines of Luther in his own dominions, and even introduced them into Courland. In other respects the

---

* Issued at the Diet of Nuremberg, 1356. Its provisions constituted the fundamental law of the German Empire.

† *Vide* page 231.

Electoral House of Hohenzollern greatly prospered during his reign. It might be said, indeed, that the foundation-stone of its future greatness was laid. In the first place, he made a family compact with Frederic II., Duke of Liegnitz, in virtue of which, on the default of heirs male in that family, the principalities of Liegnitz, Brieg, and Wohlau were to devolve upon the representative of the Hohenzollerns*; in the second, the Imperial Diet assembled at Petrikau (1563) guaranteed to the Brandenburg Hohenzollerns the reversion of the duchy of Prussia in the event of the extinction of the then ruling family of Brandenburg—Quolzbach (Ansbach).

These dispositions promised well for the future, and Joachim II., on the eve of being gathered to his fathers in 1571, must have felt that he had laid a secure foundation of greatness that would come. Under his successor, John George, the young state made a considerable stride forward. That prince, bent on the development of his country and the extension of his dominions, reunited under the Electoral sway the severed provinces of the Neumark and Courland, and, suppressing the three bishoprics of Brandenburg, Havelberg, and Lebus, annexed the lands attaching to them. He maintained, at the same time, the claims of his son to the archbishopric of Magdeburg, a see which, since 1513, had been ever occupied by a member of the House of Brandenburg. Above all, he pushed the claims of his House to the Duchy of Prussia, and to the duchies of Cleve, Julich, and Berg, the former secured to it, as I have shown, by the resolutions of the Diet of Petrikau—the reigning Duke, Albert Frederic, having no male heir; the latter, by the marriage of his grandson, John Sigismund, with Anna, only daughter of Eleonora,†

---

* The Piast family of the Dukes of Liegnitz died out in 1675. The compact referred to constituted the basis of the claim preferred to Silesia by Frederic II. of Prussia in 1741.

† Eleonora of Cleve was the sister of the last Duke of Jülich. Her only child, Anne, was, therefore, the heiress of the duchy of Prussia, and of the Jülich duchies, comprising the duchies of Jülich, Cleve, and Berg, and the counties Mark, Ravensberg, and Ravenstein. As stated in the text, Anne had married John Sigismund, grandson of the then ruling Elector of Brandenburg.

wife of Albert Frederic, and sole heiress to those duchies. Death overtook John George (1598) before the claim upon these duchies had become due, but the same end was pursued with even more vigour by his son and successor, Joachim Frederic. This prince caused the investiture over Prussia to be renewed, and endeavoured by all means to win the suffrages of the nobles in the three duchies. Besides this, he confirmed with his cousins the family compact made by their common ancestor, Albert Achilles (1603), and the year following he established the College of the Privy Council, as standing chief guardian of the fundamental rights of the family. He died (1608) before the occurrence of the event which would have gratified all his aspirations. His son, however, John Sigismund, husband of the heiress Anne, made good his claims (1614), after some hard fighting, to the possession of the three duchies, and, four years later, became, by the death of his father-in-law, ruler, under the overlordship of Poland, of the Duchy of Prussia. It will, I think, be convenient if I pause here to take a retrospective glance at the history of that duchy, from the period when it was first known to the time when it came, in the manner already shown, under the sway of the Hohenzollerns.

The lands on the shores of the Baltic, which afterwards constituted the kingdom of Prussia, are said to have been made known to the ancients by the famous Greek traveller Pytheas,* about three hundred and twenty years before Christ. Pytheas calls the lands washed by the Baltic "Mentenomon," their inhabitants Goths, and the neighbours of their inhabitants Teutons. In the course of time, the place of many of the adventurous Goths who had quitted these lands in search of other pastures was taken by Slavs, and these mingled with the Goths who had remained. The country west of the Weichsel—that part of the present West Prussia formerly known as Pomerellen,†—

---

* *Ueber Pytheas* von *Massilien*, W. Bessel. Gottingen, 1858.

† Pomerellen (Pomerania parva) was formed of the strip of West Prussia which lies between the left bank of the Weichsel, Pomerania, the grand duchy of Posen, and the Baltic. Its principal towns were Schwetz, Konitz, Stargard, and Dirschau.

was occupied by the Pomeranians; but the lands to the east of that river had fallen to a branch of the mixed race I have referred to, and who, towards the close of the tenth century, began to be known as Borussi—thence Porussi and Prussi. The religion of these people was substantially a worship of Nature, their chief divinity being Perkunos, the god of light. Their solemn feasts were held at the change of the seasons. Forests and lakes were specially dedicated to the divinities. No other people of Slav origin held with such tenacity to the old faiths as did the Prussians. Traces of heathen customs and forms of worship were to be seen in the habits of the people even so late as the beginning of the seventeenth century. The first attempts at their conversion, undertaken in the tenth century by Adalbert of Prague and Bruno of Magdeburg, were baffled by the savageness of the people. The breast of Adalbert was pierced to the death by a javelin cast by a heathen priest near Culm (997); Bruno, and eighteen of his followers, fell victims to an infuriated mob on the 14th February 1009. Up to this period the Prussi, or Prussians, had maintained their wild independence. Their priests, who exercised likewise the offices of judge and law-giver, had not been slow to point out to them that the abandonment of their old faith would be a sure precursor to the loss of the personal liberty which they enjoyed. They had not prepared them for the contrary process. It was that process, however, which prevailed. Six years after the death of Bruno, the Polish duke, Boleslaw Chobri, assumed an overlordship over East Prussia. For a long series of years this overlordship remained nominal, every attempt at subjection or conversion being fiercely repulsed. After the lapse of nearly a century and a half, his successor at a long interval, Boleslaw IV., succeeded indeed in procuring the absolute submission of the inhabitants of a small tract, but in attempting to push his conquests further he and his entire army were destroyed (1161). His successor, Casimir II., was for the moment more successful. During his reign of twenty-one years (1173–94) he managed to reduce the Prussians to obedience. But the success was only temporary. On his death the Prussians not only **threw** off **the** yoke, but, attacking in their turn the Polish possessions of Casimir's **son Conrad,** forced **its** inhabitants to **pay** them tribute!

Meanwhile, Christianity had **been introduced into the lands** west of the Weichsel. From these a **Bernardine monk named** Christian, a Pomeranian by birth, set **forth at the beginning of** the thirteenth century **to convert** his brethren in the **eastern** tracts. His efforts were crowned with **success;** many **of the** most influential of **the** Prussian population were **baptised, and** the commoner people **followed their** example. In **consideration** of these great services Pope Innocent III. nominated Christian first Bishop of Prussia **(1214).** Soon after, however, a reaction set in, the converts returned to their old faith; and their conduct, and that of the people generally, forced upon Christian the conviction that force—that is, the sword—was the only remedy. With the sanction of the Pope, then, he organised a crusade against the Prussians. The campaign opened. The Prussians offered but little opposition to the disciplined forces sent against them. **Their** appearance **of submission** seemed, then, to justify the withdrawal, after a three years' occupation, of the crusaders. No sooner, however, had they left the country than the Prussians rose **to a man (1222), re-asserted** their independence, and resumed their old habits!

Baffled in his first remedy of **force,** the **Prussian Bishop** attempted now a second. Taking example from a **measure of** the same kind which had been tried successfully **in** Livonia, **he** founded (1225) an association of " Knights of Christ," called also—from the castle Dobrin, on the other side of **the** Kulmer**land,** which had been assigned them as a residence—the Order of the Knight Brothers of Dobrin. These he **sent** forth on a **new crusade. But they were, even** at the **outset, less** successful than their predecessors. **Joining Duke Conrad, they** entered East Prussia, but were attacked, defeated, and **nearly entirely** destroyed (1225) by the warlike inhabitants at Strassburg* (on the Drewenz). Not content with their victory, the Prussian hordes spread over all the lands watered by the Weichsel, poured into Pomerellen, took Danzig, and destroyed the Cistercian monastery at Oliva. In terror at their devastations, Christian and Duke Conrad implored the German Order of Chivalry to come to their aid. Conrad was forced to add to his supplications substantial gifts, and it was only by the cession of the territories represented by Culm and Löbau that he induced the Grand Master of the Order, Hermann of Salza, to despatch a small number of knights to his assistance (1228). At their head came the gallant Hermann Balk. For the first year or two they avoided contact with the enemy, preferring to repair destroyed castles and to build others.† Gradually their number increased to a hundred, but it was not till the year 1233 that they ventured upon decisive operations against the enemy.

In that year the tide turned in their favour. Wearing a black cross on their white mantles, and aided by volunteers, knights, and warriors from all parts of Northern Germany, they gained a great battle on the Sirguna. This first success was the prelude to many others. The opposition, however, was fierce and resolute. The war lasted exactly fifty years, nor was it till 1283 that East Prussia was completely conquered and its people were subdued! By means of German colonists, who flocked to the conquered territory from all parts of the empire, especially from the lands watered by the Lower Rhine, a German character was gradually impressed upon it. To the peasantry was secured free administration of their communities; to the inhabitants of the town fixed privileges. Whilst the war was still progressing the victors had founded the city of Königsberg, in eternal memory of the conquest, after a hard-fought contest, of the district still known as the Samland,‡ under the splendid leading of Ottokar,

---

* Strassburg lies forty miles south-east of Marienwerder.

† They repaired Culm, and built castles at Thorn, Marienwerder, and Elbing.

‡ The Samland is the territory bounded on the north by the Kurishe-Haff—a lagoon or backwater of the Baltic—and the Baltic; on the east by the Deime; on

King of Bohemia. Bishop Christian, who may be considered the author of the war, died before it had been decided (1243). After the subjection of Prussia, the Knights turned their attention to Lithuania, and aided Margrave Waldemar of Brandenburg in the conquest of Pomerania, which then became his by purchase (1309).

The part which the German orders of chivalry had taken in the subjection of Prussia and the adjoining territories gave them naturally very great influence. Under their protection the towns and cities waxed rich, formed guilds, and became great centres of trade. But after a time the discipline of the knights relaxed. With that relaxation the sympathetic relations which had existed between them and the great towns gradually disappeared. The Knights had failed, after a war which lasted a century, to conquer Lithuania. In 1386 that province had been united to Poland, and, the war still continuing, the Knights suffered at Tannenberg a defeat (1410) so decisive as to compel them to accept at Thorn a peace (1411) in which they renounced their long-contested pretensions. From that moment their downfall became a question of time. The great towns of Prussia combined with the Poles to effect their overthrow. Gradually their fortunes decayed, and in a second Peace of Thorn (1466) they were compelled to assign to Poland, in complete sovereignty, the territories west of the Weichsel, and to accept for the eastern portion the overlordship (Lehns-oberhoheit) of the sovereign of that kingdom. The separation of East from West Prussia was a consequence of this treaty.

A period followed marked by the rule of weak Grandmasters who lived upon the recollections of the past, without attempting to remedy the actual present. At length it dawned upon the ruling minds of the community that deliverance from foreign yoke could only be attained by drawing closer the ties which

the south by the Frische-Haff—a fresh-water sea separated from the Baltic by a tongue of land—and the Pregel. The whole forms a right-angled parallelogram, divided into two by a line running from Königsberg to Crantz.

bound the Order to the German Empire. In 1511 the Order had elected as Grandmaster Margrave Albert of Brandenburg—Quolzbach (Ansbach)—grandson of the Elector Albert Achilles, to whom reference has already been made.* Trusting to the aid promised him by the Emperor, the new Grandmaster refused to take the oath of overlordship to the King of Poland. That sovereign asserted and sustained his rights by force of arms. The promised help never came to Albert. To obtain it, the latter, after many defeats, proceeded to Germany to seek it in person. When it was even then denied him, he came to a heroic resolution. Already, in 1523, Luther had exhorted the German Orders of Chivalry to renounce the vow which forbade them to marry. To Wittenberg, then, the Grandmaster Albert made his way, saw the great Reformer, and was advised by him to marry and to form Prussia into a hereditary principality. The Grandmaster consented, and, that nothing might be wanting to the success of the project, Poland agreed to cede Prussia to him as a hereditary principality on the condition of his acknowledging her King as his feudal sovereign. The delight with which this arrangement was accepted in Prussia was the main cause of the easy and rapid spread of the Reformed doctrines in that country.

Duke Albert left one child, Albert Frederic. He, however, died, without male issue, in 1618. To provide for the succession the Imperial Diet at Petrikau had arranged (1563) that in the event of the failure of the line of which he was the sole representative, Poland should agree to the reversion to the Electoral House of Brandenburg of the duchy over which he ruled. On the death, then, of Albert Frederic in 1618, the duchy of Prussia at once came into possession of the Hohenzollerns, represented at the time by the Elector John Sigismund. At this point I resume the thread of the story of the Hohenzollerns, which I had laid down to sketch the antecedents of the province thus

* Page 232.

devolving upon them, and which was to give its name and character to their increasing dominions.

John Sigismund did not long enjoy his new dignities. Very severe illness forced him to abdicate the following year (December 1619), and he died shortly afterwards. His son, George William, possessed neither the intellect nor the disposition necessary to enable a man to guide the destinies of a young country in very difficult times. The Thirty Years' War had just broken out. A foreign invader, professing to secure the religious rights of the German people, was landing in Pomerania, whilst, on the other side, the Emperor Ferdinand II. was taking measures to oppose with all the steadfastness of his nature a cause which he considered to be indissolubly allied with anarchy and revolution. At the outset, George William seemed inclined to cast in his lot with the Reformers. Falling, however, under the influence of his minister, Adam of Schwarzenberg, a Catholic in religion and an Austrian in politics, he drew back at the critical moment, and showed unmistakable leanings to his feudal lord. His covert hostility towards Gustavus Adolphus caused the terrible sacking of Magdeburg; and if, for a moment before the battle of Breitenfeld (Leipzig), he came to terms with the Swedish invader, the apparent friendliness was of a very transitory character. When, after Lützen, the fortunes of the Reformers seemed to be on the wane, the Elector of Saxony signed a separate peace with the Emperor (1635), and George William followed his example. The consequence was that Brandenburg, which had been before devastated by the Imperialists, now suffered terribly from the exactions of the Swedes. It was still so suffering when George William died (1640).

His son, Frederic William, known in history as the Great Elector, was only twenty years old when he succeeded his father. He found everything in disorder: his country desolate, his fortresses garrisoned by troops under a solemn order to obey only the mandates of the Emperor, his army to be counted

16

almost on the fingers. His first care was to conclude a truce with the Swedes; his second to secure his western borders by an alliance with Holland; his third—not in order of action, for in that respect it took first place—to raise the nucleus of an army; his fourth, to cause the evacuation of his fortresses. During the first year of his rule he raised a solid, well-trained force of three thousand men, and induced the commanders of the garrisons to quit the fortresses they held. To allay the wrath of the Emperor, he temporised until his armed force had attained the number of eight thousand. That force once under arms, he boldly asserted his position, and with so much effect that in the discussions preceding the Peace of Westphalia he could exercise a considerable influence. By the terms of that treaty, the part of Pomerania known as Hinter Pommern, the principalities of Magdeburg and Halberstadt, and the bishoprics of Minden and Kammin were ceded to Brandenburg. Frederic William tried hard to obtain the other part of Pomerania (Vor Pommern) as opening to him the coast of the Baltic, but in this he failed.

The Peace once signed, Frederic William set diligently to work to heal the disorders and to repair the mischief which the long war had caused in his dominions. To the development of trade and commerce, to the encouragement of agriculture, he contributed so largely by his measures, that during his reign, subsequent to the war, of forty years, the income of the State more than quadrupled itself. Nor did unwise parsimony contribute in the slightest degree to this end. He specially cherished his army. We have seen its small beginning in 1640–42. Fifteen years later, in 1655, or seven years after the conclusion of the Peace of Westphalia, it amounted to twenty-five thousand men, well drilled and well disciplined, disposing of seventy-two pieces of cannon.

In the times in which he lived he had need of such an army. In 1654, Christina, the wayward and gifted daughter of Gustavus Adolphus, had abdicated. Her successor on the throne of

Sweden was her cousin, Charles Gustavus, Duke of Zweibrücken, the same whom we have seen vainly endeavouring to triumph over the persistent gallantry of the citizens of Prague.* The right of Charles Gustavus to the succession was, however, contested by John Casimir, King of Poland. Vainly did the great Elector use all his efforts to induce both parties to agree to an accommodation. Those were the days—and they have not yet entirely died out—when possession was to the warrior who could most effectually wield the sword. War ensued. In that war the star of Charles Gustavus was in the ascendant, and the unfortunate John Casimir was forced to abandon his own dominions and to flee into Silesia. The vicinity of the two rivals to his own outlying territories was, however, too near not to render anxious Frederic William of Brandenburg. To protect Prussia, then held in fief from the King of Poland, he marched with eight thousand men to its borders. But even with such a force he was unable, or perhaps, more correctly, he was prudently unwilling, to resist the insistance put upon him at Königsberg by the victorious King of Sweden (1656) to transfer to him the feudal overlordship of that province. Great results followed from this compliance. Hardly had the treaty been signed, when John Casimir, returning from Silesia with an Imperial army at his back, drove the Swedes from Poland, and recovered his dominions. He did not evidently intend to stop there. Then it was that the opportunity arrived to the Great Elector. Earnestly solicited by the King of Sweden to aid him in a contest which had assumed dimensions so formidable, Frederic William consented, but only on the condition that he should receive the Polish palatinates (*Woiwodshaften*) of Posen and Kalisch as the price of a victorious campaign. He then joined the King with his army, met the enemy at Warsaw, fought with him close to that city a great battle, which lasted three days (28th to 30th July 1656), and which terminated then, thanks mainly to the pertinacity of the Brandenburgers—

* *Vide* page 220.

in the comple defeat of the Poles. The victory gained, Frederic William withdrew his troops. He declined, on grounds of policy, to aid further in a course which would have resulted in greatly adding to the strength of a neighbour already sufficiently powerful. His withdrawal, in almost bringing the King of Sweden to destruction, was soon to give him an evidence of his own power, and of the direction in which it might be most advantageously employed. Again did John Casimir recover from his defeat; again, aided by the Imperialists, did he march to the front, reoccupy Warsaw, and take up a threatening position opposite to the Swedish camp. The King of Sweden beheld in this action on the part of his enemy the prelude to his own certain destruction, unless by any means he could induce the Elector of Brandenburg once more to save him. He sent, then, urgent messengers after him to beg him to return. The messengers found Frederic William at Labian.* There the Elector halted, and there, joined the next day, 20th November 1656, by King Charles Gustavus, he signed a treaty, by which, on condition of his material aid in the war, the latter renounced his feudal overlordship over Prussia, and agreed to acknowledge the Elector and his male descendants as sovereign dukes of that province. In the war which followed, the enemies of Sweden and Brandenburg multiplied on every side. The Danes and Lithuanians espoused the cause of John Casimir. Its issue seemed to Frederic William more than doubtful. He asked himself, then, whether—the new enemies who had arisen being the enemies of Sweden and not of himself—he had not more to gain by sharing in the victories of the Poles than in the defeats of the Swedes. Replying to himself affirmatively, he concluded, 29th September 1657, through the intermediation of the Emperor, with the Poles, at Wehlau,† a treaty whereby the dukedom of Prussia was ceded in absolute sovereignty

---

* A town on the Deime, twenty-five miles to the north-east of Königsberg.

† A town at the confluence of the Alle and Pregel, twenty-eight miles east of Königsberg.

to the Elector of Brandenburg and his male issue, with reversion to Poland in case of the extinction of the family of the Franconian Hohenzollerns; in return, Frederic William engaged himself to support the Poles in their war against Sweden with a corps of four thousand men.

But before this convention could be acted upon, fortune had again smiled upon Charles Gustavus. Turning in the height of winter against the Danes, the King of Sweden had defeated them in the open field, pursued them across the frozen waters of the Belt to Fünen and Seeland, and had imposed upon their king the humiliating peace of Roeskilde (1658). He seemed inclined to proceed still further in the destruction of the ancient rival of his country, when a combined army of Poles and Brandenburgers suddenly poured through Mecklenburg into Holstein, drove thence the Swedes, and gave them no rest till they had evacuated likewise Schleswig and Jutland (1659). In a battle which took place shortly afterwards on the island of Fünen, at Nyborg, the Swedes suffered a defeat. This defeat made Charles Gustavus despair of success, and he had already begun to treat for peace, when death snatched him from the scene (January 1660). The negotiations which had begun, however, continued, and finally peace was signed on the 1st May 1660, in the monastery of Oliva, close to Danzig. This peace confirmed to the Elector of Brandenburg his sovereign rights over the duchy of Prussia. From this epoch dates the complete union of Brandenburg and Prussia—a union upon which a great man was able to lay the foundation of a powerful North German kingdom!

Frederic William possessed something more than a dim consciousness of the future in store for his country. To him, he felt, was assigned the task of preparing the way to greatness, of making the country over which he ruled thoroughly ready to make the next spring forward. How he had effected this in the past; how, from the crushed population in 1640-2, he had gradually formed an army, and how, by means of that army, he had rid himself of an overlordship which had fettered his ancestors and would equally have paralysed himself, has been told. But now, though the army was still to do much, there were internal reforms to be effected—grievances crying for removal, and which would have to be removed before the position of the Hohenzollerns, as rulers, would be secure.

The first of the evils which he felt must be repressed was the exorbitant power of the nobles, especially in the duchy of Prussia. Frederic William did not act until all his measures were ready. Then, and then only, he took the first step; he imposed a tax which particularly affected the well-born and wealthy. The nobles and the great commercial houses, ever up to that time exempted from all taxation, banded together to resist the new impost, refused to take the oath of fealty, and appealed for support to their ancient feudal lord, the King of Poland. Two men showed themselves specially active in fomenting this agitation: the one, Roth, chief magistrate of Königsberg, the representative of the city guilds; the other, Colonel von Kalkstein, acting on behalf of the nobility. Frederic William, seeing the necessity of strong measures, caused these two men to be seized and cast into prison. He then forced the recusants (1663) to take the oath of fealty. But his troubles in this respect were not yet over. Roth died in captivity; Kalkstein, on the submission of the Orders, had been released. Instead of recognising the inevitable, this turbulent spirit crossed the border into Poland, and appealed to the Diet of Warsaw to resume its ancient overlordship over the duchy. In vain did Frederic William demand his expulsion. Resolved, however, to terminate an incident which caused an open sore to rankle in the heart of his own dominions, he contrived a crafty scheme to seize the inciter to rebellion. Succeeding in his purpose, he hurried him off to Memel, and there had him beheaded (1671) as a warning to others. From that moment the authority of the Hohenzollerns to tax all classes alike was unquestioned.

Hardly had Frederic William thus made himself **master in his own** dominions, when his attention was called to foreign affairs. In 1672 Louis XIV., more than ever desirous to incorporate the Netherlands in his own dominions, declared war with Holland. Never had his chances of success seemed so certain; for not only had he England, then ruled by Charles II., as an ally, but he had made a pact with the Emperor Leopold, whereby that prince engaged not to act seriously against him, although as head of the Empire he could not help sending an Imperial corps to guard the Rhenish provinces against invasion. In addition, the French King had subsidised Sweden, and bound its King to attack Brandenburg **in case its Elector should make** any active demonstration **against France.**

When the war broke out, Frederic William **had marched with** his contingent **to join the confederated army of the Empire, commanded by Montecucculi, on the Upper Rhine.** Montecucculi had secret instructions **to avoid all** occasion for **a contest** with France, **to make merely** a military promenade. In obedience to these **instructions he spent the entire season in** marching and counter-marching, **always taking care to avoid the direction in which the enemy were to be found.** Meanwhile the French, under Turenne, **had invaded Westphalia.** Tired of the purposeless marches of Montecucculi, and penetrating his designs, Frederic William insisted that the **German army should march against Turenne.** Montecucculi **not only complied, but so** arranged, that in the first skirmishes which **took place when the two armies arrived within striking** distance **of each other the Germans should have all the** advantage. The Elector of Brandenburg pressed Montecucculi **to follow up these advantages, and for** some time the expectation prevailed **that** a great battle **would decide the** campaign. But Turenne and Montecucculi understood each other thoroughly. **The days passed in empty** manœuvring. **The Elector** felt **that** he was **beaten without** having fought ("**ohne** Schlacht **geschlagen**"). **The only consolation** he had was **that a considerable French army, which** would have decided the campaign in the Netherlands, was kept for a time inactive in Westphalia. Weary at length of thus playing at soldiers, and unable, unsupported, to make head against France, Frederic William signed, very unwillingly, with France, the Treaty of Vossem, whereby, in consideration of the complete evacuation by the latter of the duchy of Cleve and its fortresses, he renounced his alliance with Holland (16th June 1673).

Frederic William signed the Treaty of Vossem under very hard compulsion. It went sorely against every feeling of his heart, every inner conviction, against his sympathies, to agree to its terms. He signed it with the determination to break it on the first convenient opportunity. To the States-General he excused himself by pointing to the difficulties of his own position, the soft-heartedness of his allies, and by assuring them that when the opportunity should arise he would not hold back.

That opportunity came more quickly than even he had expected. The Emperor Leopold had become at last alive to the danger of allowing free course to the ambition of Louis XIV. He appealed to Frederic William to come forward once more to the defence of the Fatherland. Vainly did Louis try by promises and blandishments to induce the Elector of Brandenburg to agree to remain neutral. On the 1st July 1674, the Elector signed with the Emperor, Spain, and the Netherlands a convention which was virtually a declaration of war against France. In the October following, at the head of twenty thousand well-armed and well-disciplined troops, he marched to Strasbourg and joined the Imperial army in Alsace.

The commander of the Imperialists was Bournonville, a man unfit to command under any circumstances, still less to make head against so perfect a master of the art of war as was Turenne. Bournonville had, however, for a long time the advantage in numbers. But he did not utilise them. The campaign is considered as Turenne's masterpiece. He out-manœuvred the Imperial army; then beat it near Mulhausen (29th December);

again at Türckheim (5th January 1675); and by the 11th had driven it entirely out of Alsace. "There is no longer any enemy in Alsace," he wrote, "except the prisoners I have taken!"

To Frederic William the campaign was full of disappointment and disaster. For its untoward result he blamed the Imperial commander. His incapacity he had detected long before the catastrophe arrived. But another misfortune had touched him even more nearly than the loss of Alsace. His eldest son, Charles Emilius, one of the most promising princes of the age, had been carried off at Strasbourg by fever during the campaign. He was still suffering under the deep affliction caused him by this loss, when information reached him (14th January) that the Swedes had invaded his dominions!

It was too true. The reader will recollect that, to hinder the co-operation of the princes of North Germany in the defence of the Fatherland, Louis XIV. had, by the promise of an annual subsidy,* bound the King of Sweden to attack any German Power which should ally itself with the Dutch. Brandenburg was naturally indicated in this contract; and now that the Elector was far away in Alsace, his troops severely handled by Turenne, the French King called upon Sweden to carry it out. It is due to the councillors of Charles XI., King of Sweden—who, the son and successor of the Charles Augustus whom we have already met, had but little more than two years before (December 1672) terminated his minority—to state that he very unwillingly complied. But the King of France insisted; Charles himself was young and weak; finally, then, in the month of January 1675, General Wrangel led a Swedish army, twenty thousand strong, and invaded the dominions of the Elector.

The cautious proceedings of the invaders at the outset seemed to indicate that their main object was, by a diversion, to force the Elector to withdraw his troops from the army of the Empire. Soon, however, the love of gain, the sight of a defenceless

* This subsidy was to amount to six hundred thousand thalers, equivalent to ninety thousand pounds sterling.

country, changed their design. Throwing aside their caution, the Swedes marched boldly forward, plundering and burning as they advanced, until, in the month of May, they entered Havelland,* the granary of Berlin, and carried their devastations up to the very gates of that capital. Whilst they occupied the line of the Havel from Havelberg to Brandenburg, they maintained their communications with Pomerania by occupying the bridge over the little river Rhin covering the passes of Fehrbellin, of Cremmen, and of Oranienburg. Wrangel intended to concentrate his troops and, crossing the Elbe, to press forward into the Altmark, there to effect a junction with the Duke of Hanover, who only wanted a pretext to declare in favour of the French. His preparations for that purpose had nearly been completed at the middle of June; the only point still remaining to be accomplished was the concentration of the army. It was still spread in a long line along the Havel, occupying as main points Havelberg, Rathenow, and Brandenburg. In point of fact, Wrangel felt himself perfectly assured against an attack. He believed the Elector and his army to be either in Franconia—where he had taken winter quarters—or on his march thence to the Rhine.

Wrangel was still living in the paradise of fools, when suddenly information was brought to him that the centre of his line —Rathenow—had been pierced; and his troops there killed, made prisoners, or put to flight!

It had happened in this manner. Frederic William had, we have seen, first learned the invasion of the Swedes as he himself was retreating from Alsace before Turenne. His first thought was a joyful one. During the negotiations preceding the Peace of Westphalia Frederic William had tried hard to obtain Pomerania. He had not prevailed. The claims of Sweden had been

---

* Havelland comprises the country bordered by the Havel on one side, and by the low grounds watered by the overflowings of the Rhin and the Dosse. The Rhin is a small river which, after running a course of sixty miles, joins the Havel twenty-six miles north-north-west of Brandenburg.

preferred to his claims. **Now**, without cause, Sweden **was invading his territory.** The **longing for Pomerania, which had never left him, showed itself in the words which he exclaimed when he heard of the invasion : " I shall make them give me Pomerania."** He was **forced to give his army a few weeks' rest in and about Schweinfurt, in Franconia ; but he was not idle there.** He filled up **the gaps made** by the campaign, **repaired the** damages **in horses, in** clothing, **in** *matériel*; **then, in the third week of May,** everything being in readiness, he **set out. He had** kept his own **counsel ; not a syllable of his intentions had eked** out; **his generals even were ignorant of them.** Giving out that he **was about to occupy** Magdeburg, he pressed **on through the Thüringen Forest, and reached Magdeburg on the 11th June. Here he learned that the Swedes, unconscious of danger, still occupied their old quarters along the** Havel. The **weather was thick and rainy, the roads were muddy and** difficult ; **but,** in spite **of all, Frederic William and his Brandenburg horsemen pressed on with the** greatest **alacrity, leaving the infantry to follow as they** best might. **Those daring horsemen reached Rathenow in the early grey** dawn **of the 15th, seized by a stratagem the bridge over the** Havel, surprised **the garrison, cut down some, made prisoners** of others, and forced the remainder **to take refuge in flight !**

Frederic William **had thus gained a position similar to those, many in number,** which the campaign **of 1796—the most brilliant campaign in the world's** history—was **more completely to illustrate. With a force** far **inferior to the enemy's on the whole, he** had pierced **that** enemy's **centre, and cut off all** communication between **his right wing and his left. Each of those** wings **stood** now ignorant even of the **existence of the other, and tremblingly** doubting **whether it might or might not** be possible to re-unite **on a centre point** in the **rear of both.** But Frederic William **had foreseen their doubts and** difficulties. Though his **infantry** was **still behind, yet from** the very **hour of his victory at** Rathenow **he had** begun to take measures to render retreat and combination alike impossible. One small party of picked men sent out on the instant had burnt the bridge at Fehrbellin; others, of larger dimensions, had occupied the passes of Cremmen and Oranienburg.

More Frederic William could not do until his infantry should arrive. There still seemed to remain, then, one chance for Wrangel. That general was at Brandenburg with his left wing, which constituted the bulk of the army which remained to him, when he heard of the disaster at Rathenow. Had he marched with vigour against Rathenow and attacked, with superior forces, the Brandenburgers as they were lengthening their line towards Fehrbellin, he might with good leading have counted on success. Ignorant, however, of the fact that Frederic William had only cavalry, and to a certain extent demoralised by the rude awakening he had received, Wrangel thought of nothing but escape. Unable to take the main road by Rathenow, he resolved to follow the banks of the Beetz as far as Gross Behnitz, and to gain thence the main road at Nauen. He carried out this resolve, and, pushing forward as fast as possible, reached Nauen on the afternoon of the 16th.

On the morning of the same day, the Brandenburg infantry had reached Frederic William at Rathenow. The high road led from that place to Gross Behnitz. Could he reach Gross Behnitz before Wrangel, the latter was doomed. He pushed forward, then, with great vigour, reached Gross Behnitz at two o'clock, only to find that his enemy had quitted it an hour before. Again he started in pursuit, and caught the Swedes just as their vanguard was entering Nauen. A skirmish between the Brandenburg horsemen and the Swedish horsemen who formed the rearguard of Wrangel's force, terminated to the advantage of the former.

But the Swedes had gained Nauen—a great gain, for not only was the place very defensible, but it was within easy distance of Fehrbellin. It was still within Wrangel's power, by calling to himself his left wing, to oppose a superior force to Frederic

William on a decisive point, and, beating him, to overwhelm the small detachments who occupied the passes. He had, in fact, reversed the conditions; for at Nauen he was between Frederic William and the rest of the Brandenburg army. But Wrangel, instead of calling to himself the force at Fehrbellin, preferred to fall back himself on that place. He evacuated Nauen, then, during the night of the 16th, and pushed forward in the direction of his right wing. He had already reached, at 6 o'clock on the morning of the 18th, Linum, a village a little more than two miles from Fehrbellin, when the horsemen of the Brandenburg advanced guard, led by Landgrave Frederic of Hesse-Homburg, charged his rearguard with so much fury, that Wrangel was forced to halt his main column to repulse the attack. Few as were the Landgrave's number in comparison with those of the Swedes, he yet made such an impression, and gained so great an advantage, that Frederic William—whom the news of the attack had at first greatly displeased, as it interfered with his intention to make a flank movement to cut off the enemy's retreat—resolved to hurry forward with all his troops to his support.

At 8 o'clock in the morning Frederic William joined the Landgrave with all his cavalry—the infantry being still a long way in the rear. The united force counted five thousand cavalry, and six hundred dragoons or mounted infantry.* It had thirteen pieces of cannon. Wrangel, on the other hand, disposed of seven thousand infantry, four thousand cavalry, and thirty-eight guns. The difference in numbers was, however, more than compensated for by the higher spirit which animated the Brandenburgers,— by the superior skill of their leaders.

Amongst the latter was one man who deserves special mention. This was Dorflinger, who commanded the guns under Frederic William. He had only thirteen pieces, but he took care to dispose of these in such a manner that when the battle began the Swedes found the position they had taken up, between

---

* The dragoons of those days were really mounted infantry and nothing more.

the villages of Linum and Hakenberg, quite untenable. Wrangel fell back, then, into a new position out of range. But again did Dorflinger outwit him. A heavy mist hung over the battlefield. Under cover of this mist, Dorflinger took his thirteen guns to a height commanding the flank of the new Swedish line, and which Wrangel had neglected to occupy. This height, known as the Hill of Hakenberg, was, in point of fact, the key of the position. Dorflinger had conducted his movement with so much secrecy that it had not been detected by the Swedes, and he displayed a prudence equal to his skill when he resolved to defer the fire until the charge which the Brandenburg horsemen were preparing should be made. At last the critical moment arrived. The horsemen of Brandenburg dashed forward to a front attack. Then did Dorflinger open his fire, and by his sudden assault deprive the surprised enemy of all power of effective resistance.

It must be admitted in justice to Wrangel that his head remained cool, even under this terrible surprise. Recognising at once his error in having neglected to occupy the hill of Hakenberg, he wheeled his infantry to the right, led them up the height and attempted to storm the death-dealing batteries. So fierce was the rush of the Swedish veterans, that the greater number of the horsemen posted to guard the guns were overthrown and put to flight. But for the strenuous efforts of the Elector himself, the fate of the day might have been changed. But one Brandenburg regiment remained on the hill intact. As the Swedish veterans pressed on, its colonel, fighting in the front, was slain; a few seconds later, and the lieutenant-colonel was hurled, sorely wounded, from the saddle; the regiment reeled back: a minute later, and its defeat had been assured, the battle had been lost for the Brandenburgers, when, just at the critical moment, the Elector himself, leading his last reserves, rushed to the spot. Again the combat joined. With desperate energy the Swedes, strong in their prestige, pressed forward; with firm tenacity the Great Elector strove to repel them. The murderous nature of the conflict may be judged from the fact that the Master of the Horse of the Elector was killed by his side, that he himself, surrounded by Swedish horsemen, was being whirled away a prisoner, when nine daring Brandenburgers dashed forward and rescued him from their grasp. It was a hand-to-hand fight, a *mêlée*, each man striking out for himself. There was no manœuvring; it was strength against strength, Swede against Brandenburger; the prize, the supremacy over North Germany!

In such a contest,—despite the darkness caused by the all-shrouding mist, despite the valour of the Swedes,—the strong Northmen of Germany, inspired by the love of the Fatherland, felt that they were making way, that gradually, though slowly, the foe was falling back before them. After two hours of a contest, resembling in its intensity those described as taking place before the walls of Troy, the mist suddenly lifted, the sun shone forth in all its brightness! Then the truth stood nakedly revealed. The right wing of the Swedes was crushed and broken; the centre and left wing were in full retreat towards Fehrbellin. The victors, utterly exhausted,—they had scarcely quitted their saddles for eleven days—were too worn out to pursue. It was not till the following morning that, refreshed and recovered, they followed the retreating foe to the borders of Mecklenburg.

Such was the battle of Fehrbellin—a battle which not only freed Brandenburg from a dangerous enemy and paved the way for the surrender of Pomerania to its Elector, but which broke for ever the spell of invincibility which for more than half a century had attached itself to Sweden—a spell which, gained at Leipzig, at Lützen, had indeed vanished for an instant at Nördlingen, but had been recovered and confirmed by the many splendid victories gained by Banner, by Torstenson, and by Wrangel. That spell was now vanished—vanished for ever. Henceforward, the Germans of North Germany were animated by the resolution to become masters on their own soil, proudly independent of their neighbours.

For the great Elector promptly followed up his victory till he had compelled the Swedes to evacuate all Pomerania. Three years later, when they once more crossed the border from Livonia, he forced them again to retreat; and although in the treaty signed at St. Germain in 1679 he was forced to renounce his Pomeranian conquests, he did not the less establish the ultimate right of the State of which he was the real founder to those lands on the Baltic for which he had so hardly struggled at the negotiations which preceded the peace of Westphalia. When he died (9th May 1688) he left the kingdom already made in a position of prosperity sufficient to justify his son and successor in assuming, thirteen years later, on the anniversary of the victory of Fehrbellin, the title of King—a title which a descendant was to exchange, a hundred and seventy years later, for the higher dignity of Emperor!

The degree of importance attached by the Brandenburg-Prussian people to the victory of Fehrbellin is proved by the monuments which, from time to time, have been raised on the field of battle. In 1800 the canons of Rochow erected on a hill at Linum a monument bearing this inscription: "Here did the brave Brandenburgers lay the foundation of **Prussia's** greatness" (Hier legten die braven Brandenburger den Grund zu Preussen's Grösse). In 1857 the Warrior's Club (Kriegerverein) of the Havelland placed a second monument on the battle-field. And, lastly, on the 18th June 1875, the two hundredth anniversary of the victory, the present Crown Prince of the German Empire laid with his own hand the foundation stone of a third monument which has subsequently been erected on the hill of Hakenberg, the hill the opportune seizure of which by Dorflinger had given the gallant horsemen of Brandenburg the opportunity which their courage, directed by their great leader, had known how to make decisive.

CHAPTER IX.

VIENNA.

THE year 1526 saw an immense increase to the power of the House of Habsburg. The death of Louis II., King of Hungary and Bohemia, on the fatal field of Mohács, 29th August 1526, and the extinction by that death of the Hungarian branch of the Jagellons, had, in virtue of the then existing treaties, brought the crowns of those kingdoms within reach of the Archduke Ferdinand, brother of the Emperor Charles V., subsequently to become King of the Romans and Emperor of Germany as Ferdinand I. Ferdinand stretched out his hand to take the fallen heritage. The 24th October 1526, at an assembly of the three orders (Landtag) held at Prague, at which the nobles, the knights, and the burghers were fully represented, he was unanimously elected King of Bohemia. Some weeks later, at a meeting of the Hungarian Diet held at Pressburg, Ferdinand was chosen by a majority King of Hungary. He was crowned at Stuhlweissenburg* a year later (3rd November 1527).

To examine the claims of Ferdinand to the crowns of the two kingdoms, it may be interesting to trace back for three or four generations the history of the family to whose extinction he owed his succession.

* The Roman Alba Regalis, or Alba Regia, a town on the road from Vienna to Ofen, a hundred and twenty-six miles from the former and sixty-four from the latter where the Kings of Hungary were always crowned up to the time of Ferdinand inclusive.

George of Podébrad, the **son of Victorin** Bocek of Kunstadt, a Bohemian **magnate, the intimate friend of** Ziska, **and** brother-**in-law of** Ulric **of** Rosenberg, **the first of the** nobles and chief of the Catholic **party in Bohemia, had** succeeded, **by** force of character **and by** military **skill, in so influencing the Diet and the** Emperor (Frederic III.) **that he was elected (April 1452)** regent **of that** kingdom, to act in **that capacity for Ladislas I., King of Hungary, and** who had been **also chosen King of Bohemia. On the death** of Ladislas I. just as he was about to **assume the government of Bohemia (23rd** November 1457), **George of Podébrad, still Regent of** Bohemia, marched with an **army into Hungary to secure the crown** of that kingdom **for** Mathias Corvinus, **who lay in the prison to which** he had been consigned **by Ladislas. His influence** with Ujlak Voivode of Transylvania and the **Hungarian Palatine Gara** gained the election for Mathias Corvinus. **In return** Corvinus promised an eternal gratitude to Podébrad, **and married** his daughter. In supporting the election **of** Corvinus, of an eminent Hungarian to rule over Hungary **to the** displacement **of a prince of the** House of Austria, George **of** Podébrad had really **been fighting for his own** hand. The example became contagious. **The** Bohemians caught the infection, and, the 2nd March 1458, their Diet unanimously **elected** George as their King.

This is not the place to record the **history of his** brilliant reign. **It is, however, necessary to mention** that the course of events **impelled Corvinus, King of Hungary, who owed to him his crown, to turn against him. During a** war in which the Bohemians had **suffered many reverses,** Podébrad succeeded **(March 1469) in** drawing the **army** commanded by Corvinus **into a position in** which it might be exterminated. He showed his signal generosity **by** allowing it **to depart free and** unmolested. Corvinus, who **in the hour of his danger had** given his word of honour **to** cease from all hostility, avowed or secret, proceeded at once to repay Podébrad by intriguing **to** cause himself **to be elected King** of Bohemia. Two months after he had been spared, he was so elected by the chiefs of the Catholic League assembled at Olmütz. The news of this treachery changed the nature of George of Podébrad. He raised an army, and, to obtain the aid of the Poles, he assembled a diet, at which, solemnly renouncing for his own family the rights of succession, he caused its members to elect Ladislas Jagellon, son of King Casimir IV., King of Poland, and who, on his mother's side, could boast of Bohemian blood. In the war which followed, complete success attended the armies of Podébrand. The success had effects which survived him. On his death (14th March 1471), Ladislas succeeded him in Bohemia, and on the death of Mathias Corvinus nineteen years later, Ladislas obtained also the throne of Hungary. The two crowns were thus united on the head of a Jagellon.

Ladislas, known in history as Ladislas II., ruled over the united kingdoms for twenty-five years. He was succeeded in both (13th March 1516), by his son, Louis II., then only ten years old. From that moment until the date on which he attained his majority, Louis was the centre point round which the ambitious nobles of Hungary intrigued and fought to gain personal power. If we look at the position of Edward VI. of England, and add to it a jealous enemy on the border eager to foment and to take advantage of the internal divisions of the country, we obtain an accurate bird's-eye view of the position in Hungary of Louis II. during the first eight years of his reign.

At the time of his accession peace reigned between Hungary and her powerful eastern neighbour, the Sultan of Turkey, then Selim I. On the death of Selim four years later (22nd September 1520), his son, Sulaimán II., better known in history as Sulaimán the Great, then in all the vigour of active youth—he was just twenty-five—sent an embassy to propose a continuance of the existing treaty, but on terms which would secure to himself considerable advantages. The faction which at that moment predominated at the Hungarian Court, knowing that a war with Turkey would affect injuriously the interests of the party which was pressing it very hardly for power, replied to this demand, first, by receiving the Turkish envoys with contumely, and then by cutting off their noses and their ears. Exasperated by this cowardly and cruel treatment of the men to whom in all good faith he had confided a sacred mission, Sulaimán invaded without delay the country whose ministers had afforded him an insult so gross and so barbarous.

On the 20th August he took Belgrade. Salankemen, Peterwardein, and many other places fell in quick succession into his hands. Vainly did the boy king strive to rouse amongst his nobles a spirit of patriotism. Every feeling of honour and love of country disappeared before the more prevailing greed for selfish interests. Did one great nobleman summon his vassals to fight on behalf of the national cause, another at once withdrew with all his following to his estates. Thus it happened that throughout that war the Turks were never opposed by the full strength of the kingdom. Nor even did matters mend when, having attained his majority, the young King, leading an army into the field, summoned all his great vassals to accompany him in the national crusade. But few responded to his call, and when, on the 29th August 1520, Louis faced the army of Sulaimán on the field of Moháces, his own following did not represent one third even of the nobility of his country.

It is not to be wondered that under such circumstances the battle was lost for Hungary. The victory of Sulaimán was complete. The young King, after distinguishing himself by courage and conduct, was forced from the field. The night was dark and the road little known. Crossing a swamp near the village of Czecze he and his horse sank and perished. It was only two months later that the bodies of both were discovered.

Sulaimán took advantage of his victory by marching directly to Ofen (Buda), and seizing that important town. Meanwhile, Ferdinand, afterwards Ferdinand I. Emperor of Germany, but then Vicegerent for his brother, the Emperor Charles V., put in his claims to the succession to the vacant crowns of Hungary and Bohemia, in virtue of the compact made in 1491 by the Emperor Maximilian with King Ladislas II., and confirmed in 1515 by his own marriage with the Princess Anna, sister of Louis II., whereby it had been agreed that in the event of the representative of the one family dying without issue, his dominions should devolve upon the representative of the other. The Estates of Bohemia were the first to recognise the validity of this claim. On the 24th October 1526, the three orders composing those Estates—the nobility, the knights, and the representatives of the towns—unanimously elected Ferdinand as their King.

In Hungary the unanimity was not so perfect. The great territorial nobles had not left the last of the Jagellons without support on the field of battle with the object of placing themselves under the power of the Habsburg. If they had objected to be beaten with whips, it was certainly with no desire that they should be chastised with scorpions. But the necessities of Hungary were great. The Turk was in Ofen: the Hungarians had no army to oppose to him.

Under such circumstances the Estates met in December at Pressburg. Vainly, meanwhile, had the most powerful of the self-seeking nobles, John Zápolya, Voivode of Transylvania, supported by another great noble, Stephen Verböcz, summoned his adherents and proclaimed himself king. His pretensions were laughed to scorn by the greater number of the other great magnates. On the 16th December, when the Diet voted, Ferdinand of Habsburg was, on the proposal of Stephen Báthory, elected by a large majority; a year later he was, as already stated, crowned King of Hungary at Stuhlweissenburg!

If Hungary was in many respects a valuable acquisition for the House of Habsburg, it was an inheritance which brought with it many responsibilities and many cares. Prominent amongst these were a turbulent nobility and incessant warfare with the Turk!

No long time was to elapse before Ferdinand was made to feel the weight of these responsibilities and of these cares. Furious at his own rejection for the Kingship, John Zápolya had thrown himself into the arms of Sulaimán, and Sulaimán, after taking possession of Moldavia and ravaging Hungary with fire and the sword, had marched with an army of a hundred and fifty thousand men against Vienna. The garrison of the city consisted of sixteen thousand soldiers and five thousand armed citizens under the command of Count Nicholas of Salm. Sulaimán appeared before the city the 27th September (1529). For eighteen days the garrison offered a stubborn resistance, repulsing, during that time, no less than twenty assaults. It would, however, have gone hard with them, but that three circumstances hindered on every occasion the success of the assailants, and finally forced them to retreat. These were (1) the incessant rains, (2) the overflowing of the Danube, and (3) the indiscipline of the Janissaries. Sulaimán returned, furious with disappointment, to Constantinople. The check his arms had received so preyed upon him that, in the spring of the following year, he tore himself from the festivals which were rejoicing the hearts of the citizens of Constantinople, entered Hungary, and again conquered the greater part of that country and of Slavonia. The cries of Hungary at length reached the ears of the brother of Ferdinand, the Emperor Charles V., and that prince, just released from his contest with the Protestant princes of Germany, marched to release her from her agony. Near the little town of Günz * the two armies came (May 1532) in sight of each other, the Ottomans superior in numbers, the Germans bearing the palm in discipline and leading. The Turks had already spent nearly three weeks in besieging Günz, and had delivered nineteen attacks. Vainly, however; the garrison, though but eight hundred strong, was commanded by

* Günz or Güns, in the Hungarian language Köszeg, lies on the river of the same name in the county (Komität) of Eisenburg. On the north side of it rises the castle of the Esterhazys dominating the numerous possessions of that family in the vicinity.

a hero, a Croat named Nicholas Jurisic, and, under his guidance, had repulsed them all. The arrival of the Emperor, whilst it cheered the garrison, dispirited the enemy. Sulaimán had already begun to fall back when the news reached him that the Genoese fleet, led by the famous Doria, had captured some of the principal towns in the Morea. He concluded, then, a truce with the Emperor (September 1532), and evacuated Hungary.

The rebel prince of Transylvania, John Zápolya, still refused, however, to bend his head to the House of Habsburg. So fiercely did he continue to fight, and so persistently did he maintain his claims, that six years elapsed after the last departure of Sulaimán before he would agree to come to terms, and he agreed then only on conditions which were eminently favourable to himself. By the Peace of Grosswardein he obtained not only Transylvania, but a great part of lower Hungary (the Theiss circles), with the title of King; with the reserve, however, that on his death the Theiss circles should revert to the Habsburgs.

John Zápolya died two years later (21st July 1540). He had married, the 16th February of the preceding year, Isabella, daughter of Sigismund, King of Poland, and she had borne him a son. No sooner was the breath out of his body than Martinuzzi, a brother of the Paulino order, proclaimed on the field of Rákos his son, John Sigismund, as King, successor to all his father's possessions. As soon as the news reached Constantinople, Sulaimán declared Hungary to be a Turkish satrapy, the young Zápolya to be a tributary prince of Transylvania and of the circles watered by the Theiss!

This declaration meant war with the Emperor. Such a war, indeed, it was impossible to avoid. A considerable number of the nobility had adhered to Martinuzzi, who in his capacity as one of the nominated guardians of the baby prince had carried John Sigismund and his mother to Ofen, and had despatched thence messengers to the Sultan imploring his protection. Considerable as was the number of the nobility who adhered to this plan, those who opposed it were more numerous still. These appealed to Ferdinand. Meanwhile Sulaimán had promptly responded to the call of the Zápolya party, had declared all Hungary to be part and parcel of the Ottoman Empire, and had summoned Ferdinand to do homage to him for all his hereditary possessions! Ferdinand replied by sending an army to besiege Ofen. Had he succeeded in capturing that city and the important personages within its walls, he might then and there have concluded the war. But the slowness of the Austrians gave time to the Pasha of Belgrade to march to the aid of the garrison, and the besiegers were compelled to renounce the fruit of their labours just as the city was on the point of capitulation. From that time—1541—for nearly a century and a half—till 1686—Ofen—or, as it is now better known, Buda—remained in the possession of the Turks—the third city of the Ottoman Empire!

Sulaimán was prepared to maintain his pretensions with the sword. Following the Pasha of Belgrade, he threw ten thousand Janissaries into Ofen, occupied Pesth, and so held both banks of the Danube as to command his communications with the southern provinces.

Ferdinand had no means of resisting him. His own provinces were exhausted; he could expect no help from his brother; he had no money. Under these circumstances he signed, with a heavy heart (August 1547), a truce with the Sultan, whereby he bound himself to make to Sulaimán an annual payment of thirty thousand ducats! On his side the Sultan forced the widow and guardians of John Sigismund Zápolya to renounce in his favour all claim to the crown of Hungary, and bound them to accept for their ward the position of tributary prince of Transylvania and of the Theiss circle.

The conditions of this peace were highly displeasing to the great majority of the Hungarian nobility. At a diet (Landtag) held at Tyrnau the same year, they formally recognised the rights of Ferdinand I. and his issue to hereditary dominion over their lands. Many intrigues followed, accompanied by incessant warfare between the adherents of the Habsburgs and the followers of the Zápolya. The monk Martinuzzi, who had originally invoked the assistance of Sulaimán, now worked for the restoration of the country to Ferdinand. But, whilst he was so engaged, Castaldo, the commander-in-chief of the latter, a Spanish officer of distinction, suspecting him of renewed treason, caused him to be murdered (15th December 1551). Then recommenced the war, the fate of Hungary following the rise and fall of the fortunes of the Turk. At length, by the exertions of Auger Gislain Busbek, the son of a Flemish nobleman, a man well skilled in the mode of conducting war against an Oriental people, a truce for eight years was concluded (7th June 1562). By the terms of this truce the provinces still occupied by the Turks were to remain Turkish; John Sigismund Zápolya was to possess Transylvania and Upper Hungary as far as Kaschau;* the Austrians were to retain what they held. In the interim Isabella, the mother of the young Zápolya, had died, and Ferdinand had become Emperor of Germany.

Ferdinand did what he could to introduce law and order into the part of Hungary which still remained to him, and to provide for the defence of the military frontier. But on his death two years later (25th July 1564) his son Maximilian II., then thirty-seven years old, a prince of a firm though gentle and tolerant character, who had been brought up under the eyes of his uncle, the renowned Charles V., was called upon to meet difficulties of no ordinary character.

No sooner was the death of Ferdinand notified than John Sigismund Zápolya, who inherited all the turbulent ambition of his father, broke the truce and invaded the Hungarian dominions of the Habsburgs. Surprise assured him momentary success. But the Austrian armies were led then by one of the most famous warriors of the age, Lazarus of Schwendi.

---

* Kaschau lies nearly a hundred and seventy miles north-east by east of Buda-Pesth.

This general raised a considerable force, set it in action in the winter of 1566, reconquered all the strong places which Zápolya had taken, captured in addition Tokay and Erdöd, and completely defeated the army of the Transylvanian prince at Szathmár.

In his distress John Sigismund invoked the aid of the Sultan. That Sultan was still Sulaimán the Great. In spite of his burden of seventy-six years, Sulaimán responded to the call made upon him, and, in May 1566, appeared in Hungary at the head of an army, and laid siege to Gyula. To meet him Maximilian had the victorious corps of Schwendi in the Theiss country, fronting Transylvania; a second, led by his brother, the Archduke Charles, covering Illyria; whilst with a third, a hundred thousand strong, he occupied an intrenched camp at Raab, watching the movements of the Turks. Those movements had been somewhat hampered by the jealousy displayed by Zápolya, and for the first two months were restricted to the siege and capture of fortified places. At length Sulaimán moved against Szigeth on the Theiss, the capital of the district of Marmaros. This town was defended by a hero, whose name and fame have descended to posterity; no other, in fact, than Count Nicholas Zriny, Ban of Croatia and Slavonia. With a garrison consisting only of fifteen hundred soldiers this courageous man bade defiance to Sulaimán, and repulsed attack after attack. Vainly did Sulaimán ply him with promises as well as threats. To one and to the other the answer of Zriny was the answer which Leonidas gave to Xerxes!

Human resistance, well directed, can do much; but there is a limit even to its splendid capabilities. By degrees the constant attacks completely demolished the outer walls of the town. Zriny's garrison of fifteen hundred men had by this time been reduced to six hundred. Still, with undiminished energy and unabated firmness of purpose, the gallant warrior opposed a firm front to his enemy. Unable, at last, to continue resistance behind the outer walls, he withdrew within the inner fortifications and made preparations for a sortie. The spirit which animated him inspired every man of his garrison. They stood there, those six hundred, ready to fight, ready to die, prepared to do aught but yield!

At length the hour for the sortie arrived. Opening the gates, the gallant band, led by Zriny, dashed on the countless foe. How they fought, the slaughter they caused, the death they died, has been told in many a ballad on that wild frontier. Zriny himself was one of the first to fall, covered with wounds. He was at once slain. A similar fate befell all but a very few of his daring followers; and those very few owed their lives, not to a desire to live, but to the admiration which their splendid courage extorted even from the ruthless Janissaries!

Zriny did not give his life in vain. He had left behind him in the fortress adherents, incapable of fighting, but as devoted as himself to the cause for which he had combated. When, on his death, the Turkish bands rushed in to seize the fortress, one of these adherents applied a match to the powder-magazine, and blew into the air three thousand enemies!

But his gallant defence had produced a result by many degrees more important still. Sulaimán had been specially angered by the stubborn defence of Szigeth. Before that place he had lost twenty thousand men. The unsalubrious air of the marshes of the Theiss had affected his health considerably. The bad air combined with the vexation to bring in a serious disorder. His constitution was not proof against the attack, and, three days before the feat of arms I have recorded—the night of the 5th September (1566)—he died, if not the last, yet the last but one, of the great commanders of the race of Othmán! *

The death of Sulaimán had all the effect for Maximilian of a victory in the field. The Turkish army, shaken by it more even

---

* His son, Selim II., was the actual last of the successful conquerors of the race, and Selim, far inferior to his father, succeeded only because he inherited the impulse which Sulaimán had given.

than by the dearly-bought conquest of Szigeth, promptly evacuated Hungary, and, within two years Maximilian had concluded peace (1568) with the Porte. Zápolya, however, still continued the war; but on his death, three years later (14th March 1571), the **contest collapsed for want of a** competitor to the Habsburg. The ambition **of one family had maintained it for** fifty **years.** The extinction of that family **freed the Habsburgs from a** race whose members had, **from the first, contested their** pretensions to Hungary as well as Transylvania.

To prevent further danger from that quarter, **and to incorporate Transylvania more** closely within his dominions, **Maximilian proposed to the Diet Caspar Békes, a** nobleman on whose loyalty **and fidelity he could absolutely rely; but the nobles had not yet been so** humiliated **as to** respond, without question, to **the choice of the** Emperor. Instead of Békes they **elected** Stephen Báthory, **a man of great** abilities, who had **served with** distinction **as minister and** commander-in-chief **under their** late **ruler.** This election, **leaving** Transylvania practically independent, **or,** if dependent, **dependent rather** on the Porte, presaged a continuance of **the** troubles which the want of cohesion between **that** principality **and the** other hereditary **possessions** had caused for so many **years. It is** worthy of **note that the election of** Báthory **was** confirmed by Selim II.

Caspar Békes tried in vain to **wrest Transylvania from Stephen** Báthory. **He was completely defeated, taken prisoner, and** beheaded (1575). **The** year following **Stephen** was elected King **of Poland,** and **was succeeded** in **Transylvania** by his brother **Christopher. On the death** of Christopher Báthory in 1581 **the rule over Transylvania devolved upon his** brother Sigismund.

Under the sway **of** Sigismund Báthory **the** policy of Transylvania changed. **In the interval,** Maximilian II. **had** died; **and** his son and successor **in the Empire, Rudolph II.,** hating **war,** and especially **war** in Hungary, had transferred the border territories as an imperial **fief** (Reichslehen) to his uncle Charles,

Duke of **Styria,** father of **Ferdinand** of Gratz. To protect that border, Charles had built on the banks of the river Kulda the fortress of Carlstadt; and, dividing the fief into districts, had assigned the lands in each to adventurers of all nations. These men were the forerunners of the famous Pandours. The frontier line assigned to them stretched along the borders of **Slavonia and Croatia.**

Whilst matters were thus progressing in those **two provinces,** in Transylvania matters had been taking a turn still **more decisive.** Sigismund Báthory was an enthusiast, an **idealist, a man who, strong for the moment in his own** convictions, shrank from no means **to** force those convictions **upon others.** His brother had brought the **Jesuits into** Transylvania. **Sigismund** made their **influence predominant; and when his nobles** resisted he **stifled their resistance in blood.** He then **married a** sister **of the Emperor Rudolph, and proposed to the** latter that **in the event of his dying** without issue **the estates of** Transylvania **should be transferred to the Imperial House.** Almost **immediately afterwards, still** under the **influence of the** Jesuits, **he abdicated, embraced the** ecclesiastical state, **and,** despite the **opposition of** his nobles—the **most eloquent** of whom, Stephen **Josibia, he** caused to be beheaded—transferred **Transylvania bodily** to Austria (1588). As a reward **for** this transfer **he had been** promised **a** Cardinal's hat; **but as** the Emperor **hesitated, or was unable, to keep** his engagement, Sigismund **re-entered Transylvania** (1591) **with the** view of **placing the crown** upon **the head of his brother,** Balthazar. **The same year** Sultan Amurath broke the **truce which** existed between Turkey and the **Empire,** and invaded **Hungary.**

It is unnecessary to do more **than** give the results **of this long and desultory war of** fifteen years. In 1592, the Pasha of **Bosnia,** after **some trifling successes,** was completely defeated **and slain—with him also a nephew of the** Sultan—under the walls **of** Sissek. **Amurath, however, continued the war.**

During its continuance, Balthazar Báthory had been **beaten** in Transylvania and killed by his own people. For a moment, then, the Austrians were able to use the resources of that province and of Wallachia against the Turks; and by means of those resources the fortresses of Gran and Visegrad were recovered (1593). Meanwhile, Amurath had died, and been succeeded by his son, Muhammad III. This prince entered Hungary and took Erlau. The war then took a very changing character. The Turks regained Visegrad and Gran,* and captured Stuhlweissenburg. Finally, on the 11th November 1606, a peace was concluded—the Peace of Sitvarok—in virtue of which, whilst the Turks retained all their conquests, the Emperor was freed from the payment of the annual tribute by which he had been bound.

Meanwhile, anarchy had prevailed in Transylvania. The nobles had risen against Austrian domination (1601), and Sigismund Báthory had been restored. No sooner had the Imperial generals, George Baster and Michael, Voivode of Wallachia, expelled him, than his place was taken, with Turkish assistance, by his uncle, Stephen Bocskay, the first nobleman of Upper Hungary. The title of Bocskay was recognised by the Emperor in the Peace of Sitvarok (1606). On his death, the following year, the estates of Transylvania elected as his successor Sigismund Rákóczy. After one year's experience of government in Transylvania, Rákóczy abdicated (1608) in favour of Gabriel Báthory, younger brother of Sigismund of that name. The cruelties perpetrated by Gabriel roused his subjects to insurrection (1610), and a civil war ensued. This war resulted, after a duration of three years, in the murder of Gabriel, and the establishment, by Turkish aid, of Gabriel Bethlen, better known as Bethlen-Gabor, cousin of the Báthorys, on the princely and quasi-independent throne of Transylvania (1613).

It seemed as though a better era were about to dawn upon that long-distracted principality and upon Hungary. On the 14th June 1615, the truce which still existed with Turkey, then

* They held Gran for the seventy-eight years that were to follow.

ruled by Sultan Achmed III., was prolonged for a year; again for two years, the 1st May 1616; and once again, the 27th February 1618, for twenty years. At the same time the Emperor Mathias, who had become King of Hungary, the 24th May 1611, and Emperor of Germany the following year, entered into an alliance with Bethlen-Gabor, in which he recognised not only the inherent right of the Estates of Transylvania to elect their prince, but the absolute independence of that principality.

But, despite these concessions and the promise of peace with which they seemed to be fraught, the hopes of those who believed in the dawn of a new era proved to be entirely illusory. Bethlen-Gabor was a Protestant. In no other part of the dominions of the Habsburgs had Protestantism spread so widely as in Bohemia. The nobles of that kingdom were during the reigns of Rudolph and Mathias in a chronic state of revolt against their sovereign. The very year which saw the grant to Bethlen-Gabor of the concessions I have noted, witnessed likewise the outbreak of the Thirty Years' War. The year which followed saw also the conclusion of an alliance between Bethlen-Gabor and the revolted nobles of Bohemia, and the invasion of that kingdom by a Transylvanian army!

Thenceforth, and during the thirty years which followed, Transylvania was an open sore in the side of Austria. If the successes of her ruler were fitful and transitory, the inconvenience to the House of Habsburg was not the less keenly felt. A great ruler in Transylvania might at any moment during those years have overthrown the Imperial House. Bethlen-Gabor, though in many respects a superior man, a protector of letters and the arts, did not possess the resolute nature which, having fixed upon a point, directs all its efforts to gain it. In 1619–20, at a period when the fortunes of Austria were at their lowest, he took Pressburg, threatened Vienna, and caused himself to be elected King of Hungary; but the year following he was induced, in consequence of some slight reverses, to renounce that title in consideration of obtaining from Ferdinand II.—who had succeeded Mathias in 1619—the town of Kaschau, seven Hungarian counties (Komität), and the Silesian principalities of Oppeln and Ratibor. For nearly a year he contented himself with the task of administering these additions to his dominions. But in 1623, tired of peace, he levied an army of sixty thousand men, and advanced as far as Brunn in Moravia, with the intention of joining his troops to those of Prince Christian of Brunswick, and marching on Vienna. But as Christian did not come, Bethlen-Gabor made peace with the Emperor and returned. The year following he engaged to support Mansfeld, just then defeated by Wallenstein at Dessau, in North Germany. But the complete collapse of that partisan leader, in consequence of the vigorous pursuit of his antagonist, caused Bethlen-Gabor to draw back in time. Three years later he died, leaving no children. By his will—a very remarkable document—whilst recommending his country and his wife to the care of the Emperor Ferdinand II., he nominated as the executor of his last wishes the Sultan of Turkey. To each of these sovereigns he left legacies.

On the death of Bethlen-Gabor, the Estates of Transylvania confided the nominal chief office of the government to his widow, Catherine of Brandenburg, with her brother-in-law, Stephen Bethlen, as Gubernator or administrator. The difference of religion between the two—Catherine being a Catholic and Stephen a Protestant—caused so much inconvenience, that, after a brief interval, the Estates, on the proposal of Stephen, decreed the deposition of Catherine. Stephen meanwhile, uncertain of the result of his contention with Catherine, had offered the throne of Transylvania to George Rákóczi, son of the Sigismund Rákóczy who had momentarily occupied it in 1608. Rákóczy had accepted the offer, and had advanced at the head of a considerable army as far as Grosswardein, when he heard that Stephen Bethlen had disposed of the pretensions of Catherine, and was eager to occupy the throne himself. To settle the claims of the two pretenders, a Diet was summoned to meet at Segesvar in 1631. At that Diet, by means of the support of Catherine, whom he had known how to conciliate, and of presents to the most influential nobles, George Rákóczy was elected almost unanimously. But he possessed none of the qualities which should distinguish a ruler. His avarice, his cruelties, and his injustice provoked a general hatred on the part of his subjects. For a long time they bore the evil they could not cure; but in 1636 Stephen Bethlen fled to Constantinople, the interpreter of the views of the majority, and implored the intervention of the Sultan. The Sultan was not disposed at the moment to do more than to insist upon the restoration to Stephen Bethlen of his estates. On his expression of satisfaction, after this had been accomplished, the tyranny of Rákóczy became more unbearable than ever. Nor did he make amends for his tyranny by capacity. In 1643-44 he allied himself with the Swedish general, Torstenson, in the attempt which the latter made upon Vienna. Had he conducted his part of the operations seriously, Vienna must have fallen.* But his avarice made him as bad an ally as it had made him a bad ruler. The Emperor excited the Sultan against him on the one side, whilst on the other he offered the Transylvanian prince the cession for his life of the revenues of five shires (Gespannschaften) in Hungary if he would withdraw his troops. Under this double influence, Rákóczy abandoned his ally and concluded a peace with the Emperor (July 1645.)

Irritated at the part which Turkey had played in this arrangement, Rákóczy refused to increase to fifteen thousand ducats the tribute demanded by the Sultan, and which in the time of Bethlen-Gabor had not exceeded two-thirds of that sum. The Sultan Ibrahim, therefore, declared war against him. The death of that prince (1648), and the consequent succession of a Sultan personally more favourably disposed towards himself, Muhammad IV., relieved Rákóczy of the dread caused him

* *Vide* pages 154-5.

by this declaration. His hopes were never higher than at this period of his life. He had become a candidate for the vacant throne of Poland, and his election seemed assured, when he suddenly died (24th October 1648).

Rákóczy was succeeded in Transylvania by his son George, known as George II. His first act was to pay to the Porte the arrears of tribute due at the rate which had been fixed by Sultan Ibrahim; his next to restore to the Emperor the five shires which had been ceded to his father for life. For nine years no incident of importance marked his reign. But, having failed, on the death, in 1655, of Casimir V., to be elected King of Poland, he united his armies with those of Sweden, two years later, to wage war against that country. The expedition was in every respect very disastrous. Rákóczy was abandoned by the Swedes, his own army was destroyed, and he had provoked the hostility of the Sultan against whose positive orders he had acted. A war with the Porte followed, which, after some vicissitudes, resulted in the overthrow and death of Rákóczy (26th June 1660).*

Transylvania now lay at the mercy of the Porte. The Sultan, by his famous Grand Vizier, Koprili Muhammad Pasha, nominated Alexander Barcsay to be tributary ruler of the principality; and when the Diet dismissed Barcsay in favour of the national favourite, John Keményi, Koprili marched at the head of an army to expel him. Keményi was defeated and slain in 1662. In his place the Sultan appointed Michel Apaffy to the tributary throne.

This interference of the Sultan in the affairs of Transylvania brought about war between Turkey and Austria. In 1663, a Turkish army, led by the son and successor of the late prime minister, Koprili Ahmad Pasha, invaded Hungary, gained a great victory at Gran, took Forgács, Neuhäusel, Neutra, and

* At the battle of Klausenburg which preceded the death of Rákóczy by four days, the Transylvanians had slightly the advantage. But the death of their leader, who had received four mortal wounds in the fight, transferred that advantage to the Turks.

other strong places, whilst its Tartar horsemen spread terror and desolation in Moravia and Silesia.

To check the progress of his formidable enemy, the Emperor despatched towards the close of the year an army under the command of Nicholas Zriny, Ban of Croatia, great-grandson of the hero of the same name, who had covered himself with glory at the siege of Szigeth.*

Zriny's winter campaign was a masterpiece. With an army far inferior in number to that of the invaders, he beat up their quarters, cut off their supplies, and especially at the bridge of Essegg, which he held against them with a handful of men, hindered their advance. As the spring came on he fell back on another Imperial army, led by the famous Raymond, Count of Montecucculi. The union of two armies under two such leaders afforded another example—for the world has many of them, alike in public and in private life—how easily divergences of character in two leaders, each excellent in his way, can neutralise the best-laid schemes. Zriny was daring, enterprising, even audacious; Montecucculi was methodical, careful, circumspect. The scheme which commended itself to the one was invariably condemned by the other; and this difference of opinion led naturally to inaction. It caused, first, the raising of the siege of Kanizsa; and, again, the surrender to the Turks of the fortress of Zrinevar, a fortress built by Zriny and called after his own name, and to succour which he in vain implored Montecucculi. The inaction became so pronounced that it emboldened Sultan Muhammad IV. to invade Styria. In falling back to cover that province, Montecucculi was reinforced by the contingent of the Diet and by six thousand French levies —an addition which raised his army to sixty thousand men. Thus strengthened, he resolved to contest with the enemy the passage of the Raab at St. Gotthardt, on the high road leading from Ofen to Gratz. Here on the 1st August (1664) he was attacked by the Turkish army. The furious assault

* *Vide* page 267.

of the spahis threw the right wing of the Imperialists into
disorder, and fugitives from it announced in Gratz the complete
defeat of the army. But it was at such a conjuncture that
Montecucculi invariably displayed the calmness and presence of
mind which gained for him his great reputation. Despatching
his cavalry to take the spahis in flank, he led against the
Janissaries the *élite* of his infantry, broke their serried ranks, recovered the position his right wing had lost, and forced back the
enemy with a loss on their part of sixteen thousand men! Nine
days later a truce for twenty years was signed with the Grand
Vizier at Eisenburg (Vasvár), in virtue of which the latter
retained Neuhäusel and Grosswardein, and obtained the recognition of the Emperor for the Turkish nominee, Prince Apaffy,
as ruler of Transylvania. In return for these concessions, the
advantages gained by the Emperor for Hungary were little more
than nominal!

It can easily be imagined that the Peace of Eisenburg, or,
as it is sometimes called, of St. Gotthardt, in which, after
a great victory, Leopold conceded infinitely more than he
gained, did not tend to increase the power of the Emperor in
Hungary. And, as no concessions were simultaneously made
on questions affecting the rights and privileges of the nobles of
Hungary, many of these openly expressed their determination
to disregard it. Prominent amongst them were the Palatin,
Vesselényi; the representative of the Rákóczis, Francis Rákóczi; and Peter Zriny, brother of the illustrious Nicholas,
who had been killed whilst hunting shortly before the battle
of St. Gotthardt. These three noblemen went so far as to
sign at Trentschin (Trencin, on the Waag) a bond of confederacy against the Emperor Leopold. They were very serious
in their design. And when, before they could bring their plans
to maturity, Vesselényi died, Peter Zriny, whose vindictiveness
was boundless, brought, amongst others, as adherents to the
cause, from Croatia, Count Frangepani, from Hungary Count
Nádasdy, and from Styria Count Tättenbach.

Notwithstanding these weighty adhesions the conspiracy
failed. Caught red-handed in the act, the leaders, with the
exception of Rákóczy, who was condemned to pay a heavy fine,
were beheaded (1671). For the moment, order reigned in Hungary. Only, however, for the moment. Emerich Tököly,* who
had escaped when the other confederate nobles were captured,
returned in 1672 to Hungary, the leader of the insurrection.
At one moment, somewhat later, an accommodation with the
Emperor seemed possible; but the opportunity was allowed to
slip, and then Tököly, active, daring, adventurous, implored

* Few men have lived a more romantic career than Emerich Tököly. Born in
1656, the son of one of the most powerful magnates in Hungary, Tököly had, at
the age of fifteen, become a proficient alike in learning and in arms. When the
conspiracy referred to in the text broke out, the Imperial Government, suspecting
with some reason that the elder Tököly, the father of Emerich, was privy to it,
sent troops to besiege him in his castle of Likavoka. Conscious of his inability to
make a long resistance, the father confided Emerich to two devoted servants, who
conveyed him, in the disguise of a woman, into Poland. Soon after the father died,
and Emerich Tököly, now head of the House, proceeded to the court of Apaffy, Ban
of Transylvania, and so won upon him by his intelligence and ability, that he was
shortly afterwards appointed first minister, then commander-in-chief, of the troops
despatched by the Ban into Hungary on his learning of the execution of Nadasdy,
Zriny, and the other chiefs. The insurgent Hungarians at once saluted Tököly as
their leader.
   Tököly was still leader of the Hungarian nationalists, in the pay of France and
coining money in the name of the King of that country, when, in 1678, the Princess
Rákóczi informed the Emperor Leopold that the young chief was an aspirant for
the hand of her daughter-in-law, Helena Zriny, widow of the Francis Rákóczy
above referred to, who died in 1676. As Tököly was already engaged to the widow
of Nicholas Apaffy, the Princess saw that a marriage with Helena would deprive
Tököly of Transylvanian aid, and she urged the support of it upon Leopold as a
means for gaining the Hungarian chief. Leopold refused at first to interfere; and
when, at last, he did so, the benefits to be derived from the marriage and from the
annuity which followed were neutralised by the insertion in the agreement of a
clause reserving the manorial rights of the large landowners. These latter, with
Tököly at their head, took advantage of the vagueness of the clause to remain in
insurrection and to ally themselves closely with the Porte.
   The events which followed are told in the text. On the failure of the campaign,
Tököly, suspected by the Turks, was sent prisoner to Adrianople. It was the
greatest political fault ever committed. Whilst he still languished in confinement,
entire Hungary had been recovered for the House of Habsburg; and when the
Sultan released him and urged him once again to action, it was too late. In the
civil war which followed, his wife Helena distinguished herself by her courage, her
daring, and her enterprise. The gallantry with which she defended Munkács is
still told in the Hungarian ballads. She and her husband continued their opposition
to the Habsburgs to their last days. Tököly was created by the Sultan Prince of
Widdin, and he (1705) and Helena (1703) died subjects of the Porte.

the assistance of the Ottoman Porte. The Porte, without hesitation, responded.

At the head of an army, two hundred thousand strong, the Grand Vizier, Kara Mustapha, who on the death of his brother-in-law, Koprili Ahmed Pasha (30th October 1676), had succeeded to that office, marched direct upon Vienna!

Let us glance for a moment at the means which the Emperor Leopold had at his disposal to protect his capital.

His own army, thirty-three thousand strong, was commanded by his brother-in-law, Duke Charles of Lorraine. Lorraine had, on the news of the invasion, marched on Pressburg, some forty miles from Vienna, to observe the movements of the enemy. At the same time the Emperor ordered a levy *en masse* in Hungary; sent imploring letters to the Elector Max. Emanuel of Bavaria, to the Elector John George III. of Saxony, and, above all, to John Sobieski, King of Poland, who, nine years before, 11th November 1673, had inflicted a crushing defeat upon the Turkish army, then led by Koprili Ahmed Pasha, at Choczim, to come to his aid.

From the princes to whom he wrote those letters Leopold received assuring answers. Maximilian promised eight thousand men; John George, the whole force of which he could dispose; John Sobieski, forty thousand men; but the levy *en masse* in Hungary produced only three thousand men.

Kara Mustapha meanwhile advanced, plundering and devastating. As he approached the capital, the Duke of Lorraine fell back towards it; not so quickly, however, but that his rear-guard was badly maltreated at Petronell, about one-third of the distance from Pressburg to Vienna. On the 14th July Kara Mustapha appeared before the capital. Lorraine had thrown his infantry, thirteen thousand strong, into the city; and these, with seven thousand armed citizens, formed the garrison, the command of which was entrusted to Count Rüdiger Starhemberg. The number was not sufficient to prevent the complete investment of Vienna by the Turks. So rapid were their movements, that it was by a miracle that the Emperor and his family were not captured as they fled to Linz and Passau. Lorraine, unable to stop the progress of the enemy, had, after having been driven from [the islands in the vicinity of the Leopoldstadt, taken up a position first at the Jedlesee, later at Krems, nearly fifty miles from the capital, but so placed on the outer rim of a bend of the Danube as to give the general holding it opportunities for communicating with the garrisons of Pressburg and Komorn, which had not as yet been assailed. Here also he might hope to receive the promised reinforcements from Southern Germany and Saxony.

In spite of this, notwithstanding, too, the courage of the garrison and citizens of Vienna, the task which Kara Mustapha had undertaken was comparatively an easy one. Nothing could be more deplorable, according to modern notions, than were the defensive means of Vienna. The front, watered by the Danube, was protected by a simple wall, strengthened at intervals by towers for the most part crumbling and in decay. The other portion, facing the country, was covered similarly by a rampart, twelve feet high, with two bastions, the curtains of which were covered by ravelins and by a ditch. But little attention had been paid, since the abortive siege of the city by Torstenson, to the repair of the works. Of artillery, three hundred and seventy-one pieces, guns and mortars, were available.

The Turks directed their principal attacks against the following points:—the segment of the fortifications between the Burgthor and the Schottenthor;* the Burg bastion with its cavalier, and the Augustin ravelin to the left of it; and the Löwel curtain and bastion. To destroy these by mining they approached by way of the Red House (in the Alsergrund) and St. Ulrich, and erected batteries there and at the Kroatendörfel (Spittelberg). From these points they began to mine the Burg and Löwel bastions.

The modern Volksgarten represents the space, between the old

* Of these gates the Burgthor alone remains.

Wiedenerthor and the Schottenthor, on which the besieged won eternal glory by deeds of valour and endurance. Well did those gallant men know the fate which would befall their wives and children if their enemy were to force his way into the city! To describe in detail their watchfulness, their energy, and their valour, would lead me beyond the limits I have marked out. Otherwise, I could describe how the regiment of Stahremberg repulsed, from the advanced front of the covered way before the Burg ravelin, four successive attacks of vastly superior numbers; how the gallant Duke of Würtemberg attacked the Turks in the Graben and forced them to retire with heavy loss; the proofs of extraordinary vigilance, energy, and courage, in his defence of the ravelin and ditch of the Löwel bastion given by the captain of the city, Hofner; how Captain Heistermann, with but fifty men at his disposal, extinguished the fire applied by the Turks to the palisades of the Burg bastion, and victoriously repulsed the swarms who, upon the kindling of the fire, had rushed to the storm! On every point of defence did the men prove themselves worthy of their gallant leaders. Thrice during the day, and once during the night, did Stahremberg make the rounds of the city and of the defences. Compelled by wounds in the head and arm to desist for two days, he was seen on the third day resuming his work, and ascending, as was his custom, the tower of St. Stephen's, to notice from that elevated spot the movements of the enemy. The stone on which he used to sit is shown at the present day. It was to his watchfulness, his calmness in danger, his careful supervision, and, withal, to the perfect discipline he maintained, that the prolongation of the defence was mainly due.

 The Turks had begun the siege on the 14th July. From that date their guns, their mines, their assaults had afflicted the beleaguered city. Slowly but steadily, notwithstanding the repulses to which I have adverted, they continued to make progress. On the 16th August they made a firm lodgment in the ditch in front of the Löwel bastion; and though they were driven thence a few days later, they succeeded, by means of repeated mining and the persistent attacks following, in gaining possession of the Burg ravelin—a most important post, because from it they were able to maintain a constant fire on the Burg and Löwel bastions, and on the curtain between those bastions.

The result of the gain of the Burg ravelin was displayed a few days later. On the 23rd, 24th, and 26th August the Turks made desperate efforts to storm the bastions. Though they were repulsed with heavy loss, the defenders were nevertheless compelled, on the 3rd September, to abandon the ravelin of the Löwel bastion. The following day the Turks sprang one of their principal mines under the Burg bastion with such a loss of life to the besieged that the Janissaries, dashing forward, stormed the bastion and planted two horse-tails on its summit. But neither the crash and destruction of the explosion, nor the whirl of the storm which followed, abated one jot the courage and persistance of the gallant Austrians. Rallying behind the *débris* they came fearlessly to the assault and succeeded, by a great effort, in expelling the Janissaries from the bastion they believed they had won.

But, not discouraged by such occasional failures, the besiegers continued to pursue their mining system, and, spite of the heroism of the garrison, they gradually made their way. On the 6th, 7th, and 8th September they sprang fresh mines under the Burg and Löwel bastions. By means of these they succeeded in boring a way underneath the Minorite Church,* through which they were able to despatch to the scene of action a constant supply of fresh troops to replace those who had fallen. Every day's work thus increased the imminence of the fall of Vienna.

Meanwhile the Duke of Lorraine, with the remnant of his army, had, as I have already stated, taken up a post at Krems.

* Still existing, close to the Niederösterreichishes Landhaus in Minoriten-Platz.

Thence he endeavoured to maintain an intermittent communication with the garrison of the beleaguered city. But between himself and that city lay the besiegers: the country, too, was scoured by bands of disaffected Hungarians. Communication was therefore almost impossible. Of the many who attempted to carry despatches some were killed, some returned frustrated. In the third week of August, however, Lorraine received a despatch dated the 18th, gallantly conveyed by a Pole named Kolschitzki, informing him that the besiegers were still full of hope. Sending back by Kolschitzki a message in which he promised to do his utmost to deliver the city, Lorraine, whose troops had been gradually increasing, marched suddenly upon Pressburg, defeated there the Hungarian army under Tököly; then, learning that the Pasha of Grosswardein had reached Stammersdorf (in the Marchfeld) with reinforcements, he turned suddenly upon him and smote his rearguard badly; then proceeding to the Tullner Feld, a vast plain near Tulln on the Danube,* he effected at Hollabrunn (30th August) a junction with the King of Poland. In the interval he learned that the Bavarian, Saxon, and Franconian reinforcements had reached Krems.

John Sobieski, King of Poland, has left a name which will never die.† He was in all respects a hero, and a hero of the purest type. Alike in character, in foresight, in the simplicity of his mind, and in the brilliancy of his achievements, he was one of the most remarkable men the world has ever seen. Born in Galicia in 1624, he had, at the age of twenty-one, followed the example then prevailing in aristocratic circles in

---

* Near the point where the Danube is now crossed by the Franz-Joseph railway.

† "To strive constantly against the jealousies and factions of the aristocracy," writes M. Leonard Chodzko, "to resist the intrigues of his wife; to oppose the Machiavelism of foreign cabinets which were labouring unceasingly to destroy the Polish republic; to devote himself body and soul to defend the glory and the grandeur of the Polish name; to surrender his own personal property for the public cause; to astonish Europe, during a period of forty years, by his victories; to ascend by all the steps until, by his personal merit, he had reached the highest, that is to say, the throne; to leave, finally, a name that will be popular in ages to come;—such are the titles of John Sobieski to the admiration of posterity!"

Poland by entering the French army. The regiment in which he served was the "Mousquetaires rouges"—one of the most brilliant of those reserved for the personal guard of the King. Whilst in that regiment he made the acquaintance and gained the friendship of the famous Condé; and it is a proof of the power of thought which he even then evinced that when Condé asked him how he would remedy the evils then even beginning to undermine the French monarchy, Sobieski suggested the convocation of the States-General! After a short sojourn in France, and a visit to Turkey, Sobieski returned to Poland and consecrated his life to the defence of his country. I must unwillingly pass over the many services he rendered her. It must suffice to state that they were so great, so brilliant, so visible, so compelling admiration, that on the 21st May 1674,* nearly six months after he had destroyed the Ottoman army at Choczim, 11th November 1673, he was elected King of Poland.

War was then raging between Poland and Turkey. Scarcely had Sobieski mounted the throne when he had to drive the enemy across the frontier. The following year they returned, only, however, to be completely defeated (24th August). The war seemed terminated when, thanks to the intrigues of the Emperor Leopold, jealous of the success of the Polish King, it broke out with renewed fury. The genius of Sobieski, however, triumphed over all difficulties, and on the 27th October 1676 he forced upon his enemies a peace glorious for Poland. He was in alliance with the Emperor when the Muhammadan attack upon the dominions of the latter, which forms the main subject of this chapter, took place. We have seen how, in his agony, the Emperor sent pressing solicitations to Sobieski to march to his aid. Those solicitations were urgently supported by the

---

* The Diet, for the election of a king in room of the deceased sovereign, Michael, met the 20th April. Sobieski vehemently supported the candidature of Condé; the other candidates were the Duke of Lorraine and the Duke of Neuburg. When, after many days of sitting, an agreement seemed impossible, Stanislaus Jablonovsky made an eloquent appeal in favour of Sobieski, who was thereupon elected with unanimity.

prayers of the Papal nuncio. Whilst the one implored him to save the Empire, the other besought him to preserve Christianity. There were not wanting entreaties to him to abstain from all interference with the fate of Austria. The Court of Versailles brought up in review before him the many injuries he had received from Leopold, and urged a policy of non-intervention. This policy was supported by no inconsiderable number of Polish nobles, who would have preferred, if they fought at all, to fight for the immediate advantage of their own country. But Sobieski never hesitated. Troubled though he was with an accumulation of flesh which no exercise could lessen,* Sobieski, his finances recruited by the sum of one million two hundred thousand florins (about one hundred thousand pounds) sent him by the Emperor, raised an army of twenty-five thousand men with thirty pieces of cannon, and set out from Cracow the 15th August. Marching rapidly in the direction of Vienna, he reached Hollabrunn the 30th, and there effected his junction with Lorraine.

· I will pass over the meeting of the two commanders. A council of war was held the same day. By the consent of all present, the command-in-chief devolved upon the renowned King of Poland. It was resolved to wait for the arrival of the Bavarian, Saxon, and Franconian troops, then hastening from Krems, and then to march through the Wiener Wald and occupy the Kahlenberg.

On the 6th September the German contingents crossed the river: on the 7th the entire army, amounting to eighty-four thousand men—of whom forty-six thousand one hundred were cavalry—furnished with one hundred and eighty-six pieces of artillery,† was concentrated in the Tullner Feld. It was ranged in three divisions: the left wing, composed of Imperial‡

---

* The French ambassador wrote from Cracow to his master that the extreme *embonpoint* of the King would not allow him to enter on the campaign.

† The Imperial troops numbered 27,100, the Poles, 26,600, the Saxons 11,400, the Bavarians 11,300, the Franconians 8,400.

‡ Amongst these served as Lieutenant-Colonel of the Imperial Cavalry, Prince Eugene of Savoy, then nineteen years old. It was his first campaign. Of other men afterwards to become famous, present with the army, were George Frederick,

and Saxon troops, being commanded by Lorraine; the right, consisting of the Polish army—strengthened by one regiment from each of the contingents furnished by the Empire, by Saxony, by Bavaria, and by Franconia—by the King of Poland; the centre formed of Saxons, Bavarians, and Franconians, by the Prince of Waldeck and the Electors of Bavaria and Saxony. The army set out the next day, directing its march on the Kahlenberg, its left wing feeling the Danube.

What, meanwhile, was Kara Mustapha doing? On learning of the defeats of Tököly and of the Pacha of Grosswardein, and of the junction of Lorraine with Sobieski, Kara Mustapha had mustered his army. He had found that, deducting the forty-eight thousand five hundred who had already perished before the walls of Vienna, he could still dispose of a hundred and seventy-three thousand seven hundred warriors. Not for a moment, then, did he lose courage. He knew that the beleaguered city was at its last gasp; that of its thirteen thousand regular defenders little more than one-half remained. He took his measures, then, with resolution, if not with skill. Before the walls of the city he left the pick of the Janissaries, under the command of Kuhaja Bey, with the strictest orders to pursue the siege without the smallest relaxation. He then, having first slaughtered his Christian prisoners—to the number, it is said, of thirty thousand—led the rest of his army to the foot of the Kahlenburg, placed the centre, under his own personal command, at Währing and Weinhaus; the right wing, under Osman Oglu Pasha, at Nussdorf; the left, commanded by the beaten Pasha of Grosswardein, at Dornbach. A worse disposition could scarcely have been made. The hill of Kahlenberg, now the Sunday resort of the happy Viennese, commanded the villages occupied by the Turks. Granting that an excuse might be found for Kara Mustapha, though it is difficult to conceive

Prince of Waldeck, afterwards Imperial Field-Marshal and comrade of William III. in the Netherlands; Prince Louis of Baden, victor of Salankemen; Count Taafe, indirect ancestor of the present Prime Minister of Austria; the Scotchman, Leslie. If I do not enumerate more, it is because the list is too long.

one, for failing to deal with his enemies before the several particles which formed their army had united, his neglect to occupy the Kahlenberg and his occupation of positions commanded by that hill were deviations from the rules of war which stamped him as absolutely ignorant of his art. Well might Sobieski exclaim, as he reconnoitred from the summit of the Kahlenberg: "This man is badly encamped; he knows nothing of war; we shall beat him!"

Sobieski had, in fact, gained the Kahlenberg on the evening of the 11th September. From its summit he beheld the doomed Turkish army, with its horses, its tents, its camels, spread out in the plain before him. Beyond that army the beleaguered city, now verily at its last gasp.* He at once signified to the garrison his presence by a salute of three guns and the discharge of rockets. He then made the necessary preparations to attack by the morrow's early dawn.

His examination of the ground between Kahlenberg and Vienna—a distance of about four miles—had disclosed to Sobieski difficulties on which he had not counted. The ground, in fact, was not only undulating, broken by hillocks and valleys, but it was covered by vineyards and villages or ruins of villages burnt by the Turks. He resolved, then, whilst sending Lorraine to drive the Turks from Nussdorf, to march himself with the centre over the Cobenzlberg† and the right over the Hermannskogel, and attack the enemy at Dornbach.

It followed from this arrangement that Lorraine would be first under fire. With the red dawn of the Sunday morning that general pressed forward to accomplish the work allotted to him, and, descending the hill, attacked the Turkish right wing. But in Osman Oglu Pasha, Lorraine encountered no mean adversary. He had to fight every step of his way. Twelve o'clock sounded before he could make good his footing in Nussdorf and the

---

* **Two days** before he had received the following message from Stahremberg: "No time to be lost; no time, indeed, to be lost."

† Then known as the **Reisenberg**.

neighbouring village of Heiligenstadt, **and when there he had to repulse five attempts made with splendid courage by Osman Oglu to regain them.** His position **even then was far from assured, for Osman Oglu still held Döbling and the Hummelberg, on which strong batteries had been erected. Instead, then, of attempting a further forward movement, Lorraine very prudently tried to feel towards** the centre, which, though hidden by the trees, he was sure could not be far from him.

Meanwhile, the centre, composed **as** we have seen **of Germans,** had, though long delayed by the difficulties of the ground and the opposition of **the** enemy, made at last good its way over the Cobenzlberg. The Poles, led by their gallant King, had likewise about the same time accomplished the long detour over the Hermannskogel and through **the gorges leading** to **Dornbach.** The clock had struck **two,** however, **before the left of the centre** had made touch with the right of the left **and the whole army** was in **line. Then the advance was made. Too rashly, indeed, by a few! One regiment of** Polish Uhlans, dashing forward hurriedly **and without support, was** surrounded and cut **down; and, Kara Mustapha, who beheld** the deed, and who observed **that Osman Olgu** still **held** Döbling **and the** Hummelberg, flattered himself **for a** moment with the hope that he would repulse his assailants. **But the** hope soon gave way to despair. Whilst the **Polish cavalry, directed** now **by their** King, renewed the fight, supported by the Germans, **on the right** and in the centre, Lorraine, advancing with desperate courage, **stormed the** batteries **of** Döbling, and, following up the fleeing enemy, drove them **from** the great redoubt at Währing and Weinhaus—called to the present day the Turkish trenches—then wheeling to the **right,** fell upon the right flank of the still fiercely **contending** Ottomans.

This movement **made victory certain. Hitherto Sobieski, conscious of the vastly** superior **numbers of the enemy, had advanced** with a **certain** amount of **caution;** but the carrying of Döbling and the masterly movements that followed it, removed whatever there might have been of doubt from his mind. He threw all his force upon the now discouraged foe. Meanwhile, Louis of Baden, who had nobly seconded the efforts of Lorraine against Döbling, anxious to be the first to convey to the defenders of the beleagured city the first news of their deliverance, galloped through the Ross-Au, his trumpets sounding, to the counterscarp before the Schottenthor, and, aided by a vigorous sally of the garrison, drove the besiegers from the approaches. Vainly, meanwhile, had the enemy, sensible of the imminence of the danger, tried to turn the siege guns upon the assailants. Vainly had Kara Mustapha endeavoured to re-form and concentrate his line. The fatal "too late" was stamped upon all he attempted. It soon became clear that the battle was lost beyond redemption. At half-past five, indeed, the Turks made a final rally at St. Ulrich. It was their last. Half-an-hour later they were fleeing in wild disorder over the Wienerberg on the lines leading to Raab!

Vienna was saved. The bodies of close upon twenty-five thousand Turks, the gain of three hundred and seventy guns, of many colours, standards, and horsetails, and of fifteen thousand tents, proclaimed the decisive nature of the victory. Amongst the tents was the palace-tent of Kara Mustapha himself, containing within it, in gold coins, a sum equal to two hundred thousand pounds; his arms, his horse, and his secret correspondence. The amount of provender found was enormous. Fifteen thousand buffaloes, oxen, camels, and mules; more than ten thousand sheep; a hundred thousand measures of corn; whole magazines of coffee, sugar, and rice—besides large sums of gold and many golden ornaments—became the spoil of the victors.

The following morning the King of Poland and the Duke of Lorraine met and exchanged congratulations on the brilliant victory. Then, accompanied by the gallant Rüdiger Stahremberg, they made a solem entry, through the Stubenthor, into the city. Whilst a salute of three hundred guns proclaimed the grandeur of the occasion, the shouts and tears—for joy can call forth tears—of the citizens, more than compensated the victors for the peril and privations they had overcome.

A victory is not complete until it shall have been followed up. Of the truth of this sound military maxim no one was more convinced than the illustrious warrior who had saved Vienna. As soon, then, as matters could be arranged in that city, Sobieski entered Hungary at the head of a Polish-Imperial army—the imperial portion commanded by Stahremberg. Following up the Turks, he caught and beat them (9th October) at Párkány,* and twelve days later forced Gran to surrender. He then returned to his own kingdom, leaving to the Imperialists to complete the work he had so well begun.

It is impossible on this occasion to give in full detail an account of the manner in which the Imperialists accomplished that task. A short summary of the consequences which resulted from the great victory before Vienna is, however, necessary for the full comprehension of the importance of the crisis, of the decided nature of the turn it gave to the history of affairs in Eastern Europe. From 1684 to 1688, Prince Charles of Lorraine carried on the war against the Turks with brilliant success. That success, indeed, was rendered much more feasible than it otherwise would have been by the conciliatory conduct of the Emperor towards the Hungarians, and the concession to them in 1684 of religious freedom. With the exception of excited spirits, such as Tököly and others, urged by real or fancied wrongs, the whole nation threw its strength into the scale on behalf of the House of Habsburg. The consequences were most marked. Under the command-in-chief of Lorraine, the several corps of the Imperial army, led by Louis of Baden, Count Caprara, Eugene of Savoy, and the Max-Emanuel of Bavaria, stormed during 1685-6 the important towns of Vysegrad, Waitzen, Neuhäusel, Kaschau, and Erlau. But perhaps the most important gain of all was that of the city of Ofen (Buda). For a century and a half this city had been in the

* The victory of the 9th was preceded by a repulse on the 7th.

19

hands of the Turks—the base **from** which they could threaten Vienna. On **the 2nd September 1686 it** surrendered **to Max-Emanuel** in Bavaria.

A little more than eleven months later the Duke of Lorraine wiped out the stain which a hundred and sixty-one years before **had** marked the Hungarian **banners at Mohács.** On the field **which** had been fatal to the **last of the** Jagëllon rulers **of** Hungary, the brother-in-law of the Emperor completely defeated the Turkish **army** (12th August 1687).*

The **victory of Mohács was** followed by the capture of many **strong places in Lower** Hungary **and** in Croatia. Munkács surrendered the beginning of 1688. During the same year, the Ban of **Transylvania, Michael** Apaffy, renounced his connection with Turkey, and **admitted** Imperial garrisons into his strong place. Wallachia **even** offered **to** submit. On the 6th September Belgrade **was stormed by** the Imperialists. Several fortresses in Slavonia were also taken.

The war, which in 1689 had seemed to languish, was renewed in 1691. On the **19th August of that year,** Prince Louis of Baden, **who** had **succeeded to the** command-in-chief on the death on the 18th April **of the preceding year** of the **Duke of Lorraine, inflicted a crushing defeat upon** the Turks at Salankemen.† **This blow** brought into the field the Sultan Mustapha II. in person. Leading **a large** army into Hungary, **in** 1695, **he defeated the Imperial general,** Veterani, **on the Theiss, between** Lippa **and** Lugos (22nd September), made **him** prisoner, and decapitated **him. Called** to Constantinople by other affairs, **he renewed the invasion in 1697, stormed** Titel—close to which **the Theiss flows into the Danube—and** threatened Peterwardein. **With the intention to recover** **Transylvania and** Lower Hungary **he then** crossed the **Danube** and marched **up** the Theiss. At

---

* One remarkable consequence of the victory **of** Mohács was the decree of a Diet at Pressburg settling the hereditary right of the Princes of the Austrian House to rule over Hungary. As a confirmation of this, Leopold's eldest son, the Archduke Joseph, then nine years old, was, on the 9th December, crowned King of Hungary.

† Twenty-one miles east-south-east **of Peterwardein.**

Zenta, however, he was met and completely defeated (11th September 1697) by Prince Eugene of Savoy.

The victory of Zenta—the after result of the famous battle which forms the subject of this chapter—was decisive. The long war had broken the power of the Turks. By the peace of Carlowitz, which was its logical conclusion (26th September 1699), **the ties between** Hungary, **Transylvania,** Slavonia, and Austria **were** riveted in a manner never again **to be** broken **by Turkish** invasion. The Peace of Carlowitz indeed constituted **a new** departure in the politics **of Eastern** Europe. It settled for the time the **Eastern** question. The Porte, after long threatening and devastating **Europe, was** forced to resign—to Austria, to Poland, to **Venice, and to Russia—more than half** her European **possessions.** Thenceforth **she ceased to be a** terror to **Christendom ;** and that she did **cease to be a terror to** Christendom **was primarily** due **to the** gallant defence made against **her armies in** Vienna in 1683, **and to the splendid foresight, the unselfishness, the** chivalry, the daring, **of the hero-**King of **Poland!**

CHAPTER X.

BLENHEIM.

THE Peace of the Pyrenees (7th November 1659) had assured supremacy to France on the continent of Europe. The conferences at the Isle of Pheasants, which preceded it—Cardinal Mazarin acting on behalf of France and Don Louis de Haro representing Spain—had bristled with difficulties. Over those difficulties the subtlety, the tact, the firmness, of Mazarin had at length triumphed, and the treaty was signed. The signature of that treaty, assuring, as I have said, the supremacy of France on the continent of Europe, gave Mazarin the right to declare that if his native tongue was not French he had proved that his heart was so. The Peace of the Pyrenees, in fact, gave to France the provinces of Artois and Roussillon and a portion of Cerdagne*; important territories in Flanders, in Hainault, and in Luxemburg; it placed the province of Lorraine within her grasp; and, worse than all for the future peace of the world, it secured to the Monarchy of France certain eventual rights. Its moral results were greater still. The gap in the Peace of Westphalia was supplied. That treaty had humiliated the Austrian Habsburgs : this dealt a very staggering blow to the branch of the same family which governed Spain!

The peace thus formulated was still existing when the death of Mazarin (9th March 1661) left Louis XIV., then in his twenty-third year, without a guiding mind to aid him in the

* Contained now in the department of Les Pyrénées Orientales.

direction of the affairs in France. The spirit which animated the rule of that prince, a spirit of intolerance in domestic and of greed and rapine in foreign affairs, sufficed in a few years to rouse all Europe against him, to throw Germany into "the dangerous arms". of the Habsburgs, to unite, on the common ground of hatred against France, nationalities whose interests were in other respects at variance, and sympathies which, except upon that one point, had little else in common.

How little the other Powers of Europe were naturally disposed to bind themselves in a league against France may be imagined if the reader will but glance at their relative positions at the time when the guiding hand of Mazarin was about to be withdrawn. He will behold a Spain ruled by an effete race, enfeebled, almost lifeless; England still absorbed by the affection awakened by the Restoration; Holland in the hands of an aristocratic party without unity in its political and military leading, almost as defenceless as Spain; the Austrian Habsburgs engaged in a ceaseless contest with Hungary and the Porte; the rest of Germany without union, and, therefore, without strength; Italy, a geographical expression; the Northern Powers fully occupied with their own concerns. Such was the state of Europe without France. What a contrast did France herself offer! She possessed a fertile soil, yielding abundant supplies for her population; a numerous and well-disciplined army; a fleet which might then have claimed supremacy on the seas; a sovereign who could dispose without question of all her resources; union within her borders! Her capital, even then, had come to be regarded as the centre of civilisation!

It was this contrast which proved the temptation to the youthful monarch. What wonder if a young man, trained in the spirit of absolutism, habituated to regard himself as the Sun round which the world revolved and to which the lesser satellites turned for light, for guidance, for instruction—gifted with a nature which, somewhat of the common order, and inclined towards the dazzling rather than towards the useful and the beneficent, was yet originally not wanting in richness—what wonder that such a man, in the lustiness of early youth and absolute power, should, beholding the contrast I have painted, give unchecked sway to the acquisitiveness which burned as a passion within him! What wonder that he should yearn to bring under his own sceptre the disunited masses of territory around him, to make his France the centre of absolute power as she was the centre of culture!

Before Louis had taken in his own hands the reins of power, his famous minister had given to him a potent weapon for fomenting disunion in Germany. On the death, in 1657, of the Emperor Ferdinand III., Mazarin had despatched to the Diet of Frankfurt the Duke of Gramont and the Marquis of Lionne with instructions to support the candidature of the Elector of Bavaria; further, if they could not prevent the election of Leopold of Habsburg, to make secret arrangements with the minor princes of Germany which should greatly limit his power. The ambassadors failed to prevent the election of Leopold, but, as a set off, they succeeded in obtaining from that prince a promise that he would not assist Spain in the war which that power was waging with France; and, what was of far greater importance, they concluded with several of the minor German princes—Catholic and Protestant—a treaty assuring to them all, and to France herself, the peaceful exercise of the privileges secured to them and to her by the Peace of Westphalia. This league, called the Confederation of the Rhine, was a wedge which at any moment might be thrust very deeply into the vitals of the loosely-confederated German Empire. Formed in 1658, it was renewed and re-constituted and supplied with a governing Council, in 1660 and 1663.

Very few years elapsed before Louis, freed from Mazarin, used this wedge to promote the ambitious projects to which the sight of a disunited Europe round a powerful and united France had given birth in his mind. In 1665, his father-in-law, Philip IV.,

King of Spain, died. Disregarding the renunciation which the Queen, Maria Theresa, had made, on her marriage, to all the rights of inheritance, Louis at once laid claim to Spanish Flanders. After some successful negotiation with the Emperor, whom he lured by promises of division of the spoil, Louis entered Flanders, and in three weeks made himself master of that portion of the country which has ever since been known as French Flanders. A month later and the entire province submitted to his arms. From first to last his was a triumphal march. This easy conquest flattered the hopes which had long dwelt within him; and although, on the formation of an alliance against him of the sea powers—England and Holland, with Sweden—Louis agreed, whilst retaining French Flanders, to restore Franche-Comté, he restored it (1668) with the mental resolution to take the first opportunity to punish "the nation of pedlars" which, under the guidance of de Witt, had been the soul of the league against him.

The opportunity soon came. The necessities of Charles II. of England, arising from his never-ceasing schemes to undermine the liberties of Englishmen, had made him a pensioner of Louis, and as a pensioner Charles was forced to assist the French king in his schemes for universal dominion. In 1670 Charles subscribed to the conditions insisted upon by Louis for the humiliation of Holland. Two years later Sweden gave her adhesion. The Emperor was pacified by promises; and the smaller princes of Germany, the Archbishops of Mainz, of Cologne, and of Münster, openly tendered their support to the prince whom they regarded as their protector. Secure in his alliances, Louis then, the same year, invaded Holland. Vainly did Holland try to conjure the storm. To the ambassadors who asked the King what reparation he demanded for the unintentional offence* the States-General

---

* The pretext for the invasion was, of all pretexts, the most frivolous. Louis complained that the States-General had struck and circulated medals representing Holland as the arbitress of Europe. The medals bore a Latin inscription, of which the following is a translation: "Laws established, religion reformed, kings succoured, defended, and re-united, the liberty of the seas avenged, Europe pacified."

had committed, Louis deigned the following haughty answer: "I shall employ my troops in the manner which my dignity requires, and I recognise in no one the right to ask of me any explanations on the subject."

Holland had but 25,000 men to oppose to the army four times that number, at the head of which Louis, accompanied by Turenne, Condé, Vauban, and Louvois, opened the campaign. William of Orange, who commanded the Dutch, avoided for the moment risking the fortunes of his country in a battle which could have had but one result. He was compelled to see three provinces and forty strong places submit, in less than three months, to the French king. It was not, however, till Amsterdam was threatened that the States-General, torn by internal dissensions, submitted to Louis proposals of peace of a nature which, made before he had crossed the Rhine, would have found ready acceptance. Had Louis been the great statesman he believed himself to be, it had gone hard with the liberties of Europe. The acceptance of that peace would have assured to France a permanent predominance in her councils. But, throughout his reign, brilliant in many respects though it was, Louis XIV. showed himself but a poor administrator of foreign affairs. He constantly neglected the substance to grasp at the shadow. It happened so on this occasion. Much as Holland offered, Louis demanded more. He demanded, too, concessions which Holland could not grant without sacrificing her independence. He required the re-establishment of the Roman Catholic religion; the cession to the Romish Church of a fixed number of Protestant churches; the payment of twenty millions of francs for the expenses of the war; the cession of the territories possessed by the United Provinces on the Waal and on the Rhine; and, lastly, the striking and circulation of expiatory medals to be presented to him every year as a token that the Seven Provinces owed to his clemency their existence and their liberty!

Alone of all the princes of Europe the Great Elector of

Brandenburg, Frederic William, had penetrated the secret intentions of Louis, and had armed for the menaced liberties of Europe. But even Frederic William had been compelled to bow before the storm and to conclude a separate peace.* The terms insisted upon by Louis roused, however, the susceptibilities of every power on the continent. The Empire, Spain, Denmark, Lorraine, and again Brandenburg, entered into a league to crush the ambition the extent of which Louis had himself disclosed. The Dutch, meanwhile, driven to despair, had cut their dykes. Nature, thus left to her unrestrained course, had forced the French to evacuate the greater part of the country. The voice of the English people, raised in their still free Parliament, had forced Charles to renounce the French alliance. Of all his conquests in Holland there remained to Louis, at the close of 1673, only Grave (Graaf) and Maestricht. To revenge himself Louis turned upon Spain, and wrested once more Franche-Comté from that Power. On the German frontier Turenne, and, after Turenne's death, Condé and the Duke of Orleans, marched from success to success. On the sea the triumph of the French arms, wielded under the orders of the illustrious Duquesne, was signal. The war, unjustly undertaken, was advantageously finished. The Peace of Nymwegen, which affixed the seal to its achievements (10th August 1678), whilst it restored to Holland all that she had lost, gave to France Franche-Comté and confirmed her claims upon Alsace.

Though the gain was small in comparison to that which might have accrued had the political insight of Louis equalled his ambition, yet it was large enough to whet the passion of acquisitiveness—whatever might be the object—which was the ruling passion of Louis XIV. Thenceforward he acted as if he were above all treaties. With the concurrence of princes summoned for the purpose to Besançon, to Metz, and to Breisach, he examined the titles of territories which had at any time been under the dependence of Alsace, or of the three Bishoprics,

* *Vide* page 248.

Mainz, Cologne, and Münster, and caused them to be brought under the jurisdiction of France. He crowned these acts by the seizure of Strasburg (30th September 1681) in a time of profound peace!

For a moment it seemed as though this infraction of the law of nations would be resented. There was some very angry correspondence and some preparation for a third coalition. But the Empire was then threatened by that Turkish invasion described in the last chapter, and the Emperor, far from thinking of recovering Strasburg, was compelled to agree to a twenty years' peace with his ambitious neighbour. But although, in this peace, the Emperor recognised the right of France, temporarily, to Strasburg, to Luxemburg—of which she had also taken possession—and to the many places ceded to her by the reunions of Metz, Besançon, and Breisach, it did not last its full time. In 1688 the autocratic resolve of Louis to force Prince William Egon of Fürstenberg, Bishop of Strasburg, upon the Bishopric of Cologne, in spite of the decision of the Pope in favour of Prince Joseph Clement of Bavaria, caused the renewal of war with the Empire. Again was Louis the aggressor; and again was his enemy unprepared. Leopold of Austria, however, though still waging fierce war with the Porte, resolved, in spite of the entreaties of his councillors, to look his enemy in the face. All Germany rallied round him. He could not, indeed, prevent the ravaging of the Palatinate in 1687, nor were his allies, the English and the Dutch, able to ward off defeats at Fleurus, at Steenkerken, and at Neerwinden*; but the very victories exhausted France, still suffering from the fatal revocation of the edict of Nantes. Those victories were counterbalanced, too, by the destruction of the French fleet at Cape La Hogue (19 May 1692) and by the invasion of Provence by Victor Amadeus. The war languished still for five years. Then

---

* Fleurus, 1st July 1690, gained by Marshal Luxemburg over the Prince of Waldeck; Steenkerken, 14th July 1692, gained by the same over William III.; Neerwinden, or Landen, 19th July 1693, gained by the same over the same.

Louis, desirous to re-invigorate the energies of his country with the view to gain some profit from the approaching extinction of the Habsburg dynasty in Spain, resolved, after a war which lasted nine years, to sign (30th October 1697) a treaty of peace at Ryswick.

The Peace of Ryswick was for Louis a step backward. He preserved indeed Strasburg, but he was forced to renounce the many places which, by means of the reunions at Besançon, Metz, and Breisach, France had fraudulently annexed. What was, perhaps, more galling to his pride, he was compelled to recognise William III. as King of England!

The Peace was little more than an armed truce. The great powers of Europe were waiting with impatience the death of Charles II. of Spain. To his dominions the Emperor, France, and Bavaria alike preferred claims. For the moment, indeed, immediately after the exhaustion of the war, there seemed to be some chance of arriving at an understanding. In concert with France it was arranged that, on the death of the Spanish king, Spain and the Indies, with the Netherlands, should devolve to the Electoral Prince of Bavaria as grandson of the sister of Charles II.; the Milanese to Charles, second son of the Emperor; Naples, Sicily, Tuscany, and Guipuscoa, to Louis XIV. as grandson of Philip III. of Spain and as husband of a sister of Charles II. The death of the young Prince of Bavaria rendered this scheme abortive. Another arrangement, to which England, France, and Holland subscribed, but to which the Emperor refused to accede, was then promulgated. According to this, Charles, the second son of the Emperor Leopold, was to obtain Spain and the Indies with the Netherlands; Louis XIV., Lorraine, Naples, Sicily, and Guipuscoa; the Duke of Lorraine, the Milanese.

Such was the understanding between the maritime Powers when suddenly Charles II. died (October 1700). For some time previous to his death his palace had been the seat of intrigues carried on by agents of the rival Houses of Bourbon and

Habsburg. Just a month prior to the occurrence the superior address of the French agent had carried the day, and Charles had signed a will—his third and last—by which he bequeathed all the possessions of the Spanish Monarchy to Philip of Anjou, grandson of Louis XIV., and great grandson of his father, Philip IV. of Spain!

Louis, then at an age when the impulses of early youth have subsided—he was sixty-two—recognised all the dangers to which the acceptance of this vast inheritance would expose him. "The King listened," writes St. Simon, "to everyone's opinion, but he did not disclose his own. He said that he had listened with attention, and had thoroughly understood all that had been said on both sides; that on both good reasons had been advanced; but that it was well worth while to wait four-and-twenty hours for intelligence from the other side of the Pyrenees, to see if the Spaniards were of the same opinion as their King." The information received from Spain seeming to indicate that the people would ratify the choice of their late sovereign, Louis no longer hesitated. On the 16th November he presented the young Duke of Anjou to his Court as King of Spain, called to that high dignity by his birth, by the will of the late King, by the Spanish nation, and "by the order of Heaven." A few days later he bade farewell to the new King. When the latter had fairly started Louis gave vent to his satisfaction in the expression, "There are no longer any Pyrenees!"

Yet, the acceptance by the French King on behalf of his grandson of the testament of Charles II. meant, he well knew, war with Europe. Not only was it an infringement of the agreement anteriorly arrived at with England and Holland, but it passed by, as though they did not exist, the claims of the Emperor. Leopold did more than simply protest. He contested alike the validity of the will and the right of the late King to dispose in such a manner of the future welfare of his subjects; and, though without an ally, he declared war against France, and despatched an army under Prince Eugene into

Northern Italy. Eugene assumed command of that army at Roveredo the 20th May 1701.

Neither of the maritime Powers, England and Holland, was as much affected by the act of Louis as had been the Emperor. England, especially, would gladly have avoided war, and Holland did not care to wage it without the assistance of her powerful ally. Both, then, recognised Philip of Anjou as King of Spain and the Indies, and it is probable that had Louis conducted his affairs with ordinary prudence his grandson might have retained the greater part of the inheritance without a struggle. It was only necessary for him to avoid wounding the susceptibilities of England and Holland and he could easily have come to terms with the Emperor.

But Louis, as a politician, was incorrigible. His pride, unchecked by many reverses, scorned the dictates of prudence. When the success of his plans depended upon the forbearance of England he went out of his way to offer to that country a deliberate insult, and to indicate to her an infraction of treaty, to which, had it not been forced upon her notice, she might have blinded her eyes, yet in which it was impossible that she should acquiesce. The will of Charles II. had expressly barred to his nominated heir the right of succession to the throne of France. Louis, by letters patent, declared the clause which contained that condition to be null and void. Again, by the treaty of Ryswick, Louis had formally recognised the consequences of the Revolution of 1688 as they affected the rights of William III. and the succession in the Protestant line. Yet, standing by the side of the death-bed of the last King of the House of Stuart he swore to him solemnly to recognise his son as King of England; and on the father's death, 16th September 1761, he did publicly and officially so recognise him. This recognition, coming after the abrogation of the clause which would have prevented the union of the crowns of France and Spain upon one head, proved to the English people that it was necessary once more to fight for the liberties of Europe. At a meeting of Parliament in January 1702, the recognition by Louis of the Pretender was declared an infraction of existing treaties, and a levy of forty-five thousand men was decreed. The death of William, two months later (8th March), rather precipitated events. The first important act of his successor was to declare war against France (May 1702). Holland followed the example, and proceeded, with England and the Empire, to put in force against France the conditions of the Triple Alliance negotiated between the three Powers the preceding September.

Meanwhile, matters had prospered with the Emperor. Prince Eugene, left with a free hand, had crossed the Adige, gained a victory at Carpi, and repulsed an attack made upon him in great force by Marshal Villeroi at Chiari. He had then taken in succession Caneto, Marcaria, Brescello, Mirandola; and when winter set in, and the French took up winter quarters, he, more daring, blockaded Mantua. Alike for its conception and execution, the Italian campaign of 1701 is well worthy of study. It was solid and brilliant. During its progress, the Elector of Brandenburg, raised (18th June 1704) to the rank and dignity of a king, joined the Emperor. So, likewise, as we have seen, did England and Holland; with them also the King of Denmark and the Elector of Hanover. On the other hand, Max-Emanuel, Elector of Bavaria, joined France.

The campaign of 1702 was to be more sensational still. We left Eugene, in the winter of 1701-2 (January 1702) blockading Mantua—the French army, commanded by Villeroi, in winter quarters in and about Cremona. But supplies were scarce in Eugene's camp; the country about Mantua had been eaten up; money was not forthcoming. The possibility of striking such a blow as would alike remove the more pressing of these difficulties, and at the same time make the enemy reel under its force, presented itself to the fertile mind of the Prince. Some three months before, **Field-Marshal** Prince Commercy had entered into relations with a priest in Cremona, Antonio **Cosoli by name.** This **man had** informed Commercy that there existed an empty water-canal, unguarded by, probably unknown to, the French, which ran from the cellar of his house to the country outside the walls. It occurred to Eugene that he might, by means of this canal, surprise the place. The enterprise seemed the less difficult inasmuch as he had information that the French were so unsuspicious that the very gates were but feebly guarded and that there no sentinels on the walls!

Full of this idea Eugene summoned (30th January) Guido Starhemberg and the Prince of Vaudemont to his head-quarters at Luzzara. He gave his orders to both generals. Starhemberg was to march, as secretly as possible, with four thousand men to a point within five miles of Ustiano, whilst Vaudemont, with about the same number, should march through the territory of Parma and deliver a simultaneous attack from the other side.

On the evening of the 31st, Eugene, Commercy, and Starhemberg, and the troops told off for the surprise, were at Ustiano. Anxious and impatient, the three generals, leaving the troops to follow, rode on to within twelve hundred paces of Cremona, entered an empty cottage, and awaited there the arrival of their forces. The roads were heavy, and five o'clock had struck before all the men came up. Then—the great body under Eugene remaining halted near the Margaret gate—an intelligent guide, sent by the priest, led Major Hofman and his men, about two hundred in number, into the aqueduct. The distance thence to the priest's cellar, though short, took some time to accomplish, for they had to go in single file. Hofman was followed by two hundred men under Count Nasary, and Nasary by the same number under Count Küfstein. Whilst they were creeping along Count Mercy was sent with two hundred and fifty picked horsemen close to the Margaret gate with orders to dash through at the first signal, traverse the city, and open the Po gate, in order to allow free ingress to the troops under the Prince of Vaudemont who, it had been arranged, should be there in readiness.

Hofman, Nasary, and Küfstein, carried out their parts of the programme with perfect success. Their men, emerging from the cellar of Consoli's house, dashed to the Margaret gate, overpowered the small guard placed there, and admitted Mercy and his horsemen. These dashed in full gallop to the Po gate. Following them into the city came **Eugene, Commercy,** and Starhemberg, leading the infantry. **They marched** to the town hall, whence Eugene deemed he could best direct further operations.

Whilst these events were happening, the commander-in-chief of the French army, Marshal Villeroi, who had returned only the previous evening from Milan, was in bed. About seven o'clock in the morning he was awakened by hearing three musket-shots. Before he had time to surmise the cause of this unaccustomed explosion his valet rushed into the room exclaiming "The Germans are in the town!" Springing from his bed, and ordering his horse, Villeroi hastened to dress, ordering his secretary, as he did so, to burn all his papers. Scarcely had this been done when Villeroi threw himself on his horse and, followed by a single page, galloped to the mainguard. Before he was aware of it he found he had ridden into the midst of German soldiers. By these he was torn from his horse and made prisoner. Recognised by his captors as an officer of rank, he was in some danger from the energy with which each of them asserted his claim to regard him as his personal prisoner, when there dashed through the crowd an Irish officer, Macdonnel by name. Macdonnel took the prisoner, of whose name he was not aware, to Starhemberg, refusing on the way the offer made to him by Villeroi of ten thousand pistoles* and the command of a regiment, if he would only let him go. Eugene, fearing lest the French troops would, on hearing of his capture, make a desperate attempt to rescue their general, despatched him, under a strong escort, to Ustiano.

He had but just time to do so, for every moment rendered his position more critical. Mercy had indeed reached the Po gate, but had found no Vaudemont ready to enter. His numbers

* Equal to one hundred thousand francs, or four thousand pounds sterling.

were few; and before he could be reinforced an Irish regiment, in the service of the French, drove him from the gate. In the contest, he and many of his officers were made prisoners. Meanwhile the Marquis of Entragues had mustered his regiment, which he had ordered for parade the previous evening, on the market-place, and had opposed the further progress of the Imperialists. His resistance gave time to the bulk of the garrison to join him; and though many of their officers were taken prisoners, the natural intelligence of the French soldier supplied the absence of definite orders. Soon, the senior officer, Count Revel, found himself at the head of troops greatly outnumbering those of Eugene. His rear secured by the firm occupation of the Po gate, he assumed the offensive, drove the Imperialists from street to street, and, after a combat lasting ten hours, forced them to evacuate the town. The losses were considerable, the French losing twelve hundred, the Imperialists half that number. Eugene had tried a bold stroke. He had failed because his coadjutor, the Prince of Vaudemont, had not kept his engagement. Delayed by the roads, Vaudemont arrived before the town at two o'clock to find the gate by which he was to have entered strongly guarded.

In one respect the attempt had unfavourable consequences for Eugene. The captured Villeroi, pompous and vain,* was succeeded by the more brilliant and skilful Vendôme.†

* "C'etait un homme," writes Saint-Simon, "fait exprès pour présider à un bal, pour être le juge d'un carrousel, et, s'il avait eu de le voix, pour chanter à l'Opera les rôles de rois et de héros; fort propre encore à donner les modes, et rien du tout au delà."

† Vendôme, whose grandfather was a natural son of Henry IV. and Gabrielle d'Estrées, is thus described by a writer as caustic and often even more severe: "Il ne passait pas," wrote Voltaire, " pour méditer ses desseins avec la même profondeur que le Prince Eugène. Il négligeait trop les détails; il laissait périr la discipline militaire; la table et le sommeil lui dérobaient trop de temps. . . . Mais au jour d'action il réparait tout par une présence d'esprit et par des lumières que le péril rendait plus vives, et ces jours d'action il les cherchait toujours." He was first cousin, on the maternal side, to Prince Eugene. His natural talents were great. His father had been a very dull man. One day Philip V., King of Spain, on whose account the war of the Spanish succession was undertaken, asked him,"How comes it that you, the son of so dull a father, possess such great talents?" "It is because my genius (esprit) traces its origin further back," wittily replied Vendôme.

After the failure on Cremona, the **campaign in** Northern Italy resolved itself into a conflict between the genius of Eugene **and the genius of** Vendôme. **They** were fairly matched. At length, after much **marching and** counter-marching, Vendôme, obtaining a superiority in numbers by means of reinforcements from **Spain,** was able to gain an advantage. **He succeeded** first **in surprising** and cutting up three Imperial cavalry regiments **on the** Crostolo, then forced Eugene to raise the siege of Modena, **and a little later,** with an army exceeding his by one-third, **fought with him, 15th August, an** indecisive battle at Luzzara. Vendôme indeed claimed the victory on the ground that Eugene had lost many of **his** best officers and his choicest soldiers, and that, **in consequence of the battle, of** the four strong places in the **vicinity, Luzzara,** Borgoforte, Guastalla, and Oneglia, he **was** able to take **the first** three. But it is not the less a fact **that** Eugene maintained the field **of battle, and** that the places referred to would still have been taken had no battle been fought.

With the capture by the French **of** Luzzara, Borgoforte, and Guastalla, the campaign **of** 1702 in North Italy terminated. In Germany itself it had **been less** advantageous to the allies. **It is true that their army, led** nominally by **Joseph,** afterwards **the** Emperor Joseph I., having at his side the Margrave Louis of Baden and Field-Marshal Count von Thüngen, had, after a **siege of six weeks, taken** Landau, the defences of which were **justly regarded as Vauban's** masterpiece. But **the** action **of Bavaria had forced the** Imperial army to think rather of defence **than of conquest.** Max-Emanuel II., Elector **of** Bavaria, had cast **in his lot** with **the French.** In pursuance of an agreement entered into with the Court of Versailles he took possession (8th September) **of the** important town of Ulm. In anticipation of this **action Louis** XIV. had commissioned General **Villars to** pierce the German line of defences, and, joining the Elector, **to** carry the war into the heart of the Empire.

Claude Louis Hector Villars counted then forty-nine years. He had never **commanded an** army, but **he** possessed all the qualities to make a successful general. In action he was remarkable alike for his coolness and the sureness of his glance. He knew how to gain the affection of his men and to inspire them with confidence amid the greatest dangers. He was always the first under fire. Having to deal with adversaries circumspect, wary, prudent, closely following the rules of war, Villars astonished them alike by the promptitude of his conceptions and the rapidity and boldness of his views. In a word, it may be said, that famous as was the reign of Louis XIV. for the warriors who gave lustre to his throne, illustrated by the achievements of Turenne, Condé, Boufflers, Catinat, Berwick, and Vendôme, Villars was entitled to take his place as a general by the side even of the greatest of these!

Villars, answering to the call of his sovereign, set out, as soon as he had heard of the fall of Ulm, at the head of an army composed of thirty battalions, forty squadrons, and thirty pieces of cannon—about forty thousand men—and ascended the Rhine as far as Hüningen in the hope of being able to turn the German army, now commanded by the Margrave Louis of Baden, and which he knew to be posted in the Black Forest. But the Margrave had followed all the movements of Villars, and anticipating his design to penetrate into Bavaria, had occupied a strong position on the heights near Friedlingen, barring the road into that country. Villars turned it, then attacked the Margrave in flank and beat him. That night he was saluted by his soldiers Marshal of France, and Louis, always prompt to reward success, confirmed their election by sending Villars the bâton. His victory was, notwithstanding, resultless; for the heavy fall of snow which followed it prevented him from effecting a junction with Max-Emanuel. On the lower Rhine the campaign had been far more pronounced. An allied corps, composed mostly of Prussian and Dutch troops, twenty-five thousand strong, had taken Kaiserswerth (15th June), after a siege which had cost them one-fifth of their numbers. In the Netherlands the main English and Dutch army, sixty thousand strong, commanded till after the fall of Kaiserswerth—the operations of the army besieging which it had covered—by the Earl of Athlone, and subsequently, from 8th July, by the illustrious Earl of Marlborough, had captured the fortresses of Venlo (23rd September), Ruremonde (5th October), Stevenswaert (6th October), and, finally, the important city of Liège (23rd October). By the reduction of these places the allies had become masters of the Meuse as far as the heart of Flanders; they had broken down the barrier to the invasion of France which the possession of the fortresses of the Spanish Netherlands had offered. For his brilliant services in this campaign Marlborough was raised to the Dukedom.

The good result which might have been hoped for from these successes was temporarily retarded by an event which threatened, in 1702, the continuance of the rule over Hungary of the House of Habsburg. The first of these was the rising in Hungary of Prince Francis Leopold Rákóczy.

It is unnecessary to do more than refer very briefly to this rebellion. That it diminished the power of the Emperor to fight against the French cannot be doubted. For more than nine years—from the beginning of 1702 to the 11th May 1711—Hungary was an open sore in a very vulnerable part of the Empire. Taking care not to engage in a decisive battle, Rákóczy carried on a guerilla war, which nevertheless necessitated the despatch against him of large masses of the Imperial forces. The energies of Prince Eugene were diverted for this purpose in 1703. Afterwards, Marshal Heister, Count Rabuten, Guido Starhemberg, Prince John Pálffy, and others, employed all their energies to stamp out the rebellion. It was not, however, till May 1711 that they succeeded. And the reader should remember, when noting the efforts made by the Emperor against the French in Italy, on the Rhine, in Germany, in France, and even in Spain, that his resources were sorely taxed to meet at the same time a rebellion which was raging in Hungary, and the active agents of which often carried desolation and the sword into the two Austrias, into Silesia, and into Moravia.

After Eugene's departure from Italy the command of the Imperial army in that quarter devolved upon Count Guido Starhemberg. But it was no longer a question of opposing Vendôme south of the Adda. In the early spring of the year Max-Emanuel of Bavaria had begun to put into execution the plan which he had devised with the French King, of detaching Tirol from the House of Habsburg. The forerunner of the Andreas Hofer of the beginning of the present century was a man not inferior even to him in daring, in resources, in his power of influence over the people. His name was Martin Sterzinger. Nobly supported by his countrymen, this man held the mountain passes against the Bavarians. The success of his defence depended mainly, however, on the capacity of Starhemberg to prevent an advance on his rear from the south. Such an advance was threatened by Vendôme. Divining his opponent's plans Starhemberg, whose numbers fell short by nearly one-half of those of the French general, marched rapidly to the north, threw a strong garrison into Trent, and then pressing forward against the Bavarians, caught their army, defeated it, and then hurried back to stop the further progress of Vendôme. That general, meanwhile, had been employing all his energies to take Trent. The successful defence of that town gave time to Starhemberg to re-enter Italy. He returned at an opportune moment.

Victor Amadeus, Duke of Savoy, had long been chafing under his alliance with the French. Though not absolutely resolved to quit them, he had yet gone so far as to enter into negotiations with the Emperor's envoy, Count Auersperg. Information of these negotiations reached Louis XIV. early in September. Unable to control his anger, Louis at once despatched a categorical order to Vendôme to act in such a manner as would force the Duke to a decision. Vendôme was still before Trent when the order reached him. He promptly raised the siege and hastened to San Benedetto, where three thousand Piedmontese troops were encamped, surrounded them, caused the officers to be imprisoned, and distributed the common soldiers among his own regiments (29th September). He then despatched a messenger to Victor Amadeus, requiring him to declare his intentions within twenty-four hours. The Duke at once gave in his adhesion to the Emperor. In a treaty made shortly afterwards (9th November), he bound himself to contribute fifteen thousand men to the common cause.

The troops of which the Duke of Savoy could immediately avail himself were few in number; but, few as they were, they constituted an important reinforcement to Starhemberg's army. Still, counting them, that general could only dispose of twenty-four thousand men, whilst Vendôme had forty thousand. The utmost he could do, then, was to prevent the French army from approaching Turin; and this, during the short remaining period of the campaign of 1703, he accomplished.

In Germany, events had again been unfavourable to the allies. In January 1703, Marshal Villars, who, after his victory at Friedingen had placed his army into winter quarters near Strasburg, re-crossed the Rhine in January, took Kehl, after a siege of thirteen days, then, outmanœuvring the Margrave Louis of Baden, traversed the Black Forest and effected his junction with Max-Emanuel (8th May) at Ulm.

Villars was now on the Danube. Nothing so clearly demonstrated the military genius of the man as the proposals he made at once to the Elector. "We can dictate peace," he said, "if we can reach Vienna. The road to Vienna is before us. Between us and that capital is but one army, commanded by a man whose incapacity is notorious." He then urged Max-Emanuel to join with him in a march on Vienna. But the Elector was concerned so much about the lesser matter—the immediate aggrandisement of his own territories—that he seemed inclined to disregard the greater—the dictation of a peace which would have realised all his aspirations. Thereupon Villars laid before him an alternative plan. "Go, then," he said to Max-Emanuel, "and conquer Tirol; then effect a junction with Vendôme, and drive the Austrians from Italy."

Max-Emanuel, not so much a timid man—for he certainly was not that—as a small-minded man, accepted the second alternative. How the plan shattered against the resistance of the Tirolese and the enterprise of Starhemberg has been already told. He returned, in September, with a beaten army, to join Marshal Villars. Under the circumstances, Villars, in the very heart of Germany, wanting provisions, but sparsely provided even with gunpowder, and incommoded rather than assisted by the presence of Max-Emanuel, felt that a decisive victory was necessary to relieve him from his difficulties. He made up his mind to gain one. The Imperial army, commanded by Count Styrum, was, he learnt, at Höchstädt, twelve miles from Donauwörth, on the road to Neu-Offingen. Villars marched against him and attacked him with such fury that the battle was gained in little more than half an hour. The enemy's loss amounted to eight thousand men killed and wounded and seven thousand prisoners. Then were evidenced the possibilities which would have been assured if only Max-Emanuel had yielded to the entreaties of Villars three months before. The road to Vienna was open. But the course which would have been easy for a well-provided army Villars deemed impracticable for one destitute of everything. He declined, then, to move forward. After a violent altercation with the Elector he fell back on Memmingen The altercation of which I have spoken caused the King of France to transfer the command of the army to Marshal Tallard.

In Alsace and the Palatinate the French arms had met the same year (1703) decided success. Tallard, who commanded the corps operating in those provinces, had taken Alt-Breisach (21st September); then, descending the Rhine, laid siege to Landau. He had besieged that place a month when he learnt that the Duke of Hesse-Cassel was approaching with an army to relieve it. Leaving one-fourth of his men to blockade the place, Tallard led the remaining three-fourths to meet the Duke, encountered him at Speyer (15th November), and completely defeated him.* Two days afterwards Landau surrendered to his arms.

In the Netherlands, **Marlborough, at the** head of an army fifty-five thousand strong, **was** opposed to Villeroi, who commanded 52,000. Strong **in the** advantages he had gained the previous year, Marlborough had resolved to resume the offensive. He had designed to lay siege to Antwerp, and, after reducing that strong place, to attack Ostend. The capture of these places **would not only** have opened **a** direct sea-communication with England: **it would have** prevented the French from reinforcing **their army in Germany.** To his disappointment Marlborough found that the **States-General** were strongly **opposed** to a scheme **of that character: their** thoughts were **bent on the Lower Rhine; and, for the** moment, their great **object was the reduction** of Bonn. Constrained by force of circumstances to adopt the views **of his allies,** Marlborough **set to work** with his **usual energy to** carry them out. **He had landed at the Hague the** 17th **March**; he reached **Bonn** the **20th April; and, delayed** somewhat by the Dutch, **opened trenches on the 3rd May.** On the 15th the place surrendered.

Whilst Marlborough was before Bonn, Villeroi had made a **great effort to save the place.** Breaking up on **the** 9th May **from Montenacher, he took** Tongres on the 11th, **and** advanced **promptly on Maestricht,** which he hoped to find undefended. His movements, **however,** had been **reported to** General Overkirk, **who, posted between** Liège **and** Bonn, was covering Marlborough's siege operations; and that general, divining his **intentions, had made a** forced march to the city which he **deemed to be the first** object **of** Villeroi's movements. He

---

* Tallard announced the victory to his master in the following laconic terms: "Sire, votre armée **a** pris plus d'étendards et de drapeaux qu'elle n'a perdu de soldats."

marched so rapidly, that when Villeroi appeared before Maestricht, the morning of the 12th, he found his way barred by Overkirk's army. Very superior in numbers, the French general, with whom likewise was Marshal Boufflers, resolved to attack; but, as he approached the allied position, he found it so formidable, its left resting on Maestricht, its right on Petershorn, and its front strongly defended, that he renounced the idea and returned to Tongres.

After the fall of Bonn, Marlborough resolved to carry out his long-meditated designs against Antwerp. Between that city and himself lay the French army. He designed then that whilst one corps of the allied army under General Spaar should attack that part of the French lines which lay beyond the Scheldt, and a second, under the renowned engineer Cohorn, should force that other part which covered the territory of Hulst, a third, still stronger, under the command of General Obdam, should advance against Antwerp from the side of Bergen-op-Zoom, and make itself master of the lines covering the fortress on that side. Marlborough himself, commanding the main army, was meanwhile so to threaten the French centre as to prevent it from sending aid to the threatened points, and, on being assured of Obdam's success, to enter the enemy's lines betweeen Leine and Antwerp and form the siege of that fortress. It was a plan dangerous to carry out against a vigilant and daring enemy, placed in the very centre of the circle on the arc of which Marlborough was operating. To secure the success of the operation every move of it must be successful.

Here the failure of one move spoiled the whole plan. Spaar succeeded; Cohorn succeeded; but Boufflers, detached by Villeroi with a strong force, attacked (30th June) Obdam at Ekeren, and so totally defeated him that the Dutch general had great difficulty in effecting his escape attended by thirty horsemen. His army, left to the charge of General Schlangenberg, lost four thousand men, six hundred prisoners, and eight guns, before it could effect its retreat to Fort Lille.

Notwithstanding this defeat, Marlborough was still sanguine. His army had been strengthened to the number of sixty-four thousand men, and at the head of these he projected, on the 23rd July, an attack on Villeroi, whose army, fifty thousand strong, was drawn up in front of the French lines. The movement had already begun, but, before it could take effect, Villeroi prudently withdrew his army behind the threatened lines. Strong as those lines were, Marlborough was still anxious to attack them. He was over-ruled, however, by the Dutch deputies, and withdrew. Retracing his steps to the vicinity of Liège, he took Huy, a strong fortress on the Meuse. This capture may be said to have concluded the somewhat barren campaign of 1703 in the Netherlands.

Regarding the campaign of 1703 as a whole, the advantages preponderated on the side of the French. True it is that the Duke of Savoy had gone over to the allies, and Portugal had, likewise, declared in their favour; but whilst in the Netherlands their success had been slight, in Northern Italy they had been reduced to the defensive. They had suffered one defeat on the middle Rhine; whilst in Germany the French had not only destroyed the only army covering Vienna, but had discovered the means by which, by a rapid advance on that capital, the war with the Emperor might be brought to a speedy conclusion.

The ideas in that respect which Marshal Villars had brought with him from Bavaria had indeed found a quick response at Versailles. Already, after the defeat of the Duke of Hesse-Cassel at Speyer (15th November), the French Court had detached a considerable force, escorting a large convoy, under General Marchin,* to join the Elector. The very day of his arrival the Elector presented him with royal patent letters, dated from Versailles, conferring upon him the rank of Marshal of France. Marchin, who had accepted the ideas of Villars, at once marched upon and took possession of Augsburg (December). Max-

---

* Incorrectly styled by most writers "Marsin." He was son of the Marchin who was severely wounded at Allersheim, *vide* pages 197-8.

Emanuel, on his side, setting out from Donauwörth, followed the Danube, without opposition, as far as Passau, and occupied that place early in January (1704).

This, then, was the position at the beginning of that year. France had one army in the Netherlands under Marshal Villeroi, one in Northern Italy under Vendôme, a third on the Rhine under Tallard, a fourth in the heart of Germany under Marchin. She had, besides, troops in Spain, and others employed in repressing the insurrection of the Protestants in the Cevennes. With armies in all these countries, the Court of Versailles, thoroughly imbued with the ideas of Villars, had resolved to strike the deadly blow in Germany.

To oppose these armies, the allies, not counting the troops employed in Spain and in Hungary, possessed one army, that of Marlborough, in the Netherlands; a second, commanded by the Margrave of Baden, in Germany; a third, opposed to that of Tallard, on the Rhine and Moselle, commanded by Prince Eugene. This prince had been recalled from Hungary to meet the dangers threatening the empire from the alliance between Bavaria and France. His clear eye, closely examining the situation, had detected that France would make two serious efforts in 1704—the one in Italy, the other, and most dangerous, in the heart of Germany. It is in that direction that we must turn.

In January 1704 the troops of the Elector of Bavaria occupied the entire country between the Inn and the Lech. Besides Passau, Kufstein and several places in Upper Austria were in their hands. A strong corps was posted, likewise, in the Upper Palatinate. Max-Emanuel had his head-quarters at Munich.

Supporting and in military connection with the Bavarian troops was the army-corps of Marshal Marchin. The headquarters of this army were at Augsburg. Giving touch to the Bavarians on the Lech, it occupied the ground between that river and the Iller, and from Augsburg to the Danube.

The army of Marshal Tallard occupied, for the most part, Alsace and Franche-Comté, keeping touch, at the same time, with the army corps commanded by the Count of Coigny on the Moselle.

It must be added that whilst the **Bavarian troops and those of** Marshal Marchin **formed a united army, and the troops of** Tallard and Coigny likewise **a united army, there yet existed a space between those two armies, which prevented direct communication the one with the other. Such communication was** rendered **impossible by the fact that that space was occupied by** Imperial **troops who held Freiburg and the** passes **of the** Black **Forest. These troops were** commanded by the Margrave of Baden.

It was clear to Eugene that the **danger to be** feared **was a junction between the armies** of **Tallard and** Marchin **and a march upon Vienna, whilst Vendôme,** Villeroy, **and** Coigny, **should occupy his attention** and **that of** Marlborough and Starhemberg. He wrote these **ideas to Marlborough, and,** pointing out to him **that the Empire was totally** unable to aid him in the Netherlands **whilst the sword was pointed** at its very heart in Germany, urged **him to unite** with **him in an** attempt **to baffle the** enemy **by meeting him on the very** ground he had **selected.** The idea **entirely coincided with the views of** Marlborough, **and he at once applied for and obtained from** England and the States-General—with some difficulty **from the latter*— permission to** carry it into **execution.**

The danger was, indeed, **pressing. Acting on the** urgent **orders of** his sovereign, Tallard **had massed his** troops, now strongly **reinforced, in Alsace,** and had collected there vast **stores of supplies, laden on** carts, **which he** purposed to take **with him** into Bavaria. As soon as **he** was ready to set out he **sent word to** Marchin and Max-Emanuel, **and** these, acting on a

---

* "I expect," said Eugene to Marlborough, when **they met, "if** Alexander the Great had been obliged to await the approbation **of the Dutch** deputies before he executed his projects his conquests would not **have been quite** so rapid as they were."

pre-arranged plan, marched against Donaueschingen, where a German corps, under the Field-Marshal Lieutenant von Thüngen already mentioned, was stationed. Thüngen, alarmed, fell back on Rottweil. His thoughts were then so entirely occupied by the movements of his two opponents that he paid no heed to the movements of a third. That third, no other than Tallard, confident that his colleagues would keep fixed the attention of Thüngen, crossed the Rhine at Breisach, the 13th May, with twenty-four thousand men, thirty guns, and his enormous convoy. To support him, Coigny crossed the same river the same day at Rheinau with thirteen thousand. Pressing on with all the expedition possible on the circumstances, Tallard made his way through the Black Forest by Freiburg, and effected a junction, the 13th May, with his coadjutors between Villingen and Donaueschingen. The ease with which this important operation was effected was due mainly to the extraordinary forbearance of Margrave Louis of Baden. This general might easily have attacked Tallard before the junction had been effected. His abstaining to do so caused grave suspicions in the highest quarters in Vienna.

The instructions given to Tallard were to make over the convoy to Max-Emanuel and to return to Alsace. Carrying out these instructions to the letter, he re-crossed the Rhine the 2nd June. Max-Emanuel then took up a position at Ulm; Louis of Baden, who had taken action after the convoy had been delivered, moved to Ehingen, twenty miles to the south-west of Ulm.

Marlborough, meanwhile, acting in perfect concert with Eugene, had crossed the Rhine at Coblentz the 26th May, and traversing the Neckar at Ladenburg (3rd June), had entered Mundelsheim on the 10th. There Eugene, accompanied only by a small escort, met him. The interview which followed laid the foundation of the esteem, admiration, and regard which existed between the two men during the remainder of their lives. Three days later the two commanders, riding on in front of the English army, had an interview with the Margrave Louis of Baden in his head-quarters at Gross Heppach (on the Rems), a village on the direct road to Nördlingen. Under a tree, still living, in front of the Lamm inn, also still used as a hostelry, the three commanders deliberated over the plan of the campaign. The first matter to decide was that which should regulate the command. On this point the Margrave displayed an obstinacy only to be accounted for by the jealousy with which he had viewed the selection by the Emperor of Eugene to the chief command against the Turks in 1697, against Catinat in 1702, and his nomination to be President of the Imperial Council of War in 1703. He insisted, in the first instance, that he should command the allied armies; when this was shown to be impossible, he agreed, though with great reluctance, that he and Marlborough should command on alternate days. For him, the example of Paulus Emilius and Terentius Varro had no terrors. As a consequence of this arrangement Eugene was relegated to the command of the army of the Rhine, watching Tallard. This was especially hard upon him, as the scheme had originated in his brain. The army commanded by the Margrave Louis lay at Gross Heppach. Thither, through long and narrow defiles, Marlborough led his troops; and there, on the 18th June, the junction was effected. The two generals had resolved to become possessed of some strong place on the Danube which would give them the power of crossing that river, and they had fixed for that purpose on the important town of Donauwörth.

The town of Donauwörth has been often mentioned in these pages. It had been occupied and re-occupied, during the Thirty Years' War, by the Swedes and the Imperialists. The importance of its position, commanding the passage of the Danube contiguous to the point where the Lech flows into that river, had always given it great value. Covering the town on the north, its left resting on the covered way and its right thrown back till it reaches one of the branches of the Danube, is a conical hill, with a flat surface on the summit, half a mile in diameter, called the Schellenberg. Opposite the centre of this hill was a thick wood, called the Borchberg. Other artificial defences had been erected by Gustavus Adolphus, and these, though in a state of disrepair, might, in a few days, be greatly strengthened. The hill was occupied by Count Arco with eight thousand men. The main Anglo-Bavarian army occupied a position behind the Lech similar to that held by Tilly in 1632.

The allied commanders arrived before the place at two o'clock on the morning of the 2nd July. Their men had been marching since three in the morning—having halted only to take their meals—and were tired. Nevertheless, the generals promptly reconnoitred. Both of them recognised the great strength of the place, but the eye of Marlborough detected indications that a delay, even of eighteen hours, would cause the dilapidated artificial defences to be greatly strengthened. He, therefore, urged an immediate attack. His colleague was, at first, for delay; but, finally, realising the facts patent to Marlborough, he gave way.

The Bavarian soldiers, not expecting an attack, were at work with the spade and shovel. No sooner, however, had Arco realised the intention of the allies, than he ordered them under arms, and detached three thousand into Donauwörth to maintain a flanking fire on the enemy as he should advance. The hill was very defensible, and, had his orders been obeyed, it is probable that the attack would have been repulsed. As it was, he drove back a first attack, a second, and a third; and it was only in consequence of a turning movement made by the Margrave, which secured for his men admission to the base of the hill through the unfinished works—a movement impossible had the troops in Donauwörth obeyed their orders, and which, for a few critical moments, distracted the attention of Arco from the front—that a fourth attack succeeded. The storming of the Schellenberg cost the victors fifteen hundred killed and four thousand wounded.* The results of this victory were the surrender of Donauwörth to the allies, the retreat of Max-Emanuel to the vicinity of Augsburg.

The day before the Schellenberg had been stormed Tallard had again crossed the Rhine, at the head of twenty-six thousand men, to effect a junction with Max-Emanuel. To replace and support him, Villeroi came a few days later with an army equally strong and took post at Offenburg. Coigny still continued to occupy his old position, between Fort Louis and Drusenheim, threatening always an attack on the lines of Stolhofen. Those lines were occupied by Eugene with an army which he had not proved and which, as yet, knew him not. Its component parts were contingents from Brandenburg, the Palatinate, Denmark, the circles of Westphalia, and the Upper Rhine. The Brandenburg, or, as the world began now to call it, the Prussian contingent, was commanded by Prince Leopold of Anhalt-Dessau; and as it was the contingent upon which Eugene would have most to rely, everything depended upon the relations which should be established between that prince and himself.

Fortunately, the Prince of Anhalt-Dessau, though his manners were brusque and his bearing was stern, was a man of good sense and judgment; beloved, in spite of his rough exterior, by his men, and a very capable commander. Merit always attracts. Leopold recognised the genius of Eugene; Eugene was drawn towards the unbending warrior who placed duty above all other considerations. Thus it was that before even the tie of a common glory had united them Eugene felt that his orders would be carried out. He could not, indeed, attempt to hinder the march of Tallard towards Bavaria, for he had Villeroi in front of him. But, bent on preventing the overwhelming of

---

* Alison states that only three thousand of the garrison could be collected round the French standards after the storm. But, then, he puts the original number of the defenders at twelve thousand, whereas the best German authorities rate them only at eight thousand. *Vide*, also, Arneth's *Prinz Eugen*, page 249, "Und entsendete den Feldmarschall Grafen Arco mit acht tausend Mann zur Besetzung des Schellenberges."

the allies by an enormous superiority, he disposed twenty thousand men of his army in such a manner as completely to impose upon the French general, and hurried with the remainder, fifteen thousand, on the track of Tallard. He was fully resolved to attack that general should opportunity offer. But Tallard did not give him a chance. He effected his junction with Max-Emanuel the 4th August near Augsburg. Eugene, with his army, reached Dondorf the 31st July. On the 6th of the following month he pitched his camp, not far from the allies, at Höchstädt.

Marlborough and the Margrave had, in the meanwhile, crossed the Danube and the Lech, and had taken Rain and Aichach. Aichach is but a short sixteen miles from Augsburg. Thence, and from Friedberg, still nearer, the allies had carried on negotiations with Max-Emanuel with the hope of detaching him from the French alliance. Max-Emanuel, for a time, temporised; but as soon as he heard that Tallard was approaching he broke off the correspondence. Marlborough avenged himself by "ravaging the country with light troops, levying contributions wherever they went, and burning the villages with savage ferocity as far as the gates of Munich."*

Eugene rode over to the allied camp on the 6th to concert measures with its commanders. He found them divided in opinion. The Margrave was bent on besieging Ingolstadt. Marlborough objected to the employment of his own troops for such a purpose. The difficulty was solved by a proposal made by the Margrave, to the intense relief of Marlborough and Eugene, that he personally should undertake the siege provided Marlborough would cover his operations. This course of action was resolved upon, and Eugene, the conqueror of Zenta and the hero of Luzzara, offered, with characteristic self-

---

* Alison's *Life of the Duke of Marlborough*, page 156. He adds that "three hundred towns or villages were consumed in this savage warfare." Rightly does Alison call it savage; it deserved even a stronger epithet, for it was wholly unnecessary.

abnegation, to place himself, for the carrying out of the common purpose, under the orders of the Englishman.

Eugene stayed three days in the English camp, interesting himself in the preparations for covering the siege of Ingolstadt. He then returned to Höchstädt. He had scarcely arrived there (the 9th) when he received information that the French and Bavarians had sent a part of their army across the Danube at Neu-Offingen, and that this portion, to be followed by the remainder, was in full march on Dillingen, a town only five miles from Höchstädt. Giving strict orders to Leopold of Anhalt-Dessau to fall back behind the Wernitz on the very first indication on the part of the enemy to move along the Danube, Eugene rode back to Marlborough to request that he would reinforce him with the corps of the Duke of Würtemberg. On receiving Marlborough's promise, he returned in advance of that corps, only to find that his troops had fallen back before the enemy and were engaged in intrenching themselves on the Schellenberg. Eugene at once threw a strong detachment into Donauwörth; then, with the remainder of the cavalry at his disposal, took up a position on the Kesselbach, between Münster and Oppertshofen, there to await the arrival of the Würtemberg troops, under orders to cross the same night at Merxheim. In that position, his horses saddled and his men in readiness, Eugene waited the approach either of his reinforcements or of the enemy. The former came first. He then directed that the girths of the saddles should be loosened, and that his men should take some sleep. Though his army constituted, even with the reinforcements, but one-third of the number of the advancing enemy, he resolved not to budge without a fight.

Max-Emanuel and his French allies were, meanwhile, moving forward with the intention, at the outset, of making the attack which Eugene was awaiting behind the Kesselbach. Better had it been for them if they had adhered to their resolve, for, with their overwhelmimg numbers, they must have forced the position; and if they had then pressed on they would have met, flushed with victory, the English army hurrying forward. But the information that the fortified town of Höchstädt was but feebly occupied by their enemy, made them resolve to reduce that place in the first instance. This was their first mistake. They had two objects before them, a greater and a lesser : the greater, to prevent the junction of Eugene and Marlborough ; the lesser, to take Höchstädt. They deliberately chose the lesser. The consequence was that Eugene remained unassailed on the Kesselbach, and Marlborough, who with a full comprehension of the situation, had set his army in motion towards that brook on the morning of the 11th, effected a complete junction with Eugene by the early morning of the following day. The opportunities which were lost to the allied French and Bavarians may be judged from the fact that whereas Eugene was expecting to be attacked by them on the night of the 10th, and they might easily have assailed him, at the latest, on the early morn of the 11th, the vanguard, that is, the cavalry, of Marlborough's army, joined him only on the afternoon of that day, the main body very late the same evening, and the artillery and baggage not till the following morning !

The French took Höchstädt. Whilst they were engaged before it they spied, in the distance, clouds of dust. They ascertained that this was occasioned by a reconnaissance made by Marlborough and Eugene. It was the first intimation to their generals that a great opportunity had been lost and a junction between the allied armies effected !

Höchstädt having been captured, the French and Bavarians advanced and took up a position behind a little rivulet known as the Nebelbach. Tallard, who commanded the right, occupied the village called by the Germans Blindheim—but which we, in deference to the contempt for the spelling of foreign names displayed by our forefathers, are bound to call Blenheim— almost touching, with his extreme right, the Danube. Marchin, who commanded on the left, rested on Lutzingen and the slopes of the Goldberg. Max-Emanuel, with the cavalry of his guard, was posted at Sondernheim, a short distance in rear of Blenheim.

Marlborough had drawn up his army on the ground behind the Kesselbach, where he had joined Eugene. His left wing, which constituted nearly two-thirds of its strength, which he commanded in person, occupied Münster, on the Danube; the right, led by Eugene, Oppertshofen. The two wings, extending to the right and left from these extreme points, touched at a village called Bragstetten.

The reconnaissance which Marlborough and Eugene made on the afternoon of the 11th, and another, which followed it, on the 12th, had been careful and thorough. They had noticed that to the south-west of Donauwörth, along the left bank of the Danube, there extended for several miles a plain, which, covered to the north by wooded hills, sloped imperceptibly towards the river. This plain was intersected by several rivulets, ditches, and watercourses, and was in many places marshy, covered with coarse grasses and reeds. It counted on its surface, nevertheless, villages, isolated houses, and mills. Between Lutzingen and Blenheim its breadth was about four and a half English miles, whilst at its narrowest point—that about Schweningen and Tapfheim, immediately in front of the allied position—the wooded slopes of the hills descended to within two thousand paces from the river. The Danube itself flows here in snake-like turnings; it abounds in islands and sand-banks; brooklets run into it, and bushes in many parts cover its banks.

It had been the original intention of the two allied generals to advance to the vicinity of Höchstädt. But in their second reconnaissance they beheld, from the church-tower of Tapfheim, the masses of the enemy taking up a position just beyond that village. They came then and there to the resolution to attack them before they should have had time to add in any degree to the natural strength of the ground. They instantly gave orders for the filling-up, in their immediate front, of the ditches which otherwise would have retarded the advance of their men; and when, in the course of their operations, the fatigue-parties were attacked by, and repulsed, the enemy's horse, they caused the narrow part of the plain, where it was most defensible, to be strongly occupied. The rest of the afternoon and evening they spent in making preparations for an advance on the morrow.

At two o'clock on the morning of the 13th the allied troops were silently awakened and ordered to fall in. The men, drawn up in the order in which they were to advance, stood impatiently awaiting the dawn, which was to be the signal of their forward movement. Their total number was fifty-two thousand, with sixty-six guns, and they were composed of the contingents of many sovereigns. Germany was not then a nation; and the troops from Prussia, from Hanover, from Hesse, from the Palatinate, and from Würtemberg, were foreigners to each other. Besides these, there were Danes, Dutch, and last, but certainly not the least of all, the stalwart sons of the British Isles. Fortunately, the two men who led this army were firmly united in opinion. They were the greatest captains of their age; and their regard for each other was heightened by the respect, amounting to admiration, with which each regarded his comrade's genius.

The French and Bavarians mustered fifty-six thousand* men and ninety guns. Of these, the Bavarians counted fourteen thousand. But the slight superiority in numbers which they possessed was more than counterbalanced by the inferiority of their commanders. Tallard possessed industry, application, and coherence of ideas; he was, too, beloved by his officers and men. But he was short-sighted, and, on this occasion, he commanded only his own army corps. Marchin had served under Tallard at Speyer, but here he, too, held an independent command. This division of command constituted an enormous weakness in the

---

* Alison has rated the allies approximately at fifty-six thousand, and the French at sixty thousand. The difference between the two enemies is the same as that derived from the numbers which I have given on the authority of Arneth.

French army, and contributed not a little to the loss of the battle.

At three o'clock in the morning the order was given to the allied army to advance. The army corps of Eugene, which consisted of nearly eighteen thousand men and formed the right, was ranged in four columns—two of infantry, and the like number of cavalry. The infantry led; then followed the guns; the cavalry brought up the rear. The English * army, thirty-four thousand strong, formed the left, and was similarly disposed. A thick mist covered the plain, and necessitated the exercise of care and caution.

The army pushed on till the first rivulet, the Reichenbach, was passed. The order to halt was then given, and the men were formed in fighting order. The infantry of both wings took ground to the right, so as to allow the cavalry to occupy a position in the centre. The artillery was redistributed—portions being posted between the several cavalry brigades, the remainder being directed to follow the infantry. Pressing on again, the columns came upon and took up the battalions which had occupied Tapfheim during the night. These battalions, strengthened by other troops, formed a ninth column, destined to cover the advance of the English and Dutch cavalry and to lead the attack on Blenheim.

Silently the troops advanced. No sound from the enemy's camp reached their ears. At length, at six o'clock, under cover of a cloud of light cavalry skirmishers, they reached the slopes of the hills between the so-called Augraben and the Nebelbach. Here, again, a halt was ordered. Then, Marlborough and Eugene rode forward to reconnoitre.

The advanced posts of the enemy were alone visible. Again, then, was the order given to move forward. As the army marched on the enemy's pickets were seen to fall back. At seven

---

* The "English" army was composed of English, Dutch, Hanoverians, Hessians, and Danes. The numbers were approximately 9,000 English, 9,500 Dutch, 9,500 Hanoverians, 4,500 Hessians, and 1,500 Danes.

o'clock the army reached the elevations which stretch towards Wolpertstetten. By this time the mist had quite cleared away. The enemy's camp was visible in all its extent. The entire course of the Nebelbach, covering his front, was clear to the view. His position seemed very strong. On the right, Tallard was covered by the Danube; in his immediate front was the village of Blenheim, evidently strongly garrisoned. In front of Blenheim, on the Nebelbach, there were visible many mills and detached houses, all apparently occupied. Nor did the centre seem to present a better chance for attack. There, the village of Oberglauheim offered the main point of resistance. It, too, was occupied. Whilst the ground in front of it was a marsh, the made paths across which were guarded, that behind it was commanded by the hillocks, strongly held by hostile batteries, in its immediate rear. Its left, too, was linked to the army corps of Marchin and the troops of Max-Emanuel, whose left flank, again, was covered by the heights which have been already spoken of. There seemed but one weak spot in the arrangement. The distance between the right about Blenheim and the centre about Oberglauheim was too great to allow of touch. If this were weakly held—and it had that appearance —the concentration against it of a strong attack would inevitably sever the troops in Blenheim from the rest of their army.

Whilst Marlborough and Eugene are peering eagerly to detect that weak spot, I propose to inquire for a moment into the plans of the two French marshals and the Elector of Bavaria. Their previous conduct in attacking Höchstädt, instead of pressing on against Eugene, proved that they had no great idea of their enemy's enterprise. To the very morning of the 13th, indeed, they believed that the allies would retreat before them. Even when the latter's cavalry pressed on towards the Nebelbach they still believed it was only a demonstration designed to cover a retreat on Nördlingen.* Not till the mist had completely

* "The enemy," wrote Tallard to the French Minister of War in the early hours of that identical morning, "sounded the reveille at two o'clock this morning, the

cleared away, and the morning light displayed to their astonished gaze the allied army marching in battle array to the attack, did the deception vanish. Then, for a few moments, all was confusion. The trumpets and bugles sounded to arms. Three cannon-shots recalled to their ranks the forage parties started, or about to start, on their daily errand. There was the rush to arms, the hurry to take up the appointed position. It is on such occasions that the natural intelligence of the French soldier displays itself. It was not wanting on this occasion; and, before the allies could approach sufficiently near to fire a shot, their gallant opponents were as ready to receive them as though they had been expecting them since the early dawn!

Tallard regarded Blenheim as the key of his position. To secure it absolutely, he had concentrated in and about it sixteen thousand of his best troops, under Lieut.-General the Marquis of Clérembault. He did not take sufficient note of the fact that though he might thus secure Blenheim, he weakened the thin line which joined him to Oberglauheim, and thus gave a chance to an adventurous enemy to cut him off. He was more careful about his extreme right, for he had filled the small space between Blenheim and the Danube with a barricade of wagons, defended in their rear by four regiments of dismounted dragoons. The front of the village was protected by palisades and abattis.

To the left of Blenheim, following the course of the Nebelbach, at some little distance from its bank, was ranged the French cavalry of the right wing, about five thousand five hundred strong, supported in the centre by two weak brigades of infantry numbering about five thousand four hundred men. Baron Zurlauben, who commanded this line, had received instructions to allow the enemy to cross the brook without opposition, so that their defeat when they were repulsed might be the more complete.

assembly at three o'clock. He is ranged in battle array in front of his camp, and, according to all appearances, he will march to-day. The rumour is that he will move on Nördlingen."

The left of this long line of cavalry nearly touched Oberglauheim. This village was defended by Lieut.-General the Marquis of Blainville with seven thousand men. This village, and the village of **Lutzingen** to the left of it, formed the pivots of the left wing, which, stretching to the slopes of the hills, strongly occupied all the ground to the left of it as far as Eichbergerhof. It remains only to be added that the three villages mentioned were connected by bridges with the country which the allies were traversing.

The reconnaissance made by Marlborough and Eugene had not fully disclosed to those generals the weakness—of which we, who are behind the scenes, have been made aware—of the line of connection between Blenheim and Oberglauheim. Marlborough believed, with Tallard, that Blenheim was the key of the French position, and against it he resolved to hurl his attack. Whilst thus engaged, Eugene was to cross the Nebelbach and assail Lutzingen.

At nine o'clock, the English column of attack, commanded by Lord Cutts—the first line consisting of five English and four Hessian battalions under General Rowe, the supports of eleven battalions and fifteen squadrons led by Lord Cutts himself—advanced against Blenheim. Under a very heavy fire directed from that village Cutts stormed the two detached mills in its front, and then dashed against the palisades immediately defending it. His attack, however, shattered before the steady defence of the gallant Frenchmen. Reserving their musketry fire till the assailants were well within distance, these men then delivered it with murderous effect. Still, however, Rowe pressed on. Vainly, however. Conscious of the strength of their defences, the enemy renewed their fire. Still, always advancing, the English reached the palisades, and strove to reach the enemy with the bayonet. But they could not force the palisades. Vainly did the men, seizing them with their hands, and, clinging to them, endeavour to tear them from the earth or to break them down. The steady fire of the French infantry continued to shoot them down. Still they clung on—their leader badly wounded, the two next senior officers killed, half their own numbers vanished—hoping that their pertinacity would still succeed. Just then, a charge on their left flank from the French cavalry threw them into disorder. For a moment, indeed, they lost their colours; and though these were recovered, and an opportune charge of the English cavalry drove back their first assailants, yet, others more numerous came on; and the allied columns, beaten and baffled, fell back, in great disorder, to their original position.

The failure of this attack convinced Marlborough that it was useless to persevere in a direct assault on Blenheim. The right of the enemy was safe. Reports from his own right brought him intelligence that Eugene was preparing to fully occupy the enemy's centre. There remained, then, that line between the French right and its centre, which constituted the weakness of the French disposition, and which, he felt sure, might be pierced. His infantry had failed against palisades and houses defended by men more numerous than themselves. But if, masking those palisades and houses, he were to hurl his masses against the thin line whose only defence was a rivulet, he would surely reverse the conditions. Then, without a doubt, it would be he who could bring the greatest number to bear on the decisive point of the field of battle.

Fully impressed with this idea, Marlborough resolved without delay to hurl his cavalry, supported by infantry, across the Nebelbach. As a preliminary, it was necessary that the latter should drive the enemy from Unterglauheim, a small village midway between Blenheim and Oberglauheim, on the centre of a bend made by the Nebelbach towards the English position. To storm that village he despatched the infantry division, commanded by Lord Churchill. But, before Churchill could reach it, the French, well aware that it was not defensible, had set fire to it and retired. This incident did not much retard the advance. The English pressed forward as best they could, crossed the

Nebelbach by the bridge, and re-formed on the other side. They were followed by the Hanoverian division, **commanded by the Prince of Holstein-Beck, who had orders, on re-forming, to attack Oberglauheim. No sooner had these divisions crossed the rivulet than Marlborough ordered a general advance of** the cavalry. But the difficulties they encountered were **far greater than had been foreseen. In many parts the rivulet** was divided **into** channels, the banks **on both sides and the beds of which** were **soft and** marshy. For a time, it seemed as though the passage **could not be** accomplished; and it **was** only by dint **of the** greatest exertions, by casting in **fascines and boards, that the horses were** at length **able to** struggle through. **Even then they** reached the further **bank in twos and threes,** without order or arrangement, thus **giving a splendid opportunity to the French** leader **to deal with them in detail. But Tallard,** though he continued **to direct a constant fire from the guns of the somewhat too distant Blenheim, unaccountably neglected this** great opportunity. His action, **now about to be described,** proved that he committed **a very great** fault, **that he deemed** himself **too** sure **of** victory, **and, believing he could destroy** the whole British cavalry, would **not content himself with the few lest he** should scare the remainder.

Tallard waited till the greater part of **the allied cavalry had, after great** difficulties, **crossed the Nebelbach. Then, whilst they were** still in disorder, **still in twos and** threes, struggling to form, he directed against **them a charge of the** entire **French** horse at **his** disposal, supporting that **charge by** a flank **fire of** guns and musketry from the enclosures **of** Blenheim. **This** charge had almost decided **the day.** The French horsemen overthrew **the** struggling line **of the** allied **cavalry,** whilst the **fire I have spoken of threw** their left flank **into the direst confusion. Then occurred one** of those **critical moments peculiarly** favourable **to the** assertion of individual **power. Just as the** French deemed victory within their grasp, **Churchill, who it will be** recollected had **crossed the rivulet** with his infantry **division,**

opened a musketry-fire so severe that the enemy's attention was diverted for some minutes, and Marlborough, with great exertion, was able to bring across the Danish and Hanoverian squadrons, who had, till then, remained on the other side. With these, for a few moments, he restored the combat. Only, however, for a few moments. The French cavalry, re-forming, drove these in their turn before them in disorder; and it was only the opportune arrival of the remainder of the English infantry which prevented a total rout. Before their musketry-fire the French horsemen fell back, and gave the opportunity to the English army to cross and form up in two lines on the ground east of the Nebelbach.

This had scarcely been accomplished when information reached Marlborough that the right of the wing which he commanded was seriously compromised. The reader will recollect that, as a part of his scheme, Marlborough had directed the Prince of Holstein-Beck, who commanded the Hanoverian division, forming the right of the troops under his immediate orders, to attack Oberglauheim whilst he was pushing across his cavalry. The Prince crossed the Nebelbach; but before he could form up his two brigades, between six and seven thousand strong, General Blainville sallied from the village and attacked him. The assailants, led by Blainville, were less strong in number by about one-sixth than the assailed;* but the Frenchmen had all the impetus of the attack, and the Prince's men were not formed. The result was that the Hanoverians were completely defeated and their commander was taken prisoner. Such an advantage, if well and vigorously followed up, would have been fatal to the allies. For a rent had been made in the very centre of their army, and it needed only the pouring of a body of chosen troops through that rent to make the disaster irreparable.

* Alison gives to the Prince of Holstein-Beck eleven battalions, equal in round numbers to six thousand five hundred men, and to Blainville nine thousand. But Blainville charged at the head of only nine battalions, and the French battalions averaged about six hundred men each

Some idea of the importance of the crisis seems to have struck Marchin, for, engaged as he was, as I shall presently relate, with Eugene, he directed some of his squadrons to gallop to the spot where Blainville was engaged, and to take full advantage of his success. But before Marchin had even given that order the despairing cry of the defeated Hanoverians had reached the ear of Marlborough. Instantly he comprehended the importance of the crisis. Without a moment's delay he put himself at the head of Bernstorff's Danish brigade, originally about four thousand strong, and led it across the rivulet in the direction of Oberglauheim. Blainville's men had meanwhile fallen back upon that village. Marlborough reached then without opposition the scene of the disaster of the Hanoverians. Suddenly, however, he beheld approaching at full gallop the cavalry of Marchin. He had but just time to form up his men, all infantry, to receive them, and, what was of not less importance, to send a message to Eugene begging for instant aid in cavalry. The fate of the battle depended upon the ability of the Danes to resist that attack until the assistance from Eugene should arrive. It is time that we should inquire how, whilst matters were so progressing on the left, that commander had fared on the right.

The difficulties which Eugene had to encounter before he could reach his enemy were greater even than those which had hindered the advance of his colleague. Numberless tributary streams, covered with bushes, making the ground about them sticky and marshy, prevented a direct movement. Forced then to make a flank march, every step of which in advance brought him more and more under the fire of the enemy, Eugene only reached at eleven o'clock a position whence he could attack, opposite Lutzingen and the Eichbergerhof. The line of the enemy occupying those places was, however, so extended that he was forced to call up his reserves and bring them to the front of the battle. This operation, and the detaching of two batteries to occupy a commanding position on the edge of the forest, took up a considerable time, and twelve o'clock struck before he was ready to begin.

The task before him was no light one. He had under his orders little more than seven thousand Prussian and five thousand Danish infantry; his cavalry numbered five thousand. Opposed to him, in a strong position, were the troops of Marchin and Max-Emanuel, sixteen thousand strong in infantry and ten thousand in cavalry. But calm, cool, and resolute, he waited, exposed to the fire of the enemy's guns, posted in front of Lutzingen, until the two batteries should take up the position he had assigned to them. That accomplished, Leopold of Anhalt-Dessau advanced against Lutzingen at the head of his gallant Prussians, whilst the Danes marched to assail the French posted on the Eichbergerhof. The enemy's advanced troops were driven back, the guns posted before Lutzingen were taken; the French, after a fierce contest, were driven from the Eichbergerhof. To improve these advantages, Eugene then launched his cavalry against that of the enemy. The French front line, not awaiting the attack, fell back on the second. It was but to entice their enemy. The device succeeded. Eugene's cavalry followed, only, however, to be charged in front and flank by double their number, and driven back across the brook. A simultaneous attack made by Max-Emanuel on the Prussians, forced them also to retire, abandoning the guns which they had gained.

It was whilst the Prince, after this repulse, was re-forming his men for a second attack, that he received from Marlborough the demand for aid of which I have spoken. He immediately despatched General Fugger at the head of the Imperial cuirassiers. Then, confident that he would best assist his colleague by keeping occupied the enemy in front of him, he made a second attack. This attack, too, shattered against the vastly superior numbers of the enemy. Though victorious in his first charge, his men were again encountered on both flanks and forced to retire. Realising then that, unassisted, he could accomplish nothing against the enemy opposite to him, and noting, with the keen eye of a practised commander, that Marlborough had restored the battle on his side, Eugene despatched, in his turn, a pressing message, demanding prompt and efficient aid.

Whilst the messenger was speeding on that errand, Eugene re-formed his men, and went up and down the ranks, speaking to them words of encouragement. Then, before the hoped-for reinforcements had arrived, impatient at the delay, he directed a third attack. Leopold of Anhalt-Dessau led his Prussians with great gallantry from the slopes of the wood against the flank of the French, whilst the cavalry endeavoured to divert their attention by a front assault. But again did the good leadership of Max-Emanuel, and the conduct of his men, baffle the hopes of Eugene. Charging with his full strength, the Elector drove the assailing horsemen with great loss back across the Nebelbach. Vainly did Eugene use every effort to rally his disheartened soldiers. Two of the more prominent fugitives he shot dead. Then, feeling that panic had overmastered their reason, he left to the Duke of Württemberg and Prince Maximilian of Hanover the care of rallying them, and dashed off to his gallant Prussian infantry. He found those men steady, facing the foe, ready to obey any order to advance. With splendid daring, then, he dashed them furiously against the left flank of the Bavarians. The enemy, Germans like themselves, met them with equal intrepidity. Feeling that much depended upon the result of this encounter, Eugene exposed himself in the van of the men whom he was leading. His example made everyone of them feel that he must do or die. He almost paid with his own life the forfeit of his daring. A Bavarian dragoon had covered him with his carbine at a few paces, and was just about to fire when he was cut down. With great efforts Eugene at length succeeded in driving the enemy through the wood, and in hurling them beyond the defile near Lutzingen. Unfortunately his cavalry had, as related, been shattered, and unable, with only two squadrons in hand, to follow up his success, he was forced to content himself with maintaining the position he had gained.

That position, however, would have been fraught with danger had the Elector and Marchin been able to concentrate against him all their resources. But the splendid efforts of Marlborough against the French right and centre had so shaken them that they were forced now to direct all their attention to that quarter. We left Marlborough threatened by Marchin's cavalry, whilst, at the head of Bernstorff's Danes, he was endeavouring to repair the mischief which had been occasioned by the defeat of his Hanoverians, and despatching a messenger to Eugene for aid. Eugene had responded by sending him at full gallop a regiment of Imperial cuirassiers, led by Count Fugger. Fugger arrived just in time to throw himself on the flank of the French cavalry as they were endeavouring to break the Danes. This opportune charge enabled the latter to hold their ground until the arrival of fresh squadrons and a battery from the left gave Marlborough the strength he required to re-establish matters in the centre.

The English general felt himself now in a position to make a supreme bid for victory. Of the French army the bulk of the infantry was shut up in Blenheim: the greater portion of the remainder was in and beyond Oberglauheim; he himself stood with his whole army on the ground beyond the Nebelbach facing the weakest part of the enemy's line, that stretching between Blenheim and Oberglauheim, defended by cavalry and two weak brigades—five thousand five hundred men—of infantry. Could he pierce that line the battle would assuredly be gained, for the enemy's right would thereby be cut off from its centre.

Full of the hope that he could do so, Marlborough drew up the infantry he had at hand, composed mainly of Danes and Hessians, and led them, supported in the centre by his guns and on both flanks by his cavalry in two lines, and advanced up the gentle slope which led to the enemy's position. The French were drawn up in good order to receive him. Their centre was formed of the two brigades, Robuq and Albaret, supported likewise by artillery, and protected also on the flanks by cavalry in two lines. As the allies advanced, the French poured upon them a fire of artillery and musketry so hot, that the Hessians recoiled under its effects and fell back some sixty paces. Then occurred the last and finest opportunity for the sons of France! Tallard saw it. "I saw," he wrote in his official account of the battle, "I saw an instant in which the battle was gained by the brigades of Robuq and Albaret, if——" if his cavalry had done their duty! For a moment, indeed, it appeared that that duty would be gallantly performed. The French cavalry, encouraged by the success of the two infantry brigades, advanced with the apparent intention of ensuring victory by a charge. Had they charged boldly, who can say what might have been the result? But, tired, dismayed by the firm attitude of the English, who, far from awaiting them, charged forward to meet them, they shrank from the shock, and rode to the rear, abandoning the gallant infantry brigades to their fate. Vain were the efforts of Tallard to rally them. Single squadrons, here and there, responded to his call, but the mass, after a discharge of their carbines, fell back disheartened. Marlborough seized the propitious moment, sent his cavalry over the crest of the ridge, and in spite of the splendid resistance of the two brigades,* gained the entire space between the two villages.

The battle was, in effect, gained. Tallard, who had witnessed with an indignation he could not control the conduct of his cavalry, and who had been twice wounded whilst striving to urge them on, continued to fight, no longer for victory, but for a safe retreat. The strong body of men who were defending Blenheim must, at all hazards, be extricated. To secure a line by which they could retire he once more threw himself with all

---

* "The abandoned infantry were at once surrounded and for the most part cut down."—ARNETH. Alison says, "They made a noble resistance, and their men were found lying on their backs in their ranks as they had stood in the field."

the horsemen he could collect on the advancing English. But a charge which, made with the whole force, might have been effective, produced no result when a handful of men alone took part in it. In vain did he send a despairing appeal to Marchin. The orderly who took the message returned with the reply that Marchin was himself unable to repulse the fierce attacks of Eugene. Then, and then only, did Tallard issue the order which, expedited half an hour earlier, might have saved him from a total rout. He directed the Marquis of Clérembault to evacuate in all haste Blenheim, and to fall back on Sondernheim.

Even had the messenger who carried that order reached his destination he would probably have arrived too late. But he was taken prisoner. Meanwhile Marlborough, thoroughly convinced that by giving the enemy before him no respite, he would sever the troops in Blenheim from the centre of their army, pressed with all his energy after the retreating cavalry. Of that cavalry two bodies only continued to resist. The men of one of these, driven into an angle formed by the turning of the rivulet, endeavoured to escape by swimming their horses to the other side. Many were cut down in the act of urging their horses into the water, but some reached the opposite bank and escaped to Lauingen. The other, with which was Tallard, still attempted to defend the road leading to Höchstädt.

All this time Tallard was anxiously directing his gaze towards Blenheim in the hope of seeing carried out the order to evacuate that place. As, however, Clérembault gave no sign, he started to ride thither to see himself to the execution of his order. His shortsightedness, however, carried him into the midst of a detachment of allied cavalry whom he mistook for Frenchmen. Baron Boyneburg, aide-de-camp of the Prince of Hesse-Cassel, recognised him by his orders, and, taking him prisoner, conducted him to the Prince. "This is the revenge for Speyer," exclaimed the latter to his staff, as he observed the approach of the French marshal. Tallard was at once despatched to a place of safety, and treated with the distinction due to his rank.

We left Eugene having established his position with the Prussian infantry on the margin of the wood facing the left flank of Lutzingen. The position, I have pointed out, would have been full of danger if the Elector and Marchin had been able to direct against him their undivided forces. But by this time the fierce onslaught of Marlborough had made itself felt all along the French line, and the two commanders, recognising the danger of their own position if Marlborough should succeed in establishing himself on their left whilst Eugene was pounding on their front and right, had now no other thought but how to draw off their men. To check the advance of Eugene they set fire to the villages on the rivulet they had held, and, drawing to them all their troops, began a movement in three columns along the edge of the woods, in the direction of Mörschlingen, leaving Höchstädt to the left. Max-Emanuel, brave as a lion, commanded the rear-guard in person, and displayed so much skill and conduct that he effectually warded off pursuit. He was, indeed, much aided by the fact that Eugene at the moment had no cavalry at his disposal, but was forced to follow only with his brave Prussian infantry. When at last the cavalry, reinforced by some squadrons from the left wing, did reach him, Max Emanuel had taken up a position behind the Brunnenbach strong enough to resist attack.

The field was now cleared of the enemy. The last two French battalions which had maintained the fight had just laid down their arms to General Hompesch. Blenheim alone remained in their hands; and Blenheim, uncovered, was now exposed to the assault of the whole allied army.

Up to this time the Marquis of Clérembault had contented himself with maintaining his position in Blenheim, which he had rendered very capable of defence. But as he noticed the later events of the battle, the advance of Marlborough, the flight of the French cavalry, the overthrow of the two brigades, his heart sank within him, and, seeing that all was over, he resolved to leave his troops to their fate and to escape. With this object he spurred his horse into the Danube and attempted to swim to the opposite bank. But Fortune would not aid the man who had abandoned his own soldiers. His horse sank, and he was drowned. Count Blansac, who assumed the command on the disappearance of Clérembault, was, like his predecessor, a man incapable of taking upon himself any responsibility. Left without orders—for none of the messengers who had been sent reached him—he might yet, by a timely evacuation of the place when he saw that by the defeat of the cavalry it was about to be exposed to the full fury of the allies, have saved to France the very considerable body of men who occupied it. But he was incapable of taking a resolution. In gloomy torpidity he and his officers beheld inevitable fate closing around them. Nearer and nearer approached the solid ranks of the allies. At last, when it was too late, when success was all but impossible, Blansac made desperate efforts, constantly repeated, to cut his way through. In vain, however. Every attack was repulsed.

The situation of the French troops in Blenheim was now desperate. Yet, with the pride to which many past victories had given them a just right, those gallant men rejected every citation to surrender. No other course, then, was left to Marlborough but to storm. Force, here at least, was the only remedy. He made his dispositions accordingly. After a hardly-contested and very murderous attack and defence, signalised by one or two repulses, the troops under Lord Cutts carried the churchyard.

The occupation of the churchyard deprived the French of their strongest outer-defence. From it the way into Blenheim was comparatively easy. It happened that during the assault upon it a French officer of rank, Colonel Denonville, had been taken prisoner. When Lord Cutts had carried the position he pointed out to Denonville the futility of further resistance, and that humanity required that the French should accept the honourable terms offered to them. Denonville, convinced, returned with an

English officer to the town to endeavour to carry out this idea. Then occurred a very curious scene. Actuated, either by contempt for, or aversion to, Blansac, Denonville did not address himself to him, but harangued the troops, pointing out to them the situation, and requiring them to lay down their arms. In vain did Blansac storm, order him to be silent, and to quit the place. The words of Denonville had made a deep impression on the men, and Blansac saw that they might refuse to obey his orders. Whilst all was doubt and confusion, another herald from the English general entered the place and demanded to speak to the commanding officer. He then informed Blansac that Marlborough had ranged in front of the village forty battalions and sixty guns; that he had many more in reserve; that the capture of the churchyard had left the place open to an assault; that the rest of Tallard's army, and the entire army of the Elector and Marchin, were in full flight; that, in a word, he was in the air, without support or chance of assistance; that he had, therefore, no excuse to prolong the resistance. Blansac yielded to these representations, and gave the order accordingly. The greater part of the French soldiers, nine thousand in number, submitted to their fate with angry despair. The men of the regiment of Novarre, a regiment grown grey in victory, displayed their deep mortification by casting their colours into the flames of the burning houses and destroying their muskets.

All was now over. The army of Marchin and the Elector had been defeated, that of Tallard had been annihilated. Whilst the loss of the allies in killed and wounded had reached twelve thousand men, that of the French and Bavarians exceeded fourteen thousand. In addition, the defeated army had lost thirteen thousand men taken prisoners, forty-seven pieces of cannon, twenty-five standards, and ninety colours.

This is not the place to enter into a discussion of the merits of the two allied commanders. But this, at least, may be said, that if Marlborough struck the decisive blow, he was facing

Tallard with an army greater than that of the French general, whereas the harder task had been assigned to Eugene of confronting Marchin and the Elector with a force inferior to theirs by more than one-third. And yet it was the timely aid rendered by Eugene which enabled Marlborough to deliver the attack which decided the battle.

The effect of the victory was enormous all over Europe. It dashed to the ground the ambitious plans of Louis XIV. and of Max-Emanuel. It saved the House of Habsburg, whose hereditary dominions, had the result been different, would have fallen a prey to the Elector. It dealt a very hard blow to the insurgents in Hungary, who had counted on the help of France. And, what was scarcely of less importance, it showed the world of Europe that it was possible to defeat even the armies of Louis XIV. Blenheim was to that monarch what Moscow was, a little more than a century later, to Napoleon!

The invasion which led to Blenheim was the last offensive attack made by Louis XIV. on Germany. In 1706 Eugene beat one army at Turin, and Marlborough another at Ramilies. Two years later the two generals, once more acting in concert, triumphed at Oudenarde, and the year following at Malplaquet. When, after a contest which lasted five years longer, the Emperor and the French King signed the Peace of Baden, the former gained the Netherlands, Naples, the Milanese, and Sardinia; besides, on the Rhenish frontier, Breisach, Freiburg, and Kehl. England and Holland and Prussia had, two years before, signed a peace which, much abused at the time, secured for those countries advantages which were not contemplated at the outset of the war, and which is memorable as the first treaty which fixed the commercial intercourse of Europe on an intelligent basis. It is not too much to affirm that these advantages, and the long peace which followed them, are to be traced to the victory of Blenheim!

INDEX.

A.

Achilles, Dispositio, fundamental family law of the Hohenzollerns, 233.
Adalbert, of Prague, is slain in an attempt to introduce Christianity into Prussia, 236.
Aldringer, reinforces Tilly after Breitenfeld, 43; gallant conduct of, at the battle of the Lech, 59-60; is severely wounded, 60; presses hard Banner and Horn, 107; position of, 108; manœuvres of, with reference to Horn, 111; disobeys Wallenstein, 112.
Allersheim, description of the eminence and of the village of, 195; battle of, 196-202; is fruitless of results, 202.
Amurath, Sultan, invades Hungary, 269; dies, and is succeeded by Muhammad III., 270.
Anhalt-Dessau, Prince Leopold of, commands the Prussian contingent under Eugene; character of, 320; splendid conduct of, at Blenheim, 334-6.
Anhalt, Ernest, Prince of, commands the cavalry reserves on the left at Lützen, 91; is killed at that battle, 99.
Apaffy, Michael, is appointed Voivode of Transylvania, 274; is confirmed as such by the Treaty of Vasvár, 276; renounces his connection with Turkey, 291.
Arnheim, the adviser of John George of Saxony, 24; assumes command of the Saxon army at Prague, 49; character of, 50.

Augsburg, Imperial Diet at, **confirms provisions** of Peace of Passau, 2; is occupied by Gustavus, 61; becomes the **centre of** operations in 1647, 206.

B.

Baden-Durlach, Margrave Christopher of, is killed before Ingolstadt, 62.
Baden-Durlach, Margrave George Frederic of, is beaten by Tilly, 9; tries in vain to wrest Lower Saxony from Tilly, 14.
Baden, Margrave Louis of, serves in the campaign of 1683 against the Turks, 284-7; gains the battle of Salankemen, 290; is outmanœuvred by Villars in the Black Forest, 307; the extraordinary remissness of, enables Tallard to traverse Swabia in safety, 317; obstinacy and self-assertion of, 318; aids Marlborough in storming the Schellenberg and taking Donauwörth, 318-20; relieves Marlborough by deciding to besiege Ingolstadt, 321.
Ballandine, zeal and energy of, 71.
Bamberg, The Bishop of, negotiates with Gustavus, 42; repudiates the bargain on the approach of Tilly, 43.
Banner, accompanies Gustavus to Germany, 19; commands a brigade at Breitenfeld, 34; moves to the relief of Nuremberg, 71-2; campaign of, against Aldringer, 107; beats the Saxons at Dömitz and Wittstock, 126; and Gallas at Chemnitz, 126; overruns Bohemia and Silesia, 130; is worsted at Plauen

Banner—*cont.*
and forced to fall back on Erfurt, 131; is joined there by the Dukes of Luneberg and by Guébriant, 131; is inspired by the idea of seizing Ratisbon, 131; makes a daring march across Germany in the depth of winter, 132; reaches the Danube but is baffled by a sudden thaw, 133; in his anger bombards the city, 133; left by his French colleague and threatened by the Imperialists, is forced to retreat, 133-4; skill and daring displayed by, in the retreat, 134, 135; dies, 135; character of, 135, 136.

Barcsay, Alexander, becomes ruler of Transylvania, but has to make way for Keményi, 274.

Bathory, Stephen, becomes Voivode of Transylvania, but resigns the office on his being elected King of Poland, 268; Christopher, succeeds Stephen, and Sigismund, Christopher, 268; character and conduct of Sigismund, 269; resigns to Balthasar, but is restored, but has to make way for Stephen Bocskay, 269-70; Gabriel, becomes Voivode, but is murdered, 270.

Baudissin, accompanies Gustavus to Germany, 19; is present at Breitenfeld, 33; commands the left column in its march into Franconia, 41; receives a rap from Tilly, 54; is opposed to Pappenheim in Westphalia, 79.

Bernhard, Duke, of Saxe-Weimar, marches to the relief of Gustavus at Nuremberg, 72; obtains a temporary success at the *Alte Veste,* 76; is detached by Gustavus to hinder the march of Wallenstein, 81; rejoins Gustavus near Erfurt, 85; passes the night before Lützen in conversation with Gustavus, 90; commands the left of the army, 91; attacks Holk and carries all before him, 91; is checked by Wallenstein in person, 92; is strengthened by Gustavus, after whose death he restores the battle, 94; presses the enemy hard, 96; at nightfall, holds his ground. 97; the retirement of the enemy during the night allows, to claim the victory, 98; joins the Saxons at Leipzig and then marches into Franconia, 106; marches, on the citation of Horn, to the Danube, 107-8; the possibilities which seemed to be before, 108; ambitious schemes of, 109; tries to wrest a principality from Oxenstierna, 110; succeeds, 111; is warned by Oxenstierna regarding Wallenstein, 112; marches on, and seizes, Ratisbon, 113-4; advances along

Bernhard, Duke—*cont.*
the Danube towards Vienna, 114; when before Passau realizes the danger of his position, 115; and falls back into the Upper Palatinate, 116; want of sympathy, caused by difference of disposition between, and Horn, 118; effects a junction with Horn, 119; comes in view of the enemy at Nördlingen, 119; in his eagerness to attack overrides the caution of Horn, 120; attacks the enemy in the plain, 123; Horn's defeat forces, to retreat, 123; falls back towards the Main, 124; personal blow to, caused by the defeat, 124; is authorised by France to levy troops, 126, 127; conditions under which, placed himself wholly at the service of France, 127; efforts of, to levy troops, 127; after some skirmishing defeats the enemy at Rheinfelden, at Wittenweiher, and at Thann, 128; repulses Götz from Breisach, 129; is carrying on the war successfully when he dies, 129.

Bergstrasse, The, overrun by Gustavus, 48; description of, 48, *note.*

Bethlen-Gabor, reference to action of, in Hungary, 12; abandons Mansfeldt, 13; becomes Voivode of Transylvania, 270; obtains the independence of Transylvania, and becomes a thorn in the side of the House of Austria, 270-72; is succeeded by his widow and Stephen Bethlen, 272.

Bethlen, Stephen, succeeds his brother in copartnership with his brother's widow, 272; the partnership is dissolved, and, makes way for George Rákóczy, 272-3.

Birkenfeldt, Prince Palatine of, is left to command on the Danube, 84; action of, there, 106, 107; acts with Horn, 108, 111.

Blainville, General, sallies from Oberglauheim, overthrows the troops commanded by Marlborough, and gives his leaders a chance which they do not take, 333.

Blansac, Count, succeeds to the command in Blenheim on the death of Clérembault, 340; strange conduct of, 340-1.

Blenheim, description of the battle-field of, 324; battle of, 325-40; effect of the victory of, 342.

Bocskay, Stephen, becomes Voivode of Transylvania; is succeeded by Sigismund Rákóczy, 270.

Bohemia, wrings almost unlimited religious freedom from Rudolph II. and

Bohemia—*cont.*
Matthias, 2; pronounces against Roman Catholicism, 4; rises against the House of Habsburg, 4; offers her crown to the Elector Palatine, 5; submits to the Emperor, 8; is overrun by Banner, 130; desolation of, during the Thirty Years' War, 223, *note*, and 224; history of, under George of Podébrad, 258, 259; is handed over to the Jagellons, 259; reverts to the House of Austria, 261.

Boleslaw, Chobri, asssumes a nominal overlordship over East Prussia, 236.

Boleslaw IV., causes the submission of a small tract, but is eventually slain, 236.

Bournonville, commands the Imperialists, is outmanœuvred, beaten, and driven out of Alsace by Turenne, 248-9.

Brahé, Nicholas, commands the centre of the Swedish army at Lützen, 91; is killed at that battle, 99.

Brandenburg, George William, Elector of, makes overtures to Gustavus Adolphus, 15; character and views of, at the outset of the war, 24; thwarts Gustavus in his attempts to relieve Magdeburg, 27; engages to adhere to the Swedish alliance after the death of Gustavus, 105; makes a separate peace, after Nördlingen, with the Emperor, 124; gains of the electorate of, by the Thirty Years' War, 225; the electoral hat of, is bestowed upon Frederic VI. of Hohenzollern, 229 & *note*; tranquillity restored to, and borders of increased, by Frederic and his son, 230 & *note*; gradual progression of, under the Hohenzollerns, *q. vide* 230-256.

Braunau, tumults at, in connection with religious differences, 4.

Breitenfeld, description of, 1, 2; first battle of, 32-7; reflections on the consequences of the battle of, 37-9; Torstenson moves to the plain of, to meet the Imperialists, 142; second battle of, 143-4.

Bruno, of Magdeburg, is killed in his attempts to introduce Christianity into Prussia, 236.

Brunswick, Duke Christian of, is driven by Tilly from the Palatinate, 9.

Bucquoi, General, beats Mansfeldt at Zablati, 5.

Buda, *vide* **Ofen**, 28.

Bulach, Count, commands the cavalry reserve on the right at Lützen, 91.

Bull, The Golden, the fundamental law of the German Empire, 233 *note*.

C.

Campaign, results of the, of 1633, 117; of Nördlingen, 124; of Freiburg, 185-6; of Blenheim, 341.

Carlowitz, The Peace of, constitutes a new departure in the politics of Eastern Europe, 291.

Caspar Bekes, the nominee of the Emperor for the Government of Transylvania, is rejected and beheaded, 268.

Charles Gustavus, of Sweden, arrives to reinforce Königsmark before Prague, 220; makes many futile attempts to storm when the signature of the Peace of Westphalia puts an end to hostilities, 220-3; conducts a long, and on the whole an unsuccessful, war with the Great Elector, terminated by his own death, 243-5.

Charles II., King of England, the secret ambition of, makes him a pensioner of France, 295; is forced by his Parliament to declare war against France, 297.

Charles II., King of Spain, dies, and leaves his vast dominions to Philip of Anjou, 299.

Chemnitz, Banner beats Gallas at, 126.

Christian IV., King of Denmark, *vide* **Denmark**.

Christ, The Knights of, introduce, after much hard fighting, Christianity all over Prussia, 237-9.

Churchill, Lord, crosses the Nebelbach during the battle of Blenheim, 331; the cool and spirited conduct of, greatly neutralises the effect of the French cavalry charge, 332.

Clérembault, The Marquis of, commands the French troops in Blenheim, 328; loses his head, and is drowned attempting to cross the Danube, 339.

Coburg, the Castle of, called the Ehrenburg, successfully resists Wallenstein, 82.

Colloredo, Count, is posted to command the left of Wallenstein's army at Lützen, 89; splendid conduct of, at Lützen, 94, 97.

Condé, Prince of, *vide* **Duke of Enghien**.

Confederation, The, of the Rhine, becomes the means, in the hands of Louis XIV., of fomenting disturbance in Europe, 294.

Conti, Torquato, vainly attempts to oppose Gustavus Adolphus in Pomerania, 19; abandons his army, 20.

Corvinus, Mathias, becomes King of Hungary by the instrumentality of George of Podébrad, 258; treachery and insincerity of, 258-9; dies, 259.

Cratz, General, is recommended by Tilly to Maximilian to command his army, 62; exercises that command, 71.

Craven, Lord, gallant conduct of, at the storming of Kreuznach, 53.

Cremona, attempt made by Prince Eugene to surprise, 302-5.

Cutts, Lord, charge of, on Blenheim, repulsed, 329; carries the churchyard, 339.

D.

Dampierre, Count of, opportune arrival of, saves Vienna, 6.

Darmitz, Colonel, is taken prisoner by Gustavus, who squeezes information from him, 69.

Denmark, Christian IV., King of, becomes champion of the Protestant cause in Germany, 10; is defeated by Tilly at Lutter, 14; is forced to conclude peace, 14; the country of, is invaded and occupied by Torstenson, 147.

Domitz, Banner beats the Saxons at, 126.

Donauwörth, tumults at, in connection with the Protestant rising, 3; description of, 55-6; is abandoned by the Imperialists to Gustavus, 56; is taken by Turenne, 205; is captured by Marlborough and Margrave Louis of Baden, 318-20.

Dorflinger, splendid coolness of, at the battle of Fehrbellin, 253-4; the action of, the turning point of the battle, 256.

Dubatel, chivalrous conduct of Wallenstein with respect to, 69; forces Wallenstein to retire from the Ehrenburg, 82 & note.

E.

Enghien, Louis II., Duke of, antecedents and character of, 170-2, & note to 172; joins Turenne near Freiburg, 172, 174; resolves, against the advice of Turenne, Gramont, and another, to attack Mercy, 174; detaches Turenne to turn him whilst he attacks in front,

Enghien, Louis II., Duke of—cont.
175; gains the summit of the hill, 176; joins Turenne, after an indecisive battle, 179; reconnoitres the new position taken by Mercy, 179; notwithstanding its strength, resolves to attack it, 180; ranges his order of battle, 180; whilst reconnoitring, finds that the battle had been engaged on a wrong point by Espenan, 181; draws off his men, and with Turenne makes a vigorous but unsuccessful attack on the enemy's position, 182; gallantry of, as described by Gramont, 182 & note; resolves to attack Mercy as he retreats towards Villingen, 183; terrible race of, to cut off Mercy, 184-5; is just beaten on the post, but reaps all the advantages of the campaign, 185; joins Turenne after his defeat at Mergentheim and marches with him towards Nördlingen, 194; finds the Bavarian army drawn up before him about Allersheim, 196; reconnoitres, and contrary to the advice of Turenne resolves to attack, 196; first and second attacks of, are repulsed, 197-9; the third, in spite of the extraordinary valour of, is almost driven back, when the opportune death of Mercy enables him to recover his ground, 199; the presence of mind of, enables him to avert defeat, 200; reinforces Turenne, forces back the enemy's right and gains the day, 200-1; returns to France to cure his wounds, 202.

England, declares war against France, 302.

Espenan, Count of, commands the front attack on Enghien's army on the Schönberg, 175; again, on the Lorettoberg, where he compromises the success of the day by an attack on the wrong point, 181.

Eugene, Prince, of Savoy, is present with the Duke of Lorraine during the investment of Vienna, note to 284; and during the expulsion of the Turks from Hungary, 289; gains the battle of Zenta, 292; campaign of, against Marshal Villeroi, 302; attempts to surprise Cremona, 302-5; fights the battle of Luzzara against Vendome, 306; is employed against Rákóczy in Hungary, 308; detects the designs of the French in 1704, 315; writes his ideas to Marlborough, 316; meets him on the German side of the Rhine, 317; conference of, with Marlborough and Louis of Baden, 318; outmanœuvres Villeroi and hastens to

Eugene, Prince, of Savoy—*cont.*
join Marlborough on the Danube, 320-1;
self-abnegation of, 321-2; takes a position on the Kesselbach, 322; is joined by Marlborough, 323; arranges with Marlborough the plan of attack, 324-5; difficulties to be encountered, 334; is twice repulsed, 334-5; the success of Marlborough enables him to make way, 336-7; forces the enemy from the field, 338-9.

Europe, comparison between France and the other States of, when Louis XIV. acceded to power, 293.

F.

Fehrbellin, the pass of, is occupied by Wrangel and the Swedes, 250; battle of, 250-5; monuments erected at, 256.

Ferdinand I. is elected King of Hungary and Bohemia, 261; fails to recover Ofen, loses Pesth, and signs a truce with the Sultan, 264; does what he can to introduce law and order into the country, 265.

Ferdinand II., accession of, to the Empire, 5; the firmness of, saves the Empire, 5, 6; resolves to crush the revolution in Germany, 6; measures taken by, against the reformers, after the victory of the White Hill, 8, 9; despatches Tilly to the Weser to oppose the King of Denmark, 10; reasons of, for forming an army under Wallenstein, 10, 11; triumphant position of, after the defeat of King Christian, 14; issues the Restitution edict, 14; is forced to remove Wallenstein, 15; the harsh policy of, with respect to the Dukes of Mecklenberg, drives them to side with Gustavus Adolphus, 21, 22; the aims of, contrasted with those of Gustavus Adolphus, 37-9; makes overtures to Wallenstein, and confides to him the command of an army, 51-2 & *note*; orders Gallas to march to the defence of Ratisbon, 113; letters of, to Wallenstein, *notes* 114, 116, 117; advantageous position of, after the victory of Nördlingen, 124; dies, 130.

Ferdinand III. commands the Imperial army in the Nördlingen campaign, 118; succeeds his father, and supports peace proposals at the diet of Ratisbon, 130; splendid pertinacity displayed by, at Ratisbon, 132; is hampered by the rebellion of Rákóczy, 146; summons

Ferdinand III.—*cont.*
his generals and soldiers around him at Prague, 148; hurries, after the defeat of Jankowitz, to Vienna, 152; strengthens the fortifications of that city, and buys off Rákóczy, 153; yields to the solicitations of Maximilian of Bavaria, and summons a peace congress at Ulm, 206; resolves to continue the war, and marches in person against Wrangel, 208; is almost taken prisoner, 208; transfers the command to Melander, 209.

France, agrees to aid Gustavus in money, 21; authorises Duke Bernhard to levy troops against the Emperor, 126; engages him wholly in her service, 127; confiscates the territories promised to Duke Bernhard on his death, 129; assumes more and more the position of a chief factor in the war, 129; objects of, 166; gains, through the instrumentality of Enghien and Turenne, the frontier of the Rhine, 185-6; is the great gainer by the Thirty Years' War, 224; comparison of, with the rest of Europe, at the moment when Louis XIV. assumed the reins of power, 293; gains accruing to, by the Peace of Nymwegen, 297; one disastrous effect of the revocation of the Edict of Nantes upon, 298; the Peace of Ryswick is a step backward for, 299; the address of the agents of, secures Spain and the Indies for a prince of the House of, 299-300.

Frankfurt on the Main, declares for, and is occupied by, Gustavus, 47.

Frankfurt on the Oder, is stormed by Gustavus, 24.

Frederic V., Elector Palatine, is elected King of Bohemia, 5; weak character of, 6, 7; is completely defeated on the White Hill, and flies to Holland, 8 & *note*; returns to the Palatinate, but is again forced to retire, 9; joins Gustavus at Frankfurt, 47.

Freiburg (in the Breisgau), is besieged and taken by Mercy, 170; description of the country about, 172-3; the three battles in the vicinity of, 174-84; campaign of, eminently advantageous to France, 185-6.

Friedland, Duke of, *vide* **Wallenstein**.

Furstenberg, Count, urges Tilly to occupy the field of Breitenfeld, 31; commands the right of the army in the battle, 32; defeats the Saxons, 34; but shares the general defeat of the army, 36.

Fürth, position taken up by Wallenstein near Fürth, 67 & *note*.

G.

Gallas, Count of, is detached by Wallenstein to reinforce Holk, 80; storms Lauf, 81; is re-called and sent into Bohemia, 85; ordered by the Emperor to march to the defence of Ratisbon, receives orders from Wallenstein not to fight a general action, 113; virtually succeeds Wallenstein, 118; defeats Duke Bernhard and Horn at Nördlingen, 121-4; is beaten by Banner at Chemnitz, 126; is outmanœuvred by Torstenson, 146; and finally completely crushed by him at Jütenberg, 147-8; repairs to Prague with the remnants of his army, 148.

German Empire, situation of the, at the death of Matthias, 5; on the conclusion of the Peace of Lübeck, 14; on the signature of the Treaty of Westphalia, 224.

Germany, the smaller princes of, side with France in her war against Holland, 295.

Gleen, General, commands the Bavarian right at Allersheim, 195; repulses two attacks of Turenne, but is finally forced back and made prisoner, 200-1.

Götzen, Count of, distinguishes himself at Lützen, 97; is summoned by Ferdinand III. to Prague, 148; surprises Torstenson at Jankowitz, 150; is killed just as victory was within his grasp, 150.

Gotz, General, is repulsed by Duke Bernhard from Breisach, 129.

Gramont, Duke of, advises Enghien not to attack Mercy, 174; description of Enghien at the second battle given by, 182 & *note*; endorses Enghien's opinion, in opposition to Turenne, for an attack at Allersheim, 196; the wing commanded by, is completely defeated, and he is taken prisoner, 198.

Gran, the Turks gain a great victory at, 274; is recovered from the Turks, 289.

Gronsfeld, General, escapes with his Bavarians from the rout of Zusmarshausen, 214-5; is defeated at the Lech, 216-7.

Guébriant, Count of, joins Banner at the head of Duke Bernhard's army, 131; accompanies Banner in his raid on Ratisbon, 132; quits him to secure for France the left bank of the Rhine, 133; assumes command of the allied forces on the death of Banner, and beats the

Guébriant, Count of—cont.
Imperialists at Wolfenbüttel, 138; quits Torstenson, and proceeds to the Lower Rhine, 139, 158; resolves to attack Marshal Lamboy's army at Kempen, 158; attacks and defeats him, 159; is made a Marshal of France, 159; marches into Thüringen, but is baffled by John of Werth, and falls back on Breisgau, 159-60; journeys to Leipzig to concert measures with Torstenson, 144-5 and 160; enters Swabia, 160; ensures, by his skilful retreat, the fall of Thionville, takes Rottweil, and dies from a wound there received, 161.

Günz, or Güns, splendid defence of, by Nicholas Jurisic, 262-3.

Gustavus Adolphus, distinguishes himself at the siege of Stralsund, 14; receives overtures from Brandenburg and Saxony, 15, early history of, 16, 17; resolves to aid the reformed cause in Germany, and embarks for that country, 18; first operations of, after landing, 19; opportunities open to, after the retreat of Conti, 20; conquers Pomerania, 21; takes Frankfurt on the Oder, 24; is thwarted by George William of Brandenburg on his march to relieve Magdeburg, 26; also by John George of Saxony, 27; damaging effect of the fall of Magdeburg on the reputation of, 27, 28; proceeds to extremities against George William of Brandenburg, 28; marches against Pappenheim, 29; refuses battle to Tilly, 29, 30; restores the German princes dispossessed by Tilly, 30; is joined by the Elector of Saxony, and marches towards Leipzig to meet Tilly, 31; fights the battle of Breitenfeld, 32-7; the aims of, contrasted with those of Ferdinand II., 37-9; considerations which weighed with, after Breitenfeld, 40, 41; pushes into Franconia, 41-2; opens negotiations with the Bishop of Bamberg, 42; takes Würzburg, 43; frightens the Duke of Lorraine, 44; directs his march towards the Rhine, 45; receives the adhesion of Nuremburg, 45; enters Frankfurt, and receives reinforcements, 47; takes Oppenheim, and makes a triumphal entry into Mainz, 48; is joined by Oxenstierna and by his queen, 49; discusses the future with Oxenstierna, 50-1; takes Kreuznach, 52-3; marches by way of Franconia to Donauwörth, 55; occupies Donauwörth and advances to the Lech, 58; forces the passage of that river, 58-60; occupies the aban-

INDEX. 349

Gustavus Adolphus—*cont.*
doned position of the enemy, 60; marches against Ingolstadt, 61; narrow escape of, 62; renounces his attempt on Ingolstadt, and marches towards Munich, which he takes, 62; learning the preparations and divining the intentions of Wallenstein, occupies Nuremburg, 64; appeals to the citizens, who respond, 65; fortifies the city, 66; holds out against Wallenstein for nearly three months, 67-74; attacks Wallenstein **near** Fürth, 74; is repulsed, 74-6; falls **back to** Windsheim, 77; considerations which weighed with, 80; detaches Duke Bernhard to occupy Wallenstein while **he** marches to Ingolstadt, 81; **arrives at** Neuburg, when news of the action **of** Wallenstein reached him, 81-2; the position as it presented itself to, 83; resolves to hurry back to Saxony, 84; effect of his march on the Elector, 85; **is** joined by Duke Bernhard, **85**; **surprises** Naumburg, 86; **sets** out **to effect** a junction **with** the Saxons, 87; learning on the **way that** Wallenstein had dis**tributed his** army, **turns** to surprise him, 88; **finds** the **distance** longer and the difficulties greater than he had anticipated, and halts for the night, 89-90; picture of, before Lützen, 90; advances in the morning, and ranges his army, commanding the right, 90-1; carries all before him on the right, and hastens to reinforce his maltreated left, 92; whilst urging on his men is wounded, and then killed, 93; Was he murdered? 99-101.

H.

Halle, Colonel, is killed **at the storming** of Kreuznach, 53.
Halle, fortress of, is besieged by **Pappenheim**, 87.
Halle, town **of**, occupied by Wallenstein, 83.
Hamilton, **Alexander, zeal** and energy of, 71.
Hamilton, **Marquis of**, joins the Swedish army with six thousand men, 29 & *note*.
Haro, **Don Louis de**, negotiates with Mazarin the Peace of the Pyrenees, 292.
Hatzfeldt, **General**, **is ordered by the** Emperor to aid **in expelling Banner** from Bohemia, 130; **is summoned by**

Hatzfeldt, General—*cont.*
the Emperor to Prague, 148; is commissioned to bar the road of Torstenson to Vienna, and takes up a position near Jankowitz, 149; attacks him, 150; after a strong appearance of success, is beaten, 150-1; and taken prisoner, 152, is released, and joins Mercy in Swabia, 163; participates in the successful surprise of Tuttlingen, 164-6.
Heilbronn, Congress of, 105.
Hepburn, fights under Gustavus at Breitenfeld, 33-7; commands with Monro at Ochsenfurt, 44.
Hesse-Cassel, **Landgrave William of**, noble answer of, to Tilly, 29; is the first of the German princes to adhere to Gustavus, 30; joins him with nine thousand men at Frankfurt, 47; **joins** Oxenstierna, 71.
Hesse-Cassel, The Duke of, is defeated by Tallard at Speyer, 312; **revenge of**, for that defeat, 338.
Hesse-Homburg, Landgrave **Frederick of**, the gallant attack made by, brings on the decisive battle of Fehrbellin, 253.
Hochstadt, Villars defeats the Imperialists at, 311; the hope of the capture of, diverts the French generals from their true line, 323; capture of, 323.
Hohenzollerns, early history of the, 226; Conrad of, becomes Burgrave of Nuremberg, 227; divides into two branches, **of** which we follow the Franconian, 227; a fortunate marriage with Clementia of Habsburg brings new territories to the, 227-8; **Frederic V. of**, is created a Prince of the Empire, 228; **Frederic VI. of**, obtains the electoral hat of Brandenburg, 229 & *note*; and assumes the designation of Frederic I., **229** & *note* (2); **Frederic I. and II. of**, re**store** prosperity to Brandenburg, **and** extend its borders, 230, *note*, & **231**; achievements of **Albert Achilles of**, 232; **Joachim of**, takes the Roman Catholic side at the time of the Reformation, 232-3; **Joachim II. of**, embraces the reformed religion, 233; makes a convention with the Duke of Liegnitz which subsequently formed the bases of the claim of the Kings of Prussia to Silesia, 234 & *note*; **John George of**, claims the duchies of Prussia, and of Cleve, Jülich, and Berg, 234 & *note* (2); **John Sigismund of**, makes good those claims, 235-40; **Albert of**, Grand Master of the Teutonic Order of Chivalry, adheres to the reformed reli-

Hohenzollerns—*cont.*
gion, forms Prussia into a **hereditary principality**, 240; incapable **rule of George William of**, 241; **great character of Frederic William of**, the Great Elector, 241; acquires for his electorate the first position in Germany at the Peace of Westphalia, 242; conducts a long, but ultimately a successful war with Poland and Sweden, 243-5; puts down the great nobles and commercial grandees of Prussia, 246; unsatisfactory campaign of, against Montecucculi, 247; concludes the Treaty of Vossem, 248; is roused by the ambition of Louis XIV. to renew the war, 248 & 297; unsatisfactory character of that war, 248-9; loses his eldest son, 249; first thoughts of, on hearing that the Swedes had invaded his territory, 250; proceeds by forced marches, and takes a position which cuts the Swedish army in two, 251; has to wait for his infantry, 252; then hurries after the Swedes, attacks, and completely defeats them, at Fehrbellin, 253-5; forces the Swedes from Pomerania, 256; the achievements and conquests of, justify the assumption by his successor of the title of King of Prussia, 256.

Holk, General, is detached by Wallenstein into Saxony, 72; rejoins Wallenstein, 85; commands the right of the army at Lützen, 89; is assailed by Duke Bernhard, and driven back, 91; is rescued by Wallenstein, 92; greatly dares, 97; is wounded, 99.

Holland, is invaded by Louis XIV. on the flimsiest of pretexts, 295 & *note*; is overrun, and sues for peace, 296; is saved by the haughty insistence of Louis, 296; recovers all she had lost at the Peace of Nymwegen, 297.

Holstein-Beck, the Prince of, the defeat of, compromises the English army at Blenheim, 332.

Horn, Gustavus, accompanies his master to Germany, 19; fights at the battle of Breitenfeld, 33-6; takes Bamberg, and repulses Tilly in an attempt on that place, 54-5; is sent to occupy Landshut, 62; is left in the Lower Palatinate to oppose the Spaniards, 71; is in Alsace when Lützen is being fought, 92 & *note*; marches into Swabia, and implores the aid of Duke Bernhard, 107; manœuvres of, 108, 111; want of sympathy between, and Duke Bernhard, 118; joins Duke Bernhard, 119; endeavours to dissuade the Duke from attacking the enemy at

Horn, Gustavus—*cont.*
Nördlingen, 120; is ordered, and proceeds, to occupy the Weinberg, 121; bad tactics of, 122; is defeated, 122-3; and forced to surrender, 123; is exchanged against John of Werth, *note* & 160.

Hungary, earlier history of, under Corvinus and the Jagellons, 258-61; the **Kingdom of**, elects Ferdinand of Habsburg, 261; sketch of the history of, thence to the close of the seventeenth century, 261-91.

I.

Ingolstadt, reputation of, 61; is invested by Gustavus, 61-2; who, after eight days, withdraws, 62; invested by Margrave Louis of Baden, 322.

J.

Jankowitz, description of the district in which lies, 149; battle of, 150-2.
Jurisic, Nicholas, commands the garrison which successfully defends Günz against Sulaimán the Great, 263.

K.

Kalkstein, Colonel von, rebels against the Great Elector, and, after an interlude, is beheaded, 246.
Kara Mustapha, succeeds his brother-in-law, Koprili, in the office of Grand Vizier, and marches on Vienna, 278; opens fire against various parts of the city, 279-80; brings it to extremity, 281, & *note* to 286; on learning of the arrival of Sobieski ranges his army to oppose him, 285; is defeated with great loss, 286-8.
Keményi, John, becomes Voivode of Transylvania, but is expelled and slain by the Turks, 274.
Kempen, description of, 158 & *note*; Guébriant defeats Marshal Lamboy at, 159.
Klostergrab, tumults at, in connection with religion, 4.

Kniphausen, Baron, advice given by, to Gustavus, on the eve of Lützen, 90; commands the cavalry reserve of the centre at Lützen, 91.

Konigsmark, John Christopher, reinforces Turenne with his flying corps, 193; is offended with Enghien and withdraws, 196; is despatched by Wrangel into **Bohemia,** 217; learns from Ottwald **that it might be possible** to surprise **Prague, 217; gains the** Kleinseite, 218; **and lays siege to the** modern city, **during July, August, and** September, 219; **is reinforced by Prince** Charles Gustavus **of Sweden, 219-20;** fails in many **attempts to storm, 221-2;** the peace **of Westphalia causes, to** desist, 223.

Koprili Ahmad Pasha, Grand Vizier, invades Hungary, gains a great victory, and makes considerable progress, 274-5; is defeated at St. Gothard, 275-6; concludes the Treaty **of Vasvar,** 276; dies, 278.

Koprili Muhammad Pasha, Grand Vizier, regulates the affairs of Transylvania, 274.

Kreuznach, is stormed by the Scotch brigade of Gustavus, 52.

L.

Lambay, Marshal, occupies **a** position at Kempen, 158; is attacked, defeated, and taken prisoner, by Guébriant, 159.

Lauenburg, Franz Albert of, *vide* **Saxe-Lauenberg.**

League, The Catholic, formation **of,** 3; the superior organization of, **asserts** itself, 7.

Lech, The, description of, **56 &** *note*, **57**; battle of, 58-60, the passage of, **forced** by Turenne and Wrangel, 216-7.

Leipzig, situation of, described, **1**; contrast of the two greatest battles **fought** at and near, 2; taken by Tilly, **31**; surrenders to Gustavus, 38; is taken by Wallenstein, 83; is evacuated by that general, 101; and occupied by the Saxons, 106; besieged **by** Torstenson, **142**; taken by Torstenson, 144.

Leopold, Archduke, takes command **of** the army formed to **expel** Banner from Bohemia, 130; **delivers to** him a severe blow at Plauen, **131**; **unites** with Piccolomini against Torstenson, 139; separates, 140; refuses battle, 141; follows Torstenson, and, reuniting with Piccolo-

Leopold, Archduke—*cont.*
mini, resolves to fight his **enemy, 141**; is defeated **at** Breitenfeld and retreats into Bohemia, 143-4; joins John of Werth after Allersheim and falls back **on** Donauwörth, 202; allows Turenne **to traverse** Swabia **and** Franconia and **seize the** line **of the Lech, 205; is at length** roused, **crosses the Danube, and** takes a position **fifteen miles from** Landsberg, 205-6; **allows Turenne to** seize his magazines, 206.

Leopold I., Emperor of Germany, small army at the disposal of, when the Turks marched against Vienna, 278; asks for assistance from Germany and Poland, 278; escapes with his family to Passau, 279; the armies of, drive the Turks out of Hungary, 289-91; is forced to resent the conduct of Louis XII., 298; declares war against France, 300.

Leubelfing, page attached **to Gustavus** Adolphus at Lützen, where **he is killed,** 93.

Loretto-Berg, description of the, 178.

Lorraine, Charles IV., Duke of, joins Tilly's army, receives a slap from Gustavus, and returns, 44; is beaten by Duke Bernhard at Thann, 128; joins Mercy's army in Swabia, 163; participates in the successful surprise of Tuttlingen, 166; **Charles V., Duke of,** watches the approach of the Turkish host on Vienna, 278; retires to Krems, 279, 281; defeats Tököly at Pressburg and the Pasha of Gosswardein at Stammersdorf, 282; is joined by John Sobieski, 284; commands the left wing in the battle of Vienna, and contributes greatly to the victory, 286-7; makes **a** triumphal entry into the city, 288-9; defeats **the** Turks **at** Mohács, 289 & *note.*

Louis II., King of Hungary, position **of, during** his minority, 259; is defeated and slain by Sulaimán the **Great at** Mohács, 260.

Louis XIV., assumes the reins **of power** on the death of Mazarin, 292; the state of Europe calculated to whet the ambitious instincts of, 293-4; **a** potent weapon of disturbance had been forged for, by Mazarin, 294; uses it, 294; invades Holland **on** flimsy pretexts, 295 & *note*; overruns the country, but insists on impossible terms, 296; gains of, **by the** Peace of Nymwegen, 297; acts as though he were above all treaties and seizes Strasburg, 297-8; again forces war on the Emperor, 298; rouses

Louis XIV.—*cont.*
all Europe against him and signs the Peace of Ryswick, 298-9; conduct of, on hearing that the King of Spain had died, leaving his dominions to his grandson, 300; war declared against, by the Emperor, 300; haughtily aggravates the situation by deliberately insulting England, 301-2; the battle of Blenheim the first great blow for the subversion of the plans of, 341.

Luneberg, The Dukes of, fall off from the Swedish alliance, 124, repent and join **Banner, 131**; quit the Swedish army on **his death,** 138.

Lützen, description of the ground about, 88-9; battle of, 91-7; victory **at,** rightly claimed by the Swedes, **98**; losses **at, 98**.

M.

Macdonnel, takes Marshal Villeroi prisoner in Cremona, 304.

Magdeburg, invested by Pappenheim and Tilly, 25; storming of, 27; damaging effect of the fall of, on the reputation of Gustavus, 27, 28.

Mainz, triumphal entry of **Gustavus into,** 48; the occupation of, marks **an era in** the campaign, 48-9.

Mansfeldt, is defeated by Bucquoi, **5**; in the Palatinate, 9; **is defeated** by Wallenstein, disbands his army, and dies, 13.

Marchin, Marshal, is despatched to join Max Emanuel of Bavaria, 314 & *note*; marches with him and Tallard to Höchstädt, 323; commands the left wing **at the battle** of Blenheim, 325; sends a regiment of cavalry to support the attack on Marlborough, 333; repulses Eugene's attacks, 334-5; but the victory of Marlborough, followed by the renewed persistence of Eugene, compels him to quit the field, 338-9.

Marlborough, Duke of, campaign of 1702, in the Netherlands, **307-8**; **campaign** of, of 1703, 312-4; **concides** with **Prince** Eugene as **to the line** to be adopted in **1704,** 316; **crosses** the Rhine and has **an** interview **with** Eugene, 317; and **with Louis** of Baden, 318; line of **action** resolved upon between, and his **German** colleagues,' **318;** marches on Donauwörth, attacks **and** storms the Schellenberg, 318-20; marches near Augsburg, tries in **vain to** detach Max

Marlborough, Duke of—*cont.*
Emanuel from the French alliance, then ravages the country as far as Munich, 321 & *note*; is immensely relieved by the proposal of Louis of Baden to besiege Ingolstadt, 321; Eugene offers to serve under, 321-2; joins Eugene on the Kesselbach, 323; makes a reconnaissance and decides his plan of attack, **324-5**; first attack of, is repulsed, 330; **resolves** to attack the weak middlepart, **331**; is pressed hard and sends to Eugene **for** cavalry, 333; re-establishes his position, and makes a **supreme bid** for victory, 336; pierces **the weak** middle point, 337; **and captures Blenheim,** 340.

Martinitz, is hurled **from the window of** the Hradschin, 4.

Martinuzzi, intrigues against the Habsburgs in favour of John Sigismund Zápolya, 263; changes sides, but is suspected and slain, 265.

Masham, Mr., gallant conduct of, before Kreuznach, 53.

Matthias, Emperor, concessions made by, to the reformed party, 3; death of, 5.

Max Emanuel, Elector of Bavaria, captures Belgrade, 290; casts in his lot **with the** French, and takes Ulm, 306; **is baffled in** his attempts on Tirol, 309; rejects the advice of Villars, and quarrels with him, 310-11; moves forward **with** his French allies towards the enemy, 322; is fortunately diverted by the temptation to take Höchstädt, 323; takes up a position behind the Nebelbach, 324; commands with Marchin the left of the French army at Blenheim, and distinguishes himself by his gallantry and conduct, 334-40.

Maximilian, Duke of Bavaria, carries out the **imperial sentence** against Donauwörth, **3**; appointed executor **of** the decrees **of the Catholic** League, 3; expels Frederic V. from Bohemia, **7, 8**; asserts **his position** with reference **to** the Emperor, **15**; advises Tilly to avoid a battle, if possible, 44; orders a retreat, after the passage of the Lech by the Swedes, on Ingolstadt, 60-1; vainly urges Wallenstein to attack Gustavus at Nuremberg, 67; invokes in vain the aid of the Emperor and Wallenstein to defend Ratisbon, 113; is forced by Turenne to take refuge in Braunau, 205; in utter weariness of the war, beseeches the Emperor to call a peace congress, 206; **on the** congress separating with-

Maximilian, Duke of Bavaria—*cont.*
out coming to a conclusion, declares
himself neutral, 207; is forced by his
generals to re-enter into the war, 208,
209; is driven to despair by the defeat
at Zusmarshausen, and flees to Salzburg, 217; gains of, by the Thirty Years'
War, 225.

Maximilian II., Emperor of Germany,
succeeds Ferdinand I., 265; has to wage
war with the Sultan, 266; concludes
peace with the Porte, 268; the extinction of the family of Zápolya seems to
free him from future trouble, but it
does not, 268; dies, 268.

Mazarin, Cardinal, tact, subtlety, and
firmness of, in negotiating the Peace of
the Pyrennees, 292; had, before his
death, forged for the use of his master
a potent weapon of disturbance, 294.

Mecklenburg, the Dukes of, are driven
by Ferdinand into the arms of Gustavus,
21, 22; who returns to them their territories, 30.

Melander, Peter, Count of Holzapfel,
is nominated to the command of the
Imperial army, 209; antecedents of,
209; character of, 210; presses Wrangel
hard, when he is diverted by a desire to
revenge himself on the Landgravine of
Hesse, 210; is forced back across the
Danube and takes up a position at
Zusmarshausen, 211–3; in his fussy
anxiety crosses the Zusam when he
learns that the enemy is upon him, 213;
hurrying back, is caught in *flagrante
delicto,* defeated and slain, 213–6.

Mercy, Francis, Baron of, serves under
Marshal Lamboy, 159; is made prisoner at the battle of Kempen, 159; is
released, and endeavours to relieve
Thionville, 160; but fails, 161; resolves
to surprise Rantzau at Tuttlingen, 163;
antecedents of, 163–4; position of the
army of, south of the French, 164;
favoured by the weather, surprises and
all but annihilates his enemy, 164–6;
besieges and captures Freiburg, 170;
seizes and fortifies the height called the
Schönberg, 173; is attacked by Enghien, who gains the summit, when, by a
skilful movement, he prevents the complete success of the enemy, and takes
up a new position on the Loretto-Berg,
175–8; description of new position
occupied by, 178–9, 180; strengthens it,
180; is assailed by Enghien and Turenne and again repulses them, 181–2;
divines Enghien's plans, 183; and when
forced, by starvation, to retreat, just

Mercy, Francis, Baron of—*cont.*
manages to battle them, 183–5; is compelled, however, to allow the French to
reap all the advantages of the campaign,
185; resumes the offensive, 187; but is
outmanœuvred by Turenne and driven
back on Würzburg, 187–9; resolves to
surprise the Weimar army whilst re-
posing in the Taubergrund, 190; surprises Turenne, and forces him with
great loss, into Hesse, 191–3; retreats
before Enghien and Turenne, and occupies a position on and about Allersheim,
195; joy of, as he beheld the French
advancing to attack him, 197; repulses
the first attack, 198; and the second,
198–9; has almost repulsed a third
when he is mortally wounded, 199;
dies, 201, *note.*

Mercy, Gaspard, brother of Francis,
Baron of Mercy, is killed bravely
defending the Loretto-Berg, 182.

Mergentheim, 190; surprise and defeat
of Turenne in and near, 191–3.

Merode, Count of, distinguishes himself
at Lützen, 94, 97.

Mohács, first battle of, 260; second battle
of, 290.

Montecucculi, Raymond, Count of,
succeeds to the command at Zusmarshausen but fails to restore the battle,
214–5; ineffective campaign of, against
Turenne, 247; contrasted with Nicholas Zriny, 275; defeats the Turks at
St. Gotthardt, 275–6.

Muhammad III., succeeds Amurath as
Sultan, carries on the war with changing fortunes in Hungary, and concludes
the Peace of Sitvarok, 270.

Muhammad IV., invades Styria, 275; the
army of, commanded by Koprili Ahmad
Pasha, is defeated at St. Gotthard,
275–6.

Munich, is occupied by Gustavus, 62.

Mustapha II., invades Hungary and
obtains some successes, 290; is defeated
by Prince Eugene at Zenta, 291.

N.

Nantes, Edict of, one disastrous effect of
the revocation of the, upon France, 298.

Nördlingen, is occupied by Tilly, 51;
description of, 119; battle of, 121–4;
consequences of, 124; further description of the country about, 194–5; for
second battle of, *vide* **Allersheim**; is
taken by Turenne, 205.

Nuremberg, early history of, 45-7; declares for Gustavus, 47; threatened by Wallenstein, is occupied by Gustavus, 64; zeal of the citizens of, 65; description of fortifications thrown up around, 66; the strength of, so fortified, deters Wallenstein from an attack, 67; events at and near, during the investment of nearly three months, 67-73; retirement of both armies from, 77-8; history of the connection of the Hohenzollern family with, 227-30.

Nymwegen, gains accruing to France by the Peace of, 297.

O.

Ofen, or **Buda**, is occupied by **Sulaiman the Great**, 261; is besieged by the Imperialists in vain, 264; remains in the possession of the Turk for nearly a century and a half, 264; is recovered from the Turks, 289-90.

Ottwald, Ernest of, communicates to Königsmark the feasibility of surprising Prague, 217; guides the surprise-party thither, 218.

Osman Ogln Pasha, gallantry of, at the battle of Vienna, 286-7.

Oxenstierna, Axel, early friendship of, with Gustavus Adolphus, 16; joins Gustavus with reinforcements at Mainz, 49; discussions of Gustavus with, 50; marches from the Lower Palatinate to relieve Gustavus at Nuremberg, 70-1; character of, 103-4; succeeds in impressing his will upon the reformed princes after the death of Gustavus, 105 & *note*; calls a congress at Heilbronn, 105; is forced to submit to the ambitious exactions of Duke Bernhard, 109-11; warns Duke Bernhard against Wallenstein, with whom he is himself in correspondence, 112; appeals for material aid to France, 126; expedites a messenger to Torstenson, then approaching Vienna, requiring him to return and attack Denmark, 146.

P.

Palatinate, the, occurrences in, after the expulsion of Frederic V. from Bohemia, 9.

Palatine, Elector, *vide* **Frederic V.**

Pappenheim, Godfrey Henry of, invests Magdeburg, 25; calls for the aid of Tilly against Gustavus, 29; urges Tilly to move into the plain of Breitenfeld, 31; rash conduct of, at the outset of the battle, 32; gallantry of, 33-5; is driven from the field, 35; action of, while Gustavus and Wallenstein were opposing each other at Nuremberg, 79; is heard of as marching on Merseburg, 83; at Halle, 85; a recall despatch is sent to, by Wallenstein, 89 & *note*; gallops in all haste to the field, and restores the battle, 95; is mortally wounded, 96; last words of, 96.

Passau, Peace of, nomenclature of the, 2.

Petrikau, Diet of, the, arranges for the reversion of Prussia to the electoral House of Brandenburg, 240.

Piccolomini, Ottavio, greatly distinguishes himself at Lützen, 94; charges the advancing enemy seven times, 97; receives ten wounds, 99; is sent by the Emperor against Banner, 130; assembles the scattered Imperialists to pursue Banner, 134; is detained three days at Wald-Neuburg by the obstinate defence of Colonel Schangen, 134; misses his prey by half an hour, 135; unites with Archduke Leopold to baffle **Torstenson**, 139; after many manœuvres the united Imperialist armies come in presence of Torstenson near Leipzig, 141; some reference to, 142, *note*; is defeated at Breitenfeld, 143-4.

Podébrad, George of, becomes King of Bohemia, 258; devises the throne of Bohemia to the Jagellons, 259.

Platter, Fabricius, is hurled from the window of the Hradschin, 4.

Prague, commencement of the Thirty Years' War at, 4; is occupied by the Saxons, 49; surprise and siege of, 217-22; splendid defence of, 223.

Prussia, early history of, 235 & *notes*; futile attempts to introduce Christianity into, 236; successive attempts are baffled, 237; and fifty years elapse before the inhabitants of, succumb to the Knights of Christ, 237-9; Grandmaster Albert embraces the reformed religion, and, eventually, Prussia comes into the possession of the Hohenzollerns, 240; possession of, by the Hohenzollerns confirmed, 245; gives its name to the kingdom founded by the Hohenzollerns, 256.

INDEX.   355

Pufendorf, charges Franz Albert of Lauenburg with the murder of Gustavus, 99 & note.
Pyrenees, Peace of the, peculiar features of the, 292.

R.

Rákóczy, George I., Prince of Transylvania, negotiates with Torstenson an alliance against the Emperor, 146; is bought off by the Emperor, 153-5; Sigismund, becomes Voivode of Transylvania, but abdicates, 270; George I., succeeds Stephen Bethlen, 273; dies, and is followed by his son, George II., 274; short and disastrous reign of George II., 274; Francis Leopold, conspires against the Habsburgs, 276; is detected, and forced to pay a heavy fine, 277; rouses Hungary for nine years against the Emperor, 308.
Ramsay, Mr. Alexander, is appointed Governor of Kreuznach by Gustavus, 53.
Rantzau, Josias von, succeeds Guébriant in the command of the Weimar army, 161; antecedents and character of, 161-2 & note to 161; distributes his army in winter quarters at Tuttlingen, 162; allows his army to be surprised and almost annihilated by the Bavarians led by Mercy, 164-6; is made lieutenant-general and marshal, and is given a new command, 167 & note.
Ratisbon, proceedings at the diet of 1630 at, 15; is seized by Duke Bernhard, 113; proposals of peace fruitlessly mooted at the diet of, 130 & note; danger to which, is exposed by the daring enterprise of Banner, 132-3.
Reformation, the, political existence of, first acknowledged, 2.
Religion, Peace of, 2; the Reformers excluded from the benefits of the, 15.
Restitution Edict, issue of the, by Ferdinand II., 14; terrible weapon thereby forged, and untoward consequences of the promulgation of, 15; is felt as a great grievance even by the more moderate reformed princes, 24.
Rosen, of Grossop, pursues and vigorously attacks Mercy in his retreat, 184; the carelessness and disobedience of, causes the surprise and defeat of Turenne at Mergentheim, 191-3; is taken prisoner, 192.

Rudolph II., the Emperor, commits the chastisement of Donauwörth to Maximilian of Bavaria, 3; preferences of, 3, note; grants almost unlimited religious freedom to Bohemia, 3.
Ruthven, Sir Patrick, is nominated Governor of Ulm by Gustavus, 53.
Ryswick, the Peace of, a step backward for France, 299.

S.

Salm, Count Nicholas of, commands the garrison of Vienna, which repulses Sultan Sulaiman, 262
Savoy, Victor Amadeus, Duke of, transfers his alliance to the Emperor, 309-10.
Saxe-Lauenburg, Franz Albert of, is feeling his way, before Lützen, towards Gustavus, 86; is at the side of Gustavus at Lützen, 92; abandons him when he is wounded, 93; did he murder him? 99-101; enters the Imperial service, 100; is beaten, and wounded to the death before Schweidnitz, 139 & note.
Saxony, John George, Elector of, makes overtures to Gustavus Adolphus, 15; character and views of, at the onset of the war, 24; refuses to Gustavus a free passage through Saxony to relieve Magdeburg, 27; repels the demands of Tilly, 30; and throws himself into the arms of Gustavus, 31; flees from the field of Breitenfeld, 34; re-appears to congratulate the conqueror, 37; accompanies his army as far as Prague, and then makes it over to Arnheim, 49; fickle nature of, detrimental to the plans of Gustavus, 49-51; is reassured by the arrival of Gustavus, and occupies Torgau, 85; promises to adhere to the Swedish alliance after the death of Gustavus, 105; after Nördlingen, makes a separate peace with the Emperor, 124; obtains from the Swedes a treaty of neutrality, 152; causes the descent of Saxony from the first to the second place in the electorate, 225.
Scheverlin, inopportunely surrenders Lichtenau to Wallenstein, 77.
Schlangen, splendid defence by, of Wald-Neuburg, 134; is killed at the second battle of Breitenfeld, 143-4.
Schlierberg, description of the, 178.
Schwendi, Lazarus of, one of the most famous warriors of the age, 265; completely defeats Zápolya at Szatlamár, 266.

23 *

Seckendorf, Colonel, is brought before a council of war for holding intelligence with the enemy, 138.
Seventeenth century, great **warriors of** the, 136.
Slavata, is **hurled from the window of the** Hradschin, 4.
Sobieski, John, King of Poland, character and previous career of, 282-4 & *notes*; marches **to the** relief of Vienna, and joins Lorraine at Hollabrun, 284; **calls up the** German contingents, 284, 285; **marches** forward, and gains the **Kahlenberg,** 286; settles the order of **attack** for the next day, 286; **completely defeats the** Turkish army, and **relieves Vienna,** 286-8; **makes a triumphal** entry into the **city, 288-9;** recovers the city **of** Gran, **and returns** to his own kingdom, 289; **the expulsion of the Turks** from Europe **due to,** 291.
Spork, General, conspires **with John of Werth** against Maximilian, **and forces him to** renounce his neutrality, **208-9.**
Stalhans, Colonel, commands the **Swedish** right wing at Lützen, **when Gustavus** hurries to support his **left, 92; drives back** the enemy's **left, 94; when he is** assailed, and all **but annihilated by** Pappenheim, 95; advances again after his death, 97; joins Torstenson, and captures Franz Albert **of** Lauenburg, 139; is engaged at the second battle of Breitenfeld, 143.
Starhemberg, Count Rüdiger, commands the garrison **of Vienna during** its last siege by the **Turks, 278; daily** routine of, 280.
Starhemberg, Count Guido, baffles Max-Emanuel in his invasion of Tirol, 309.
Sterzinger, Martin, nobly defends Tirol against the Bavarians, 309.
St. Gotthard, Montecucculi **defeats the** Turks at, 275-6.
Sulaiman II., the Great, wages war with Hungary, takes **several places, and** defeats Louis II. at Mohács, **259-60;** espouses the cause **of Zápolya, invades** Hungary, is checked **before Vienna,** retires only again **to return,** 262; is **repulsed** before Günz, 262, *note,* **&** 263; makes peace, but on the death **of John Zápoyla,** declares Hungary **to be a satrapy of** the Porte, 263; again invades **Hungary,** 266; besieges Szigeth, **266; is almost** broken by the splendid **resistance of** Zriny, **and** dies three days before the place was taken, 267.
Sweden, gains of, by the Treaty **of** Westphalia, 223-4; ambition of, is baffled by

Sweden—*cont.*
the Great Elector, 250-6; **sides ultimately** with France in her **war with Europe,** 295.
Swedish army, losses of, **at Breitenfeld** 36; at and about Nuremberg, 76; at Lützen, 98-9; at Nördlingen, 124; at **the second** battle **of Breitenfeld, 144;** at Jankowitz, 152.
Szigeth, splendid defence of, **by Nicholas Zriny,** 266-7.

T.

Talbot, Colonel, gallant conduct of, at Kreuznach, 83.
Tallard, Marshal, defeats the Duke of Hesse-Cassel at Speyer, 311-2; laconic announcement of, to his master, *note to* 312; collects a convoy, escorts it safely **into** Bavaria, **and** returns, 316-7; **crosses the Rhine** and marches to the **Danube, 320**, peculiarities of, 326; **position of, at** the battle of Blenheim, **327; does not expect** to be attacked, 328; is **undeceived, calls** his troops to arms, and concentrates his right wing in and about Blenheim, 328-9; weakness of the position of, 329; repulses Marlborough's first attack, 331; opportunities before, but insufficiently taken advantage of, **332; has** the mortification **to see his** cavalry recoil, 337; orders **the** evacuation of Blenheim, **338; is taken prisoner,** 338.
Taubergrund, description of the, 190; surprise and **defeat of Turenne in the,** 191-3.
Terzky, Count, commands the centre of Wallenstein's army at Lützen, 89; greatly distinguishes himself, 97.
Teufel, Colonel, fights under Gustavus at Breitenfeld, 33-7.
Thirty Years' War, remarks upon the progress and result of the, 223-5.
Thurn, Count, hurls Martinitz and Slavata from the window of the Hradschin, 4; marches against Vienna, 5; is compelled to retire, 6.
Tilly, Count, defeats the reformers on the White Hill, 8; triumphs of, in the Palatinate, 9; marches to the Weser against Christian IV. King of Denmark, 10; description of, 22, 23; marches northwards and resolves to besiege Magdeburg, 23; gives **no** quarter to the garrison of Neubrandenburg, 24; begins

INDEX. 357

Tilly, Count—*cont.*
the siege of Magdeburg, 25; storms it, 27; ravages Thüringen, 28; receives a rebuff from the Landgrave of Cassel, 29; offers battle to Gustavus near Wolmerstädt, 29; makes demands on John George of Saxony which the latter refuses, 30; marches against Leipzig, which he takes, 31; moves to the plain of Breitenfeld to meet Gustavus, 31, 32; is defeated by Gustavus, 32–37; movements of, after the battle, 43; allows Würzburg to fall, 44; and falls back on Ansbach, 45; after a futile attempt to surprise Nuremberg, marches to Nördlingen, 51; attempts to surprise Bamberg, but fails, 54-5; falls back, on the approach of Gustavus, to Rain, 55; resolves to defend the passage of the Lech, 57; is attacked by Gustavus, 58-9; is wounded and carried **from the field**, 60; advises Maximilian **to fall** back on Ingolstadt, 60-1; **death of, 62.**

Tököly, Emerich, conspires **against the** Habsburgs, 277; sketch of **the remarkable** career of, *note to* 277; **invokes the** aid of Sultan Muhammad **IV., 278; is** defeated by Lorraine, 282.

Tököly, Helena, sketch of the remarkable character and career of, *note to* 277.

Torstenson, Lennart, Count of Ortola, earlier career of, 136; succeeds Banner in command of the Swedes, 137; joins the army, and **sets** to **work** to restore its discipline, 138; spreading rumours of a contrary nature, dashes into Silesia, 138, 139; is joined by Colonel Stalhaus, and invests Schweidnitz, 139; takes Schweidnitz and other strong places in Silesia, and makes prisoner **Franz** Albert of Lauenberg, 139; enters **Moravia**, and threatens Vienna, 139; retreats into Silesia before the Imperialists receive reinforcements, and again resumes the offensive, 140; is besieging Leipzig when the armies of Archduke Leopold and Piccolomini are signalled, 142; moves into the plain of Breitenfeld to encounter them, 142; wins the battle fought there, 143–4; takes Leipzig, 144; concerts a plan of operations with Guébriant, 144; after some marching and countermarching conquers all Moravia excepting Brünn, 145; negotiates a combined plan with Prince Rákóczy, 146; receives a message from Oxenstierna requiring him **to** retrace his steps to Denmark, 146; outmanœuvres Gallas, 146; crushes the Danes, 147; and then crushes Gallas, 147-8; returns and re-

Torstenson, Lennart—*cont.*
news his negotiations with Rákóczy, 148; invades Bohemia, and enters, on his way to Vienna, the tract between the Moldau and the Sazawa, 149; is surprised by Hatzfeldt, and almost beaten, but restores the battle and gains a great victory, 150–2; marches **on** Vienna, 152; besieges Vienna, 154; **but** is forced, by the bad faith of Rákóczy, to renounce the siege, 155; marches on, and besieges, Brünn, 155–6; is repulsed, retires into Bohemia, and resigns the command to Wrangel, 156; character of the operations conducted **by,** 156-7, and *note.*

Transylvania, sketch of the connection of, with the House of Austria, 261–78.

Turenne, aids Duke Bernhard against the Imperialists, 128; antecedents of, 167–9; character of, *note to* 169; **is** nominated to succeed Rantzau, 169; marches to relieve Freiburg, 170; waits for, **and** is joined by, the Duke of Enghien, 170, 172, 174; advises against an attack, 174; is detached to turn Mercy's position, 175; has a desperate fight with the Bavarians, neither party being able to force his way, 176–7; gives his men rest, and is joined by Enghien, 179; makes a vigorous but unsuccessful attack on the Lorettoberg, 181–2; tenderness of, 182; joins with Enghien in the race to cut off Mercy, who only just escapes, 183–5; aids Enghien to conquer the boundary of the Rhine for France, 185; remains with six thousand men to guard that boundary, 186; is attacked by Mercy, but outmanœuvres him, and forces him back on Würzburg, 187–9; great military skill displayed by, 189; gives his troops rest in the Taubergrund, 190; is surprised by Mercy and forced to retreat, with great loss, into Hesse, 190–3; judgment **of,** on the surprise, 193 *note*; **receives** reinforcements in Hesse, 193, **is joined** by Enghien, and marches with **him towards** Nördlingen, 194; **reconnoitres** the enemy's position at Allersheim, and advises against an attack, but is overruled, 196; the first and second attacks of, are repulsed, and he is wounded, 200; is reinforced by Enghien, and drives the enemy from the position, 200–1; the glory of the victory attributed to, by Enghien, 202; retreats to Philipsburg, 202; obtains with difficulty the permission of Mazarin to co-operate with Wrangel, 204; joins him at Gies-

Turenne—*cont.*
sen, 205; marches to the **Danube and Lech**, and forces the Elector **of Bavaria to take** refuge in Braunau, 205; **separates from** Wrangel and returns **to France**, 207; rejoins Wrangel **and crosses the** Danube **in** pursuit of Melander, 211-3; catches Melander *in flagrante delicto* at Zusmarshausen, and completely **defeats** him, 213-6; forces the passage of the Lech in the face **of** Gronsfeld, 216-7; campaign of, against Montecucculi, 247; beats the Imperialists at Mulhausen and Türckheim, and drives them from Alsace, 248-9.

Tuttlingen, description of the **country about**, 162; **successful surprise and destruction of the Franco-Weimar army, by Mercy, at, 164-6.**

U.

Ulm, Peace Congress held at, and **results only in a** declaration on the part **of** Maximilian of Bavaria to become neutral, 206-7; is taken by Max Emanuel, 306.

Union, The Protestant, formation of the, 3; agrees to the terms **offered by** Duke Maximilian, 8.

V.

Vane, Sir Francis, gallant conduct of, before Kreuznach, 53.

Vasvár, Treaty of, called also of Eisenburg and St. Gotthard, concluded, 276.

Vaudemont, Prince of, the tardy arrival of the, saves **the French in Cremona,** 304-5.

Vendôme, Marshal, succeeds **to the** command of the French army, **in Italy,** 305; character of, *note* to 305; **campaign of**, against Eugene, 306; against **Guido** Stahremberg, 309-10.

Vesselenyi, Palatine of Hungary, conspires against the Habsburgs, but **dies before** the conspiracy matures, 276.

Vienna, is besieged by the reformed army under **Count Thurn**, 5; is saved by **the firmness of** Ferdinand and the opportune **arrival of** Dampierre, 6; fortifications **of,** strengthened by Ferdinand III., 153; outworks of, carried by Torstenson, 154, & *notes*; Torstenson retires

Vienna—*cont.*
from before, 155 & *note*; is besieged by **Sulaiman the** Great, but repulses him, 262; small number of the garrison of, when Kara Mustapha advances to besiege it, 278; miserable state **of the fortifications of,** 279; points of, against **which the Turks** directed their attacks, 279-80; **gallantry** of the garrison of, particularised, 280; still holds out, though under great difficulties, 281, & *note* to 286; description **of the battle fought** before, 286-8; triumphal **entry** of the victors into, 288-9.

Villars, is sent by **Louis XIV., to co-operate with Max Emanuel in Germany,** 306; character of, 306-7; outmanœuvres Louis **of Baden and is named Marshal** of France, **307**; joins **Max Emanuel** at Ulm, 310; urges in vain a **march on** Vienna, 310; beats the **Imperial** army at Höchstädt, 311; transfers the command to Tallard, 311.

Villeroi, Marshal, is pitted against Prince Eugene in Italy, 302; **is taken prisoner** in Cremona, 304; character of, *note* to 305.

Vogtland, description of the, 82, *note*.

W.

Wald-Neuburg, splendid defence of, by the Swedes, 134.

Wallenstein, early life of, 11, 12; raises an army, at the call of the Emperor, and marches to the Weser, 12, 13; defeats Mansfeldt at Dessau, pursues him into Hungary and forces him to disband his army, 13; drives King Christian to extremities and forces upon him a peace, 14; is removed from command and retires into private life, 15; is again appealed to by Ferdinand, 51; accepts his offer under conditions, 52 & *note*; raises an army, and, with the intention of drawing Gustavus from Southern Germany, marches against Nuremberg, 63-4; appears before the **place,** but, impressed by the strength **of its defences,** takes up a position near **Fürth,** 67; resolving to starve his **enemy, holds** the position for nearly three months, 67-74; detaches Holk into Saxony, 72; is attacked by, and repulses Gustavus, 74-6; takes Lichtenau and marches to Forcheim, 77-8; sends Gallas to reinforce Holk, 80;

Wallenstein—*cont.*
marches towards Saxony, is repulsed at the Ehrenburg, 82; enters Saxony and takes Halle and Leipzig, 82-3; recalls Gallas and Holk and despatches the former into Bohemia, 85; glance at the position of, *vis à vis* Gustavus, 86; distributes his army, and despatches Pappenheim to Cologne, 87; is surprised by the march towards him of Gustavus and tries to reassemble his forces, 88; improvises defences, and arranges his men as they come up, 88-9; restores the battle, by his personal influence and daring, when his right wing had been broken by Duke Bernhard 91-2; is, however, gradually **forced back**, 94; when he is sensibly **relieved** by the arrival of Pappenheim, 95; **hopes** for everything, when he learns **that** Pappenheim is killed, 95-6; still **shows** himself a great leader, 96-7; **maintains his ground**, but makes the fatal **mistake of** falling back on Leipzig during **the night**, 97-8; corresponds with Oxenstierna, **and, on** the failure of the negotiation, **ravages** Lower Saxony, 112; orders **Gallas** not to fight, 113; action **of, approved** by the Emperor, 114, *note*; **checks, in the** most masterly manner, **the advance of** Duke Bernhard, 115 & *note*, 116; is murdered, 117 & *note*.

Werth, John of, fails to hinder the march of Duke Bernhard, 107, 108, & *note*; decides the victory **of Nördlingen, 123**; is defeated and taken prisoner **at Rheinfelden**, 128; splendid captivity of, in Paris, *note to* 160; baffles Guébriant, 160; joins Mercy in Swabia, 163; participates in the successful surprise **of** Tuttlingen, 163-6; completes the **defeat** of Turenne **at** Mergentheim, 192; commands the **Bavarian left at** Allersheim, 195; drives the **French right wing from** the field, but follows **it up too far, 198**; returns to find the French **victorious on** their left and in their centre, and **falls** back on Allersheim, 201; is joined by the Archduke Leopold and falls back on Donauwörth, 202; in consequence of Maximilian's declaration of neutrality forms a conspiracy against him, 208; and forces **him to** re-enter on **the** field, 209.

Westphalia, Peace of, is signed, **223**; principles asserted **in the, 224**

White Hill, triumph **of the** Catholics at the battle of the, 8.

Wittstock, Banner beats **the** Saxons at, 126.

Wrangle, Charles Gustavus, succeeds Torstenson in command of the Swedish army, 156; takes some places in Bohemia and puts his army into winter quarters in Thüringen, 157; early **career of,** 203; marches into Upper **Hesse** to co-operate with Turenne, 204-5; joins him at Giessen, 205; marches with Turenne to the Danube, and seizes the line of the Lech, 205; separates from Turenne and falls **back** on **Eger, 207**; is followed **thither by the Emperor** and a battle **appears imminent, 208**; when the action of Maximilian forces, to evacuate Bohemia, 208-9; is pressed hard by Melander and only saved by the latter's diversion into Hesse, 210-11; takes the offensive, and joined by Turenne **pursues Melander** across the Danube, **211-12**; crosses the Danube and marches on Zusmarshausen, 213; completely defeats the enemy at, 213-6; forces the Lech in the face of the Bavarian army, 216-7; despatches Königsmark into Bohemia, 217; invades the dominions of the Elector of Brandenburg, 249; learns that his centre is pierced by the troops of Frederic William, 250-1; tries **to** join his two wings by a circuitous march, 252; is attacked **by** Frederic William at Fehrbellin **and** completely defeated, 253-5.

Würzburg, besieged and taken by **Gustavus,** 43; **Turenne forces Mercy back** on, 189.

Z.

Zapolya, John opposes the **election to** the crown of Hungary of Ferdinand **of** Habsburg, 261; throws himself into the arms of Sultan Sulaimán, and ravages Hungary, 262; refuses to acknowledge the Habsburgs, and dies bequeathing the spirit of rebellion to his son, 263; **John Sigismund,** is placed under the protection of the Sultan, 263; renounces his claims **to** the crown of Hungary in favour of **the** Sultan, 264; terms accorded to, **by** the Habsburgs, 265**; on** the death of Ferdinand I., breaks **the** truce and invades Hungary, 265; is completely defeated by Lazarus **of** Schwendi at Szathmár, 266; dies, **the** last of his race, 268.

Zollern, or Zolre, early traces of the House of, 226; castle of, *note to* 226; the House of, comes to be divided into Swabian and Franconian branches, **227**; history of the Franconian branch of, 227–32; comes to be called **Hohenzollern,** *q. vide.*

Zriny, Count Nicholas, splendidly defends Szigeth against the whole army of Sulaimán the Great, 266; when further defence is impossible, sallies out and dies, 267; the gallant defence of, ensures the retreat of the Turkish army, 268.

Zriny, Count Nicholas, Ban of Croatia, great grandson of the hero of Szigeth, splendid service rendered by, against the Turks, 275; contrast with Montecucculi, 275; is killed whilst hunting, 276.

Zriny, Count Peter, brother of the preceding, conspires against the Habsburgs, 276; is beheaded, 277.

Zusmarshausen, description of the country in the vicinity of, 212–3; Melander takes post at, 213; battle of, 213–6.

WORKS BY THE SAME AUTHOR.

In One Volume, 8vo., price 20s. cloth, with a Portrait of the Author, a Map, and Plans.

The Decisive Battles of India, from 1746 to 1849 inclusive. By Colonel G. B. MALLESON, C.S.I. London: W. H. Allen & Co., 1883.

"We know of no book so well calculated as is the one we are noticing for giving the student a clear and comprehensive knowledge of the successive steps taken in conquering for ourselves the Empire of Hindostan. It is not simply the story of so many decisive battles. The causes which led to each are set forth, and the connexion between successive wars is clearly shown. The author has consulted 'as far as possible original documents, or writings published and unpublished of contemporaries'; and, to judge by the list of such given, the labour of compiling this excellent work must have been very considerable."—SATURDAY REVIEW.

"This is just the sort of book we should feel inclined to place in the hands of boys—if there are such—whom the influence of æsthetic or luxurious mammas may be in danger of rendering milksops. The annals of the Roman Proconsulate do not contain a more stimulating story of endurance, daring, and the manlier virtues generally, than that told in Colonel Malleson's twelve chapters. Almost every page of the volume shows traces of original research. The author is never dull."—SPECTATOR.

"We cannot afford space to notice the other decisive and better known battles described in this book, but we can assure the reader that they are well worthy of his attention, especially those fought with the Sikhs, the official accounts of which are untrustworthy and incorrect. As to the manner in which the author has accomplished his task, it is sufficient to say that the work before us is not unworthy of Colonel Malleson's deservedly high reputation as a writer on Indian subjects."—ATHENÆUM.

"All these battles are narrated with Colonel Malleson's usual power, combining a scientific understanding of the military events with a clear appreciation of the political situation; while his literary ability enables him to present a mass of compressed information in a pleasant and readable shape. In speaking of political events especially, he is as outspoken and uncompromising as ever; never, as a soldier, so dazzled by the brilliancy of a victory as to be blind to any wrongdoing or injustice that may have paved the way for it; never, as a politician, so overborne by the success of any scheme to be silent when it seems to him that the process by which it was gained deserves unsparing exposure or stern and even harsh reproof."—GUARDIAN.

8vo., 20s. cloth, with a Portrait and *four Plans.*

Founders of the Indian Empire: Clive, Warren Hastings, and Wellesley. Vol. I.—Lord Clive. London : W. H. Allen & Co, 1882.

"How this splendid edifice was built up, with blood and iron for the cement, forms a story which Englishmen should never tire of reading. Nor will many minds weary, we answer for it, over the graphic pages, full of life and vivid local colouring, in which the ablest of recent Indian historians tells the wondrous tale."—GLOBE.

"Unquestionably the best life of Clive that has appeared."—VANITY FAIR.

8vo., 16s.

History of the French in India, from the Founding of Pondichery in 1674 to the Capture of that place in 1761. London : Longmans & Co., 1868.

"Nous n'hésitons pas à recommander, même au gouvernement, de faciliter la lecture de ce très instructif ouvrage partout où nous avons des colonies. Il devrait être le manuel de nos gouverneurs, de nos généraux, de nos commissaires dans toutes les régions du globe où flotte le pavillon français."—L'ASSEMBLÉE NATIONALE.

"One of the most important works connected with Indian history which has appeared for many years."—FRIEND OF INDIA.

"Colonel Malleson's work exhausts all that can be said concerning this episode. His book possesses an independent interest in the literature which relates to the European occupation of India."—TIMES.

Crown 8vo., 10s. 6d.

Final French Struggles in India and on the Indian Seas, including an account of the Capture of the Isles of France and Bourbon; and a Diary of the March of the Anglo-Indian Army from Kosseir to Cairo in 1801. London : W. H. Allen & Co.

"How India escaped from the government of prefects and sub-prefects to fall under that of commissioners and deputy commissioners; why a penal code of Lord Macaulay reigns supreme instead of a Code Napoléon: why we are not looking on helplessly from Mahé Karikal and Pondichery while the French are ruling all over Madras and spending millions of francs in attempting to cultivate the slopes of the Neilgheries, may be learnt from this modest volume. Colonel

Malleson is always painstaking and generally accurate: his style is transparent, and he never loses sight of the purpose with which he commenced to write."—SATURDAY REVIEW.

In Three Volumes, 8vo., price 20s. each, Cloth.

History of the Indian Mutiny, 1857-8, commencing from the close of the second volume of Sir John Kaye's History of the Sepoy War. London: W. H. Allen & Co.

"It need only be remarked that Colonel Malleson wields his pen with so much skill that while giving a realistic account of all important operations, passing over no really noteworthy act of talent or heroism, and acutely criticising everything which demands criticism, he abstains from overlaying his narrative with details which would have increased the bulk of his book beyond all reason. . . . There are many highly-placed officials whose fame is sadly tarnished by the frank, truthful criticisms of the fearless, uncompromising author of the book before us."—ATHENÆUM.

"A brilliant narrative, in which a great number of threads of history are taken up and combined with singular skill. We have never read a volume in which this merit is more conspicuously displayed; and a history which, in unskilful hands, might have become confused to the last degree, is made remarkably clear and intelligible."—SPECTATOR.

"The second volume of Colonel Malleson's "History of the Indian Mutiny" is quite equal to the first in every respect. The style is as eloquent, the grasp of the subject as firm, the arrangement as clear, and, above all, there is the same evidence of industry, the same evident desire to be impartial."—TIMES.

"It is difficult, in speaking of a living writer, to give expression to the unqualified praise which we hold Colonel Malleson's work to merit. It is not less remarkable for its literary beauty and its loftiness of diction than it is for the research and careful inquiry which are perceptible on every page. Posterity will recognise in his book a great and true exposition of one of the crises through which his countrymen have fought their way, by characteristics truly British, to wider empire and to greater fame."—EXAMINER.

In One Volume, 8vo., with six Maps, price 15s.

An Historical Sketch of the Native States of India in Subsidiary Alliance with the British Government; with Notices of the Mediatised and Minor States. London: Longmans & Co.

"Colonel Malleson is recognised as one of the masters of Indian history; and his acquaintance with the past vicissitudes, as well as the actual condition of the feudal states of Hindostan, could not easily be surpassed."—TIMES.

"This is a book at once interesting to all who desire to gain some acquaintance with the history of the numerous mediatised and minor states of India, and very valuable as a book of reference. Its arrangement is new, its plan novel as well as useful."—DAILY TELEGRAPH.

In One Volume, 8vo., with Map, 18s.

A History of Afghanistan, from the earliest period to the Outbreak of the War of 1878. London: W. H. Allen & Co.

"The charm, vivacity, and dramatic force of Colonel Malleson's narrative style are not less conspicuous in this book than in his continuation of Kaye's history of the Indian mutiny. With rare skill and literary judgment he has disentangled the facts of Afghan history from the various chronicles and records, and has put them in the form of a clear continuous narrative."—SCOTSMAN.

In One Volume, 8vo., price 8s.

Herat, the Granary and Garden of Central Asia. London: W. H. Allen & Co.

"Colonel Malleson is an acknowledged master of Indian history, and in this volume, as in his previous works, he has shown that he is a writer of great skill. His style is admirable, his itinerary useful, and his reading in all that concerns India profound."—ACADEMY.

In One Volume, Crown 8vo., price 10s. 6d., Cloth.

Studies from Genoese History. London: Longmans & Co.

"Colonel Malleson has done well in preferring to give us rather a series of pictures of the salient points of Genoese history than a mere methodical narrative or a succinct epitome. The incidents selected by him are thoroughly typical and their grouping genuinely dramatic. The sketches of Jacopo Bonfadio and of the Doria are specimens of literary work of a high order."—THE WORLD.

JANUARY 1884.

BOOKS, &c.,

ISSUED BY

MESSRS. W. H. ALLEN & Co.,

Publishers & Literary Agents to the India Office,

COMPRISING

MISCELLANEOUS PUBLICATIONS IN GENERAL LITERATURE.

MILITARY WORKS, INCLUDING THOSE ISSUED BY THE GOVERNMENT.

INDIAN AND MILITARY LAW.

MAPS OF INDIA, &c.

13, WATERLOO PLACE, LONDON, S.W.

Works issued from the India Office, and Sold by
W. H. ALLEN & Co.

Illustrations of Ancient Buildings in Kashmir.
Prepared at the Indian Museum under the authority of the Secretary of State for India in Council. From Photographs, Plans, and Drawings taken by Order of the Government of India. By HENRY HARDY COLE, LIEUT. R.E., Superintendent Archæological Survey of India, North-West Provinces. In One vol.; half-bound, Quarto Fifty-eight plates. £3 10s.

The Illustrations in this work have been produced in Carbon from the original negatives, and are therefore permanent.

Pharmacopœia of India.
Prepared under the Authority of the Secretary of State for India. By EDWARD JOHN WARING, M.D. Assisted by a Committee appointed for the Purpose. 8vo. 6s.

The Stupa of Bharhut. A Buddhist Monument.
Ornamented with numerous Sculptures illustrative of Buddhist Legend and History in the Third Century B.C. By ALEXANDER CUNNINGHAM, C.S.I., C.I.E., Major-General, Royal Engineers (Bengal Retired); Director-General Archæological Survey of India. 4to. Fifty-seven Plates. Cloth gilt. £3 3s.

Archæological Survey of Western India.
Report of the First Season's Operations in the Belgâm and Kaladgi Districts. January to May, 1874. Prepared at the India Museum and Published under the Authority of the Secretary of State for India in Council. By JAMES BURGESS, Author of the "Rock Temples of Elephanta," &c., &c., and Editor of "The Indian Antiquary." Half-bound, Quarto. 58 Plates and Woodcuts. £2 2s.

Archæological Survey of Western India. Vol. II.
Report on the Antiquities of Kâthiâwâd and Kachh, being the
result of the Second Season's Operations of the Archæological
Survey of Western India. 1874–75. By JAMES BURGESS,
F.R.G.S., M.R.A.S., &c., Archæological Surveyor and Reporter
to Government, Western India. 1876. Half-bound. Quarto
Seventy-four Plates and Woodcuts. £3 3s.

Archæological Survey of Western India. Vol. III.
Report on the Antiquities in the Bidar and Aurungabad Districts in the Territory of H.H. the Nizam of Haidarabad,
being the result of the Third Season's Operations of the
Archæological Survey of Western India. 1875–1876. By
JAMES BURGESS, F.R.G.S., M.R.A.S., Membre de la Societé
Asiatique, &c., Archæological Surveyor and Reporter to Government, Western India. Half-bound. Quarto. Sixty-six
Plates and Woodcuts. £2 2s.

Illustrations of Buildings near Muttra and Agra,
Showing the Mixed Hindu-Mahomedan Style of Upper India
Prepared at the India Museum under the authority of the
Secretary of State for India in Council, from Photographs,
Plans, and Drawings taken by Order of the Government of
India. By HENRY HARDY COLE, Lieut. R.E., late Superintendent Archæological Survey of India, North-West Provinces.
4to. With Photographs and Plates. £3 10s.

The Cave Temples of India.
By JAMES FERGUSON, D.C.L., F.R.A.S., V.P.R.A.S., and
JAMES BURGESS, F.R.G.S., M.R.A.S., &c. Printed and Published by Order of Her Majesty's Secretary of State, &c.
Royal 8vo. With Photographs and Woodcuts. £2 2s.

Aberigh-Mackay (G.) Twenty-one Days in India.
Being the Tour of Sir ALI BABA, K.C.B. By GEORGE
ABERIGH-MACKAY. Post 8vo. 4s.
An Illustrated Edition. 8vo. 10s. 6d.

Æsop, the Fables of, and other Eminent Mythologists.
With Morals and Reflections. By Sir ROGER L'ESTRANGE, kt.
A facsimile reprint of the Edition of 1669. Folio, antique,
sheep. 21s.

Akbar. An Eastern Romance.
By Dr. P. A. S. VAN LIMBURG-BROUWER. Translated from
the Dutch by M. M. With Notes and Introductory Life of
the Emperor Akbar, by CLEMENTS R. MARKHAM, C.B., F.R.S.
Crown 8vo. 10s. 6d.

Alberg (A.) Snowdrops: Idylls for Children.
From the Swedish of Zach Topelius. By ALBERT ALBERG,
Author of "Whisperings in the Wood." 3s. 6d.

—— **Whisperings in the Wood**: Finland Idylls for Children.
From the Swedish of Zach Topelius. By ALBERT ALBERG,
Author of "Fabled Stories from the Zoo," and Editor of
"Chit-Chat by Puck," "Rose Leaves," and "Woodland
Notes." 3s. 6d.

—— **Queer People.**
A Selection of Short Stories from the Swedish of "Leah."
By ALBERT ALBERG. 2 vols. Illus. Crown 8vo. 12s.

Alexander II. (Life of) Emperor of all the Russias. By the
Author of "Science, Art, and Literature in Russia," "Life
and Times of Alexander I.," &c. Crown 8vo. 10s. 6d.

Allen's Series.
  1.—Ansted's World We Live In. 2s.
  2.—Ansted's Earth's History. 2s.
  3.—Ansted's 2000 Examination Questions in Physical Geo-
      graphy. **2s.**
  4.—Geography of India. (See page 13.) **2s.**
  5—Ansted's Elements of Physiography. 1s. 4d.
  6.—Hall's Trigonometry. (See page 14.) 2s.
  7.—Wollaston's Elementary Indian Reader. 1s. (See p. 43.)

Ameer Ali. The Personal Law of the Mahommedans (according to all the Schools). Together with a Comparative
Sketch of the Law of Inheritance among the Sunnis and
Shiahs. By SYED AMEER ALI, Moulvi, M.A., LL.B., Barrister-
at-Law, and Presidency Magistrate at Calcutta. 8vo. **15s.**

Anderson (Ed. L.) How to Ride and School a Horse.
With a System of Horse Gymnastics. By EDWARD L.
ANDERSON. Cr. 8vo. 2s. 6d.
—————— **A System of School Training for Horses.**
By EDWARD L. ANDERSON, Author of "How to Ride and
School a Horse." Crown 8vo 2s. 6d.
Anderson (P.) The English in Western India. 8vo. 14s.
Anderson (T.) History of Shorthand.
With an analysis and review of its present condition and
prospects in Europe and America. By THOMAS ANDERSON,
Parliamentary Reporter, &c. With Portraits. Crown 8vo.
12s. 6d.
—————— **Catechism of Shorthand**; being a Critical Examination
of the various Styles, with special reference to the question,
Which is the best English System of Shorthand? By
THOMAS ANDERSON, Author of " Synopsis of a New System
of Shorthand Writing," "History of Shorthand," **&c.**
Fcap. 1s.
Andrew (W. P.) India and Her Neighbours.
By W. P. ANDREW, Author of "Our Scientific Frontier,"
"The Indus and Its Provinces," "Memoir of the Euphrates
Route." With Two Maps. 8vo. 15s.
—————— **Our Scientific Frontier.**
With Sketch-Map and Appendix. 8vo. 6s.
—————— **Euphrates Valley Route**, in connection with the Central Asian and Egyptian Questions. Lecture delivered at
the National Club, 16th June 1882. By SIR WILLIAM
ANDREW, C.I.E., Author of " India and Her Neighbours,"
&c. 8vo., with 2 Maps. 5s.
—————— **Through Booking of Goods between the Interior of
India** and the United Kingdom. By SIR WILLIAM ANDREW,
C.I.E., M.R.A.S., F.R.G.S., F.S.A., Author of " India and
Her Neighbours," &c. **2s.**
Ansted (D. T.) Physical Geography.
By Professor D. T. ANSTED, M.A., F.R.S., &c. Fifth
Edition. Post 8vo., with Illustrative Maps. 7s.
CONTENTS :—PART I.—INTRODUCTION.—The Earth as **a Planet.**
—Physical Forces.—The Succession of Rocks. PART II.—
EARTH —Land.—Mountains.—Hills and Valleys.—Plateaux
and Low Plains. PART III.—WATER.—The Ocean.—Rivers.
—**Lakes** and Waterfalls.—The Phenomena of Ice.—Springs
PART IV.—AIR.—The Atmosphere. Winds and Storms.—
Dew, Clouds, and Rain.—Climate and Weather. PART V.—

FIRE.—Volcanoes and Volcanic Phenomena.—Earthquakes.
PART VI.—LIFE.—The Distribution of Plants in the different Countries of the Earth.—The Distribution of Animals on the Earth.—The Distribution of Plants and Animals in Time.—Effects of Human Agency on Inanimate Nature.

"The Book is both valuable and comprehensive, and deserves a wide circulation."—*Observer.*

Ansted (D. T.) Elements of Physiography.
For the use of Science Schools. Fcap. 8vo. 1s. 4d.

—— **The World We Live In.**
Or First Lessons in Physical Geography. For the use of Schools and Students. By D. T. ANSTED, M.A., F.R.S., &c. Fcap. 2s. 25th Thousand, with Illustrations.

—— **The Earth's History.**
Or, First Lessons in Geology. For the use of Schools and Students. By D. T. ANSTED. Third Thousand. Fcap. 2s.

—— **Two Thousand Examination Questions** in Physical Geography. pp. 180. Price 2s.

—— **Water, and Water Supply.**
Chiefly with reference to the British Islands. Part I.—Surface Waters. 8vo. With Maps. 18s.

—— **and Latham (R. G.) Channel Islands. Jersey, Guernsey,** Alderney, Sark, &c.

THE CHANNEL ISLANDS. Containing: PART I.—Physical Geography. PART II.—Natural History. PART III.—Civil History. PART IV.—Economics and Trade. By DAVID THOMAS ANSTED, M.A., F.R.S., and ROBERT GORDON LATHAM, M.A., M.D., F.R.S. New and Cheaper Edition in one handsome 8vo. Volume, with 72 Illustrations on Wood by Vizetelly, Loudon, Nicholls, and Hart; with Map. 8vo. 16s.

"This is a really valuable work. A book which will long remain the standard authority on the subject. No one who has been to the Channel Islands, or who purposes going there will be insensible of its value."—*Saturday Review.*

"It is the produce of many hands and every hand a good one."

Archer (Capt. J. H. Lawrence) Commentaries on the
Punjaub Campaign—1848-49, including some additions to the History of the Second Sikh War, from original sources. By Capt. J. H LAWRENCE-ARCHER, Bengal H. P. Crown 8vo. 8s.

Armstrong (Annie E.) Ethel's Journey to Strange Lands in
Search of Her Doll. By ANNIE E. ARMSTRONG. Cr. 8vo. With Illustrations by CHAS. WHYMPER. 2s. 6d.

Army and Navy Calendar for the Financial Year 1883-84.
Being a Compendium of General Information relating to the Army, Navy, Militia, and Volunteers, and containing Maps, Plans, Tabulated Statements, Abstracts, &c. Compiled from authentic sources. 2s. 6d.

Army and Navy Magazine.
Vols. I. to V. are issued. 7s. 6d. each.

Aynsley (Mrs.) Our Visit to Hindustan, Kashmir, and Ladakh.
By Mrs. J. C. MURRAY AYNSLEY. 8vo. 14s.

Baildon (S.) The Tea Industry in India.
A Review of Finance and Labour, and a Guide for Capitalists and Assistants. By SAMUEL BAILDON, Author of "Tea in Assam." 8vo. 10s. 6d.

Belgium of the East (The).
By the Author of "Egypt under Ismail Pasha," "Egypt for the Egyptians," &c. Crown 8vo. 6s.

Bellew (Capt.) Memoirs of a Griffin; or, A Cadet's First Year in India. By Captain BELLEW. Illustrated from Designs by the Author. A New Edition. Cr. 8vo. 10s. 6d.

Berdmore (Sept.) (Nimshivich) A Scratch Team of Essays never before put together. Reprinted from the "Quarterly" and "Westminster Reviews." On the Kitchen and the Cellar—Thackeray—Russia—Carriages, Roads, and Coaches. By SEPT. BERDMORE (NIMSHIVICH). Crown 8vo. 7s. 6d.

Black (C. I.) The Proselytes of Ishmael.
Being a short Historical Survey of the Turanian Tribes in their Western Migrations. With Notes and Appendices. By CHARLES INGRAM BLACK, M.A., Vicar of Burley-in-Wharfedale, near Leeds. Second Edition. Crown 8vo. 6s.

Blanchard (S.) Yesterday and To-day in India.
By SIDNEY LAMAN BLANCHARD. Post 8vo. 6s.

CONTENTS.—Outward Bound.—The Old Times and the New.—Domestic Life.—Houses and Bungalows.—Indian Servants.—The Great Shoe Question.—The Garrison Hack —The Long Bow in India.—Mrs. Dulcimer's Shipwreck.—A Traveller's Tale, told in a Dark Bungalow.—Punch in India.—Anglo-Indian Literature.—Christmas in India.—The Seasons in Calcutta.—Farmers in Muslin.—Homeward Bound.—India as it Is.

Blenkinsopp (Rev. E. L.) Doctrine of Development in the Bible and in the Church. By Rev. E. L. Blenkinsopp, M.A., Rector of Springthorp. 2nd edition. 12mo. 6s.

Boileau (Major-General J. T.)
A New and Complete Set of Traverse Tables, showing the Differences of Latitude and the Departures to every Minute of the Quadrant and to Five Places of Decimals. Together with a Table of the lengths of each Degree of Latitude and corresponding Degree of Longitude from the Equator to the Poles; with other Tables useful to the Surveyor and Engineer. Fourth Edition, thoroughly revised and corrected by the Author. Royal 8vo. 12s. London, 1876.

Boulger (D. C.) History of China. By Demetrius Charles Boulger, Author of "England and Russia in Central Asia," &c. 8vo. vol. I. With Portrait. 18s. Vol. II. 18s.

—— **England and Russia in Central Asia.** With Appendices and Two Maps, one being the latest Russian Official Map of Central Asia. 2 vols. 8vo. 36s.

—— **Central Asian Portraits**; or the Celebrities of the Khanates and the Neighbouring States. By Demetrius Charles Boulger, M.R.A.S. Crown 8vo. 7s. 6d.

—— **The Life of Yakoob Beg**, Athalik Ghazi and Badaulet, Ameer of Kashgar. By Demetrius Charles Boulger, M.R.A.S. 8vo. With Map and Appendix. 16s.

Bowles (Thomas Gibson) Flotsam and Jetsam. A Yachtman's Experiences at Sea and Ashore. By Thomas Gibson Bowles, Master Mariner. Cr. 8vo. 7s. 6d.

Boyd (R. Nelson) Chili and the Chilians, during the War 1879-80. By R. Nelson Boyd, F.R.G.S., F.G.S., Author of Coal Mines Inspection. Cloth, Illustrated. Cr. 8vo. 10s. 6d.

—— **Coal Mines Inspection**: Its History and Results. 8vo. 14s.

Bradshaw (John) The Poetical Works of John Milton, with Notes, explanatory and philological. By John Bradshaw, LL.D., Inspector of Schools, Madras. 2 vols., post 8vo. 12s. 6d.

Brandis' Forest Flora of North-Western and Central India. By Dr. Brandis, Inspector General of Forests to the Government of India. Text and Plates. £2 18s.

Brereton (W. H.) The Truth about Opium.
Being the Substance of Three Lectures delivered at St. James's Hall. By William H. Brereton, late of Hong Kong, Solicitor. 8vo. 7s. 6d. Cheap edition, sewed, 1s.

Bright (W.) Red Book for Sergeants.
Fifth and Revised Edition, 1880. By W. BRIGHT, late Colour-Sergeant, 19th Middlesex R.V. Fcap. interleaved. 1s.

Buckland (C. T.) Whist for Beginners. Second Edition. 1s.

Buckle (the late Capt. E.) Bengal Artillery.
A Memoir of the Services of the Bengal Artillery from the formation of the Corps. By the late CAPT. E. BUCKLE, Assist.-Adjut. Gen. Ben. Art. Edit. by SIR J. W. KAYE. 8vo. Lond, 1852. 10s.

Buckley (R. B.) The Irrigation Works of India, and their Financial Results. Being a brief History and Description of the Irrigation Works of India, and of the Profits and Losses they have caused to the State. By ROBERT B. BUCKLEY, A.M.I.C.E., Executive Engineer of the Public Works Department of India. 8vo. With Map and Appendix. 9s.

Burke (P.) Celebrated Naval and Military Trials.
By PETER BURKE, Serjeant-at-Law. Author of " Celebrated Trials connected with the Aristocracy." Post 8vo. 10s. 6d.

By the Tiber.
By the Author of " Signor Monaldini's Niece." 2 vols. 21s.

Carlyle (Thomas), Memoirs of the Life and Writings of,
With Personal Reminiscences and Selections from his Private Letters to numerous Correspondents. Edited by RICHARD HERNE SHEPHERD, Assisted by CHARLES N. WILLIAMSON. 2 Vols. With Portrait and Illustrations. Crown 8vo. 21s.

Chaffers (William) Gilda Aurifabrorum.
A History of London Goldsmiths and Plateworkers, with their Marks stamped on Plate, copied in fac-simile from celebrated Examples and the Earliest Records preserved at Goldsmiths' Hall, London, with their Names, Addresses, and Dates of Entry. 2,500 Illustrations. By WILLIAM CHAFFERS, Author of " Hall Marks on Plate." 8vo. 18s.

Challenge of Barletta (The).
By MASSIMO D'AZEGLIO. Rendered into **English by Lady Louisa Magenis.** 2 vols. Crown 8vo. 21s.

Collette (C. H.) The Roman Breviary.
A Critical and Historical Review, with Copious Classified Extracts. By CHARLES HASTINGS COLLETTE. 2nd Edition. Revised and enlarged. 8vo. 5s.

Collette (C. H.) Henry VIII.
An Historical Sketch as affecting the Reformation in England. By CHARLES HASTINGS COLLETTE. Post 8vo. 6s.

—— **St. Augustine (Aurelius Augustinus Episcopus Hipponiensis),** a Sketch of his Life and Writings as affecting the Controversy with Rome. By CHARLES HASTINGS COLLETTE. Crown 8vo. 5s.

Collins (Mabel) The Story of Helena Modjeska (Madame Chlapowska). By MABEL COLLINS. Crown 8vo. 7s. 6d.

Colquhoun (Major J. A. S.) With the Kurrum Force in the Caubul Campaign of 1878-79. By Major J. A. S. COLQUHOUN, R.A. With Illustrations from the Author's Drawings, and two Maps. 8vo. 16s.

Cooper's Hill College. Calendar of the Royal Indian Engineering College, Cooper's Hill. Published by authority in January each year. 5s.

CONTENTS.—Staff of the College; Prospectus for the Year; Table of Marks; Syllabus of Course of Study; Leave and Pension Rules of Indian Service; Class and Prize Lists; Past Students serving in India; Entrance Examination Papers, &c.

Corbet (M. E.) A Pleasure Trip to India, during the Visit of H.R.H. the Prince of Wales, and afterwards to Ceylon. By Mrs. CORBET. Illustrated with Photos. Crown 8vo. 7s. 6d.

Cowdery (Miss E.) Franz Liszt, Artist and Man.
By L. RAMANN. Translated from the German by Miss E. COWDERY. 2 vols. Crown 8vo. 21s.

Crosland (Mrs. N.) Stories of the City of London; Retold for Youthful Readers. By Mrs. NEWTON CROSLAND. With ten Illustrations. Cr. 8vo. 6s.

These Stories range from the early days of Old London Bridge and the Settlement of the Knights Templars in England to the time of the Gordon Riots; with incidents in the Life of Brunel in relation to the Thames Tunnel; narrated from Personal recollections.

Cruise of H.M.S. "Galatea,"
Captain H.R.H. the Duke of Edinburgh, K.G., in 1867—1868. By the REV. JOHN MILNER, B.A., Chaplain; and OSWALD W. BRIERLY. Illustrated by a Photograph of H.R.H. the Duke of Edinburgh; and by Chromo-Lithographs and Graphotypes from Sketches taken on the spot by O. W. BRIERLY. 8vo. 16s.

Cunningham (H. S.) British India, and its Rulers.
By H. S. CUNNINGHAM, M.A., one of the Judges of the High Court of Calcutta, and late Member of the Famine Commission. 10s 6d.

Daumas (E.) Horses of the Sahara, and the Manners of the Desert. By E. DAUMAS, General of the Division Commanding at Bordeaux, Senator, &c., &c. With Commentaries by the Emir Abd-el-Kadir (Authorized Edition). 8vo. 6s.

"We have rarely read a work giving a more picturesque and, at the same time, practical account of the manners and customs of a people, than this book on the Arabs and their horses."—*Edinburgh Courant.*

Deighton (K.) Shakespeare's King Henry the Fifth.
With Notes and an Introduction. By K. DEIGHTON, Principal of Agra College. Crown 8vo. 5s.

Destruction of Life by Snakes, Hydrophobia, &c., in Western India. By an EX-COMMISSIONER. Fcap. 2s. 6d.

Dickins, (F. V.) Chiushingura: or the Loyal League.
A Japanese Romance. Translated by FREDERICK V. DICKINS, Sc.B., of the Middle Temple, Barrister-at-Law. With Notes and an Appendix containing a Metrical Version of the Ballad of Takasako, and a specimen of the Original Text in Japanese character. Illustrated by numerous Engravings on Wood, drawn and executed by Japanese artists and printed on Japanese paper. 8vo. 10s. 6d.

Diplomatic Study on the Crimean War, 1852 to 1856. (Russian Official Publication.) 2 vols. 8vo. 28s.

Doran (Dr. J.) "Their Majesties Servants":
Annals of the English Stage. Actors, Authors, and Audiences, From Thomas Betterton to Edmund Kean. By Dr. DORAN, F.S.A., Author of "Table Traits," "Lives of the Queens of England of the House of Hanover," &c. Post 8vo. 6s.

"Every page of the work is barbed with wit, and will make its way point foremost. . . . . provides entertainment for the most diverse tastes."—*Daily News.*

Douglas (M.) Countess Violet; or, What Grandmamma saw in the Fire. A Book for Girls. By MINNIE DOUGLAS. Author of "Two Rose Trees." Illustrated. 5s.

Drury (Col. H.) The Useful Plants of India,
With Notices of their chief value in Commerce, Medicine, and the Arts. By COLONEL HEBER DRURY. Second Edition, with Additions and Corrections. Royal 8vo. 16s.

Durand (H. M.) The Life of Major-General Sir Henry Marion Durand, K.C.S.I., C.B., of the Royal Engineers. By H. M. DURAND, C.S.I., of the Bengal Civil Service, Barrister-at-Law. 2 vols. 8vo., with Portrait. 42s.

Dutton (Major Hon. C.) Life in India.
By Major the Hon. CHARLES DUTTON. Crown 8vo. 2s. 6d.

Duke (J.) Recollections of the Kabul Campaign 1879-1880. By JOSHUA DUKE, Ben. Med. Service, F.R.A.S. 8vo., with Illustrations and Map. 15s.

Dwight (H. O.) Turkish Life in War Time.
By HENRY O. DWIGHT. Crown 8vo. 12s.

Écarte. By AQUARIUS. Sq. 16mo. 1s.

Edwards (G. Sutherland) A Female Nihilist.
By ERNEST LAVIGNE. Translated from the French by G. SUTHERLAND EDWARDS. Crown 8vo. 9s.

Edwards (H. S.) The Lyrical Drama: Essays on Subjects, Composers, and Executants of Modern Opera. By H. SUTHERLAND EDWARDS, Author of "The Russians at Home and Abroad," &c. Two vols. Crown 8vo. 21s.

—— **The Russians At Home and the Russians Abroad.** Sketches, Unpolitical and Political, of Russian Life under Alexander II. By H. SUTHERLAND EDWARDS. 2 vols. Crown 8vo. 21s.

Ensor (F. Sydney) The Queen's Speeches in Parliament, from Her Accession to the present time. A Compendium of the History of Her Majesty's Reign told from the Throne. Edited and Compiled by F. SYDNEY ENSOR, Author of "Through Nubia to Darfoor." Crown 8vo. 7s. 6d.

—— **Incidents of a Journey through Nubia to Darfoor.** By F. SYDNEY ENSOR, C.E. 10s. 6d.

Eyre (Major-General Sir V.), K.C.S.I., C.B. The Kabul Insurrection of 1841-42. Revised and corrected from Lieut. Eyre's Original Manuscript. Edited by Colonel G. B. MALLESON, C.S.I. Crown 8vo., with Map and Illustrations. 9s.

Fearon (A.) Kenneth Trelawny.
By ALEC FEARON. Author of "Touch not the Nettle." 2 vols. Crown 8vo. 21s.

Forbes (Capt. C. J. F. S.) Comparative Grammar of the Languages of Further India. A Fragment; and other Essays, the Literary Remains of Captain C. J. F. S. FORBES, of the British Burma Commission. Author of " British Burma and its People: Sketches of Native Manners, Customs, and Religion." 6s.

Foreign Office, Diplomatic and Consular Sketches. Reprinted from "Vanity Fair." Cr. 8vo. 6s.

Fraser (Lieut.-Col. G. T.) Records of Sport and Military Life in Western India. By the late Lieut.-Colonel G. T. Fraser, formerly of the 1st Bombay Fusiliers, and more recently attached to the Staff of H.M.'s Indian Army. With an Introduction by Colonel G. B. MALLESON, C.S.I. 7s. 6d.

Fry (Herbert) London in 188 Its Suburbs and Environs. Illustrated with 16 Bird's-eye Views of the Principal Streets, and a Map. By HERBERT FRY. Third year of publication. Revised and Enlarged. 2s.

Gazetteers of India.
Thornton, 4 vols., 8vo. £2 16s.
,, 8vo. 21s.
,, (N.W.P., &c.) 2 vols., 8vo. 25s.

Gazetteer of Southern India.
With the Tenasserim Provinces and Singapore. Compiled from original and authentic sources. Accompanied by an Atlas, including plans of all the principal towns and cantonments. Royal 8vo. with 4to. Atlas. £3 3s.

Geography of India.
Comprising an account of British India, and the various states enclosed and adjoining. Fcap. pp. 250. 2s.

Geological Papers on Western India.
Including Cutch, Scinde, and the south-east coast of Arabia. To which is added a Summary of the Geology of India generally. Edited for the Government by HENRY J. CARTER, Assistant Surgeon, Bombay Army. Royal 8vo. with folio Atlas of maps and plates; half-bound. £2 2s.

Gibney (Major R. D.) Earnest Madement; a Tale of Wiltshire. By MAJOR R. D. GIBNEY, late Adjutant 1st Wilts Rifle Volunteers. Cr. 8vo. 6s. (Dedicated by permission to Lieut.-Gen. Sir Garnet Wolseley, G.C.B.)

Gillmore (Parker) Encounters with Wild Beasts.
By PARKER GILLMORE, Author of "The Great Thirst Land," "A Ride Through Hostile Africa," &c. With Ten full-page Illustrations. Cr. 8vo. 7s. 6d.

—— **Prairie and Forest.** A description of the Game of North America, with Personal Adventures in its Pursuit. By PARKER GILLMORE (Ubique). With Thirty-Seven Illustrations. Crown 8vo. 7s. 6d.

Goldstucker (Prof. Theodore), The late. The Literary Remains of. With a Memoir. 2 vols. 8vo. 21s.

Graham (Alex.) Genealogical and Chronological Tables, illustrative of Indian History. 4to. 5s.

Grant (Jas.) Derval Hampton: A Story of the Sea. By JAMES GRANT, Author of the "Romance of War," &c. 2 vols. Crown 8vo. 21s.

Greene (F. V.) The Russian Army and its Campaigns in Turkey in 1877–1878. By F. V. GREENE, First Lieutenant in the Corps of Engineers, U.S. Army, and lately Military Attaché to the United States Legation at St. Petersburg. 8vo. With Atlas. 32s. Second Edition.

—— **Sketches of Army Life in Russia.** Crown 8vo. 9s.

Griesinger (Theodor) The Jesuits; a Complete History of their Open and Secret Proceedings from the Foundation of the Order to the Present Time. Told to the German People. By THEODOR GRIESINGER. Translated by A. J. SCOTT, M.D. 2 vols. 8vo. Illustrated. 24s.

Griffith (Ralph T. H.) Birth of the War God, A Poem. By KALIDASA. Translated from the Sanscrit into English Verse. By RALPH T. H. GRIFFITH. 8vo. 5s.

Hall (E. H.) Lands of Plenty, for Health, Sport, and Profit. British North America. A Book for all Travellers and Settlers. By E. HEPPLE HALL, F.S.S. Crown 8vo., with Maps. 6s.

Hall's Trigonometry. The Elements of Plane and Spherical Trigonometry. With an Appendix, containing the solution of the Problems in Nautical Astronomy. For the use of Schools. By the REV. T. G. HALL, M.A., Professor of Mathematics in King's College, London. 12mo. 2s.

Hancock (E. C.) The Amateur Pottery and Glass Painter. With Directions for Gilding, Chasing, Burnishing, Bronzing, and Groundlaying. By E. CAMPBELL HANCOCK. Illustrated with Chromo-Lithographs and numerous Woodcuts. Fourth Edition. 8vo. 6s.

—— **Copies for China Painters.** By E. CAMPBELL HANCOCK. With Fourteen Chromo-Lithographs and other Illustrations. 8vo. 10s.

Handbook of Reference to the Maps of India.
Giving the Lat. and Long. of places of note. 18mo. 3s. **6d.**

⁎⁎ *This will be found a valuable Companion to Messrs. Allen & Co.'s Maps of India.*

Harcourt (Maj. A. F. P.) Down by the Drawle.
By MAJOR A. F. P. HARCOURT, Bengal Staff Corps, author of "Kooloo, Lahoul, and Spiti," "The Shakespeare Argosy," &c. **2 Vols.** in one, crown 8vo. 6s.

Hardwicke (Herbert Junius) Health Resorts and Spas; or, Climatic and Hygienic Treatment of Disease. By HERBERT JUNIUS HARDWICKE, M.D., &c. Fcap. 2s. 6d.

Harting (J. E.) Sketches of Bird Life. By JAMES EDMUND HARTING, Author of a "Handbook of British Birds." 8vo., with numerous Illustrations. 10s. 6d.

Heine (Heinrich) The Book of Songs. By HEINRICH HEINE. Translated from the German by STRATHIER. Cr. 8vo. 7s. 6d.

Helms (L. V.) Pioneering in the Far East, and Journeys to California in 1849, and to the White Sea **in 1878.** By LUDWIG VERNER HELMS. With Illustrations **from original** Sketches and Photographs, and Maps. 8vo. **18s.**

Hensman (Howard) The Afghan War, 1879-80.
Being a complete Narrative of the Capture of Cabul, the Siege of Sherpur, the Battle of Ahmed Khel, the brilliant March to Candahar, and the Defeat of Ayub Khan, with the Operations on the Helmund, and the Settlement with Abdur Rahman Khan. By HOWARD HENSMAN, **Special** Correspondent of the "Pioneer" (Allahabad) **and the** "Daily News" (London). 8vo. With Maps. 21s.

General Sir Frederick Roberts writes in regard to the letters now re-published:—

"Allow me to congratulate you most cordially on the admirable manner in which you have placed before the public the account of our march from Cabul, and the operations of 31st August and 1st September around Candahar. *Nothing could be more accurate or graphic.* I thought your description of the fight at Charasai was one that any soldier might have been proud of writing; but your recent letters are, if possible, even better."

Holden (E. S.) Sir William Herschel. His Life and Works. By EDWARD S. HOLDEN, United States Naval Observatory Washington. Cr. 8vo. 6s.

Holland.
By Edmondo de Amicis. Translated from the Italian by CAROLINE TILTON. Crown 8vo. 10s. 6d.

Holmes (T. R. E.) A History of the Indian Mutiny, and of the Disturbances which accompanied it among the Civil Population. By T. R. E. HOLMES. 8vo., with Maps and Plans. 21s.

Hough (Lieut.-Col. W.) Precedents in Military Law.
8vo. cloth. **25s**

Hughes (Rev. T. P.) Notes on Muhammadanism.
Second Edition, Revised and Enlarged. Fcap. 8vo. 6s.

Hunt and Kenny. On Duty under a Tropical Sun.
Being some Practical Suggestions for the Maintenance of Health and Bodily Comfort, and the Treatment of Simple Diseases; with Remarks on Clothing and Equipment for the Guidance of Travellers in Tropical Countries. By Major S. LEIGH HUNT, Madras Army, and ALEXANDER S. KENNY, M.R.C.S.E., A.K.C., Senior Demonstrator of Anatomy at King's College, London, Author of "The Tissues and their Structure." Second Edition. Crown 8vo. 4s.

—— **Tropical Trials.**
A Handbook for Women in the Tropics. By MAJOR S. LEIGH HUNT, and ALEXANDER S. KENNY. Cr. 8vo. 7s. 6d.

Hutton (J.) Thugs and Dacoits of India.
A Popular Account of the Thugs and Dacoits, the Hereditary Garotters and Gang Robbers of India. By JAMES HUTTON. Post 8vo. 5s.

India Directory (The).
For the Guidance of Commanders of Steamers and Sailing Vessels. Founded upon the Work of the late CAPTAIN JAMES HORSBURGH, F.R.S.

PART I —The East Indies, and Interjacent Ports of Africa and South America. Revised, Extended, and Illustrated with Charts of Winds, Currents, Passages, Variation, and Tides. By COMMANDER ALFRED DUNDAS TAYLOR, F.R.G.S., Superintendent of Marine Surveys to the Government of India. £1 18s.

PART II.—The China Sea, with the Ports of Java, Australia and Japan and the Indian Archipelago Harbours, as well as those of New Zealand. Illustrated with Charts of the Winds, Currents, Passages, &c. By the same. (*In preparation.*)

Indian and Military Law.

Mahommedan Law of Inheritance, &c. A Manual of the Mahommedan Law of Inheritance and Contract; comprising the Doctrine of the Soonee and Sheea Schools, and based upon the text of Sir H. W. MACNAGHTEN's Principles and Precedents, together with the Decisions of the Privy Council and High Courts of the Presidencies in India. For the use of Schools and Students. By STANDISH GROVE GRADY, Barrister-at-Law, Reader of Hindoo, Mahommedan, and Indian Law to the Inns of Court. 8vo. 14s.

Hedaya, or Guide, a Commentary on the Mussulman Laws, translated by order of the Governor-General and Council of Bengal. By CHARLES HAMILTON. Second Edition, with Preface and Index by STANDISH GROVE GRADY. 8vo. £1 15s.

Institutes of Menu in English. The Institutes of Hindu Law or the Ordinances of Menu, according to Gloss of Collucca. Comprising the Indian System of Duties, Religious and Civil, verbally translated from the Original, with a Preface by SIR WILLIAM JONES, and collated with the Sanscrit Text by GRAVES CHAMNEY HAUGHTON, M.A., F.R.S., Professor of Hindu Literature in the East India College. New edition, with Preface and Index by STANDISH G. GRADY, Barrister-at-Law, and Reader of Hindu, Mahommedan, and Indian Law to the Inns of Court. 8vo., cloth. 12s.

Indian Code of Criminal Procedure. Being Act X. of 1872, Passed by the Governor-General of India in Council on the 25th of April, 1872. 8vo. 12s.

Indian Code of Civil Procedure. Being Act X. of 1877. 8vo. 6s.

Indian Code of Civil Procedure. In the form of Questions and Answers, with Explanatory and Illustrative Notes. By ANGELO J. LEWIS. Barrister-at-law 12mo. 12s. 6d.

Indian Penal Code. In the Form of Questions and Answers. With Explanatory and Illustrative Notes. BY ANGELO J. LEWIS, Barrister-at-Law. Post 8vo. 7s. 6d.

Hindu Law. Defence of the Daya Bhaga. Notice of the Case on Prosoono Coomar Tajore's Will. Judgment of the Judicial Committee of the Privy Council. Examination of such Judgment. By JOHN COCHRANE, Barrister-at-Law. Royal 8vo. 20s.

Law and Customs of Hindu Castes, within the Dekhan Provinces subject to the Presidency of Bombay, chiefly affecting Civil Suits. By ARTHUR STEELE. Royal 8vo. £1 1s.

Moohummudan Law of Inheritance. (See page 35.)

Chart of Hindu Inheritance. With an Explanatory Treatise, By ALMARIC RUMSEY. 8vo. 6s. 6d.

Manual of Military Law. For all ranks of the Army, Militia and Volunteer Services. By Colonel J. K. PIPON, Assist. Adjutant

General at Head Quarters, & J. F. COLLIER, Esq., of the Inner Temple, Barrister-at-Law. Third and Revised Edition. Pocket size. 5s.

Precedents in Military Law; including the Practice of Courts-Martial; the Mode of Conducting Trials; the Duties of Officers at Military Courts of Inquests, Courts of Inquiry, Courts of Requests, &c., &c. The following are a portion of the Contents:—
1. Military Law. 2. Martial Law. 3. Courts-Martial. 4. Courts of Inquiry. 5. Courts of Inquest. 6. Courts of Request. 7. Forms of Courts-Martial. 8. Precedents of Military Law. 9. Trials of Arson to Rape (Alphabetically arranged.) 10. Rebellions. 11. Riots. 12. Miscellaneous. By Lieut.-Col. W. HOUGH, late Deputy Judge-Advocate-General, Bengal Army, and Author of several Works on Courts-Martial. One thick 8vo. vol. 25s.

The Practice of Courts Martial. By HOUGH & LONG. Thick 8vo. London, 1825. 26s.

Indian Criminal Law and Procedure,
Including the Procedure in the High Courts, as well as that in the Courts not established by Royal Charter; with Forms of Charges and Notes on Evidence, illustrated by a large number of English Cases, and Cases decided in the High Courts of India; and an APPENDIX of selected Acts passed by the Legislative Council relating to Criminal matters. By M. H. STARLING, ESQ., LL.B. & F. B. CONSTABLE, M.A. Third edition. 8vo. £2 2s.

In the Company's Service.
A Reminiscence. 8vo. 10s. 6d.

Irwin (H. C.) The Garden of India; or, Chapters on Oudh
History and Affairs. By H. C. IRWIN, B.A. Oxon., Bengal Civil Service. 8vo. 12s.

Jackson (Lt.-Col. B.) Military Surveying, &c. 8vo. 14s.
(See page 28).

Jackson (Lowis D'A.) Canal and Culvert Tables.
Based on the Formula of Kutter, under a Modified Classification. with Explanatory Text and Examples. By LOWIS D'A. JACKSON, A.M.I.C.E., author of "Hydraulic Manual and Statistics," &c. Roy. 8vo. 28s.

—— Pocket Logarithms and other Tables for Ordinary Calculations of Quantity, Cost, Interest, Annuities, Assurance, and Angular Functions, obtaining Results correct in the Fourth figure. By LOWIS D'A. JACKSON. Cloth, 2s. 6d.; leather, 3s. 6d.

Jackson (Lowis D'A.) Accented Four-Figure Logarithms, and other Tables. For purposes both of Ordinary and of Trigonometrical Calculation, and for the Correction of Altitudes and Lunar Distances. Arranged and accented by Lowis D'A. Jackson, A.M.I.C.E., Author of "Canal and Culvert Tables," "Hydraulic Manual," &c. Crown 8vo. 9s.

—— Accented Five-Figure Logarithms of Numbers from 1 to 99999, without Differences. Arranged and accented by Lowis D'A. Jackson. Royal 8vo. 16s.

—— Units of Measurement for Scientific and Professional Men. By Lowis D'A. Jackson. Cr. 4to. 2s.

James (A. G. F. Eliot) Indian Industries.
By A. G. F. Eliot James, Author of "A Guide to Indian Household Management," &c. Crown 8vo. 9s.

CONTENTS:—Indian Agriculture; Beer; Cacao; Carpets; Cereals; Chemicals; Cinchona; Coffee; Cotton; Drugs; Dyeing and Colouring Materials; Fibrous Substances; Forestry; Hides; Skins and Horns; Gums and Resins; Irrigation; Ivory; Mining; Oils; Opium; Paper; Pottery; Ryots; Seeds; Silk; Spices; Sugar; Tea; Tobacco; Wood; Wool. Table of Exports. Index.

Jenkinson (Rev. T. B.) Amazulu.
The Zulu People. their Manners, Customs, and History, with Letters from Zululand descriptive of the Present Crisis. By Thomas B. Jenkinson, B.A., sometime of Springvale, Natal, and Canon of Maritzburg. Crown 8vo. 6s.

Joyner (Mrs.) Cyprus: Historical and Descriptive.
Adapted from the German of Herr Franz Von Löher. With much additional matter. By Mrs. A. Batson Joyner. Crown 8vo. With 2 Maps. 10s. 6d.

Kaufman (R.) Our Young Folk's Plutarch.
Edited by Rosalie Kaufman. With Maps and Illustrations. 8vo. 10s. 6d.

Kaye (Sir J. W.) The Sepoy War in India.
A History of the Sepoy War in India, 1857—1858. By Sir John William Kaye, Author of "The History of the War in Afghanistan." Vol. I., 8vo. 18s, Vol. II. £1. Vol. III. £1.

CONTENTS OF VOL. I.:—BOOK I.—INTRODUCTORY.—The Conquest of the Punjab and Pegu.—The "Right of Lapse."—The Annexation of Oude.—Progress of Englishism. BOOK II.—The Sepoy Army: its Rise, Progress, and Decline.—Early History of the Native Army.—Deteriorating Influences.—The Sindh Mutinies.—The Punjaub Mutinies. Discipline of the

Bengal Army. BOOK III.—THE OUTBREAK OF THE MUTINY.—Lord Canning and his Council.—The Oude Administration and the Persian War.—The Rising of the Storm.—The First Mutiny.—Progress of Mutiny.—Excitement in Upper India.—Bursting of the Storm.—APPENDIX.

CONTENTS OF VOL II.:—BOOK IV.—THE RISING IN THE NORTH-WEST.—The Delhi History.—The Outbreak at Meerut.—The Seizure of Delhi.—Calcutta in May.—Last Days of General Anson.—The March upon Delhi. BOOK V.—PROGRESS OF REBELLION IN UPPER INDIA.—Benares and Allahabad.—Cawnpore.—The March to Cawnpore.—Re-occupation of Cawnpore. BOOK VI.—THE PUNJAB AND DELHI.—First Conflicts in the Punjab.—Peshawur and Rawul Pinder.—Progress of Events in the Punjab.—Delhi.—First Weeks of the Siege.—Progress of the Siege.—The Last Succours from the Punjab.

CONTENTS OF VOL III.:—BOOK VII.—BENGAL, BEHAR, AND THE NORTH-WEST PROVINCES.—At the Seat of Government.—The Insurrection in Behar.—The Siege of Arrah.—Behar and Bengal. BOOK VIII.—MUTINY AND REBELLION IN THE NORTH-WEST PROVINCES.—Agra in May.—Insurrection in the Districts.—Bearing of the Native Chiefs.—Agra in June, July, August and September. BOOK IX.—LUCKNOW AND DELHI.—Rebellion in Oude.—Revolt in the Districts.—Lucknow in June and July.—The siege and Capture of Delhi.

(For continuation, see " History of the Indian Mutiny," by Colonel G. B. MALLESON, p. 23.)

Kaye (Sir J. W.) History of the War in Afghanistan.
New edition. 3 Vols. Crown 8vo. £1. 6s.

—— **Lives of Indian Officers.**
By Sir JOHN WILLIAM KAYE. 3 vols. Cr. 8vo. 6s. each.

Keatinge (Mrs.) English Homes in India.
By MRS. KEATINGE. Part I.—The Three Loves. Part II.—The Wrong Turning. Two vols., Post 8vo. 16s.

Keene (H. G.) Mogul Empire.
From the death of Aurungzeb to the overthrow of the Mahratta Power, by HENRY GEORGE KEENE, B.C.S. Second edition. With Map. 8vo. 10s. 6d.

This Work fills up a blank between the ending of Elphinstone's and the commencement of Thornton's Histories.

—— **Administration in India.**
Post 8vo. 5s.

Keene (H. G.) Peepul Leaves.
Poems written in India. Post 8vo. 5s.

—— **Fifty-Seven.**
Some account of the Administration of Indian Districts during the Revolt of the Bengal Army. By HENRY GEORGE KEENE, C.I.E., M.R.A.S., Author of "The Fall of the Mughal Empire." 8vo. 6s.

—— **The Turks in India.**
Historical Chapters on the Administration of Hindostan by the Chugtai Tartar, Babar, and his Descendants. 12s. 6d.

King (D. B.) The Irish Question. By DAVID BENNETT KING, Professor in Lafayette College, U.S.A. Cr. 8vo. 9s.

Lane-Poole (S.) Studies in a Mosque. By STANLEY LANE-POOLE, Laureat de l'Institut de France. 8vo.

Latham (Dr. R. G.) Russian and Turk,
From a Geographical, Ethnological, and Historical Point of View. 8vo. 18s.

Laurie (Col. W. F. B.) Our Burmese Wars and Relations
with Burma. With a Summary of Events from 1826 to 1879, including a Sketch of King Theebau's Progress. With various Local, Statistical, and Commercial Information. By Colonel W. F. B. LAURIE, Author of "Rangoon," "Narrative of the Second Burmese War," &c. 8vo. With Plans and Map. 16s.

—— **Ashé Pyee, the Superior Country;** or the great attractions of Burma to British Enterprise and Commerce. By Col. W. F. B. LAURIE, Author of "Our Burmese Wars and Relations with Burma." Crown 8vo. 5s.

Lee (F. G.) The Church under Queen Elizabeth.
An Historical Sketch. By the Rev. F. G. LEE, D.D. Two Vols., Crown 8vo. 21s.

—— **Reginald Barentyne;** or Liberty Without Limit. A Tale of the Times. By FREDERICK GEORGE LEE. With Portrait of the Author. Crown 8vo. Second Edition. 5s.

—— **The Words from the Cross:** Seven Sermons for Lent, Passion-Tide, and Holy Week. By the Rev. F. G. LEE, D.D. Third Edition revised. Fcap. 3s. 6d.

—— **Order Out of Chaos.** Two Sermons. By the Rev. FREDERICK GEORGE LEE, D.D. Fcap. 2s. 6d.

Lee's (Dr. W. N.) Drain of Silver to the East.
Post 8vo. 8s.

Le Messurier (Maj. A.) Kandahar in 1879.
Being the Diary of Major A. LE MESSURIER, R.E., Brigade Major R.E. with the Quetta Column. Crown 8vo. 8s.

Lethbridge (R.) High Education in India. A Plea for the State Colleges. By ROPER LETHBRIDGE, C.I.E., M.A. Crown 8vo. 5s.

Lewin (T. H.) Wild Races of the South Eastern Frontier of India. Including an Account of the Loshai Country. By Capt. T. H LEWIN, Dep. Comm. of Hill Tracts. Post 8vo. 10s. 6d.

Lewis (A. J.) Indian Penal Code
In the Form of Questions and Answers. With Explanatory and Illustrative Notes. By ANGELO J. LEWIS. Post 8vo. 7s. 6d.

—— **Indian Code of Civil Procedure.**
In the Form of Questions and Answers. With Explanatory and Illustrative Notes. By ANGELO J. LEWIS. Post 8vo. 12s. 6d.

Liancourt's and Pincott's Primitive and Universal Laws of the Formation and Development of Language; a Rational and Inductive System founded on the Natural Basis of Onomatops. 8vo. 12s. 6d.

Lloyd (J. S.) Shadows of the Past.
Being the Autobiography of General Kenyon. Edited by J. S. LLOYD, Authoress of "Ruth Everingham," "The Silent Shadow," &c. Second Edition. Crown 8vo. 6s.

—— **Honesty Seeds, and How they Grew**; or, Tony Wigston's Firm Bank. Cr. 8vo. Illustrated. 2s. 6d.

Lockwood (Ed.) Natural History, Sport and Travel.
By EDWARD LOCKWOOD, Bengal Civil Service, late Magistrate of Monghyr. Crown 8vo. With numerous Illustrations. 9s.

Lovell (Vice-Adm.) Personal Narrative of Events from 1799 to 1815. With Anecdotes. By the late Vice-Adm. WM. STANHOPE LOVELL, R.N., K.H. Second edition. Crown 8vo. 4s.

Low (Charles Rathbone) Major-General Sir Frederick S. Roberts, Bart., V.C., G.C.B., C.I.E., R.A.: a Memoir. By CHARLES RATHBONE **Low**, Author of "History of the Indian Navy," &c. 8vo., with Portrait. 18s.

Lupton (J. I.) The Horse, as he Was, as he Is, and as he Ought to Be. By JAMES IRVINE LUPTON, F.R.C.V.S., Author of "The External Anatomy of the Horse," &c. &c. Illustrated. 3s. 6d.

Macdonald (D. G. F.) Grouse Disease; its Causes and Remedies. By DUNCAN GEORGE FORBES MACDONALD, LL.D., C.E., J.P., F.R.G.S., Author of "What the Farmers may do with the Land," "Estate Management," "Cattle, Sheep, and Deer," &c. 8vo. Illustrated. Third Edition. 10s. 6d.

MacGregor (Col. C. M.) Narrative of a Journey through the Province of Khorassan and on the N. W. Frontier of Afghanistan in 1875. By Colonel C. M. MACGREGOR, C.S.I., C.I.E., Bengal Staff Corps. 2 vols. 8vo. With map and numerous illustrations. 30s.

—— **Wanderings in Balochistan.** By MAJOR-GENERAL SIR C. M. MACGREGOR, K.C.B., C.S.I., C.I.E., Bengal Staff Corps, and Quartermaster-General in India. 8vo. With Illustrations and Map. 18s.

Mackay (C.) Luck, and what came of it. A Tale of our Times. By CHARLES MACKAY, LL.D. Three vols. 31s. 6d.

Mackenzie (Capt. C. F.) The Romantic Land of Hind. By EL MUSANNIF (Capt. C. F. MACKENZIE). Crown 8vo. 6s.

Maggs (J.) Round Europe with the Crowd. Crown 8vo. 5s.

Magenis (Lady Louisa) The Challenge of Barletta. By Massimo D'Azeglio. Rendered into English by Lady LOUISA MAGENIS. 2 vols., crown 8vo. 21s.

Malabari (B. M.) Gujerat and the Gujeratis. Pictures of Men and Manners taken from Life. By BEHRAMJI M. MALABARI, Author of "The Indian Muse in English Garb," "Pleasures of Morality," &c. Crown 8vo. 6s.

Malleson (Col. G. B.) Final French Struggles in India and on the Indian Seas. Including an Account of the Capture of the Isles of France and Bourbon, and Sketches of the most eminent Foreign Adventurers in India up to the period of that Capture. With an Appendix containing an Account of the Expedition from India to Egypt in 1801 By Colonel G. B. MALLESON, C.S.I. Crown 8vo. 10s. 6d.

—— **History of the Indian Mutiny, 1857-1858,** commencing from the close of the Second Volume of Sir John Kaye's History of the Sepoy War. Vol. I. 8vo With Map. 20s.

CONTENTS.—Calcutta in May and June.—William Tayler and Vincent Eyre.—How Bihar and Calcutta were saved.—Mr. Colvin and Agra.—Jhansi and Bandalkhand.—Colonel Durand and Holkar.—Sir George Lawrence and Rajputana.—Brigadier Polwhele's great battle and its results.—Bareli, Rohilkhand, and Farakhabad.—The relation of the annexation of Oudh to the Mutiny.—Sir Henry Lawrence and the Mutiny in Oudh.—The siege of Lakhnao.—The first relief of Lakhnao.

VOL. II.—The Storming of Delhi, the Relief of Lucknow, the Two Battles of Cawnpore, the Campaign in Rohilkhand, and the movements of the several Columns in the N.W. Provinces, the Azimgurh District, and on the Eastern and South-Eastern Frontiers. 8vo. With 4 Plans. 20s.

VOL. III.—Bombay in 1857. Lord Elphinstone. March of Woodburn's Column. Mr. Seton-Karr and the Southern Maratha Country. Mr. Forjett and Bombay. Asirgarh. Sir Henry Durand. March of Stuart's Column. Holkar and Durand. Malwa Campaign. Haidarabad. Major C. Davidson and Salar Jang Sagar and Narbadi Territory. Sir Robert Hamilton and Sir Hugh Rose. Central India Campaign. Whitlock and Kirwi. Sir Hugh Rose and Gwaliar Le Grand Jacob and Western India. Lord Canning's Oudh policy. Last Campaign in, and pacification of, Oudh. Sir Robert Napier, Smith, Michell, and Tantia Topi. Civil Districts during the Mutiny. Minor Actions at Out-stations. Conclusion 8vo. With Plans. 20s.

Malleson (Col. G. B.) History of Afghanistan, from the Earliest Period to the Outbreak of the War of 1878. 8vo. Second Edition. With Map. 18s.

—— The Decisive Battles of India, from 1746–1849. With a Portrait of the Author, a Map, and Three Plans. By Col. G. B. MALLESON, C.S.I., Author of the "Life of Lord Clive," &c. 8vo. 18s.

—— Herat: The Garden and Granary of Central Asia. With Map and Index. 8vo. 8s.

—— Founders of the Indian Empire. Clive, Warren Hastings, and Wellesley. Vol. I.—LORD CLIVE. By Colonel G. B. MALLESON, C.S.I., Author of "History of the French in India," &c. 8vo., with Portraits and 4 Plans. 20s.

Manning (Mrs.) Ancient and Mediæval India.
Being the History, Religion, Laws, Caste, Manners and
Customs, Language, Literature, Poetry, Philosophy, Astronomy,
Algebra, Medicine, Architecture, Manufactures, Commerce,
&c., of the Hindus, taken from their writings. Amongst the
works consulted and gleaned from may be named the Rig Veda,
Sama Veda, Yajur Veda, Sathapatha Brahmana, Bhagavat
Gita, The Puranas, Code of Manu, Code of Yajnavalkya,
Mitakshara, Daya Bhaga, Mahabharata, Atriya, Charaka,
Susruta, Ramayana, Raghu Vansa, Bhattikavya, Sakuntala,
Vikramorvasi, Malati and Madhava, Mudra Rakshasa, Ratna-
vali Kumara Sambhava, Prabodha, Chandrodaya, Megha Duta,
Gita Govinda, Panchatantra, Hitopadesa, Katha Sarit, Sagara,
Ketaia, Pancoavinsati, Dasa Kumara Charita, &c. By Mrs.
MANNING, with Illustrations. 2 vols., 8vo. 30s.

Marvin (Chas.) Merv, the Queen of the World and the Scourge
of the Men-stealing Turcomans. By CHARLES MARVIN, author
of "The Disastrous Turcoman Campaign," and "Grodekoff's
Ride to Herat." With Portraits and Maps. **8vo. 18s.**

——— **Colonel Grodekoff's Ride from Samarcand to Herat,**
through Balkh and the Uzbek States of Afghan Turkestan.
With his own March-route from the Oxus to Herat. By
CHARLES MARVIN. Crown 8vo. With Portrait. 8s.

——— **The Eye-Witnesses' Account of the Disastrous Russian**
Campaign against the Akhal Tekke Turcomans; Describing
the March across the Burning Desert, the Storming of Den-
geel Tepe, and the Disastrous Retreat to the Caspian. By
CHARLES MARVIN. With numerous Maps and Plans. 8vo.
18s.

——— **The Russians at Merv and Herat,** and their Power
of Invading India. By CHARLES MARVIN, Author **of**
"Disastrous Russian Campaign against the Turcomans,"
"Merv, the Queen of the World," &c. **8vo.,** with Twenty-
four Illustrations and Three Maps. **24s.**

Mateer (Samuel) Native Life in Travancore.
By the Rev. SAMUEL MATEER, of the London Missionary
Society, Author of "The Land of Charity." With Nume-
rous Illustrations and Map. 8vo. 18s.

Matson (Nellie) Hilda Desmond, or Riches and Poverty.
Crown 8vo. 10s. 6d.

Mayhew (Edward) Illustrated Horse Doctor.
Being an Accurate and Detailed Account, accompanied by more than 400 Pictorial Representations, characteristic of the various Diseases to which the Equine Race are subjected; together with the latest Mode of Treatment, and all the requisite Prescriptions written in Plain English By EDWARD MAYHEW, M.R.C.V.S. 8vo. 18s. 6d.

CONTENTS.—The Brain and Nervous System.—The Eyes.—The Mouth.—The Nostrils.—The Throat.—The Chest and its contents.—The Stomach, Liver, &c.—The Abdomen.—The Urinary Organs.—The Skin.—Specific Diseases.—Limbs.—The Feet.—Injuries.—Operations.

"The book contains nearly 600 pages of valuable matter, which reflects great credit on its author, and, owing to its practical details, the result of deep scientific research, deserves a place in the library of medical, veterinary, and non-professional readers."—*Field.*

"The book furnishes at once the bane and the antidote, as the drawings show the horse not only suffering from every kind of disease, but in the different stages of it, while the alphabetical summary at the end gives the cause, symptoms and treatment of each."—*Illustrated London News.*

—— Illustrated Horse Management.
Containing descriptive remarks upon Anatomy, Medicine, Shoeing, Teeth, Food, Vices, Stables; likewise a plain account of the situation, nature, and value of the various points; together with comments on grooms, dealers, breeders, breakers, and trainers; Embellished with more than 400 engravings from original designs made expressly for this work. By E. MAYHEW. A new Edition, revised and improved by J. I. LUPTON. M.R.C.V.S. 8vo. 12s.

CONTENTS.—The body of the horse anatomically considered. PHYSIC.—The mode of administering it, and minor operations SHOEING.—Its origin, its uses, and its varieties. THE TEETH. —Their natural growth, and the abuses to which they are liable.

FOOD.—The fittest time for feeding, and the kind of food which the horse naturally consumes. The evils which are occasioned by modern stables. The faults inseparable from stables. The so-called "incapacitating vices," which are the results of injury or of disease. Stables as they should be. GROOMS.—Their prejudices, their injuries, and their duties. POINTS.—Their relative importance and where to look for their development. BREEDING.—Its inconsistencies and its disappointments BREAKING AND TRAINING.—Their errors and their results

Mayhew (Henry) German Life and Manners.
As seen in Saxony. With an account of Town Life—Village
Life—Fashionable Life—Married Life—School and University
Life, &c. Illustrated with Songs and Pictures of the Student
Customs at the University of Jena. By HENRY MAYHEW,
2 vols., 8vo., with numerous illustrations. 18s.
A Popular Edition of the above. With illustrations. Cr. 8vo. **7s**
"Full of original thought and observation, and may be studied with profit by both German and English—especially by the German."*Athenæum.*

Mayo (Earl of) De Rebus Africanus.
The Claims of Portugal to the Congo and Adjacent
Littoral. With Remarks on the French Annexation. By
the EARL OF MAYO, F.R.G.S. 8vo., with Map. 3s. **6d.**

McCarthy (T. A.) An Easy System of Calisthenics and
Drilling. Including Light Dumb-Bell and Indian **Club**
Exercises. By T. A. MCCARTHY, Chief Instructor at
Mr. Moss's Gymnasium, Brighton. Fcap. **1s. 6d.**

McCosh (J.) Advice to Officers in India.
By JOHN MCCOSH, M.D. Post 8vo. 8s.

Meadow (T.) Notes on China.
Desultory Notes on the Government and People of China and
on the Chinese Language. By T. T. MEADOWS. 8vo. 9s.

Menzies (S.) Turkey Old and New: Historical, Geographical,
and Statistical. By SUTHERLAND MENZIES. With Map and
numerous Illustrations. Second Edition. 2 vols., 8vo. **21s.**

Military Works—chiefly issued by the Government.
Field Exercises and Evolutions of Infantry. Pocket edition, **1s.**
Queen's Regulations and Orders for the Army. Corrected **to**
1881. 8vo. 3s. 6d. Interleaved, 5s. 6d. Pocket Edition, 1s. 6d.
Musketry Regulations, as used at Hythe. 1s.
Dress Regulations for the Army. (Reprinting.)
Infantry Sword Exercise. 1875. 6d.
Infantry Bugle Sounds. **6d.**
Red Book for Sergeants. By WILLIAM BRIGHT, Colour-
Sergeant, 19th Middlesex R.V. 1s.
Cavalry Regulations. **For** the Instruction, Formations, and
Movements of Cavalry. Royal 8vo. 4s. 6d.
Manual of Artillery Exercises, 1873. 8vo. 5s.
Manual of Field Artillery Exercises. 1877. 3s.

Principles and Practice of Modern Artillery. By Lt.-Col. C. H. OWEN, R.A. 8vo. Illustrated. 15s.

Volunteer Artillery Drill-Book. By Captain W. BROOKE HOGGAN, R.A., Adjutant 1st Shropshire and Staffordshire V.A. 2s.

Artillerist's Manual and British Soldiers' Compendium. By Major F. A. GRIFFITHS. 11th Edition. 5s.

Compendium of Artillery Exercises—Smooth Bore, Field, and Garrison Artillery for Reserve Forces. By Captain J. M. McKenzie. 3s. 6d.

Principles of Gunnery. By JOHN T. HYDE, M.A., late Professor of Fortification and Artillery, Royal Indian Military College, Addiscombe. Second edition, revised and enlarged. With many Plates and Cuts, and Photograph of Armstrong Gun. Royal 8vo. 14s.

Text Book of the Construction and Manufacture of Rifled Ordnance in the British Service. By STONEY & JONES. Second Edition. Paper, 3s. 6d., Cloth, 4s. 6d.

Treatise on Fortification and Artillery. By Major HECTOR STRAITH. Revised and re-arranged by THOMAS COOK, R.N., by JOHN T. HYDE, M.A. 7th Edition. Royal 8vo. Illustrated and Four Hundred Plans, Cuts, &c. £2 2s.

Elementary Principles of Fortification. A Text-Book for Military Examinations. By J. T. HYDE, M.A. Royal 8vo. With numerous Plans and Illustrations. 10s. 6d.

Military Surveying and Field Sketching. The Various Methods of Contouring, Levelling, Sketching without Instruments, Scale of Shade, Examples in Military Drawing, &c., &c., &c. As at present taught in the Military Colleges. By Major W. H. RICHARDS, 55th Regiment, Chief Garrison Instructor in India, Late Instructor in Military Surveying, Royal Military College, Sandhurst. Second Edition, Revised and Corrected. 12s.

Treatise on Military Surveying; including Sketching in the Field, Plan-Drawing, Levelling, Military Reconnaissance, &c. By Lieut.-Col. BASIL JACKSON, late of the Royal Staff Corps. The Fifth Edition. 8vo. Illustrated by Plans, &c. 14s.

Instruction in Military Engineering. Vol. 1., Part III. 4s.

Military Train Manual. 1s.

The Sappers' Manual. Compiled for the use of Engineer Volunteer Corps. By Col. W. A. FRANKLAND, R.E. With numerous Illustrations. 2s.

Ammunition. A descriptive treatise on the different Projectiles Charges, Fuzes, Rockets, &c., at present in use for Land and Sea Service, and on other war stores manufactured in the Royal Laboratory. 6s.

Hand-book on the Manufacture and Proof of Gunpowder, as carried on at the Royal Gunpowder Factory, Waltham Abbey. 5s.

Regulations for the Training of Troops for service in the Field and for the conduct of Peace Manœuvres. 2s.

Hand-book Dictionary for the Militia and Volunteer Services, Containing a variety of useful information, Alphabetically arranged. Pocket size, 3s. 6d.; by post, 3s. 8d.

Gymnastic Exercises, System of Fencing, and Exercises for the Regulation Clubs. In one volume. Crown 8vo. 1877. 2s.

Text-Book on the Theory and Motion of Projectiles; the History, Manufacture, and Explosive Force of Gunpowder; the History of Small Arms. For Officers sent to School of Musketry. 1s. 6d.

Notes on Ammunition. 4th Edition. 1877. 2s. 6d.

Regulations and Instructions for Encampments. 6d.

Rules for the Conduct of the War Game. 2s.

Medical Regulations for the Army, Instructions for the Army, Comprising duties of Officers, Attendants, and Nurses, &c. 1s. 6d.

Purveyors' Regulations and Instructions, for Guidance of Officers of Purveyors' Department of the Army. 3s.

Priced Vocabulary of Stores used in Her Majesty's Service. 4s.

Lectures on Tactics for Officers of the Army, Militia, and Volunteers. By Major F. H. DYKE, Garrison Instructor, E.D. 3s. 6d.

Transport of Sick and Wounded Troops. By DR. LONGMORE. 5s.

Precedents in Military Law. By LT-COL. W. HOUGH. 8vo. 25s.

The Practice of Courts-Martial, by HOUGH & LONG. 8vo. 26s.

Reserve Force; Guide to Examinations, for the use of Captains and Subalterns of Infantry, Militia, and Rifle Volunteers, and for Serjeants of Volunteers. By Capt. G. H. GREAVES. 2nd edit. 2s.

The Military Encyclopædia; referring exclusively to the Military Sciences, Memoirs of distinguished Soldiers, and the Narratives of Remarkable Battles. By J. H. STOCQUELER. 8vo. 12s.

The Operations of War Explained and Illustrated. By Col HAMLEY. New Edition Revised, with Plates. Royal 8vo. 30s.

Lessons of War. As taught by the Great Masters and Others; Selected and Arranged from the various operations in War. By FRANCE JAMES SOADY, Lieut.-Col., R.A. **Royal** 8vo. **21s.**

The Surgeon's Pocket Book, **an** Essay on the **best** Treatment of Wounded in War. By **Surgeon** Major J. H. **PORTER.** 7s. 6d.

A Precis of Modern **Tactics.** By COLONEL HOME. 8vo. 8s. 6d.

Armed Strength of Austria. By Capt. COOKE. 2 pts. £1 2s.

Armed Strength of Denmark. 3s.

Armed Strength of Russia. Translated from the German. **7s.**
Armed Strength of Sweden and Norway. 3s. 6d.
Armed Strength of Italy. 5s. 6d.
Armed Strength of Germany. **Part I. 8s. 6d.**
The Franco-German War of 1870—71. By CAPT. **C. H. CLARKE.** Vol. I. £1 6s. Sixth Section. 5s. Seventh Section 6s. Eighth Section. 3s. Ninth Section. 4s. 6d. Tenth Section. 6s. Eleventh Section. 5s. 3d. Twelfth Section. 4s. 6d.
The Campaign of 1866 in Germany. Royal 8vo. With Atlas, 21s.
Celebrated Naval and Military Trials. By PETER BURKE. Post 8vo., cloth. 10s. 6d.
Military Sketches. By SIR LASCELLES WRAXALL. Post 8vo. 6s.
Military Life of the Duke of Wellington. By JACKSON and SCOTT. 2 Vols. 8vo. Maps, Plans, &c. 12s.
Single Stick Exercise of the Aldershot Gymnasium. 6d.
Treatise on Military Carriages, and other Manufactures of the Royal Carriage Department. 5s.
Steppe Campaign Lectures. 2s.
Manual of Instructions for Army Surgeons. 1s.
Regulations for Army Hospital Corps. 9d.
Manual of Instructions for Non-Commissioned Officers, Army Hospital Corps. 2s.
Handbook for Military Artificers. 3s.
Instructions for the use of Auxiliary Cavalry. 2s. 6d.
Equipment Regulations for the Army. 5s. 6d.
Statute Law relating to the Army. 1s. 3d.
Regulations for Commissariat and Ordnance Department 2s.
Regulations for the Commissariat Department. 1s. 6d.
Regulations for the Ordnance Department. 1s. 6d.
Artillerist's Handbook of Reference for the use of the Royal and Reserve Artillery, by WILL and DALTON. 5s.
An Essay on the Principles and Construction of Military Bridges. by SIR HOWARD DOUGLAS. 1853. 15s.

Mill's History of British India,
With Notes and Continuation. By H. H. WILSON. 9 vols. **cr.** 8vo. **£2** 10s.

Mitchinson (A. W.) The Expiring Continent; A Narrative of Travel in Senegambia, with Observations on Native Character; Present Condition and Future Prospects of Africa and Colonisation. By ALEX. WILL. MITCHINSON. With Sixteen full-page Illustrations and Map. 8vo. 18s.

Mitford (Maj. R. C. W.) To Caubul with the Cavalry Brigade. A Narrative of Personal Experiences with the Force under General Sir F. S. Roberts, G.C.B. With Map and Illustrations from Sketches by the Author. By Major R. C. W. MITFORD, 14th Beng. Lancers. 8vo. Second Edit. 9s.

Modern Parallels to the Ancient Evidences of Christianity. Being an Attempt to Illustrate the Force of those Evidences by the Light of Parallels supplied by Modern Affairs. 8vo. 10s. 6d.

Muller's (Max) Rig-Veda-Sanhita. The Sacred Hymns of the Brahmins; together with the Commentary of Sayanacharya. Published under the Patronage of the Right Honourable the Secretary of State for India in Council. 6 vols., 4to. £2 10s. per volume.

Misterton, or, Through Shadow to Sunlight. By UNUS. Crown 8vo. 5s.

Mysteries of the Vatican; Or Crimes of the Papacy. From the German of DR. THEODOR GRIESENGER. 2 Vols. post 8vo. 21s.

Neville (Ralph) The Squire's Heir. By RALPH NEVILLE, Author of "Lloyd Pennant." Two Vols. 21s.

Nicholson (Capt. H. W.) From Sword to Share; or, a Fortune in Five Years at Hawaii. By Capt. H. WHALLEY NICHOLSON. Crown 8vo. With Map and Photographs. 12s. 6d.

Nirgis and Bismillah. NIRGIS; a Tale of the Indian Mutiny, from the Diary of a Slave Girl: and BISMILLAH; or, Happy Days in Cashmere. By HAFIZ ALLARD. Post 8vo. 10s. 6d.

Norris-Newman (C. L.) In Zululand with the British, throughout the War of 1879. By CHARLES L. NORRIS-NEWMAN, Special Correspondent of the London "Standard," Cape Town "Standard and Mail," and the "Times" of Natal. With Plans and Four Portraits. 8vo. 16s.

Norris-Newman (C. L.) With the Boers in the Transvaal and Orange Free State in 1880-81. By C. L. NORRIS-NEWMAN, Special War Correspondent, Author of "In Zululand with the British." 8vo. With Maps. 14s.

Notes on the North Western Provinces of India.
By a District Officer. 2nd Edition. Post 8vo., cloth. 5s.
CONTENTS.—Area and Population.—Soils.—Crops.—Irrigation.—Rent.—Rates.—Land Tenures.

O'Donoghue (Mrs. P.) Ladies on Horseback.
Learning, Park Riding, and Hunting. With Notes upon Costume, and numerous Anecdotes. By Mrs. POWER O'DONOGHUE, Authoress of "The Knave of Clubs," "Horses and Horsemen," "Grandfather's Hunter," "One in Ten Thousand," &c. &c. Cr. 8vo. With Portrait. Second Edition. **5s.**

Oldfield (H. A.) Sketches from Nipal, Historical and Descriptive; with Anecdotes of the Court Life and Wild Sports of the Country in the time of Maharaja Jang Bahadur, G.C.B.; to which is added an Essay on Nipalese Buddhism, and Illustrations of Religious Monuments, Architecture, and Scenery, from the **Author's own** Drawings. By the late HENRY AMBROSE OLDFIELD, **M.D.,** of H. M.'s Indian Army, many years Resident at Khatmandu. Two vols. 8vo. 36s.

Oliver (Capt. S. P.) On and Off Duty.
Being Leaves from an Officer's Note Book. Part I.—Turania; **Part** II.—Lemuria; Part III.—Columbia. By Captain S. P. OLIVER. Crown 4to. With 38 Illustrations. 14s.

—— **On Board a Union Steamer.**
A compilation. By Captain S. P. OLIVER. To which is added "A Sketch Abroad," by MISS DOVETON. 8vo. With Frontispiece. 8s.

Osborne (Mrs. W.) Pilgrimage to Mecca (A).
By the Nawab Sikandar Begum of Bhopal. Translated from the Original Urdu. By MRS. WILLOUGHBY OSBORNE. Followed by **a** Sketch of the History of Bhopal. By COL. WILLOUGHBY OSBORNE, C.B. With Photographs, and dedicated, by permission, to HER MAJESTY, QUEEN VICTORIA. Post 8vo. £1. 1s.

This is a highly important book, not only for its literary merit, and the information it contains, but also from the fact of its being the first work written by an Indian lady, and that lady a Queen.

Oswald (Felix S.) Zoological Sketches: a Contribution to the Out-door Study of Natural History. By FELIX S. OSWALD, Author of " Summer-land Sketches of Mexico and Central America." 8vo., with 36 Illustrations by Hermann Faber. 7s. 6d.

Owen (Sidney) India on the Eve of the British Conquest. A Historical Sketch. By SIDNEY OWEN, M.A. Reader in Indian Law and History in the University of Oxford. Formerly Professor of History in the Elphinstone College, Bombay. Post 8vo. 8s.

Oxenham (Rev. H. N.) Catholic Eschatology and Universalism. An Essay on the Doctrine of Future Retribution. Second Edition, revised and enlarged. Crown 8vo. 7s. 6d.

—— **Catholic Doctrine of the Atonement.** An Historical Inquiry into its Development in the Church, with an Introduction on the Principle of Theological Development. By H. NUTCOMBE OXENHAM, M.A. 3rd Edition and Enlarged. 8vo. 14s.

" It is one of the ablest and probably one of the most charmingly written treatises on the subject which exists in our language."—*Times*.

—— **The First Age of Christianity and the Church.** By JOHN IGNATIUS DÖLLINGER, D.D., Professor of Ecclesiastical History in the University of Munich, &c., &c. Translated from the German by HENRY NUTCOMBE OXENHAM, M.A., late Scholar of Baliol College, Oxford. Third Edition. 2 vols. Crown 8vo. 18s.

Ozanam's (A. F.) History of Civilisation in the Fifth Century. From the French. By The Hon. A. C. GLYN. 2 Vols., post 8vo. 21s.

Pebody (Charles) Authors at Work. Francis Jeffrey—Sir Walter Scott—Robert Burns—Charles Lamb—R. B. Sheridan—Sydney Smith—Macaulay—Byron Wordsworth—Tom Moore—Sir James Mackintosh. Post 8vo. 10s. 6d.

Pelly (Sir Lewis). The Miracle Play of Hasan and Husain. Collected from Oral Tradition by Colonel Sir LEWIS PELLY, K.C.B., K.C.S.I., formerly serving in Persia as Secretary of Legation, and Political Resident in the Persian Gulf.

Revised, with Explanatory Notes, by ARTHUR N. WOLLASTON, H.M. Indian (Home) Service, Translator of Anwar-i-Suhaili, &c. 2 Vols. royal 8vo. 32s.

Pen and Ink Sketches of Military Subjects. By "IGNOTUS." Reprinted by permission from the "Saturday Review." Crown 8vo. 5s.

Pincott (F.) Analytical Index to Sir JOHN KAYE's History of the Sepoy War, and Col. G. B. MALLESON's History of the Indian Mutiny. (Combined in one volume.) By FREDERIC PINCOTT, M.R.A.S. 8vo. 10s. 6d.

Pinkerton (Thomas A.) Agnes Moran.
A Story of Innocence and Experience. By THOMAS A. PINKERTON. 3 vols. 31s. 6d.

Pittenger (Rev. W.) Capturing a Locomotive.
A History of Secret Service in the late American War. By Rev. W. PITTENGER. Crown 8vo. With 13 Illustrations. 6s.

Pollock (Field Marshal Sir George) Life & Correspondence.
By C. R. Low. 8vo. With portrait. 18s.

Pope (G. U.) Text-book of Indian History; with Geographical Notes, Genealogical Tables, Examination Questions, and Chronological, Biographical, Geographical, and General Indexes. For the use of Schools, Colleges, and Private Students. By the Rev. G. U. POPE, D D., Principal of Bishop Cotton's Grammar School and College, Bangalore; Fellow of the Madras University. Third Edition, thoroughly revised. Fcap. 4to. 12s.

Practice of Courts Martial.
By HOUGH & LONG. 8vo. London. 1825. 26s.

Prichard's Chronicles of Budgepore, &c.
Or Sketches of Life in Upper India. 2 Vols., Foolscap 8vo. 12s.

Prinsep (H. T.) Historical Results.
Deducible from Recent Discoveries in Affghanistan. By H. T. PRINSEP. 8vo. Lond. 1844. 15s.

—— **Tibet, Tartary, and Mongolia.**
By HENRY T. PRINSEP. Esq. Second edition. Post 8vo. 5s.

Prinsep (H. T.) Political and Military Transactions in
India. 2 Vols. 8vo. London, 1825. 18s.

Private Theatricals.
Being a Practical Guide to the Home Stage, both before
and behind the Curtain. By AN OLD STAGER. Illustrated with Suggestions for Scenes after designs by
Shirley Hodson. Crown 8vo. 3s. 6d.

Ramann (L.) Franz Liszt, Artist and Man, 1811-1840. By
L. RAMANN. Translated from the German by Miss E.
Cowdery. 2 vols. 21s.

Richards (Major W. H.) Military Surveying, &c.
12s. (See page 28.)

Rowe (R.) Picked up in the Streets; or, Struggles for Life
among the London Poor. By RICHARD ROWE, "Good Words"
Commissioner, Author of "Jack Afloat and Ashore," &c
Crown 8vo. Illustrated. 6s.

Rumsey (Almaric) Moohummudan Law of Inheritance, and
Rights and Relations affecting it. Sunni Doctrine. Comprising, together with much collateral information, the substance, greatly expanded, of the author's "Chart of Family
Inheritance." By ALMARIC RUMSEY, of Lincoln's Inn, Barrister-at-Law, Professor of Indian Jurisprudence at King's
College, London. Author of "A Chart of Hindu Family
Inheritance." 8vo. 12s.

—— A Chart of Hindu Family Inheritance.
Second Edition, much enlarged. 8vo. 6s. 6d.

Sachau (Dr. C. Ed.) The Chronology of Ancient Nations. An
English Version of the Arabic Text of the Athar-ut Bâkiya of
Albîrûnî, or "Vestiges of the Past." Collected and reduced
to writing by the Author in A.H. 390-1, A.D. 1,000. Translated and Edited, with Notes and Index, by Dr. C. EDWARD
SACHAU, Professor in the Royal University of Berlin. Published for the Oriental Translation Fund of Great Britain and
Ireland. Royal 8vo. 42s.

Sanderson (G. P.) Thirteen Years among the Wild
Beasts of India; their Haunts and Habits, from Personal
Observation; with an account of the Modes of Capturing and
Taming Wild Elephants. By G. P. SANDERSON, Officer in

Charge of the Government Elephant Keddahs at Mysore. With 21 full page Illustrations and three Maps. Second Edition. Fcp. 4to. £1 5s.

Scudamore (F. I.) France in the East.
A Contribution towards the consideration of the Eastern Question. By FRANK IVES SCUDAMORE, C.B. Crown 8vo. 6s.

Sewell (R.) Analytical History of India.
From the earliest times to the Abolition of the East India Company in 1858. By ROBERT SEWELL, Madras Civil Service. Post 8vo. 8s.

⁎ The object of this work is to supply the want which has been felt by students for a condensed outline of Indian History which would serve at once to recall the memory and guide the eye, while at the same time it has been attempted to render it interesting to the general reader by preserving a medium between a bare analysis and a complete history.

Shadow of a Life (The) A Girl's Story.
By BERYL HOPE. 3 vols., post 8vo. 31s. 6d.

Sherer (J. W.) The Conjuror's Daughter.
A Tale. By J. W. SHERER, C.S.I. With Illustrations by Alf. T. Elwes and J. Jellicoe. Cr. 8vo. 6s.

—— **Who is Mary?**
A Cabinet Novel, in one volume. **By J. W.** SHERER, Esq., C.S.I. 10s. 6d.

—— **At Home and in India.**
A Volume of Miscellanies. By J. W. SHERER, C.S.I. Crown 8vo., with Frontispiece. 5s.

Signor Monaldini's Niece.
A Novel of Italian Life. Crown 8vo. 6s.

Simpson (H. T.) Archæologia Adelensis; or, a History of the Parish of Adel, in the West Riding of Yorkshire. **Being** an attempt to delineate its Past and Present Associations, Archæological, Topographical, and Scriptural. By HENRY TRAILL SIMPSON, M.A., late Rector of Adel. With numerous etchings by W. LLOYD FERGUSON. Roy. 8vo. 21s.

Small (Rev. G.) A Dictionary of Naval Terms, English and Hindustani. For the use of Nautical Men trading to India, &c. By Rev. G. SMALL, Interpreter to the Strangers' Home for Asiatics. Fcap. 2s. 6d.

Solymos (B.) Desert Life. Recollections of an Expedition in the Soudan. By B. Solymos (B. E. Falkonberg), Civil Engineer. 8vo. 15s.

Songs of a Lost World.
By a New Hand. Crown 8vo. 6s.

Starling (M. H.) Indian Criminal Law and Procedure.
Third edition. 8vo. £2 2s. See page 18.

Steele (A.) Law and Customs of Hindu Castes.
By Arthur Steele. Royal 8vo. £1. 1s. (See page 18.)

Stent (G. C.) Entombed Alive,
And other Songs and Ballads. (From the Chinese.) By George Carter Stent, M.R.A.S., of the Chinese Imperial Maritime Customs Service. Crown 8vo. With four Illustrations. 9s.

—— **Scraps from my Sabretasche.** Being Personal Adventures while in the 14th (King's Light) Dragoons. By George Carter Stent, M.R.A.S. Crown 8vo. 6s.

—— **The Jade Chaplet,** in Twenty-four Beads. A Collection of Songs, Ballads, &c. from the Chinese. By George Carter Stent, M.R.A.S. Second Edition. Crown 8vo. 5s.

Stothard (R. T.) The A B C of Art.
Being a system of delineating forms and objects in nature necessary for the attainments of a draughtsman. By Robert T. Stothard, F.S.A., late H.D.S.A. Fcap. 1s.

Swinnerton (Rev. C.) The Afghan War. Gough's Action at Futtehabad. By the Rev. C. Swinnerton, Chaplain in the Field with the First Division, Peshawur Valley Field Force. With Frontispiece and Two Plans. Crown 8vo. 5s.

Taunton (A. G.) The Family Register. A Key to such Official Entries of Births, Marriages, and Deaths at the Registrar-General's Office as may refer to any particular family. Edited by Alfred George Taunton. Folio Cloth. 21s.

Tayler (W.) Thirty-eight Years in India, from Juganath to the Himalaya Mountains. By William Tayler, Esq., Retired B.C.S., late Commissioner of Patna. In 2 vols. 25s. each.

Contains a memoir of the life of Mr. William Tayler, from 1829 to 1867—during the Government of eight Governors General—from Lord William Bentinck to Lord Lawrence, comprising numerous incidents and adventures, official, personal, tragic, and comic, "from grave to gay, from lively to severe" throughout that period. These volumes contain upwards of two hundred illustrations, reproduced by Mr. Tayler himself, from original sketches taken by him on the spot, in Bengal, Behar, N.W. Provinces, Darjeeling, Nipal, and Simla.

Tayler (Wm.) The Patna Crisis; or Three Months at Patna during the Insurrection of 1857. By WILLIAM TAYLER, late Commissioner of Patna. Third Edition. Fcap. 2s.

Thoms (J. A.) A Complete Concordance to the Revised Version of the New Testament, embracing the Marginal Readings of the English Revisers as well as those of the American Committee. By JOHN ALEXANDER THOMS. 6s.

Thomson's Lunar and Horary Tables.
For New and Concise Methods of Performing the Calculations necessary for ascertaining the Longitude by Lunar Observations, or Chronometers; with directions for acquiring a knowledge of the Principal Fixed Stars and finding the Latitude of them. By DAVID THOMSON. Sixty-fifth edit. Royal 8vo. 10s.

Thornton (P. M.) Foreign Secretaries of the Nineteenth Century. By PERCY M. THORNTON.

Contains—Memoirs of Lord Grenville, Lord Hawkesbury, Lord Harrowby, Lord Mulgrave, C. J. Fox, Lord Howick, George Canning, Lord Bathurst, Lord Wellesley (together with estimate of his Indian Rule by Col. G. B. Malleson, C.S.I.), **Lord Castlereagh**, Lord Dudley, Lord Aberdeen, and Lord Palmerston. Also, Extracts from Lord Bexley's Papers, including lithographed letters of Lords Castlereagh and Canning, which, bearing on important points of public policy, have never yet been published; together with other important information culled from private and other sources. With Ten Portraits, and a View shewing Interior of the old House of Lords. (Second Edition.) 2 vols. 8vo. 32s. 6d.

Vol. III. **8vo.** With Portraits. 18s

Thornton's History of India.
The History of the British Empire in India, by Edward Thornton, Esq. Containing a Copious Glossary of Indian Terms, and a Complete Chronological Index of Events, to aid the Aspirant for Public Examinations. Third edition. 1 vol. 8vo. With Map. 12s.

₀ *The Library Edition of the above in 6 volumes, 8vo., may be had, price £2 8s.*

Thornton's Gazetteer of India.
Compiled chiefly from the records at the India Office. By EDWARD THORNTON. 1 vol., 8vo., pp. 1015. With Map. 21s.

⁎ *The chief objects in view in compiling this Gazetteer are:—*

1st. *To fix the relative position of the various cities, towns, and villages with as much precision as possible, and to exhibit with the greatest practicable brevity all that is known respecting them; and*

2ndly. *To note the various countries, provinces, or territorial divisions, and to describe the physical characteristics of each, together with their statistical, social, and political circumstances.*

To these are added minute descriptions of the principal rivers and chains of mountains; thus presenting to the reader, within a brief compass, a mass of information which cannot otherwise be obtained, except from a multiplicity of volumes and manuscript records.

The Library Edition.
4 vols., 8vo. Notes, Marginal References, and Map. £2 16s.

—— **Gazetteer of the Punjaub, Affghanistan, &c.**
Gazetteer of the Countries adjacent to India, on the northwest, including Scinde, Affghanistan, Beloochistan, the Punjaub, and the neighbouring States. By EDWARD THORNTON, Esq. 2 vols. 8vo. £1 5s.

Thornton (T.) East India Calculator.
By T. THORNTON. 8vo. London, 1823. 10s.

—— **History of the Punjaub,**
And of the Rise, Progress, and Present Condition of the Sikhs. By T. THORNTON. 2 Vols. Post 8vo. 8s.

Tilley (H. A.) Japan, the Amoor and the Pacific.
With notices of other Places, comprised in a Voyage of Circumnavigation in the Imperial Russian Corvette *Rynda*, in 1858–1860. By HENRY A. TILLEY. Eight Illustrations. 8vo. 16s.

Tincker (Mary Agnes) The Jewel in the Lotos.
A Novel. By the Author of "Signor Monaldini's Niece," &c. Crown 8vo., with 5 Illustrations. 7s. 6d.

Tod (Col. Jas.) Travels in Western India.
Embracing a visit to the Sacred Mounts of the Jains, and the most Celebrated Shrines of Hindu Faith between Rajpootana and the Indus, with an account of the Ancient City of Nehrwalla. By the late Lieut.-Col. JAMES TOD. Illustrations. Royal 4to. £3 3s.

⁎ *This is a companion volume to Colonel Tod's Rajasthan.*

Torrens (W. T. McC.) Reform of Procedure in Parliament
to Clear the Block of Public Business. By W. T. McCullagh
Torrens, M.P. Second Edition. Crown 8vo. 5s.

Trimen (Capt. R.) Regiments of the British Army,
Chronologically arranged. Showing their History, Services,
Uniform, &c By Captain R. Trimen, late 35th Regiment.
8vo. 10s. 6d.

Trotter (L. J.) History of India.
The History of the British Empire in India, from the
Appointment of Lord Hardinge to the Death of Lord Canning
(1844 to 1862). By Captain Lionel James Trotter, late
Bengal Fusiliers. 2 vols. 8vo. 16s. each.

—— **Lord Lawrence.**
A Sketch of his Career. Fcap. 1s. 6d.

—— **Warren Hastings, a Biography.**
By Captain Lionel James Trotter, Bengal H. P., author
of a "History of India," "Studies in Biography," &c.
Crown 8vo. 9s.

Tupper (M. F.) Three Five-Act Plays and Twelve Dramatic
Scenes. Suitable for Private Theatricals or Drawing-room
Recitation. By Martin F. Tupper, Author of "Proverbial Philosophy," &c. Crown 8vo. Gilt. 5s.

Under Orders: a Novel. By the Author of "Invasions of
India from Central Asia." Third Edition. 3 vols. 31s. 6d.

Underwood (A. S.) Surgery for Dental Students.
By Arthur S. Underwood, M.R.C.S., L.D.S.E., Assistant
Surgeon to the Dental Hospital of London. 5s.

Valbezen (E. De) The English and India. New Sketches.
By E. De Valbezen, late Consul-General at Calcutta,
Minister Plenipotentiary. Translated from the French
(with the Author's permission) by a Diplomate. 8vo. 18s.

Vambery (A.) Sketches of Central Asia.
Additional Chapters on My Travels and Adventures, and of the
Ethnology of Central Asia. By Armenius Vambery. 8vo. 16s.

"A valuable guide on almost untrodden ground."—*Athenæum*.

Vibart (Major H. M.) The Military History of the Madras Engineers and Pioneers. By Major H. M. VIBART, Royal (late Madras) Engineers. In 2 vols., with numerous Maps and Plans. 2 vols. 8vo. 32s. each.

Victoria Cross (The) An Official Chronicle of Deeds of Personal Valour achieved in the presence of the Enemy during the Crimean and Baltic Campaigns and the Indian, Chinese, New Zealand, and African Wars. From the Institution of the Order in 1856 to 1880. Edited by ROBERT W. O'BYRNE. Crown 8vo. With Plate. 5s.

Vyse (G. W.) Egypt : Political, Financial, and Strategical. Together with an Account of its Engineering Capabilities and Agricultural Resources. By GRIFFIN W. VYSE, late on special duty in Egypt and Afghanistan for H.M.'s Government. Crown 8vo. With Maps. 9s.

Wall (A. J.) Indian Snake Poisons, their Nature and Effects. By A. J: WALL, M.D., F.R.C.S. England, of the Medical Staff H.M.'s Indian Army. Crown 8vo. 6s.

Waring (E. J.) Pharmacopœia of India.
By EDWARD JOHN WARING, M.D., &c. 8vo. 6s. (See page 2.)

Watson (M.) Money.
By JULES TARDIEU. Translated from the French by MARGARET WATSON. Crown 8vo. 7s. 6d.

Watson (Dr. J. F.) and J. W. Kaye, Races and Tribes of Hindostan. The People of India. A series of Photographic Illustrations of the Races and Tribes of Hindustan. Prepared under the Authority of the Government of India, by J. FORBES WATSON, and JOHN WILLIAM KAYE. The Work contains about 450 Photographs on mounts, in Eight Volumes, super royal 4to. £2. 5s. per volume.

Webb (Dr. A.) Pathologia Indica.
Based upon Morbid Specimens from all parts of the Indian Empire. By ALLAN WEBB, B.M.S. Second Edit. 8vo. 14s.

Wellesley's Despatches.
The Despatches, Minutes, and Correspondence of the Marquis Wellesley, K.G., during his Administration in India. 5 vols. 8vo. With Portrait, Map, &c. £6. 10s.

This work should be perused by all who proceed to India in the Civil Services.

Wellington in India.
Military History of the Duke of Wellington in India

White (S. D.) Indian Reminiscences.
By Colonel S. Dewe' White, late Bengal Staff Corps. 8vo. With 10 Photographs. 14s.

Wilberforce (E.) Franz Schubert.
A Musical Biography, from the German of Dr. Heinrich Kreisle von Hellborn. By Edward Wilberforce, Esq., Author of "Social Life in Munich." Post 8vo. 6s.

Wilk's South of India.
3 vols. 4to. £5. 5s.

Wilkin (Mrs.) The Shackles of an Old Love.
By Mara (Mrs. Wilkin). Crown 8vo. 7s. 6d.

Wilkins (W. N.) Visual Art; or Nature through the Healthy Eye. With some remarks on Originality and Free Trade, Artistic Copyright, and Durability. By Wm. Noy Wilkins, Author of " Art Impressions of Dresden," &c. 8vo. 6s.

Williams (F.) Lives of the English Cardinals.
The Lives of the English Cardinals, from Nicholas Breakspeare (Pope Adrien IV.) to Thomas Wolsey, Cardinal Legate. With Historical Notices of the Papal Court. By Folkestone Williams. 2 vols., 8vo. 14s.

—— **Life, &c., of Bishop Atterbury.**
The Memoir and Correspondence of Francis Atterbury, Bishop of Rochester, with his distinguished contemporaries. Compiled chiefly from the Atterbury and Stuart Papers. By Folkestone Williams, Author of "Lives of the English Cardinals," &c., 2 vols. 8vo. 14s.

Williams (S. Wells) The Middle Kingdom.
A Survey of the Geography, Government, Literature, Social Life, Arts, and History of the Chinese Empire and Its Inhabitants. By S. Wells Willams, LL D., Professor of the Chinese Language and Literature at Yale College, Author of Tonic and Syllabic Dictionaries of the Chinese Language. Revised Edition, with 74 Illustrations and a New Map of the Empire. 2 vols. Demy 8vo. 42s.

Wilson (H. H.) Glossary of Judicial and Revenue Terms, and of useful Words occurring in Official Documents relating to the Administration of the Government of British India. From the Arabic, Persian, Hindustani, Sanskrit, Hindi, Bengali, Uriya, Marathi, Guzarathi, Telugu, Karnata, Tamil, Malayalam, and other Languages. Compiled and published under the authority of the Hon. the Court of Directors of the E. I. Company. 4to., cloth. £1 10s.

Wollaston (Arthur N.) Anwari Suhaili, or Lights of Canopus. Commonly known as Kalilah and Damnah, being an adaptation of the Fables of Bidpai. Translated from the Persian. Royal 8vo., 42s.; also in royal 4to., with illuminated borders, designed specially for the work, cloth, extra gilt. £3 13s. 6d.

—— **Elementary Indian Reader.**
Designed for the use of Students in the Anglo-Vernacular Schools in India. Fcap. 1s.

Woolrych (Serjeant W. H.)
Lives of Eminent Serjeants-at-Law of the English Bar. By Humphry W. Woolrych, Serjeant-at-Law. 2 vols. 8vo. 30s.

Wraxall (Sir L., Bart.) Caroline Matilda.
Queen of Denmark, Sister of George 3rd. From Family and State Papers. By Sir Lascelles Wraxall, Bart. 3 vols., 8vo. 18s.

Young (J. R.) Course of Mathematics.
A Course of Elementary Mathematics for the use of candidates for admission into either of the Military Colleges; of applicants for appointments in the Home or Indian Civil Services, and of mathematical students generally. By Professor J. R. Young. In one closely-printed volume. 8vo., pp. 648. 12s.

"In the work before us he has digested a complete Elementary Course, by aid of his long experience as a teacher and writer; and he has produced a very useful book. Mr. Young has not allowed his own taste to rule the distribution, but has adjusted his parts with the skill of a veteran."—*Athenæum.*

Young (M.) and Trent (R.) A Home Ruler.
A Story for Girls. By Minnie Young and Rachel Trent, Illustrated by C. P. Colnaghi. Crown 8vo. 3s. 6d.

Works in the Press.

Malleson's Capt Musafir's Rambles in Alpine Lands.
By Colonel G. B. MALLESON, C.S.I. 4to. 10s. 6d.

Life of Gustave Doré.
By BLANCHARD JERROLD.

Personal Reminiscences of General Skobeleff.
By NEMIROVITCH-DANTCHENKO. Translated by E. A. BRAYLEY HODGETTS. With 3 Portraits.

A Land March from England to Ceylon Forty Years Ago.
By EDWARD MITFORD. With Map and Numerous Illustrations.

At Home in Paris.
By BLANCHARD JERROLD. 2 Vols., Crown 8vo. 21s.

My Musical Life.
By the Rev. H. R. HAWEIS, Author of "Music and Morals." With Portraits.

Coruña to Sevastopal.
By Colonel F. A. WHINYATES.

Thoughts on Reading Shakespeare.
By The Hon. A. S. G. CANNING.

Games of Cards for Three Players.
By "AQUARIUS." Author of "Écarté."

Piquet and Cribbage.
By the same Author.

THE
ARMY AND NAVY MAGAZINE,

A

MONTHLY SERVICE REVIEW.

ONE SHILLING.

London: W. H. ALLEN & CO., 13, Waterloo Place.

LONDON IN 1884.

ILLUSTRATED WITH SIXTEEN BIRD'S-EYE VIEWS OF THE PRINCIPAL STREETS AND A MAP.

By HERBERT FRY.

New Edition, Revised and Enlarged. Crown 8vo. Cloth, 2s.

London: W. H. ALLEN & CO., 13, Waterloo Place.

Price, 2s.

ACADEMY SKETCHES,

INCLUDING

VARIOUS EXHIBITIONS.

WITH ABOUT

200 ILLUSTRATIONS.

EDITED BY

HENRY BLACKBURN,

EDITOR OF THE "ACADEMY" AND "GROSVENOR NOTES."

1883.

London: W. H. ALLEN & CO., 13, Waterloo Place, S.W.

In January and July of each year is published in 8vo., price 10s. 6d.,

THE INDIA LIST, CIVIL AND MILITARY.

BY PERMISSION OF THE SECRETARY OF STATE FOR INDIA IN COUNCIL.

CONTENTS.

CIVIL.—Gradation Lists of Civil Service, Bengal, Madras, and Bombay. Civil Annuitants. Legislative Council, Ecclesiastical Establishments, Educational, Public Works, Judicial, Marine, Medical, Land Revenue, Political, Postal, Police, Customs and Salt, Forest, Registration and Railway and Telegraph Departments, Law Courts, Surveys, &c. &c.

MILITARY.—Gradation List of the General and Field Officers (British and Local) of the three Presidencies, Staff Corps, Adjutants-General's and Quartermasters-General's Offices, Army Commissariat Departments, British Troops serving in India (including Royal Artillery, Royal Engineers, Cavalry, Infantry, and Medical Department), List of Native Regiments, Commander-in-Chief and Staff, Garrison Instruction Staff, Indian Medical Department, Ordnance Departments, Punjab Frontier Force, Military Departments of the three Presidencies, Veterinary Departments, Tables showing the Distribution of the Army in India, Lists of Retired Officers of the three Presidencies.

HOME.—Departments of the Officer of the Secretary of State, Coopers Hill College, List of Selected Candidates for the Civil and Forest Services, Indian Troop Service.

MISCELLANEOUS.—Orders of the Bath, Star of India, and St. Michael and St. George. Order of Precedence in India. Regulations for Admission to Civil Service. Regulations for Admission of Chaplains. Civil Leave Code and Supplements. Civil Service Pension Code—relating to the Covenanted and Uncovenanted Services. Rules for the Indian Medical Service. Furlough and Retirement Regulations of the Indian Army. Family Pension Fund. Staff Corps Regulations. Salaries of Staff Officers. Regulations for Promotion. English Furlough Pay.

THE ROYAL KALENDAR,
AND COURT AND CITY REGISTER,
FOR ENGLAND, IRELAND, SCOTLAND, AND THE COLONIES,

For the Year 1883.

CONTAINING A CORRECT LIST OF THE TWENTY-FIRST IMPERIAL PARLIAMENT, SUMMONED TO MEET FOR THEIR FIRST SESSION—MARCH 5TH, 1874.

House of Peers—House of Commons—Sovereigns and Rulers of States of Europe—Orders of Knighthood—Science and Art Department—Queen's Household—Government Offices—Mint—Customs—Inland Revenue—Post Office—Foreign Ministers and Consuls—Queen's Consuls Abroad—Naval Department—Navy List—Army Department—Army List—Law Courts—Police—Ecclesiastical Department—Clergy List—Foundation Schools—Literary Institutions—City of London—Banks—Railway Companies—Hospitals and Institutions—Charities—Miscellaneous Institutions—Scotland, Ireland, India, and the Colonies; and other useful information.

Price with Index, 7s.; without Index, 5s.

Published on the arrival of each overland Mail from India. Subscription 26s. per annum. Specimen copy, 6d.

ALLEN'S INDIAN MAIL,
AND

Official Gazette
FROM

INDIA, CHINA, AND ALL PARTS OF THE EAST.

ALLEN'S INDIAN MAIL contains the fullest and most authentic Reports of all important Occurrences in the Countries to which it is devoted, compiled chiefly from private and exclusive sources. It has been pronounced by the Press in general to be *indispensable* to all who have Friends or Relatives in the East, as affording the only *correct* information regarding the Services, Movements of Troops, Shipping, and all events of Domestic and individual interest.

The subjoined list of the usual Contents will show the importance and variety of the information concentrated in ALLEN'S INDIAN MAIL.

Summary and Review of Eastern News.

Precis of Public Intelligence	Shipping—Arrival of Ships
Selections from the Indian Press	,, ,, Passengers
Movements of Troops	,, **Departure of Ships**
The Government Gazette	,, ,, Passengers
Courts Martial	Commercial—State of the Markets
Domestic Intelligence—Births	,, Indian Securities
,, ,, Marriages	,, **Freights**
,, ,, Deaths	&c. &c. &c.

Home Intelligence relating to India, &c.

Original Articles	Arrivals reported in England
Miscellaneous Information	Departures ,, ,,
Appointments, Extensions of Furloughs, &c., &c.	Shipping—Arrival of Ships
,,   ,,   Passengers
,, Civil	, Departure of Ships
,, Military	,, ,, Passengers
,, Ecclesiastical and	,, Vessel spoken with
,, Marine	&c. &c. &c.

Review of Works on the East, and Notices of all affairs connected with India **and the Services.**

Throughout the Paper one uniform system of arrangement prevails, and at the conclusion of each year an INDEX is furnished, to enable Subscribers to bind up the Volume, which forms a complete

ASIATIC ANNUAL REGISTER AND LIBRARY OF REFERENCE.

LONDON: W. H. ALLEN & Co., 13, WATERLOO PLACE, S.W.
(PUBLISHERS TO THE INDIA OFFICE),

To whom Communications for the Editor, and Advertisements, are requested to be addressed.

Crown 8vo., 3s. 6d. each.

EMINENT WOMEN SERIES

Edited by JOHN H. INGRAM.

Already issued :—

GEORGE ELIOT.
By MATHILDE BLIND.

EMILY BRONTË.
By A. MARY F. ROBINSON.

GEORGE SAND.
By BERTHA THOMAS.

MARY LAMB.
By ANNE GILCHRIST.

MARGARET FULLER.
By JULIA WARD HOWE.

MARIA EDGEWORTH.
By HELEN ZIMMERN.

London: W. H. Allen & Co., 13 Waterloo Place. S.W.

www.ingramcontent.com/pod-product-compliance
Lightning Source LLC
Chambersburg PA
CBHW022107290426
44112CB00008B/576